The Knopf Collectors' Guides to American Antiques

Robert Bishop & William C. Ketchum, Jr.
Series Consultants

A Chanticleer Press Edition

Dolls

Wendy Lavitt

With photographs by Schecter Me Sun Lee

Alfred A. Knopf, New York

This is a Borzoi Book
Published by Alfred A. Knopf, Inc.

Prepared and produced by
Chanticleer Press, Inc., New York.

Color reproductions by Nievergelt Repro AG, Zurich,
Switzerland. Type set in Century Expanded by Dix Type Inc.,
Syracuse, New York. Printed and bound by Dai Nippon Printing
Co., Ltd., Tokyo, Japan.

First Printing

Library of Congress Catalog Number: 83-47987
ISBN: 0-394-71542-X

Contents

Acknowledgments

Many people were kind enough to assist in the preparation of this book. I want to express my appreciation to all the antiques shops, institutions, and individuals for supplying information and for making their collections available to us. In particular, I want to thank the staff of The Margaret Woodbury Strong Museum in Rochester, New York, The Brooklyn Children's Museum and Aunt Len's Doll and Toy Museum in New York City, and Auctions by Theriault in Annapolis, Maryland. Schecter Me Sun Lee tirelessly photographed all of the dolls in this book. William C. Ketchum, Jr., reviewed the manuscript, made many worthwhile suggestions, and compiled the price guide. Robert Bishop deserves special thanks for his enthusiastic participation in the project. Margaret Whitton, Curator of Dolls at the Strong Museum, read the entire manuscript, and her far-reaching knowledge, particularly in the field of 18th- and 19th-century dolls, was invaluable. Melissa Morgan researched much of the information on dolls from the Strong Museum. Nancy Paine, Curator of Collections at The Brooklyn Children's Museum, thoughtfully reviewed the text and generously shared her expertise. Mary Davis, Head Librarian at The Museum of the American Indian, looked over the manuscript on Indian dolls. Barbara Jendrick helped with the price guide. Kathleen Swan and Michael Goldman copyedited the text.

I am grateful to Paul Steiner and the staff of Chanticleer Press: Gudrun Buettner and Susan Costello, who developed the idea for the series; Carol Nehring, who supervised the art and layouts; Helga Lose, who directed the production of the book; and most of all, Lenore Malen, who, with the assistance of Marian Appellof, edited and coordinated this guide through completion. Finally, I want to thank Charles Elliott, Senior Editor at Alfred A. Knopf, for his encouragement and support.

About the Author, Photographer, and Consultants

Wendy Lavitt
Author Wendy Lavitt has written *American Folk Dolls*, published by Alfred A. Knopf, as well as articles on folk art and antiques. She has lectured at the Cooper-Hewitt Museum of the Smithsonian Institution and at other museums, and is the guest curator of "Children's Children: American Folk Dolls" at the Museum of American Folk Art in New York City. She is the co-owner of Made in America, an antiques shop specializing in Americana.

Schecter Me Sun Lee
A New York-based freelance photographer, Schecter Lee has had works published in national and international magazines. Among his most recent books are *American Folk Dolls*, as well as *Pottery and Porcelain* and *Folk Art*, new volumes in *The Knopf Collectors' Guides to American Antiques*.

Margaret Whitton
Consultant Margaret Whitton serves as Curator of Dolls at The Margaret Woodbury Strong Museum in Rochester, New York, which houses about 20,000 dolls. She is the author of *The Jumeau Doll* and co-author of *Playthings by the Yard*, a reference book on cloth dolls and toys. A frequent lecturer on dolls, Mrs. Whitton has been the regional director of the United Federation of Doll Clubs and president of several local doll clubs.

Nancy Paine
As Curator of Collections at The Brooklyn Children's Museum since 1969, consultant Nancy Paine is in charge of holdings that include some 2500 dolls as well as a rich array of ethnographic artifacts. She recently organized the exhibition "Dolls: Reflections of Ourselves" at the museum.

Robert Bishop
Director of the Museum of American Folk Art in New York City, consultant Robert Bishop is author of more than 30 books, among them *Folk Art* and *Quilts* in *The Knopf Collectors' Guides to American Antiques*. He established this country's first master's degree program in folk art studies at New York University. Dr. Bishop is on the editorial boards of *Art & Antiques*, *Horizon Magazine*, and *Antique Monthly*.

William C. Ketchum, Jr.
A member of the faculty of The New School for Social Research, consultant William C. Ketchum, Jr., is also a guest curator at the Museum of American Folk Art in New York City and a consultant to several major auction houses. Dr. Ketchum has written 18 books, including *Pottery and Porcelain* and *Furniture 2* in *The Knopf Collectors' Guides to American Antiques*. He is an associate editor at *Antique Monthly*.

Preface

Victor Hugo, the 19th-century French writer, once remarked: "In the same way as birds make a nest of anything, children make a doll of no matter what." As early as 3000 and 2000 B.C. in Ancient Egypt and Babylonia, children and their parents made dolls of old rags, wood, and clay. The earliest American dolls were made of these materials and other more unusual substances, such as dried apples, corncobs and husks, bottles, pipes, and shells. Created by anonymous craftsmen for their own pleasure, many were so imaginatively fashioned that they may be called folk art. In early American portraits, children were often depicted holding their favorite dolls in their laps as a sentimental touch.

At the same time, well-to-do American colonists sought to maintain the culture and refinement that Europe represented by importing its goods, including sophisticated English, French, and German dolls. Brought to America by even the earliest settlers, European dolls continued to be imported in great numbers until the First World War, constituting the majority of commercial dolls sold in this country. 20th-century collectors have traditionally favored these fine European dolls. Only in very recent years have tastes broadened to include charming American folk dolls, printed-cloth figures, and whimsical dolls based on comic-strip or cartoon characters.

This guide covers the entire spectrum of dolls acquired by Americans from the 18th century until the mid-1970s and even includes dolls created by American doll artists in the past few years.

Although their appeal is immediate and universal, dolls are frequently difficult to evaluate. This book is therefore designed to help readers identify and judge the wide variety of dolls—from lathe-turned wooden figures imported from England, seen at auction and at fine shops, to mass-produced plastic dolls by American toy manufacturers, likely to be found in small shops, flea markets, or attics.

To help collectors identify the examples they find, the dolls illustrated are arranged by subject or material rather than by period, style, or maker. Each entry describes in detail a representative doll and tells where, when, by whom (if known), and of what materials it was made. In addition, it provides historical background along with practical hints, including what to look for and what to avoid. To acquaint collectors with what they can expect to pay for dolls, the Price Guide in the appendix lists current price ranges for the types illustrated. The high prices given for some dolls may be the result of their rarity, fine craftsmanship, or popular appeal; low prices may indicate undervalued kinds of dolls that are worth investigating. Thus, this guide will help readers to assemble a distinctive collection and to expand their appreciation of the rich variety of dolls.

A Simple Way to Identify Dolls

Dolls come in an incredible variety, ranging from humble, homemade American cloth babies to exquisitely dressed, fragile French bisque ladies to durable plastic figures that walk or talk. To help collectors choose from this vast array, we have selected 357 representative American and imported examples for full picture-and-text coverage. These include not only some of the most common, readily available types of dolls, but also rare examples that are important for an overall understanding of the history and development of doll design and manufacture.

The color plates and accompanying text are arranged in a visual sequence organized by basic types (for example, all lady dolls are together) and material (for example, all lady dolls made of wood are together), so that a beginning collector can find a doll quickly without knowing its maker or date. Each group of color plates is preceded by a brief essay that surveys the history of the examples covered and supplies additional facts about style and manufacture. Collectors who want to refer directly to entries about dolls made of specific materials can turn to the List of Plates by Material, in which dolls are organized by head type (china or papier-mâché, for example) and major body material.

Because it is impossible to illustrate every type of doll made in America and abroad, this guide is also designed to assist you in identifying examples that are not shown. The introductory essay called History of Dolls furnishes valuable background information on sociological and technological developments that have affected dollmaking over the centuries. This is followed by an essay on the History of Doll Clothes, covering another important aspect of doll collecting and discussing some prevailing fashions. In addition, Parts of a Doll illustrates distinctive elements of design and construction of some major types of dolls from the 18th century to the present. The essay on How to Evaluate Dolls provides useful pointers on identifying and selecting dolls, including a discussion of the features that make specific examples desirable, as well as some general remarks on how a doll's condition affects its value.

A section on Doll Advertisements indicates how these can be used to identify dolls and their makers and dates. The Glossary defines specialized terms used in this book. The table of Makers and Marks offers a quick reference for the names of major doll manufacturers, their trademarks and signatures, locations, and dates of operation. Finally, the up-to-date Price Guide lists current prices for all the types of dolls illustrated. Using these tools—photographs, descriptions, essays, illustrations, and charts—both the beginner and the connoisseur will find doll collecting an easier and more rewarding experience.

History of Dolls

Defined as children's toys representing human figures, dolls
range from charred sticks wrapped in rags to exquisitely carved
miniature sculptures. Although none have been found at
prehistoric sites, dolls may be some of mankind's earliest
playthings. Dolls delight adults, but they serve primarily as
mute and gentle presences on which children project their
fantasies and fears. The most poignant evidence of the timeless
love children have for their dolls may be the preserved body of a
little girl found at Herculaneum, the ancient Roman city buried
along with Pompeii during the eruption of Mt. Vesuvius in A.D.
79; excavators discovered the child still clutching her doll.

Ancient Dolls

Most ancient Egyptian dolls that have survived have been found
in the tombs of their young owners. Paddle-shaped dolls, for
example, discovered in tombs dating from 2000 B.C., were made
of wood with hair fashioned from strands of clay beads affixed to
the heads with wax. Other Egyptian dolls had linen bodies with
embroidered faces and thread hair. Ancient Greek and Roman
dolls made of such materials as bone, ivory, wood, wax, terra-
cotta, and lead were commonly sold by itinerant merchants and
in marketplaces. In Sardis, a dollmaking center in ancient Asia
Minor, wax was frequently used to coat wooden dolls to give
them a smooth and lifelike finish. Custom required children to
dedicate their dolls to the gods as they grew up. The poet
Sappho, for example, gave one of her dolls to the goddess
Aphrodite and wrote, "Despise not my doll's little purple
neckerchief. I, Sappho, dedicate this precious gift to you."

The Middle Ages

Because of the scarcity of written documentation, little is known
about dolls made during the early Middle Ages. Unlike the
priests of ancient Egypt, the Catholic Church frowned upon the
practice of burying children with their toys, so that practically no
dolls from the period were preserved in tombs. In the later
Middle Ages dolls are mentioned in diaries, in letters, and
occasionally in treatises about raising children. It is known that
well-to-do young boys played with jointed dolls that depicted
knights mounted on horses. In Europe during the 12th century
and possibly earlier, dolls of bread and gingerbread were sold at
fairs. In the 14th century dolls of wood, solid wax, or a molded
paper-pulp waste material much like composition appeared at
Florentine and Venetian fairs; at such fairs marionettes
entertained children with parables of Christian life, and second-
hand examples were probably sold as toys.

An early type of German wooden doll was called a *Docke*,
meaning a block of wood, probably because it had a simple
rectangular torso. As early as the 14th century, the German
towns of Nuremberg and Sonneberg developed as dollmaking
centers and helped establish Germany's preeminence in this field,
a status that lasted until the early 20th century. German craft
guilds, which grew quickly in the later Middle Ages, facilitated
the production of dolls. Each guild specialized in a different craft
and produced dolls out of the materials it used for its major
products. The first recorded dollmakers were Ott and Mess,
mentioned in 1465 as *Docken Macher*. While this term referred
to toymakers in general, it is widely believed that Ott and Mess
made wooden dolls along with other items. In the 15th century,
white clay used for making pipes was another popular dollmaking
material. By the 16th century dollmaking in Germany was a
sophisticated art, and some dolls were so beautifully made that

they disturbed Martin Luther, the leader of the Protestant Reformation, who condemned their frivolity and admonished children for playing with them.

Early French Dolls

A dollmaking industry thrived in Paris as early as the 14th century. Most early French dolls were fashion manikins designed to display clothing and amuse adults. Made of wood or wax and called *Pandores* or, if life-size, *grandes Pandores*, these figures were sent to remote provincial towns and distant courts to display the latest French fashions. They were frequently given as gifts from French nobles to foreign lords and ladies. In the 15th century, for example, Anne of Brittany commissioned such a doll for Queen Isabella of Spain. Because of social and political change, these dolls gradually became outmoded after the French Revolution. Today they are widely regarded as the ancestors of the French fashion dolls of the 19th century.

The 16th and 17th Centuries

A great deal is known about dolls from the 16th and 17th centuries because they were frequently depicted in paintings, etchings, and engravings of everyday scenes. They ranged from stumplike wooden figures to fully articulated, life-size artists' manikins. Small dolls made of wax or precious metals were created for the aristocracy and were often displayed in cabinets designed to look like miniature houses. In 17th-century Germany finely crafted wooden dolls were made in towns such as Oberammergau, Sonneberg, and Nuremberg; the last town alone had 17 active dollmakers. Many other dolls produced in Nuremberg were made from the pulp waste discarded by nearby industrial mills.

The 18th Century

The growth of the middle class during the 18th century meant that the market for fine dolls was greatly increased because more families could afford them. Moreover, the strict rules governing the behavior of children were relaxed somewhat, and educators and philosophers such as Jean Jacques Rousseau encouraged little girls to play with dolls. In England children's toy shops were established for the first time.

Many kinds of inexpensive plaster and earthenware dolls were made during this century. This was also the time when significant materials such as papier-mâché, porcelain, and wax were perfected or refined for use in dollmaking. It was during the Industrial Revolution in the late 18th and early 19th centuries that the means were discovered to mass produce dolls on the vast scale with which we are familiar today.

Queen Anne Dolls

The dolls usually associated with the 18th century are the English jointed wooden figures collectors commonly refer to as Queen Anne dolls. Although they were made from 1690 until the 1840s, these dolls were most popular from 1750 to 1800. They can be easily recognized by their one-piece heads and torsos, high foreheads, close-set features, and glass, porcelain, or carved pupil-less eyes. Many have fork-type hands. While the very earliest were hand-carved, most were lathe-turned, which made it possible to produce them in large numbers.

The 19th Century

Some of the finest 19th-century jointed wooden dolls were made in the Grödner Tal, a region in the southern Alps that is now part of Italy. These figures are sometimes called Dutch dolls (a corruption of the word *Deutsch*, meaning German), peg-woodens, or penny-woodens (referring to their moderate price). The best of these, dating from the early part of the century, are elegant, delicate figures with carved upswept hairdos and tuck combs and Empire-style outfits. By mid-century the quality of these dolls had declined. Instead of having carefully modeled arms and hands, later examples have sticklike arms and so-called spoon hands, which were easy to mass produce. By the end of the century, cheaply made dolls from the Grödner Tal were distributed worldwide.

Papier-Mâché and Wax Dolls
Some of the most popular moderately priced dolls made in the 19th century had papier-mâché or composition heads attached to cloth or kid bodies. Most were made in Germany, particularly in the towns of Sonneberg and Coburg, and some in France. The heads were mechanically pressed in 2-part molds using a technique invented about 1810. Some heads, however, had such elaborate hairdos that they required 8 to 10 molds. After the papier-mâché heads were removed from the molds and dried, they were painted or varnished, or dipped in wax for a more naturalistic finish. Molds were also used to make poured-wax dolls, which were produced primarily in England. Because of its malleability, wax was a material favored for baby dolls, portrait dolls, and fashion dolls, all requiring realistically modeled features. Many of these wax dolls were of a very high quality and had hair inserted directly into their wax scalps.

China-Head Dolls
Fine china was first used to make decorative and household items in Meissen, Germany, about 1710. Although china heads for dolls were made there in the 1750s, they were expensive and extremely fragile and did not become widely popular until the 1840s, when production costs declined considerably. The heads, then manufactured primarily in the provinces of Thuringia and Bavaria, were often sold separately and attached to homemade bodies. Although some dolls had bald heads to which wigs were attached, most were produced with molded hairstyles that were often quite elaborate, incorporating snoods, combs, flowers, and other ornaments.

Industrial Innovations
The social and economic developments that transformed Europe and America into industrial powers in the 19th century strongly influenced dollmaking. Steam-powered transportation allowed for increasingly wide distribution of dolls. The availability of the sewing machine for home use in the 1860s made it possible to produce expertly stitched homemade doll bodies and clothes. Moreover, there was a growing interest in making dolls of synthetic materials that were both durable and soft to the touch. Manufacturers improved the articulation of their dolls' joints and patented these innovations. However, mechanization also encouraged shoddy workmanship, so that the quality of some types of dolls, especially wooden ones, actually declined during the course of the 19th century. At the same time, the publishing industry began to grow as paper became inexpensive, and many of the fashion magazines that proliferated included sections of doll clothes. Some magazines and books were devoted exclusively to dolls.

Innovations in dolls were achieved in rapid succession. In 1844

Charles Goodyear patented the process of vulcanization for rubber, which was applied to dollmaking. About 1855 Charles Motschmann produced one of the first commercially made baby dolls, a flexible-jointed figure with an infant's broad shape, a type that remained popular for the rest of the century. In 1858 Ludwig Greiner obtained the first American patent for his papier-mâché doll heads. Also in the 1850s, diminutive one-piece china dolls called *Badekinder* were produced by the thousands in Germany and England.

French Lady Dolls

Lady dolls with bisque heads were among the finest and most popular dolls of the 1860s and '70s. Bisque, an unglazed porcelain, was favored in France during the mid- to late 19th century because it has a soft, mat surface quite unlike the hard, shiny glazed surface of china. Some of the most elaborately costumed dolls in history were made during this era. Pleats, frills, rosettes, braids, and fringe literally covered gowns, and pockets were sewn in almost every skirt to hold handkerchiefs, card cases, and trinkets. Hundreds of dressmakers and shoemakers, many working for as little as 50¢ a day, fashioned clothes, footwear, and accessories exclusively for dolls. French lady dolls were often sold in trunks containing tea sets, vanity cases, fans, and parasols, as well as clothes. Among the best-known dollmakers of the era were Huret, Bru, Rohmer, and Pierre Jumeau. The later success of the Jumeau firm, under the direction of Emile Jumeau, depended partially on its skillful marketing, a factor that became increasingly important to the doll industry in the coming decades. For the first time children were an audience for advertising.

Late 19th-Century Dolls

In the 1870s the French bébé gradually replaced the lady doll in popularity. Bébés had bisque heads, idealized faces, and fully jointed children's bodies usually made of composition. Jumeau bébés, with their heavy brows and luminous glass eyes, were particularly successful. By the 1890s German firms, including Armand Marseille, J. D. Kestner, Jr., and others, successfully produced less expensive versions of these dolls, attracting a large share of the market.

In turn-of-the-century America, mass-produced printed-cloth dolls were the rage. Though dollmakers such as Izannah Walker and Martha Chase had already turned the production of homemade rag dolls into successful commercial ventures, printed dolls sold by the yard in uncut sheets by Arnold Print Works and Art Fabric Mills reached thousands more homes.

The 20th Century

Most dolls sold in America from 1900 to 1910 continued to come from Europe. Character dolls, designed to look like real children, revolutionized the doll industry about 1910. The pouting, crying, or laughing faces and the new bent limbs produced an unprecedented naturalness that became the keynote of 20th-century dolls. Cloth advertising dolls, including Aunt Jemima and Buster Brown, appeared shortly after 1900.

An amusing cuteness characterized many of the dolls designed between 1910 and 1915, such as the chubby-faced Campbell Kids, based on drawings by Grace Drayton, and Rose O'Neill's Kewpies. The latter, elflike creatures with googly eyes and blue wings, swept the doll world and became an instant fad. The First World War largely halted the production of French and German bisque dolls. In America, cloth-bodied "Mama" dolls, Fulper Pottery's bisque dolls, and composition or bisque dolls produced by Japanese firms replaced the European dolls. After the war German manufacturers began producing some bisque dolls created by American designers, including Grace Putnam's Bye-Lo Baby. This doll, modeled after a newborn infant, was an immediate success in the 1920s. American and European firms jumped on the bandwagon with countless imitations of this "million-dollar baby."

Cloth dolls were popular in the 1920s. Raggedy Ann was based on an old doll its designer, Johnny Gruelle, found in his mother's attic. Madame Alexander's first dolls were made of cloth in 1923. In Europe, cloth dolls by Käthe Kruse, Norah Wellings, Lenci, and Steiff were so popular that they were shipped all over the world.

The girl dolls of the 1920s, such as EFFanBEE's Patsy, ushered in an era of "companion" dolls. Boudoir dolls, designed for adults and featuring flapper and harlequin costumes, captured the flavor of the era. Cartoon-character dolls began their long reign in the early 20th century, and no one has been able to resist Popeye or Betty Boop dolls ever since. In the 1930s, the emphasis was on dolls that "did things." Baby dolls that could "drink and wet" appealed to little girls, and American companies manufactured many versions of them. However, the Depression adversely affected the doll business, causing numerous firms to close. A few manufacturers stayed active by selling dolls based on celebrities.

Modern Dolls

The Second World War disrupted dollmaking, and it was not until 1949 that a new breakthrough invigorated the industry. The invention of hard plastic in that year solved problems that had long plagued dollmakers, namely, materials that peeled, flaked, and crazed. In the 1950s the introduction of soft vinyl dolls with rooted hair (reminiscent of early wax dolls) resulted in even more realistic toddler and baby dolls. Another interesting phenomenon of the 1950s was the Barbie doll made by Mattel. Little girls were enamored of this small doll, which had an extensive wardrobe that was as large as those of the French fashion dolls of the 1870s. Barbie dolls represented a new marketing technique, that of selling an inexpensive doll while offering expensive clothes and accessories to accompany it. In the 1960s the male action dolls made by many American companies followed Mattel's example by providing dolls such as G.I. Joe with separately packaged uniforms and equipment. Mattel also introduced its talking dolls at this time.

The 1970s brought a revival of the cloth advertising dolls that had lost favor in the 1940s, but now the dolls were prestuffed and included such contemporary favorites as the Cheetos Mouse Man and the Eskimo-Pie Boy.

Many recent dolls are throwbacks to dolls made long ago. Trends come into style only to lose popularity in a decade, and 50 or 100 years later similar dolls reappear, different but reminiscent of the originals. Many contemporary doll artists, working at home or in studios, base their dolls on vintage masterpieces or create original, one-of-a-kind or limited-edition figures. By utilizing the traditional dollmaking techniques that are best suited to their work and by emphasizing research and artistic independence, they remind us of early dollmakers, working alone and intent

upon creating objects of beauty and usefulness.

History of Doll Clothes

The history of doll clothes parallels the history of men's and women's fashions and offers a fascinating glimpse into the tastes and social customs of past generations. This section primarily describes clothes worn by European dolls imported to America during the 18th and 19th centuries. During this period most American dolls wore handmade miniature versions of simple everyday garments. Only in the 20th century did the American doll industry begin to produce doll fashions commercially.

Earliest Clothes (1700–1820)
With the exception of a few rare garments, the earliest surviving doll clothes date from the 18th century. For much of the century, upper-class women and their dolls wore loose-fitting robes called sack gowns over tight bodices and enormous elliptical or round hoop skirts. Less elaborate dresses had pointed, long-waisted bodices, low necklines, loose-fitting sleeves, and full skirts. The French Revolution and Napoleonic era gave rise to a radical shift in taste. Ornate, voluminous gowns were replaced by simple high-waisted dresses. These garments, supposedly based on ancient Roman fashion, were part of the so-called Empire style. Miniature versions are sometimes found on early French or German papier-mâché dolls or on wooden Grödner Tal dolls.

The Victorian Era (1837–1901)
The introduction of fashion plates and fashion magazines meant that elegant clothing styles quickly filtered down the social ladder. The proliferation of textile mills and the invention of the sewing machine for use in the factory and, later, in the home vastly increased the production of doll clothes. From the late 1830s through the turn of the century, lady dolls wore elaborate costumes modeled after rapidly changing dress styles. However, the style of doll clothes was sometimes a decade or more behind that of adult fashions. In the 1830s the waistlines of women's dresses were lowered and tightened, and sleeves were puffed. By the 1840s dresses had narrower sleeves, and evening gowns, low necklines. During the 1850s skirts became so wide that they sometimes measured up to 10 yards in circumference; these were supported by horsehair crinolines rather than by the whalebones or willow reeds that had been in vogue a century before. In the 1860s skirts gradually narrowed and various types of bustles came into fashion. Bustles nearly disappeared in the 1870s, only to be reintroduced in the 1880s. In the 1870s most adult-style dresses had long trains. The popular French bébés, dolls representing young girls, wore ornate, long-waisted dresses that complemented their full, stocky proportions. During this period boy dolls wore sailor suits and Little Lord Fauntleroy outfits. By the 1880s ladies' dresses became tight at the hips and narrow at the hem. At the turn of the century they had wide balloonlike or leg-of-mutton sleeves and bell-shaped skirts.

The 20th Century
The introduction of child character dolls with naturalistic facial features and bent limbs about 1910 inspired a new look in doll clothes. Simple outfits such as rompers and tunics over bloomers were modeled after clothes children wore at play. As the century progressed, adult-doll costumes became more and more casual. Making a debut in 1958, Mattel's teenage Barbie doll was itself relatively inexpensive, but the wide array of clothes and accessories that were available for separate purchase induced children to add to the doll's wardrobe as new outfits reflecting current trends came on the market.

Doll Clothes Illustrations

English costume (mid-18th century)

Empire-style dress (1825–50)

Homemade dress with pantalettes (1850–75)

French bébé's outfit (1875–90)

Infant gown (mid-19th century)

Bye-Lo Baby gown (1922–30)

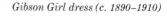

French lady's dress (late 19th century)

Gibson Girl dress (c. 1890–1910)

Man's dress suit (mid-19th century)

Young boy's outfit (c. 1890–1910)

Peddler doll outfit (19th century)

Apache Indian costume (mid-19th century)

Parts of a Doll: Bodies

Gusseted kid body (1880–1900)

Gesland-type body with bisque head (1860–1920)

Stuffed cloth "mama" body (mid-20th century)

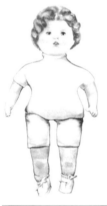

English jointed wooden body (1750–1810)

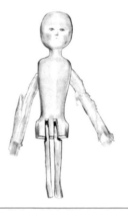

Schoenhut wooden body (1910–20)

Bébé with ball-jointed composition body (1875–1910)

Motschmann-type body (mid- to late 19th century)

Montanari-type body with wax head and limbs (c. 1850–60)

Peg-wooden body (mid-19th to early 20th century)

Lady doll with articulated wooden body (1870–1900)

Male doll with metal torso (c. 1920)

Jumeau phonograph doll (1895–1900)

Parts of a Doll: Hands and Feet

Leather hand on bisque doll (mid- to late 19th century)

Metal hand on Joel Ellis doll (mid- to late 19th century)

Wooden fork hand on wooden doll (c. 1750)

Wooden spoon hand on wooden doll (mid-19th century)

Stitched fingers on cloth hand (19th and 20th centuries)

Cloth hand with applied thumb (early 20th century)

High-heeled china boot on china doll (1860–1900)

Molded composition shoe on bébé (early 20th century)

Painted slipper on all-wooden doll (mid-19th century)

Wooden foot on Schoenhut doll (early 20th century)

French kid foot (1875–1900)

Composition foot on Steiner bébé (1875–1910)

China hand on china doll (mid-19th century)

Jointed composition hand on French bébé (1875–1910)

Wooden hand on Schoenhut doll (early 20th century)

Starfish hand on Kewpie doll (early 20th century)

Mitten hand on cloth doll (19th and 20th centuries)

Gauntlet hand on cloth doll (mid-20th century)

Cloth and leather foot on Goldsmith doll (1870–94)

Embroidered foot on homemade doll (19th and 20th centuries)

Cloth foot on Steiff doll (early 20th century)

Cloth foot on homemade doll (mid-19th to early 20th century)

Poured-wax foot on wax doll (mid- to late 19th century)

Motschmann-type composition foot (mid- to late 19th century)

Parts of a Doll: Hairstyles and Ears

Painted pate on china head (mid-19th century)

Painted child's hairstyle on china head (1840–75)

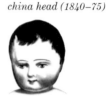

Molded braid and curls on china head (c. 1860)

Molded, side-parted male hairstyle on china head (1840–75)

Molded upswept braid on china head (mid-19th century)

Molded snood on china or bisque head (mid-19th century)

Lamb's-wool wig on bisque head (1880–1910)

Horsehair wig on Sioux Indian doll (19th century)

Molded ear on poured-wax head (1850–75)

Molded ear on china-head doll (1850–75)

Applied ear on French bébé with bisque head (1875–1900)

Felt ear on Lenci doll (early 20th century)

Molded Apollo-knot hairstyle on papier-mâché head (1830–40)

Molded sausage curls on china head (mid- to late 19th century)

Inserted hair on poured-wax head (1850–75)

Inserted hair on waxed slit-head doll (mid-19th century)

Molded hair on papier-mâché head (mid-19th century)

Molded low-brow hairstyle on china head (1840–1910)

Molded topknot on bisque Kewpie head (c. 1920)

Molded hair on composition head (1910–30)

Molded ear on parian-type head (1870–80)

Molded pierced ear on parian-type head (1870–80)

Molded cloth ear on Izannah Walker doll (late 19th century)

Applied homemade cloth ear (late 19th to early 20th century)

Parts of a Doll: Eyes and Mouths

Dot brows and pupil-less eyes on wooden head (18th century)

Painted brows and eyes on china head (mid-19th century)

Painted brows and sleep-eyes on bisque head (1875–1910)

Lithographed brows and eyes on cloth head (c. 1910)

Painted side-glancing eyes on cloth head (early 20th century)

Embroidered face on cloth head (19th and 20th centuries)

Closed mouth on French bébé (1880–1920)

Open mouth with teeth on French bébé (1880–1920)

Molded tongue on French bébé (late 19th century)

Rosebud mouth on composition head (mid-20th century)

Watermelon mouth on bisque head (early 20th century)

Crying mouth on bisque head (early 20th century)

Inserted brows on wax head (c. 1875)

Painted brows and paperweight eyes on Jumeau head (1875–1910)

Side-glancing eyes on bisque head (1890–1920)

Googly eyes on bisque head (early 20th century)

Button eyes on cloth head (late 19th to mid-20th century)

Carved eyes and brows on wooden head (c. 1900)

French bébé with painted outline mouth (1875–1910)

Open-closed mouth with teeth on Steiner bébé (c. 1880)

Open-closed mouth on bisque head (early 20th century)

Whistling mouth on German bisque head (c. 1910)

Molded mouth on Bye-Lo Baby (1922–30)

Nurser mouth on rubber doll (mid-20th century)

How to Evaluate Dolls

Although dolls vary greatly in style, age, and the characters they represent, there are some general guidelines by which they may all be evaluated. These are materials, rarity, attribution and marks, condition and restoration, authenticity, workmanship, beauty, and age.

Materials

One of the first steps in becoming a knowledgeable collector is to learn to identify dolls by their materials. Almost every doll is classified by the material of its head. For example, a doll with a bisque head, kid-over-wood body, and kid hands is considered a bisque doll. Doll heads are made from a wide range of substances, including cloth, wood, papier-mâché, composition, china, bisque, parian (untinted bisque), wax, vinyl, hard plastic, and, less frequently, celluloid, metal, rubber, and gutta-percha. Sometimes a doll's head and body are fashioned from the same material; this is often true of cloth, wooden, and plastic dolls.

Rarity

Only by studying many dolls can a collector know which ones are rare. Contrary to popular belief, rare dolls are not always the most valuable or most desirable. Rarity is but one variable among many that determine the worth of a doll. For example, a widely known doll sometimes attracts more interest than a rare but less familiar example. Moreover, a well-known doll in an unusual size—the very largest or smallest in a company's line—will often bring the greatest return on an investment.

Listed here are a few types of dolls that are considered rare. Old dolls wearing their original clothes or carrying original accessories are generally rare. Fad dolls that were made for only a short time are often rare, as are dolls made of experimental materials, such as celluloid. Also rare are folk dolls with a known provenance and Indian dolls made prior to the Second World War. Black dolls are less common and more costly than their white counterparts. Male dolls of any kind have always been a minority and are consequently desirable today. China-head dolls with pierced ears are unusual, as are those with glass eyes.

Attribution and Marks

A maker's mark or artist's signature significantly adds to a doll's value. A doll may be marked or labeled almost anywhere—on its head, body, soles of shoes or feet, inside the shoulder plate, or on a separate tag or label. The mark usually includes the name or initials and frequently the trademark of the manufacturer, designer, or craftsman; occasionally, a patent or copyright number or date appears alongside the mark. A mold number, usually indicating head style or size, may also be marked on a doll head, but not all manufacturers employed the same system of numbering, and size indications were not standardized among the various makers. Distributors sometimes affixed their own labels on dolls made by other firms. Some mass-produced dolls bear the names of their designers as well.

Unmarked Dolls

Some dolls were never marked, and others have lost their original identifying labels or tags. An unmarked doll is worth considerably more if it can be firmly attributed to a maker. It is always wise to check documentation upon which an attribution is based before acquiring a doll. The attribution of unmarked dolls can sometimes be verified through illustrations and descriptions in 19th- and 20th-century doll catalogues and in doll advertisements from old periodicals.

Try to learn as much as you can about a doll and its possible maker, place of origin, and previous owners. By studying a variety of dolls by one maker, it is sometimes possible to establish identifying traits that might not be evident when studying a single doll. Such information may help you attribute dolls in the future. For example, by examining many Steiff dolls, a collector will learn that all early examples have unusually large feet and a seam running down the center of their faces, or, by viewing a variety of Kewpie dolls, a collector will quickly discover that they all have starfish-shaped hands. Occasionally a tag or label may be found on one example belonging to a line of dolls previously thought to be unmarked.

If a dollmaker's place of residence is known, further information about him or her may often be provided by a chamber of commerce, historical society, or doll club in that area.

Condition and Restoration

A doll in mint condition with paint or finish intact is naturally the most desirable and considerably more valuable than one that is damaged, excessively worn, or restored.

Fragile Materials

Ordinary signs of age are acceptable on dolls that are made of fragile substances. For example, practically no 19th-century wax dolls are in mint condition today, since they have usually been altered by changes in temperature; the cold causes them to crack, while the heat softens and misshapes them and makes them susceptible to fingerprints. Rubber dolls made prior to the Second World War are also extremely vulnerable to temperature changes; early examples are usually brittle and cracked, and their heads are often flattened in the back from long periods of storage. Composition dolls made before the war are prone to cracking and crazing. The few surviving celluloid dolls are generally brittle and cracked as well. The limbs and heads of 19th-century china dolls often broke and were replaced; if the replaced limbs are from the same period as the rest of the figure, the doll's value is only moderately affected.

When to Restore

If a doll is damaged, careful restoration may recoup some of its lost value. Over-restoration, however, diminishes the appeal and value of a doll. Prior to 1960, when antique dolls began to be viewed as historical artifacts, numerous collectors removed the original clothing and wigs of extremely rare dolls and sometimes even replaced their heads and limbs; the dolls were then reclothed in imaginative re-creations of period garments to conform to prevailing tastes. This practice is strongly discouraged today, and a very early doll that has not been retouched will fetch a premium, even though its condition may not be perfect. Moreover, an original wig, even in matted condition, is an asset on a doll. Such a wig can sometimes be untangled by a professional at a doll hospital. If an old doll's outfit is so worn that it must be removed, do not throw it out; instead, use it as a pattern for a new garment and then store it in acid-free paper, since it may be of historical interest.

Authenticity

On occasion, dolls are repaired or restored to enhance their value and then are passed off as mint-condition examples. The best way to guarantee a doll's authenticity is to purchase it from a reliable dealer. Also, learn to recognize the warning signals that suggest a doll has been restored. For example, clothing that is glued to the body and cannot be removed may hide repairs, replacements, or makeshift construction. Keep in mind, however, that a few old dolls, especially automata, had their clothes glued to their bodies to facilitate easy movement of their limbs. Examine the paint on a doll's face: If the paint is translucent and appears to be beneath the surface, it is probably original; if it is bright, opaque, and seems to lie on the surface, the paint may have been applied recently. Before buying a china or bisque doll, try to examine the underside of its shoulder-head to see that cracks or chips are not hidden by porcelainlike repair material. If possible, carefully inspect a doll's wig and see how it is attached to the crown. French dolls have their wigs either glued or tacked to their cork pates, while nearly all German dolls have wigs glued on. Be wary of a wig that is very tightly affixed to the head, since it may hide a cracked or damaged crown.

Reproductions
Because antique bisque and china dolls are so costly and difficult to find, there is a large market for modern reproductions of them. Many of these new dolls are of an extremely high quality, and nearly all are marked as reproductions. However, on occasion such a doll is passed off as an antique.
Also much reproduced, either in printed sheets or as finished figures, are popular turn-of-the-century cloth dolls. The fresh, bright colors of the new versions distinguish them from older printed-cloth dolls, many of which have acquired a brownish tint. Once you have examined numerous old dolls, it is often quite easy to distinguish an original from a reproduction.

Workmanship
The quality of a doll's materials and the care taken in construction are important considerations when evaluating a doll. Collectors should learn the traits of each doll material and its desirable properties. For example, fine china heads are characterized by delicate modeling and glazing, and by such details as light brushstrokes around the face simulating a natural hairline. High-quality bisque should have a soft, smooth surface with a fine grain. The best wax doll heads are delicate and translucent and often have inserted hair covering the entire crown. Look for well-made joints on wooden dolls and soft white or pink kid bodies on French bisque-head dolls.

Beauty
Of all the criteria for evaluating dolls, aesthetic appeal is the hardest to measure. Though some dolls are universally considered beautiful, others appeal only to certain collectors. For example, the stately forms of old kachina dolls appeal to some people, while others prefer modern kachinas, colored with bright acrylic paint and posed as if ready for action. Perhaps the most difficult to judge are folk dolls. The distinction between a folk doll and an ordinary homemade doll is often determined by subjective criteria such as spirit, ingenuity, charm, and quaint or amusing details. It is also important to distinguish folk dolls, which are naive but charmingly whimsical or poignant, from dolls that are simply poorly designed and clumsily made.

Dating of Dolls
Determining the age of dolls is often difficult because so many of them are unmarked, and because even those that are marked do not necessarily bear a date. Moreover, some popular dolls were made for generations, and others were dressed in costumes of earlier periods to heighten their appeal. Early doll

advertisements and catalogues are excellent resources for dating dolls. Another way to establish a date is to examine a doll's materials and construction and then learn when these were invented and used, keeping in mind, however, that manufacturers did not always register their innovations right away. The following guidelines will help to establish approximate dates for many dolls.

Patents and Trademarks

Patent dates and trademarks can help to date many dolls. Some dolls, however, such as those by Izannah Walker and A. Schoenhut, were sold even before a patent date was applied for or a trademark was registered. The earliest doll patents were registered in the mid-19th century; trademarks came into favor only during the last quarter of the 19th century.

Dating Imports

Collectors can often determine if an imported doll was made before or after 1891 by whether or not it is stamped with the name of its country of origin. Beginning in that year an American customs law, the McKinley Act, required foreign products intended for sale in America to be thus stamped. While some foreign dolls made before 1891 were so marked, afterwards all such dolls had to be labeled.

Japanese dolls marked "Nippon"—the Japanese word for Japan—were probably made prior to the Second World War; most dolls made after the war say "Made in Japan."

Dating Homemade and Folk Dolls

A homemade doll can sometimes be dated approximately by examining the fabric and style of its clothing. This method is not precise, however, because dollmakers often saved fabric for years before using it. Keep in mind that rural families generally made and used homespun cloth for a longer period of time than did city dwellers, and that commercially made cloth was not widely used until the mid-19th century.

Dolls made of household objects can sometimes be dated by when such objects were made. The origin and date of clay-pipe dolls, for example, can be established by learning when smoking clay pipes was popular and in what geographical areas.

Dating Lady Dolls

Many 19th- and early 20th-century lady dolls can be dated within 20 years by their molded hairstyles or wigs, which followed the fashions of the time. Remember, however, that some popular dolls continued to be made for decades and thus featured out-of-date coiffures. In general, papier-mâché dolls produced in the 1830s and '40s have molded Apollo-knot hairstyles. China dolls from the same period are often designed with long molded hair parted in the center, draped below the ears, and swept back into a bun or twist in the style supposedly worn by the young Queen Victoria. Many mid-19th-century china dolls have molded snoods or other ornaments in their hair. China dolls from the late 19th and early 20th centuries feature low-brow hairstyles, so named for the wavy curls that fall low on the forehead. Wax dolls with slit heads or hair inserted in individual strands or clusters generally date from the second half of the 19th century. Even with these guidelines, however, by far the best way to date lady dolls and fine dolls in general is to study in depth the history of each type.

How to Use This Guide

Successful doll collectors rely on a combination of many skills, including a knowledge of types of dolls, materials, methods of construction, as well as a familiarity with the doll and toy markets. The simple steps outlined below should enable you to identify, date, and evaluate the dolls you will come across at auctions, antiques shops, flea markets, yard sales, and perhaps even in your attic.

Preparation
1. Turn to the Visual Key to become acquainted with how the dolls in this book are organized. There are sixteen groups based on type. Four of these groups feature boy and girl dolls; these dolls are grouped together according to materials. Three groups feature lady and gentleman dolls, also grouped by materials.
2. Consult Information-at-a-Glance for an explanation of the separate headings used in the entries and the type of information given under each.
3. Read the brief introductions that precede each group; these define the types of dolls illustrated, survey their history, and provide information about construction techniques.

Using the Color Plates to Identify Your Doll
1. Turn to the Visual Key and find the representative picture that stands for the doll you wish to identify. Then turn to the entry numbers listed above it.
2. Narrow your choice to the single color plate that most resembles your doll. Your doll may not match it exactly; for example, the hairstyle or eye color may differ, and clothing almost invariably will be different; materials, too, can vary, especially since a doll head made of one material may be attached to a body made of another.
3. Read the text account to check your identification. Here you will find a detailed description of the doll, its dimensions, and significant marks. The rest of the entry tells when it was made and provides historical notes as well as collecting hints.
4. Another way to identify your doll is to refer to the List of Plates by Material, in which dolls are classified by head type and major body material. Or, if you know who created your doll, look in the Index under the maker's name for other illustrated dolls by that specific person or firm.
5. After identifying your doll, turn to the Price Guide for an estimate of its current market value. Choose an amount at the low end of the range if your doll is damaged and toward the high end of the range if it is in mint condition.

Developing Expertise
1. Begin by reading the essays on the History of Dolls and the History of Doll Clothes.
2. Consult the section called Parts of a Doll, which helps increase your doll vocabulary by illustrating such distinctive elements as individual facial features and body parts. In addition, the section Makers and Marks will familiarize you with the names, dates, locations, and trademarks of some major makers.
3. Read the section How to Evaluate Dolls to learn about dating dolls and about judging their condition and quality.
4. Visit museums to learn about dolls. The section Public Collections lists those near you.
5. Read the section Building a Collection, which discusses the sources of dolls and organizations for collectors and doll artists.
6. Consult Buying at Auction, which describes how an auction works and how to bid effectively.

Information-at-a-Glance

Each color plate in this guide is accompanied by a full description
pointing out the significant features that help identify the doll.
The entry title gives the specific name of the doll, if it is known,
or the generic type, often accompanied by the maker's name.
The plate number is repeated in the Price Guide and in cross
references throughout the book. Technical terms are defined in
the Glossary.

Description
The description covers the essential elements of a doll,
including head and body materials, facial features, type of hair,
construction, and clothing and accessories. Each doll is described
starting at the head and continuing down to the feet.

Materials, Marks, and Dimensions
This section notes the materials utilized for the head, body, and
limbs of the doll illustrated. All marks are fully described, and
their location on the doll is given. The height is always in inches
and measured at the tallest point.

Maker, Origin, and Period
This category indicates the name of the craftsman, designer,
or manufacturer of the doll, if known, and sometimes its
distributor, as well as where and when it was created.

Comment
Here we provide information about the history of the specific doll
or the general type illustrated, including notes on the maker,
facts about construction techniques, and descriptions of related
dolls and common variations.

Hints for Collectors
These tips point out how to identify the type of doll illustrated,
what qualities to look for and what to avoid, which factors affect
value, how to detect repairs, and the most reliable signs of age
and authenticity. Hints are also given on caring for dolls.

Visual Key

The dolls in this guide are divided into 16 groups, among them 4 of boy and girl dolls and 3 of lady and gentleman dolls. For each group a symbol appears at left, along with a brief description of the types of dolls in the group. Photographs of dolls representing subgroups are shown at right with plate numbers indicated above them. The symbol representing the group is repeated on the opening page of the section concerning that group and again in the price guide.

Folk Dolls (*Plates 1–42*)
The diverse and imaginative 19th- and 20th-century folk dolls in this section are either one-of-a-kind items made from discarded household objects or from whatever materials were lying about, or were produced as souvenirs or craft objects by cottage industries in the South, the Appalachians, and seaside communities in Maine, California, and Florida. The subgroups in this section include dolls made of: 1) leaves; 2) miscellaneous materials; 3) cloth; 4) fruits and nuts; 5) shells; 6) wood.

Indian Dolls (*Plates 43–58*)
Originally used as ceremonial objects, figures to teach children about sacred lore, or as playthings, Indian dolls began to be made for tourists only when tribes were confined to reservations. This group includes Indian and Eskimo dolls made by these peoples as well as by others. The subgroups are: 1) dolls carved from wood or vegetable roots; 2) dolls made by combining such materials as bisque, composition, and wood; 3) dolls with stuffed bodies made of skins, cloth, or vegetable fibers.

National Costume Dolls (*Plates 59–74*)
These dolls are notable for their elaborate or fanciful costumes, which represent the traditional outfits worn by people in a wide variety of cultures. The subgroups include dolls dressed in costumes from: 1) the Far East; 2) the Middle East; 3) Europe. Craft and souvenir dolls are represented, along with dolls used in national ceremonies, dolls made by well-known European firms, and one-of-a-kind figures by prominent doll artists.

1–4   5–8, 12–13,   9–11, 31–42   14–17
       28–30

18–20   21–27

43–46   47–48, 56   49–55, 57–58

59–66   67–68   69–74

Famous Figures, Families, and Other Dolls (*Plates 75–100*)
The dolls in this section are divided into the following subgroups:
1) historical figures; 2) political personalities; 3) figures engaged
in work; 4) family members. Within this group are many elegant
and finely crafted one-of-a-kind dolls made by well-known
contemporary doll artists, several rare 19th-century novelty
dolls, as well as some best-selling examples by major American
doll companies.

Storybook, Celebrity, and Cartoon-Character Dolls
(*Plates 101–132*)
Many of the figures in this group portray popular show-business
personalities or fictional or comic-strip characters; others depict
clowns or cowboys, while still others have stuffed-animal bodies.
The subgroups are determined by the dolls' materials and
include: 1) cloth dolls; 2) dolls made of composition or other
materials; 3) wooden dolls.

Paper Dolls (*Plates 133–146*)
Inexpensive to produce, paper dolls became extremely common
in the latter half of the 19th century with the growth of the
commercial printing and publishing industries. Featured here are
a simple, homemade cutout doll, mass-produced advertising
premiums, popular characters with elaborate wardrobes, as well
as dolls that have skirts made of pages inscribed with fortunes.
The subgroups are: 1) printed-sheet, booklet, and cutout dolls;
2) celebrity dolls; 3) fortune-telling dolls.

Printed-Cloth Dolls (*Plates 147–159*)
Commercial printed-cloth dolls were first introduced in the late
19th century. They were sold in sheets that were cut and stuffed
at home, or were sold pre-assembled. The subgroups include:
1) fictional characters; 2) figures that promoted nationally
advertised products and were often distributed as premiums;
3) miscellaneous examples, such as a topsy-turvy doll and a girl
doll with a detachable coat and bonnet.

Baby Dolls (*Plates 160–189*)
This section contains baby dolls made of: 1) composition; 2) china
or bisque; 3) rubber, vinyl, or celluloid; 4) wax, wood, or papier-
mâché. Many are of historical interest, including early infant
dolls made in the 1850s and '60s of rubber or wax, popular
Victorian all-china bathing dolls, German character dolls that
realistically reflect children's expressions, as well as Grace
Putnam's famous newborn Bye-Lo Baby. Several best-selling
imitations of the Bye-Lo doll are included here as well.

Boy and Girl Dolls: China and Bisque (*Plates 190–225*)
Largely composed of bébés—bisque or china dolls representing
young children—this group includes some of the finest products
of the famous 19th-century French and German dollmakers. Also
illustrated are some later examples that reflect a decline in the
quality of materials and manufacturing standards, due primarily
to mass production and fierce international competition. The
subgroups are: 1) bisque dolls with wigs; 2) bisque dolls with
molded hair; 3) china dolls.

Boy and Girl Dolls: Wax and Wood (*Plates 226–235*)
The boy and girl dolls in this section range from fragile wax
dolls and unbreakable metal dolls to carved or molded wooden
examples. Most of the wooden dolls were produced by the
renowned firm, A. Schoenhut & Company. Included are dolls
made of: 1) wax; 2) metal; 3) wood with molded or carved hair;
4) wood with wigs.

Boy and Girl Dolls: Cloth (*Plates 236–253*)
This group contains dolls by such noted dollmakers as Izannah
Walker, Käthe Kruse, Martha Chase, Gertrude Rollinson,
Norah Wellings, Lenci, and Madame Alexander. Unlike fine
19th-century bisque or china dolls, many of the cloth figures
illustrated here were sturdy playthings, suitable for rough
handling by children. The subgroups are dolls with: 1) painted
hair; 2) applied hair or wigs; 3) molded hair.

Boy and Girl Dolls: Miscellaneous Materials (*Plates 254–283*)
The dolls in this section reflect the 20th-century search for
durable, inexpensive manmade materials. Composition was
favored through the 1940s, but other materials, especially
plastic, came into widespread use in the 1950s. The subgroups
include: 1) all-rubber dolls; 2) dolls with composition heads and
cloth or wooden bodies; 3) celluloid dolls; 4) all-composition dolls;
5) dolls with celluloid heads and composition or cloth bodies;
6) plastic or vinyl dolls; 7) a doll with a pressed cardboard head
and composition body; 8) dolls with plastic heads and cloth
bodies.

190–215   216–224   225

226–228   229   230–233   234–235

236, 239–243   237, 246–253   238, 244–245

254–255   256–257, 259,   258, 263   260, 262, 266,
                 261, 264, 267   269, 272–274,
                                                          276–278, 282

265, 271   268, 275, 279–   270   281
                 280, 283

Lady and Gentleman Dolls: China and Bisque (*Plates 284–310*)
Most of the dolls in this group are fine French or German
examples made from about 1850 to the early 20th century. These
fashionably attired dolls have either cloth or ingenious, gusseted
kid bodies, which were sometimes patented. The subgroups are:
1) china dolls with molded and painted hair; 2) bisque dolls with
molded and painted hair; 3) china dolls with wigs; 4) bisque dolls
with wigs.

Lady and Gentleman Dolls: Wood (*Plates 311–321*)
This group of wooden dolls features some of the earliest
commercially made doll types, including late 18th-century jointed
wooden lady dolls commonly known as Queen Anne dolls and a
few 19th-century German and American peg-wooden figures.
This section also contains dolls by several noted American
dollmakers as well as some charming 19th-century folk dolls. The
subgroups are: 1) dolls with wigs; 2) dolls with carved and
painted hair.

Lady and Gentleman Dolls: Miscellaneous Materials
(*Plates 322–341*)
Some of the most popular 19th-century dolls were made of such
sturdy materials as papier-mâché, composition, or wax-over-
composition. Early dollmakers also experimented with less
popular, but equally durable substances, including rubber, metal,
and rawhide. Wax, a common but fragile material, was
frequently used for expensive portrait dolls and fashion dolls. In
the 20th century some unusual fashion dolls were also made of
cloth. The subgroups here are dolls of: 1) papier-mâché; 2) wax;
3) composition; 4) rubber or metal; 5) rawhide; 6) cloth.

Mechanical Dolls (*Plates 342–357*)
Most mechanical dolls were made between 1840 and the
beginning of the First World War. Many of those shown here are
elegant French or German dolls that have movements and music
boxes operated by clockwork mechanisms. The subgroups are:
1) clowns and other characters; 2) children; 3) ladies.

284–290, 294–295, 299   *291, 296–298, 307–308*   *292–293*   *300–306, 309–310*

311–312, 320   *313–319, 321*

322–323, 326   *324, 333–336, 339*   *325, 327, 331–332, 337*   *328–329, 338*

330   *340–341*

342–343, 347, 353   *344–346, 351–352, 354–357*   *348–350*

Folk Dolls

Although they are the products of such diverse groups as Indians and Amish folk, black seamstresses and Appalachian mountain people, all folk dolls are characterized by an unmistakable boldness, simplicity, and unconventional beauty. Like other forms of folk art, they were made primarily by anonymous craftsmen, most of whom were self-taught nonprofessionals working for their own pleasure, creating primitive figures that were little influenced by the technological innovations of the day. These dolls have a timeless quality.

Some folk dolls were fashioned from one simple, readily available material, such as cloth or wood, while others were made from unusual substances or discarded objects, such as cornhusks, nuts, wishbones, fishnet, clothespins, or a patchwork of any of these. Homemade dolls that copy unavailable or costly commercial dolls are considered folk objects because of their imaginative use of materials and ingenious construction. Rustic dolls—such as the "poppets" made in Appalachia—that were created as souvenir or craft items by local cottage industries or artisans' guilds are also considered folk art. Though such craft dolls were made in significant numbers, they exhibit many of the unique personal touches found in other folk art objects. For the most part, craft dolls were designed for display rather than as playthings.

Cloth and Wooden Dolls

The two most common types of folk dolls are those made of cloth and those of wood. Usually fashioned from scrap-bag fabrics, cloth dolls range from roughly shaped figures with uneven stitching and painted or penciled faces to carefully proportioned, graceful dolls with the same kind of loving details found on many quilts. Among the simplest yet most sought-after cloth dolls are those made by Amish people; the lack of faces and the somber clothes of these figures reflect the customs and beliefs of their makers. Other more detailed cloth dolls, such as the George Washington included in this section, imitate fashionable, store-bought examples.

The spectrum of wooden folk dolls is as broad as that of cloth dolls. While many of them are crudely whittled, others show fine craftsmanship and detailing. Like folk painters, rural dollmakers were often unschooled and had difficulty in portraying the human figure, particularly hands, which resulted in charming but awkwardly proportioned dolls.

Other Mediums

Nearly every conceivable material has been shaped or incorporated into a folk doll. Indians used cornhusks to create striking dolls that ranged from unclothed, faceless figures to well-constructed dolls outfitted in pioneer or Indian costumes. Apples and other fruits and vegetables, dried and crinkled to resemble flesh, were also used by Indians and pioneers, as well as by some dollmakers today. Shells, fishnet, and even lobster claws have been ingeniously shaped into dolls in many coastal communities. A special type of folk doll is the black doll, which appears in virtually every medium. While many such figures are disturbing because they are racial stereotypes, others stand out as some of the most vibrant folk creations.

1 Iroquois cornhusk doll

Description
Cornhusk doll with simple painted features. Tall headdress. Braided arms, brown-dyed husks bound around legs. Garment tied at waist with natural and green-tinted cornhusk strips.

Materials, Marks, and Dimensions
Cornhusks. Height: 12″.

Maker, Origin, and Period
Iroquois. Probably New York State. c. 1900.

Comment
American Indians cultivated corn as early as 5000 years ago. It was the mainstay of the Iroquois people, who fashioned dolls from the husks. In keeping with a belief shared by many tribes, early 19th-century Iroquois dolls were often faceless. Their makers feared that if they defined its features a doll might literally become the person it portrayed. Some of the dolls' wigs were made with human hair or horsehair, while others had tall cornhusk headdresses. Very early Iroquois dolls are usually unclothed or wear only rudimentary cornhusk garments. Later dolls often wear costumes that are combinations of pioneer and Indian styles of dress, reflecting gradual cultural exchange. Many pioneer settlers copied the techniques and style of Iroquois and other Woodlands Indian dolls.

Hints for Collectors
The Iroquois people continue to make dolls. Fine examples can be purchased at museums and through such organizations as the Indian Arts and Crafts Board of the United States Department of the Interior. However, older dolls, as shown here, are becoming increasingly hard to find.

2 Cornhusk doll

Description
Lady doll with brown-dyed husk face. Painted features. Brown-dyed husk arms. Cornhusk costume of yellow turban and cape, natural-colored apron, and green-dyed skirt.

Materials, Marks, and Dimensions
Cornhusks. Height: 4".

Maker, Origin, and Period
Maker unknown. Probably southern United States. Early 20th century.

Comment
Some cornhusk dolls are crude and hastily made, while others are the result of hours of painstaking work. The tiny doll shown here was probably one of a set and may have portrayed a black servant, since she is dressed in the traditional outfit of a mammy. In an article published by the Brooklyn Children's Museum in 1963, Jane Adams, a midwestern woman, fondly remembered making cornhusk dolls: "About half an hour before supper we'd go into the garden, pick a dozen good fat ears of corn, shuck them, and pop them in boiling water. I'd make a little wad or ball for the head, place it in the center of the leaves, and fold them over in half, tying the husks just under the head. Then I'd twist two leaves together to make the arms, tying them at the wrist. . . . If I was making a woman I trimmed the leaves to make a skirt, maybe taking some berries to color it, making a shawl from the bottom edge of the outer leaves. . . . If I was making a man I cut the leaves and tied them at the knees and ankles."

Hints for Collectors
Cornhusk dolls that depict black people are considered rare and are eagerly sought after by collectors.

3 Cornhusk lady

Description
Lady doll with corn-silk hair and painted features. Cornhusk body stuffed with cotton. Costume of short cape tied with bow over dress with bustle and leg-of-mutton sleeves. Stylish bonnet has ribbons of shredded husk. Carries cornhusk parasol.

Materials, Marks, and Dimensions
Cornhusks and cotton. Height: 12″.

Maker, Origin, and Period
Maker unknown. New England. c. 1890.

Comment
This doll is fashioned almost entirely of cornhusks in their natural, undyed state. Her stylish dress, curly corn-silk hair, and elaborate bonnet, designed to be seen from all angles, suggest that she was patterned after a fashion-type doll. She was mentioned in *Connoisseur* magazine in the 1930s and dated to the late 19th century. A picture of an identical doll appears in Lewis Sorensen's *Doll Scrapbook*, published in 1976, and a similar version is in the collection of the Essex Institute in Salem, Massachusetts. While it is unusual to find such elegantly attired dolls made out of a rustic material, the fact that so many of these cornhusk ladies are in known collections suggests that many more exist. They must have been quite popular in the 19th century.

Hints for Collectors
The doll shown here is not expensive despite her fine quality and documented provenance. The cornhusk medium does not yet command high prices. Look for dolls with their original accessories. Female cornhusk dolls often carried items in both hands, and this one may have once owned a purse along with her parasol.

4 Walnut and leaf doll

Description
Lady doll with walnut head. Painted features including round eyes and large smiling red mouth. Multilayered dress of leaves tied with sash. Woven straw cape and sun hat. Holds bouquet of dried flowers.

Materials, Marks, and Dimensions
Walnut, leaves, and straw. Height: 13″.

Maker, Origin, and Period
Maker unknown. Possibly southern United States. c. 1930–40.

Comment
Although the doll shown here was purchased in the southern United States, she could easily have been made elsewhere. The provenance of craft dolls is difficult to determine, since their manufacture is not patented and they are generally made in private homes for sale to the tourist trade. Many souvenir dolls travel far from their origins and turn up in new places as novelties, only to be copied by local craftspeople. This spirited doll resembles figures made in Europe and Bermuda, as well as throughout the United States.

Hints for Collectors
This doll has a body composed of leaves that resemble the banana leaves that are used to make dolls in Bermuda, but they could also be tobacco leaves grown in the continental United States. There is a nearly identical walnut-head doll made with tobacco leaves at the Children's Museum in Indianapolis. A botanist's expertise might be sought for a doll like the one shown here, but such analysis is only advised if a doll is unusual or especially valuable.

5 Fishnet doll

Description
Seated girl with cork head. Painted features including side-glancing eyes and red rosebud mouth. Black fishnet hair. Body and limbs made of knotted gray fishnet. Sewn fishnet clothing of gray skirt, white apron and cap. Holds felt book with black cover and white pages.

Materials, Marks, and Dimensions
Fishnet and cork. Height: 6".

Maker, Origin, and Period
Maker unknown. California. c. 1950.

Comment
At first glance this seems to be a one-of-a-kind craft doll created spontaneously from materials lying on the beach—a stray piece of cork and multicolored remnants of fishnet. More likely, she is one of a significant number of similar dolls produced in a seaside community by a local handicraft group. Despite the seemingly haphazard arrangement of this doll's net skirt, she was fashioned with care and ingenuity. Notice her tiny felt book and the coy expression on her delicately painted face.

Hints for Collectors
American dolls fashioned out of such materials as fishnet, shells, and lobster claws can most often be found in the coastal towns of Maine and Florida. Some, however, were made in California, as was this figure. Such dolls are within the reach of even the most budget-conscious collector, and can add flavor to a craft or homemade doll collection at little expense.

Wooden moss man

Description
Male doll with carved wooden head. Inked-on features. Dried
moss mustache and beard. Wooden torso and legs; pinecone
arms. Dried moss suit tied with straw belt; tree-bark hat and
straw sandals. Carries wooden walking stick. Carved wooden
base.

Materials, Marks, and Dimensions
Wood, dried moss, and pinecones. Height: 9½″.

Maker, Origin, and Period
Maker and locale unknown. c. 1910–20.

Comment
This shaggy backwoodsman has an enigmatic past. Because of his
unusual construction he appears to be a unique doll. However,
nearly identical male and female versions exist in the Shelburne
Museum in Vermont, and in the Pitt Rivers Museum in Oxford,
England. This doll's origin has not been firmly established,
although a letter dated 1909 accompanying the two Oxford dolls,
signed "Juliet Morse, 14 Airlie Gardens, London," suggests a
Russian provenance: "I am sending the dear Uncle for New
Year, a little Russian Moss Man, made in the far 'districts' where
the forest-god rules in the natives' hearts till now. . . . The arm
being of pine-cone is a particular point, the Russians say. I
thought New Year would be the right time as he isn't a bit of a
Christian, he guarded the forests from time immemorial."

Hints for Collectors
The value of a folk doll like this one does not depend on whether
it was made in Europe or the United States, but where it is
available for purchase now. Since folk dolls are rarely mentioned
in price guides or in doll literature, it is still possible to pick up
an unusual example for a pittance, but prices do vary.

7 Wishbone dolls

Description
Dolls made of wishbones with brown wax heads and molded and carved features. Wax feet. Brown thread inserted at back of heads for hair. Prominent ears and noses. Left: Doll wears buckskin dress and cloak. Right: Doll wears shapeless buckskin garment gathered at neck.

Materials, Marks, and Dimensions
Chicken or turkey wishbones and wax. Height: 3½" (left); 3" (right).

Maker, Origin, and Period
Maker and locale unknown. c. 1875–1900.

Comment
Wishbones were fashioned into dolls by some of America's earliest settlers, who saw in them the rudiments of the human figure. They were imaginatively transformed into tiny creatures by modeling a head at the juncture of the bone with wax or other readily available materials. The dolls shown here are crude specimens, perhaps made by children; note the cross-stitched pink thread used to fasten their buckskin clothing. The presence of buckskin may indicate an Indian origin or influence. Children of many tribes made dolls from wishbones, apples, and other found objects.

Hints for Collectors
Dolls like those illustrated are likely to be found in shops specializing in Americana. Collectors can often purchase figures made of unusual materials for less than the prices asked for conventionally made dolls. Although they do not yet command wide interest, such figures do belong in collections of historical dolls, and are exhibited by various museums across the country.

8 Clothespin doll

Description
Doll fashioned from handmade wooden clothespin. Buckskin head with faintly inked-on features. Long braid of light brown human hair. Buckskin hands shaped into crude fists. Chinese-style costume of brown velvet smock over silk robe, and tall pointed silk hat with tassel.

Materials, Marks, and Dimensions
Wood and buckskin. Height: 7".

Maker, Origin, and Period
Maker unknown. Utah. c. 1875–1900.

Comment
This figure reflects the pioneer practice of creating dolls from discarded household objects—a wooden spoon or a potato peeler could just as easily have served as its base. This doll's origin is especially perplexing, because its buckskin head is typically western, but its braid is the traditional Oriental queue. Perhaps it was made by one of the many Chinese who were recruited to build the railroads in the American West during the 19th century, or fashioned by a pioneer mother inspired by the Chinese workers around her.

Hints for Collectors
Modeled from a handmade clothespin, the doll shown here can probably be dated prior to the time when clothespins were first commercially mass-produced, a change that did not come about until the late 19th century. Information provided by the manufacturer's imprint that usually appears on commercial clothespins can help in determining the geographic origin and approximate date for later dolls made from them.

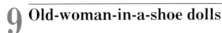

9 Old-woman-in-a-shoe dolls

Description
Cloth dolls with embroidered features and silk hair, arranged on black leather shoe. Original costumes of printed cotton dresses and suits; black caps on boys. Dolls engaged in various activities —mother holds baby, 2 boys carry bows and arrows, child reads newspaper fragment on which the word "Boston" is visible, 2 tiny heads protrude from toe of shoe.

Materials, Marks, and Dimensions
Cotton and silk dolls; leather shoe. "Old Woman in a Shoe" nursery rhyme written on sole. Height of dolls: 2–3".

Maker, Origin, and Period
Maker unknown. Probably New England. c. 1870.

Comment
Like any respectable dollhouse family, this whimsical group comes equipped with its own residence. Most likely homemade, the ensemble illustrates the popular nursery rhyme, "There was an old woman / Who lived in a shoe." The dolls' bodies are made of fabric that is rolled, a simple technique frequently used to make figures too tiny to be easily stuffed and sewn. The Victorians' love of detail is reflected in the dolls' delicately embroidered features, the variety of their costumes, and their elaborate poses.

Hints for Collectors
The theme of dolls in a shoe was popular as early as the mid-19th century. Collectors can sometimes determine the age and origin of dolls by their accessories. For example, a date has been ascribed to the group shown here based on the age of the shoe. It is likely that these dolls were made in the Boston area, since the name of that city appears on the accompanying newspaper fragment.

Dollhouse family

Description
Cloth dolls with embroidered features and threadlike hair. Six from a set of 14. Left to right: Girl with wispy blond hair, red and white striped dress, red hair ribbon and sash. Black lady in white cotton print blouse with red, white, and blue striped sash, white cotton and lace skirt. Little girl with golden hair, blue and white striped cotton dress with ruffle at neck. Lady with black hair, black silk blouse with lace collar and print skirt. Boy in black and blue checked suit, red tie and shoes. Lady wearing scarf, puffed-sleeve blouse, gray wool skirt, and crocheted apron.

Materials, Marks, and Dimensions
Cotton, silk, and wool. Height: 2–3″ (children); 5–6¼″ (ladies).

Maker, Origin, and Period
Maker unknown. United States. c. 1900.

Comment
The dolls pictured here, dressed as if on a Sunday outing, are obviously homemade creations sewn from a number of beautiful scrap-bag fabrics. Note the large, uneven basting stitches on the ladies' hems.

Hints for Collectors
One way to establish a date for a homemade doll is to examine the fabric and style of its clothing. This method is not precise, however, because dollmakers sometimes saved fabrics for years before using them. Collectors can also approximate a date based on a doll's hairstyle, since this tends to follow the fashion of the times. Such dating methods should be used with caution.

Linen-wrapped doll

Description
Cloth doll with features penciled on face. Head stuffed and stitched closed at top; body and limbs formed by folded fabric. Wears linen dress without finished collar, crudely gathered at waist and sewn over separate sleeves. Dress fabric faded to mottled tan, with original sky-blue print visible in folds. Muslin slip.

Materials, Marks, and Dimensions
Homespun linen. Height: 6″.

Maker, Origin, and Period
Maker unknown. Found in Pennsylvania. Early 19th century.

Comment
This doll is typical of the many homemade dolls that were actually played with rather than admired on a shelf. Few such figures survived the rigors of play, and they were usually discarded once they became too worn.

Hints for Collectors
It is impossible to date the utterly simple doll shown here by its appearance alone. Its age can be estimated by examining its fabric, which was spun at home in the early 1800s. Keep in mind that rural families generally made and used homespun cloth for a longer period of time than did city dwellers, and that commercially made cloth was not widely used until the mid-19th century. Always inspect the underside or seam of a doll's dress to determine its original, unfaded color. Serious doll collectors often study old fabrics, or may even consult textile experts for authentication. Dolls like this one are sometimes undervalued, and may appeal more to historians than to doll collectors.

12 Clay-pipe doll

Description
Lady doll fashioned from clay pipe. Bowl of pipe forms face; ridge on bottom of bowl serves as prominent nose and chin. Painted features including brown hair parted in center, light brown brows, blue eyes, rosy cheeks, and spectacles. Padded cotton arms and hands. Elaborate taffeta and linen bonnet; striped silk dress with homespun linen apron. Layers of petticoats allow doll to stand upright.

Materials, Marks, and Dimensions
Clay pipe and cotton. Height: 7".

Maker, Origin, and Period
Maker unknown. New England. c. 1860.

Comment
Clay-pipe figures reflect the ingenuity of 19th-century dollmakers, who transformed common objects into some of the liveliest of dolls. Many pipe figures were used as penwipers; others were sewing dolls that were made to carry needlework paraphernalia in their aprons and on their backs. The stems of some sewing dolls fit into spools of thread, which served as stable bases. Occasionally pipe dolls are found with delicate tissue-paper clothing and cotton hair, making them especially fragile.

Hints for Collectors
Because clay pipes are so easily broken, few of the dolls made from them have survived. The remaining examples are elaborately dressed, which suggests that they were kept on shelves and out of the hands of children. Valued for their rarity, they are most often found in localities where smoking clay pipes was popular, especially in New York and New England.

13 Nipple dolls

Description
Mammy dolls with heads made of rubber nipples. Simple embroidered features. Left: Doll in black dress with white linen cap, shawl, and apron. Cradles white infant in arms made of black shoelaces. Cloth baby with minute embroidered features and yellow hair; wears homespun linen dress matching mammy's outfit. Right: Doll wears red bandanna, white linen apron with matching tatted shawl over red plaid dress. Wads of white flannel underneath dresses allow dolls to stand upright.

Materials, Marks, and Dimensions
Rubber and cotton. Height: 5″ (left); 3″ (right).

Maker, Origin, and Period
Maker unknown. Southern United States. c. 1920–30.

Comment
Black dolls made from nipples and other household objects originated in the antebellum South. Some were made as late as the 1940s. Many such dolls were fashioned by the black women who cared for white children, which may explain why a number of these mammy figures hold white baby dolls in their arms. Considerable skill was needed to embroider the small faces on these nipple dolls.

Hints for Collectors
Nipple dolls have remained a well-kept secret among knowing collectors, who prize them for their charm. It is still possible to find them for a few dollars at flea markets. At stores and antiques shows specializing in Americana, however, they sell for considerably more. They are relatively scarce, since rubber nipples disintegrate over time. Keep an eye out for the rare examples depicting boys.

Chestnut and pecan dolls

Description
Mammy dolls. Left: Doll with chestnut head. Painted
caricaturized features; white cotton hair. Wears red bandanna,
black and white checked cotton dress with linen shawl and apron.
Holds white cloth baby doll with painted blue eyes and rosebud
mouth, wearing long white dress and lace-edged cap. Right:
Pincushion doll with pecan head and inked-on eyes and brows.
Mouth formed by natural split of nut. Wears red satin dress, lace
cap with matching red satin bow, lace shawl, silk organdy apron.
Beige silk hands with stitched fingers. Skirt hides satin
pincushion body.

Materials, Marks, and Dimensions
Left: Chestnut and cotton. Right: Pecan, satin, and silk. Height:
8½″ (left); 6″ (right).

Maker, Origin, and Period
Maker unknown. Left: Southern United States. Right: New
England. Early 20th century.

Comment
A pincushion doll, such as the one shown at right, served both as
a doll and as a receptacle for pins, spools of thread, needles, and
fine scissors. These dolls were made at home to encourage young
girls to sew and were also made commercially.

Hints for Collectors
Collectors try to acquire a variety of nut-head dolls. Though
walnut and hickory-nut dolls are easier to find than chestnut or
pecan figures, the type of nut has no bearing on the cost of
the doll.

15 Walnut couple

Description
Dolls with walnut heads. Painted features and gray cotton hair.
Cotton bodies over wire armatures, papier-mâché feet. Left:
Bearded gentleman in black flannel suit and bow tie; tips hat
with one hand and carries walking stick in the other. Right:
Elderly lady in elegant purple satin gown with lace jabot
and beaded brooch. Lace-covered felt hat. Carries lace
handkerchief and velvet purse.

Materials, Marks, and Dimensions
Walnuts, cotton, wire, and papier-mâché. Height: 13″ (left);
11″ (right).

Maker, Origin, and Period
Maker unknown. Southern United States. Early 20th century.

Comment
These dolls are unusual because they are dignified portraits of
black people, not the caricatures more typical of early nut-head
figures. Dressed in Sunday finery, they represent the growing
black middle class of the early 20th century.

Hints for Collectors
From time to time nut-head dolls similar to these but with slight
variations in clothing and accessories are seen at antiques shows.
This is not surprising, since nut-head dolls of this size were
frequently made in numbers of 100 or more by various groups
and small craft industries in the South, particularly in South
Carolina. To determine if dolls found separately belong together,
compare facial features, body types, and shoes. Although most
nut-head dolls are unsigned, it is wise to check the soles of their
feet for a maker's label or signature, which would enhance
value.

16 Apple-head couple

Description
Dolls with apple heads. Cloth bodies over wire armatures.
Left: Man with white bead eyes and dried apple hands. Wears
fisherman's outfit of yellow oilcloth hat and overalls, blue cotton
workshirt, and black oilcloth boots. Carries fishnet bag over
shoulder and smokes a pipe. Right: Lady with white cotton hair
parted in center, and tiny wire spectacles. Wears brown silk
jacket and skirt with black lace overskirt, beaded black lace
bonnet, black net gloves over white cotton hands. Homespun
cotton petticoat, white bloomers with floral embroidery.
Tan kid shoes.

Materials, Marks, and Dimensions
Dried apples, cotton, and wire. Height: 8½″ (left); 8″ (right).

Maker, Origin, and Period
Maker unknown. Left: Probably Maine. Right: Found in Ohio.
c. 1875–1900.

Comment
Inspired by American Indian dollmaking, pioneer settlers
created their own dolls out of apples, cornhusks, and other
local fruits and vegetables. Apple-head dolls are still made today.
Features are pinched or carved into the apple while it is still
fresh, and as the fruit dries, it darkens and shrinks. The
resulting wrinkles give the dolls personality.

Hints for Collectors
Novelty dolls like those shown here often carried little cards with
their life stories and occasionally the names of their makers.
Unfortunately, most of these tags have been lost or removed,
leaving today's collector with little definite information about the
dolls' origins.

Apple-head jazz band

Description
Trumpet player, drummer, and guitarist from a 6-man band.
Apple heads and hands, wigs of gray human hair. Cloth bodies
over wire armatures. Dressed in satin shirts, black ribbon ties,
cummerbunds, and black serge trousers. Black cardboard hats
with floral satin ribbon bands. Brass chains suggest elegant
watch fobs. Dolls attached to wooden stands.

Materials, Marks, and Dimensions
Dolls: Dried apples, cloth, and wire. Instruments: Plastic, wood,
and metal. Height: 10″ (left); 8″ (center); 10″ (right).

Maker, Origin, and Period
Maker unknown. Maine. c. 1920–30.

Comment
This lively group originally included a clarinetist, pianist, and
banjo player in addition to the dolls shown here. With their
wrinkled faces and gray hair, they seem to be veterans of Tin
Pan Alley in its heyday. Like many apple-head figures, they
were created especially for adults and were often grouped in
shadow boxes depicting vignettes of American life.

Hints for Collectors
Many apple-head dolls are products of cottage industries, made
to be sold by mail or in craft or museum shops. Older dolls are
usually found in their original clothing, since it was sewn directly
onto their bodies and was too difficult to remove or replace. The
fabric and style of the garments can often help establish an
approximate date for these dolls. Figures dressed in synthetics
were probably made since the 1930s, when such fabrics became
common.

Lobster-claw couple

Description
Dolls with lobster-claw heads. White lamb's-wool hair, black
glass bead eyes, cloth bodies and limbs, rolled paper hands.
Black electrical tape shoes. Original costumes. Left: Man wears
gray felt hat, 3-piece gray wool suit with jet buttons, watch fob,
white collar, and red tie. Carries cane. Right: Woman wears
brown felt and velvet hat, long brown printed cotton jacket and
skirt with matching purse, white lace blouse with cameo pin.
Carries lace handkerchief.

Materials, Marks, and Dimensions
Lobster claws, cloth, paper, electrical tape, and lamb's wool.
Height: 13″ (left); 12½″ (right).

Maker, Origin, and Period
Maker unknown. Possibly United States. c. 1900–10.

Comment
These comical lobster-claw dolls are novelty items meant for
display rather than play. A considerable number of such craft
dolls were made in seaside towns in Europe and the United
States from the 19th century to the present. Some were
fashioned at home and others were the commercial products of
local cottage industries. Many of the lobster-claw dolls made in
the 20th century originated on the Maine coast.

Hints for Collectors
Collectors sometimes mistake handcrafted dolls that were
produced by the hundreds for one-of-a-kind examples. Many
handcrafted dolls were originally made to delight family and
friends, and the imaginative qualities of the best of them were
retained when they were reproduced for sale.

19 Shell dolls

Description
Dolls clothed entirely in shells on wooden bases. Composition heads with painted features. Wooden bodies. Left: Lady dressed in white blouse and black skirt created from multicolored shells glued to body. Paper underskirt. Painted paper sun hat with glitter, and pointed yellow wooden shoes. Right: Man dressed in shell outfit of gray coat, black pants, white shirt with gray and black tie. Wears large black paper stovepipe hat. Carries wicker basket.

Materials, Marks, and Dimensions
Shells, wood, composition, and paper. Height: 12″ (left); 13″ (right).

Maker, Origin, and Period
Maker unknown. Possibly Germany or France. c. 1850.

Comment
These 19th-century novelty dolls are precursors to 20th-century shell dolls sold as souvenirs at seaside resorts. It is widely believed that the wooden bodies and composition heads of dolls like these were made in Germany, then exported to France to be dressed. The dolls shown here may have been outfitted in Brittany, since their outfits resemble those of Breton men and women.

Hints for Collectors
Early shell dolls are usually found in museums, both in the United States and abroad. The shells are so delicate that few such dolls have survived; those extant must be held by their stands to avoid breakage. Many of them were made in pairs that have long since become separated. This couple is therefore a rare find.

Shell wedding dolls

Description
Dolls made of shells. Painted features. Pipe-cleaner arms. Left: Bridesmaid has black hair adorned with 3 pink roses. Tiered dress of brown scallop shells and matching shell cape. White gloves, bonnet tied with ribbon. Carries bouquet of pink cloth flowers, matching flower buttons on dress. Right: Flower girl has blond hair adorned with 3 yellow roses. Tiered dress of white scallop shells with matching cape and green satin sash. Tiny pink shell buttons on bodice. Shell bonnet with flowers and ribbon on brim, tied with green bow. Carries straw basket of dried flowers.

Materials, Marks, and Dimensions
Scallop shells, pipe cleaners, and cloth. Signed "LAYTON" in ink on bases. Height: 6½″ (left); 5½″ (right).

Maker, Origin, and Period
Captain and Mrs. L. J. Layton. Florida. c. 1935.

Comment
The delicate ladies shown here, originally from a wedding party set, were among many figures produced by the Laytons, a retired Florida couple. They collected shells along the Gulf Coast, sorted them by size and color, and cleaned and bleached them. Captain Layton built the dolls' bodies; Mrs. Layton painted them and added accessories. The Laytons' dolls are known for their fine quality and sturdy construction.

Hints for Collectors
Shell ladies can be considered both bric-a-brac ornaments and true dolls. Some are only an inch high. Look for figures that are very finely detailed.

Wooden couple

Description
Pair of small wooden dolls with hand-carved and painted features
and hair. Block torsos, flexible wire arms and legs, wooden hands
and feet. Original costumes. Left: Elderly gentleman with gray
hair, beard, and mustache. Wears long-sleeved yellow cotton
shirt, brown tie, black wool vest and trousers, and painted black
wooden shoes. Right: Elderly lady with gray topknot. Wears
long brown satin dress with lace collar and gold buttons, green
beaded necklace, and painted black wooden shoes.

Materials, Marks, and Dimensions
Wood and wire. Height: 6½″ (left); 6″ (right).

Maker, Origin, and Period
Maker unknown. New Hampshire. c. 1860–80.

Comment
In 19th-century America, whittling was a favorite pastime
of boys and men, who relaxed at the end of a hard day by
carving dolls, toys, and whimsies from scraps of wood. Such
craftsmanship was especially prized among New Englanders,
who valued their woodworking abilities as part of a long and
proud tradition. The quaint couple shown here was made by a
skilled whittler. Attired in their sober Sunday best, this elderly
lady and gentleman seem the picture of respectability.

Hints for Collectors
Because homemade dolls are not only charming for their
individuality, but are also important for what they reveal about
family and social history, doll collectors must vie with museum
curators and historians for the best examples. Collectors should
be wary of modern copies of 19th-century whittled dolls that are
presented as originals. These will lack the wear and faded paint
found on earlier dolls.

Carved wooden doll

Description
Wooden doll with hand-carved features and hair. Swivel head.
Jointed at shoulders, hips, and knees. Original costume of black
cotton bonnet, black cotton apron over simple polka-dot dress,
white underskirt, and painted black wooden shoes.

Materials, Marks, and Dimensions
Wood. Label on underskirt reads "Kimcraft/American Type/
Dolls/INDEPENDENCE MO." Height: 9¼".

Maker, Origin, and Period
Maker unknown. Appalachia. Distributed by Kimcraft.
Independence, Missouri. c. 1940–50.

Comment
Carved wooden dolls like this one, often called poppets,
belong to the rich craft heritage of the mountain people of the
South. Whittled from native woods, their dolls portray hard-
working folk. Craft guilds were formed in the early 20th
century to help rural people supplement their incomes by selling
their handicrafts. Kimcraft, a Missouri mail-order company
established in 1940, actively sought works by Appalachian
dollmakers to sell through their catalogues and newsletters. The
doll shown here was distributed with the name "Ursey."

Hints for Collectors
Appalachian artisans have been making different versions of the
same dolls over a number of years. Some are still distributed by
Kimcraft. Naturally, vintage wooden dolls are the most valuable.
They can be identified by their dark patina and by costumes
made of homespun, nonsynthetic fabrics. Originally, all the early
women dolls wore bonnets, and all the men, caps, but these
accessories may now be missing.

Bedpost doll

Description
Homemade doll with dark brown wooden head fashioned from bedpost finial. Carved features. Cloth body. Original long-sleeved homespun cotton dress, 2 cotton underskirts, and lace-trimmed pantalettes.

Materials, Marks, and Dimensions
Wood and cloth. Height: 20½".

Maker, Origin, and Period
Maker unknown. United States. c. 1850.

Comment
In the 19th century, many worn-out utilitarian objects were transformed into dolls, although very few achieved the stark beauty of this bedpost figure. She is quite striking in her simplicity. The scars on the bedpost reveal her origin, but the doll's carefully modeled face tells of a new life gained in the loving hands of an expert dollmaker eager to please a child.

Hints for Collectors
In general, folk dolls made from a combination of cloth and wood are rarer and more valuable than all-cloth or all-wood examples. A knowledge of wood types and antique textiles can help in determining a doll's provenance. For example, some woods are indigenous only to certain areas of the country. Collectors interested in old dolls whose origins are unknown should view numerous dolls firsthand, become acquainted with the literature about wood and textiles, and seek the occasional advice of skilled woodworkers and textile experts. Early homemade dolls of the high quality shown here, however, seldom appear on the market.

24 Carved wooden doll

Description
Lady doll with wooden shoulder-head. Carved close-set features, and hair styled in roll. Cloth upper arms and body, painted wooden lower arms and legs. Red paper bands at elbows. Wears sleeveless dress with white cotton bodice and pleated, full-length piqué skirt.

Materials, Marks, and Dimensions
Wood and cloth. Height: 14″.

Maker, Origin, and Period
Maker and locale unknown. c. 1850–1900.

Comment
The hand-carved wooden head on the doll illustrated is a fine example of folk art because of its distinctive rolled hairstyle and expressive face. The limbs, however, are commercially made. It is possible that this doll once had all-cloth arms that were later replaced with wooden arms from another doll when the original limbs became too worn. On the other hand, the figure may have been assembled recently from available spare parts by a collector or dealer wishing to make a complete doll.

Hints for Collectors
The arms on this doll can be recognized easily as replacements because they are poorly attached to the body and out of character with the figure's hand-carved, obviously homemade head. The limbs with red paper bands were probably imported from Germany, where they were commonly used in the 19th century on papier-mâché dolls.

Description
Pair of wooden dolls with jointed bodies. Left: Carved and painted head, short black hair, green glass eyes, wooden knob nose, incised mouth. Arms and legs attached to simple carved torso with wire nails, limbs pegged together. Knoblike hands. Painted black shoes. Right: Carved head with short blond mohair wig. Wire nailheads for eyes, sharply angled nose, incised mouth. Body of laminated wood carved into woman's shape with ample bust. Arms and legs joined to torso with wooden dowels. Painted high-heeled boots.

Materials, Marks, and Dimensions
Wood. Height: 17¼″ (left); 15½″ (right).

Maker, Origin, and Period
Maker and locale unknown. c. 1850–1900.

Comment
These homemade dolls illustrate various woodworking techniques commonly used in the 19th century. The sturdy proportions and Pinocchio-type nose of the amusing figure at left suggest that it is a male doll. His nose, which nearly hides his big grin, may have been the knob of a bureau drawer. He is fastened together with the peg joints often found on homemade dolls from this period. The carved, laminated wooden body of the female doll on the right appears to be the creation of a skilled craftsman.

Hints for Collectors
Often the value of a simple homemade or folk doll can only be determined by subjective criteria, such as spirit, ingenuity, and charm. Look for quaint or amusing details like the comical nose seen on the doll at left.

Wooden girl doll

Description
Varnished wooden girl doll. Features carved in relief on flat face.
Yellow burlap hair tied in single braid with red raffia ribbon.
Arms and legs attached to body with carpentry nails. Fingernails
painted red. Green calico print dress. White bloomers edged with
rickrack. Carved boots.

Materials, Marks, and Dimensions
Poplar. Height: 9½".

Maker, Origin, and Period
Maker unknown. Possibly southern United States. c. 1920–40.

Comment
The broad-faced child shown here, with eyes nearly closed, is so
finely carved that she can be considered a folk art object. It is
not unusual that she is only partially varnished. Amateur and
professional dollmakers alike commonly painted or varnished
only a doll's head and limbs, leaving the body unpainted because
it would be covered by clothing. This doll's bright red fingernails
suggest that she was made after 1920, when cosmetics became
socially acceptable.

Hints for Collectors
A knowledge of wood types and their native origins may help
in determining a carved doll's provenance, but additional
information is usually necessary. Many wooden dolls were made
in the Appalachian Mountains, where whittling was a favorite
pastime. Regarded merely as playthings, these dolls were
usually unsigned.

Dancing stick man

Description
Black wooden dancing man worked by stick attached to back.
Carved and painted features. Arms, hips, and legs loosely
jointed to allow for dancing movement. Painted clothing of green
jacket with orange lapels, red vest and bow tie, white high-
necked shirt with rhinestone brooch, orange pants. Brass
buttons on vest and jacket. White gloves, large black shoes.

Materials, Marks, and Dimensions
Wood. Height of doll: 10½". Length of stick: 17".

Maker, Origin, and Period
Maker unknown. Maryland. c. 1920–30.

Comment
Dancing stick figures are sometimes considered toys rather than
dolls. Shaking the stick causes the dancing movement. They are
known to have been made as early as 1850, but reached the
height of their popularity in the late 19th and early 20th
centuries. During this period, they were often painted black and
dressed as dandies. The doll shown here may have originally
worn a hat to cover his bald head. He is a fine example of his
type. Average examples have flat faces, poorly articulated stick
bodies, and crudely painted clothing.

Hints for Collectors
Dancing stick dolls can be found at flea markets and in shops
specializing in toys or collectibles. Good examples command high
prices because they appeal to collectors in different fields. Avoid
rough, unfinished dolls; these are of little value. In general, early
20th-century black dancing dolls are worth more than their white
counterparts. Beware of modern reproductions.

Broom dolls

Description
Mammy dolls with children's toy brooms as bases. Cloth heads and torsos stuffed with straw, cloth arms stuffed with cotton padding. Left: Painted features, black steel-wool hair. Wears red calico bandanna and matching 3-tiered apron, yellow calico blouse, and long black skirt with gingham trim. Brass earrings, white necklace with coral bead in center. Right: Embroidered features. Wears white dust cap and white cotton apron over red and white print blouse and green skirt.

Materials, Marks, and Dimensions
Cotton. Straw brooms with wooden handles. Height: Doll 17″, broom 36″ (left); doll 12″, broom 35″ (right).

Maker, Origin, and Period
Maker unknown. United States. Early 20th century.

Comment
The figures shown here are commonly referred to as household or utility dolls. Produced as late as the 1950s, household dolls were most popular in the 1920s and '30s, when they were generally dressed in brightly colored Art Deco print outfits. 19th-century examples, now rarely seen, had dresses of calico, homespun, or gingham; the early 20th-century dolls illustrated wear calico. The necklace on the figure at left is an unusual touch of finery for a utility doll.

Hints for Collectors
People who collect broom dolls often try to find figures fashioned from other household items such as feather dusters, potato mashers, and spoons. Most broom dolls represent black figures, although a few white dolls were made in New England in the 19th century. Despite their caricaturelike features, these dolls are valued by collectors of black Americana.

Sewing dolls

Description
Cloth dolls attached to spools of thread. Embroidered features including tiny teeth. Wool hair. Black silk bodies stuffed with cotton. Black silk limbs attached with metal hooks and eyes. Left: Lady wears red hat, net blouse fastened with rhinestone brooch at collar, and silk print skirt over net slip. Sequin at wrist imitates diamond bracelet. Right: Man wears tasseled velvet hat, embroidered silk blouse, and red silk pantaloons.

Materials, Marks, and Dimensions
Silk and cotton; wooden spools. Spools labeled "M. Heminway & Sons, Watertown, Conn. Established 1849." Height: 8".

Maker, Origin, and Period
Maker unknown. Found in New Jersey. c. 1890.

Comment
Fancy needlework was a favorite 19th-century pastime, and sewing paraphernalia was often ornately decorated by amateur sewing enthusiasts. The rich fabrics and expert needlework of these imaginative dolls, however, suggest that they were made by an experienced dressmaker out of remnants from a scrap bag. Because the dolls are black, perhaps a black seamstress created them, since dressmaking was one of the few professional occupations open to black women during this period.

Hints for Collectors
Black dolls dressed in fashionable, rich clothing are highly prized, particularly when the bodies and faces are so skillfully defined. The dolls illustrated are of additional interest because they are made from spools of thread labeled with information about the manufacturer that may help to date them.

Description
Mammy dolls with stuffed cotton stocking faces and appliquéd and embroidered features. Cloth bodies fashioned over sand-filled bottles. Left: Doll with side-glancing round eyes and wide red mouth. Curly gray hair. Wears black and white checked bandanna, red floral print dress with long white apron, beige cotton slip. Brass earring. Right: Doll with round eyes made of "page-saver" reinforcements, nose of 2 white beads, and embroidered red mouth with row of tiny white beads for teeth. Wears matching bandanna and kerchief, floral print dress, and linen apron. Brass earrings. Carries black baby in short print dress and apron.

Materials, Marks, and Dimensions
Cotton; glass bottles. Height: 15″ (left); 13″ (right).

Maker, Origin, and Period
Maker unknown. Probably southern United States. c. 1920–30.

Comment
Bottle dolls are also referred to as doorstop dolls because they were made to be used as both doorstops and playthings, although a child had to be careful to avoid breaking the bottle. These dolls were often fashioned in the image of black domestic servants. They were produced commercially as well as in the home and were made by schoolchildren as classroom projects. Bottle dolls date from the early 19th century to the mid-20th century and are most commonly found in the South and in New England.

Hints for Collectors
The bottle doll illustrated here holding a black baby is an unusual find, since mammy dolls were more often shown carrying white children. White bottle dolls are quite rare.

Topsy-turvy doll

Description
Black-and-white topsy-turvy doll. Stuffed with cotton batting.
Black doll has painted features and hair. Wears yellow calico
print bonnet and dress with high-necked, pleated linen bodice.
White doll has features and hair drawn in black India ink. Wears
red calico dress and bonnet identical in style to that of black doll.
Doll can be switched from black to white by flipping its long skirt
to reveal either side.

Materials, Marks, and Dimensions
Linen and cotton. Height: 14″.

Maker, Origin, and Period
Maker unknown. Southern United States. c. 1880–1900.

Comment
Black-and-white topsy-turvy dolls originated in the antebellum
South, where they were made by black women who cared for
white children, and by black children who sometimes played with
white dolls. Slave children would flip their dolls to the black side
when an overseer or plantation owner appeared. Topsy-turvy
dolls are also called double-enders.

Hints for Collectors
This doll is unusual in that both sides are identical except for the
color of the clothing and complexions, a factor that increases its
value. Most early black-and-white topsy-turvy dolls were racial
stereotypes. The black side often had caricaturelike facial
features and was dressed as a mammy. Topsy-turvy dolls made
before 1900 are increasingly hard to find and command high
prices. Those made in the 20th century include fairy-tale or
nursery-rhyme characters, and crying-smiling figures.

Description
Elderly lady doll made of black cotton stocking with applied
features. Curly gray wool hair, brown button eyes with painted
black pupils, and brown leather lips. Body stuffed with wool.
Legs ribbed at bottom. Brown kid mitten-shaped hands. Wears
long white cotton and homespun linen dress and bloomers
adorned with lace, embroidery, and tatting. High lace-up shoes.

Materials, Marks, and Dimensions
Cotton, leather, and wool. Height: 21".

Maker, Origin, and Period
Maker unknown. United States. c. 1880–1900.

Comment
This benevolent figure, perhaps modeled after a black child's
grandmother or a white child's beloved mammy, has many
unusual features. Instead of a painted or embroidered mouth,
she has applied leather lips. Her limbs, well hidden by clothing,
are unusually proportioned. While most rag dolls have shapeless
bodies, this figure has distinctive sausagelike arms, long skinny
legs, and prominent buttocks and hips. She wears a child's worn-
out, castoff shoes that fit her perfectly; new laces have replaced
the original ones. Judging from the many times this doll was
mended, she must have been cherished by her owners. Note the
gray repair stitches on her forehead and body.

Hints for Collectors
Look for homemade dolls with distinctively fashioned bodies,
especially those made from imaginative combinations of materials
like this example. Leather hands, lips, or feet are seldom seen
and add interest to a homemade doll.

Homemade Raggedy Ann dolls

Description
Cloth dolls with embroidered and appliquéd features. Stuffed with cotton batting. Left: Bright orange yarn hair, closed eyes. Linen head and body. Pink and white candy-striped muslin legs. Blue and white checked gingham dress, white linen pantalettes, and black oilcloth shoes. Right: Red yarn hair. Muslin head, body, and limbs. Cotton floral print dress over yellow overalls. Socks of mattress ticking, black rayon boots.

Materials, Marks, and Dimensions
Left: Linen, muslin, and wool yarn. Right: Muslin, cotton, and wool yarn. Height: 23″ (left); 15″ (right).

Maker, Origin, and Period
Maker unknown. United States. c. 1920.

Comment
During the 1920s and '30s, the characters Raggedy Ann and Andy were so popular that parents who could not afford store-bought dolls fashioned their own. The original Raggedy Ann was patented by John Gruelle in 1915 and modeled after a rag doll he found in his mother's attic. The yarn hair and mitten hands of the doll on the right resemble those of Gruelle's commercial Raggedy Ann. The long-legged, sleepy-eyed doll on the left is less faithful to the original (*see* 109).

Hints for Collectors
Early commercial Raggedy Ann dolls often had red celluloid hearts attached to their bodies. Similar hearts were sometimes embroidered or painted on homemade figures. Pairs of homemade Raggedy Ann and Andy dolls are hard to find and are considered quite valuable. Some collectors amass dozens of them.

Description
Girl dolls with oilcloth heads and nearly identical painted features. Left: Doll with short hair made of brown fur. Body of mattress ticking and rough linen. Brown leather lower arms and feet. Wears brown felt hat, blue striped cotton blouse and bloomers, and blue calico skirt tied at waist with brown cotton sash. Remnants of black wool stockings. Right: Sister has short brown wool hair. Muslin body and limbs. Wears short-sleeved, smocked floral blouse, gray skirt, and ruffled brown plaid apron. One black sock missing.

Materials, Marks, and Dimensions
Left: Oilcloth, linen, cotton, and leather. Right: Oilcloth, muslin, and cotton. Height: 19″.

Maker, Origin, and Period
Maker unknown. Found in Vermont. c. 1875.

Comment
Found together, these appealing dolls were probably made as playmates for a little girl. Although sewn from such cast-off materials as mattress ticking, they are endowed with a grace all their own. The smocking on the floral blouse, for example, is the kind of loving detail that went into the figure's costuming. The fact that the dolls are so well preserved indicates that they played an important role in their owner's life.

Hints for Collectors
These homemade cloth dolls are considered excellent examples because of their charming appearance, detailed stitching, and unique combination of materials. Moreover, they are definitely a pair. Such dolls are a valuable find.

35 Amish cloth couple

Description
Amish dolls with featureless oilcloth faces and traditional Amish clothing. Muslin bodies. Left: Girl wears brown smock over purple dress. Black silk stockings and flannel shoes. Right: Boy wears simple blue shirt and plain brown cotton pants. Ribbed black woolen stockings, flannel shoes.

Materials, Marks, and Dimensions
Muslin and oilcloth. Height: 16″.

Maker, Origin, and Period
Maker unknown. Pennsylvania. c. 1920.

Comment
Amish dolls reflect the customs and beliefs of their makers. They are faceless because the Amish believed that it was sinful to capture one's likeness in photographs, portraits, or dolls. Since children wore miniature versions of their parents' clothing, so did their dolls. The figures shown here are dressed in typical Amish colors of brown, purple, and blue. Plain, often somber, clothing was the rule and printed fabrics were not allowed. Similar dolls in patterned clothing are probably Mennonite. The Mennonites, who emigrated to America from Europe in the 17th century, are somewhat less strict about dress codes than the Amish.

Hints for Collectors
Of all Amish dolls, boys and couples are the most sought after and command very high prices. On rare occasions, an Amish doll will have lightly penciled features—perhaps the work of a child who could not resist sketching in the forbidden eyes, nose, and mouth.

Cloth girl doll

Description
Girl doll with faded painted features. Brown wig of human hair that is glued and sewn on crown. Stitched fingers, separate thumbs. Original costume of striped flannel cape with shawl collar, beige linen dress with pink piping at collar and sleeves, and pink linen belt fastened by pearl button. Underskirt and pantaloons. Knit hat and stockings. Black velvet shoes with bows of gold metallic thread.

Materials, Marks, and Dimensions
Muslin. Height: 27″.

Maker, Origin, and Period
Maker unknown. Iowa. c. 1910.

Comment
The doll shown here is unusually large for a homemade figure. Perhaps she was modeled after a popular commercial doll. Judging from her carefully designed outfit, complete with cape, hat, and black velvet shoes, she was especially cherished by her young owner. However, her smudged features and sparse hair suggest that she was inadvertently exposed to the sun and rain. Although cloth dolls should not be washed, many children bathed them frequently, a factor that could also account for the doll's ill-defined features.

Hints for Collectors
Despite her somewhat ungainly appearance, this homemade doll was fashioned with care and forethought. Her long, graceful, individually stitched fingers and separate thumbs and the original costume fit for a Sunday outing set her apart from less detailed homemade dolls.

Description
Boy doll with features and ears drawn in brown ink. Body stuffed with cotton batting. Stitched fingers and thumbs. Wears black velvet cap with brim, short black velvet jacket and knickers, high-necked ecru lace blouse with red satin tie. Ribbed black cotton stockings.

Materials, Marks, and Dimensions
Muslin. Height: 15″.

Maker, Origin, and Period
Maker unknown. Found in Iowa. c. 1900.

Comment
The clumsy body beneath dapper clothing, the wide-eyed stare, and the hint of a smile give this doll the whimsical look of a rustic Little Lord Fauntleroy.

Hints for Collectors
Although his outfit is made from elegant materials, this doll is not finely constructed. The blouse is only a half-blouse, perhaps made to conserve fabric. Lifting the jacket in the back reveals that lace was sewn to the sides of the body, leaving the doll's back bare. Notice, too, that no attempt was made to give the doll hair. Such shortcuts are characteristic of many homemade figures. Collectors should not only inspect a cloth doll visually, but also carefully press it to determine what kind of stuffing was used. If the doll is filled with bran or straw, it will feel crinkly rather than soft. These fillers were used less often than cloth or cotton batting after the turn of the century.

Description
Portrait doll with linen head; features painted and drawn in ink. White cotton hair tied with black velvet bow. Cardboard body, white kid lower arms. Original clothing of pleated white linen shirtfront with white felt bow tie. Brown brocade vest with wooden buttons, black velvet jacket lined in purple silk, white lace cuffs sewn in sleeves. Black velvet breeches and hat. White cotton knit stockings, black suede shoes with grosgrain ribbon bows.

Materials, Marks, and Dimensions
Linen, cardboard, and kid. Height: 18″.

Maker, Origin, and Period
Maker unknown. United States. Early 20th century.

Comment
George Washington is thought to have inspired more patriotic dolls than any other person in American history. The Centennial, Bicentennial, and other national celebrations always precipitate a rash of George Washington dolls, in both homemade and commercial versions. He is often seen paired with his wife, Martha. These dolls are generally fashioned from combinations of silk, velvet, lace, and other costly materials that suggest the finery worn by statesmen and ladies of the late 18th century.

Hints for Collectors
Museums such as the New-York Historical Society and the West Chester Historical Society of Pennsylvania have wonderful homemade George Washington dolls in their collections. The President is usually portrayed—as he is here—with white hair tied back in a ribbon, and wearing a tricornered hat, formal jacket, and breeches.

Description
Boy doll with cloth head and painted features. Wavy brown hair parted on side. Cloth body, china hands. High boots painted on wooden feet. Wears blue wool coat with metal buttons, brown wool trousers, white cotton shirt, black cotton tie.

Materials, Marks, and Dimensions
Cloth, china, and wood. Height: 14″.

Maker, Origin, and Period
Maker unknown. United States. c. 1890–1900.

Comment
This well-tailored young man may have been patterned after a popular store-bought doll. In the 19th century it was common practice for parents to fashion homemade figures after commercial dolls that were either unavailable or too expensive to purchase. This doll's light brown hair is painted in the same style as the hair of china boy dolls. His painted facial features resemble those of the lithographed cloth dolls introduced at the end of the 19th century. His china hands may have been salvaged from a cast-off lady doll, for it was certainly easier for a parent to attach ready-made hands to a cloth figure than to stitch individual fingers for it.

Hints for Collectors
It is difficult to determine whether a homemade doll's limbs are original. Many dolls were fashioned initially from a combination of materials, and parents often replaced worn and broken parts more than once in a doll's lifetime. A doll's value is not affected by such replacements as long as the parts themselves are of the same period as the rest of the figure.

Betty and Martha Ann

Description
Homemade cloth girl dolls with painted features. Cropped brown hair with wispy bangs. Bodies stuffed with sawdust. Large painted hands with carefully stitched fingers. Dolls wear original costumes of white cotton infant dresses, undershirts, slips, and ribbed stockings. Woolen booties. Right: Martha Ann has stitched toes.

Materials, Marks, and Dimensions
Muslin. Height: 24″.

Maker, Origin, and Period
Letta Vanderhoof. Left: Michigan. 1897. Right: Woodsworth, Wisconsin. 1923.

Comment
The cloth dolls illustrated here were painted with rare sensitivity by their maker, Letta Vanderhoof. She made Betty, at left, for her 7-year-old daughter in 1897, while Martha Ann was sewn for her granddaughter in 1923. Although these dolls were fashioned 26 years apart, they are nearly identical in appearance, which suggests that the granddaughter must have requested a doll just like her mother's. The dolls traveled with the Vanderhoof family from Chicago to Kalamazoo, Michigan; Sarasota, Florida; and ultimately Las Cruces, New Mexico, where they were purchased by their current owner.

Hints for Collectors
Dolls with firmly established provenances are usually found only in museums and state historical societies. Should unique dolls like these become available, try to obtain any existing documentation about them.

Pointed-head doll

Description
Girl doll with pointed head and oil-painted features and hair.
Body and limbs stuffed with bran. Deep blue eyes, brown hair,
rosy cheeks, and thin red mouth. Sturdy body with simple arms
and no hands. Feet jut out at right angles. Wears red and white
calico print dress embroidered with French bowknots at sleeves
and collar.

Materials, Marks, and Dimensions
Muslin. Height: 13½".

Maker, Origin, and Period
Maker unknown. Found in Utah. Late 19th century.

Comment
This doll may have been the work of a child who had difficulty
constructing a round head, but who lavished great care on the
features. Note the attempt to define the nose and the sensitive
shading around the eyes. The doll's feet point outward, a
common trait of 19th-century cloth dolls.

Hints for Collectors
The value of the doll shown here is greatly enhanced by its
unusual pointed head. Features like this, as well as the doll's
whimsical and poignant face, can elevate what at first may seem
a clumsy and crude doll to the level of folk art. This doll was
reclothed in a 19th-century calico print outfit purchased by its
present owner. It is not uncommon for a collector to search for
quite some time before locating a costume of the proper size and
period for a particular doll.

Chinese doll

Description
Child doll with painted features and hair. Body and limbs stuffed with sawdust. Legs attached to body with pink buttons to allow back-and-forth movement. Feet point inward. Hands with stitched fingers and separate thumbs. Traditional Chinese-style robe of printed muslin with mandarin collar and black silk frog fasteners at neck and sides.

Materials, Marks, and Dimensions
Muslin, silk, and plastic. Height: 10″.

Maker, Origin, and Period
Maker unknown. Utah. c. 1920–30.

Comment
The doll shown here was found in Utah, where there was a large Chinese population around the turn of the century. Chinese laborers originally settled in the West in the mid-19th century to help build the railroads, bringing their families with them. This tender figure was probably made by an Oriental mother for her child. Unlike the formal figures made in China, this doll was intended as a plaything.

Hints for Collectors
This type of doll has a special meaning for doll fanciers interested in Chinese-American history. Such examples are most often found in California, Colorado, Utah, and New York. The geometric Art Deco print of her robe, her short hairstyle, and the plastic buttons that join her legs to her body indicate that she was probably made in the 1920s. She is fashioned from muslin, which was cheaper than cotton. A doll like this is a potential "sleeper"—one that may easily sell for less than its actual value.

Indian Dolls

 Dolls reveal much about the different customs and lifestyles of the many Indian tribes that made them. Early dolls were meant for play as well as for teaching children tribal traditions. By the late 19th century, when Indian groups were confined to reservations, some dolls began to be made specifically for tourists; such dolls continue to be fashioned and are today the most readily available types. Also included in this section are figures made by non-Indians, which show outsiders' idealized or stereotyped perceptions of native American groups.

Kachinas

Usually carved of cottonwood root or pine, kachina dolls are part of the religious cults of two Pueblo tribes of the American Southwest, the Hopi and the Zuni. The dolls are representations of the Kachina spirits in each tribe's pantheon as well as of their human impersonators, who are also known as Kachinas. The latter dress in elaborate costumes and masks and assume the roles of the spirits on special occasions. The dolls' outfits, based on these costumes and masks, are painted in bright symbolic colors and feature geometric shapes that identify the spirits they represent. Children are given the ceremonial kachina dolls as reminders of their religious heritage and to instruct them in the ways of sacred lore.

Dolls of the Woodlands and Plains Indians and Other Tribes

The Iroquois, Seneca, and other Woodlands Indians of the northeastern United States fashioned dolls of cornhusks and corncobs, reflecting the tribes' economic dependence on corn. Early cornhusk figures often had blank faces because of a belief that if their features were delineated, dolls might come to life. The Seminoles, a tribe that eventually settled in the South, made dolls of the palmetto leaves native to that region and dressed them in colorful ribbon or patchwork outfits based on the traditional geometric patterns of their own clothing.

Buckskin, a soft, suedelike leather that served a variety of purposes, was a dollmaking material favored by the Plains Indians. These tribes were also noted for the striking beadwork with which they decorated innumerable objects, including dolls; children practiced beadwork on doll clothing, using beads of all shapes, sizes, and colors to create patterns that were relatively simple.

Navajo cloth dolls reflect the influence of white settlers on Indian culture. For instance, these dolls show that Indian women adopted commercially woven calico fabrics for their clothing; yet their love of silver and turquoise jewelry was undiminished, inducing them to adorn their dolls with elaborate earrings, necklaces, and concha belts.

Though most Indian dolls represent adults, a few, such as the baby snuggled inside its cradleboard seen in this section, depict infants or children. In Alaska, where dolls are still made from the bone, antler, ivory, and skins that are that region's raw materials, Eskimo children act out adult roles through dolls. Boys, who usually become fishermen and hunters as adults, play with male dolls equipped with spears and kayaks; girls often carry baby dolls in their furry hoods, just as their mothers carried them when they were small.

Description
Dolls with carved cylindrical bodies. Bent arms nailed to shoulders, tiny feet. Left: Carved face painted in geometric designs. Painted chest, arms, and lower legs. Unpainted lower trunk and upper legs. May originally have worn a kilt. Carries ritual knife. Right: Kachina with painted case mask, painted body, unpainted legs flexed at knees. Rolled cotton collar, white leather kilt.

Materials, Marks, and Dimensions
Pine. Height: 11″ (left); 6¾″ (right).

Maker, Origin, and Period
Zuni Pueblo. New Mexico. Early 20th century.

Comment
Collectors frequently confuse Zuni and Hopi kachinas because those made for tourists in the last 25 years are indeed very similar in appearance. However, in early examples, differences between the dolls of each tribe are more obvious. For instance, Zuni dolls are often made of pine rather than cottonwood root, and have bent arms nailed to their shoulders. Zuni figures are also more realistically proportioned than the blocklike Hopi kachinas, and their decoration consists of cloth, leather, and feathers rather than overall body paint. Because it lacks a mask, the ceremonial dancer doll at left is technically not a kachina, but probably functioned like one, since it was used to teach children sacred lore. The kachina at right wears a case mask—so called because it covers the doll's entire head.

Hints for Collectors
Although Zuni dolls are not as varied in appearance as Hopi kachinas, their rarity makes them very desirable and costly.

Hopi kachina

Description
Butterfly Maiden kachina. White face mask with protruding carved forehead and brown spots on cheeks, chin painted with lines radiating from mouth. Elaborate tablita tied together and joined to body with wooden pins. Painted white and brown ceremonial robe.

Materials, Marks, and Dimensions
Cottonwood root. Height: 11¾".

Maker, Origin, and Period
Hopi Pueblo. Arizona. c. 1930–40.

Comment
The Kachina cult is an important aspect of the Hopi religion. A Kachina is both a supernatural power and its masked human impersonator. At the same time, "kachina" is the term for the miniature likeness of this spirit, carved and painted in the form of a doll used to teach children the Hopi pantheon. Between ceremonial dances, masked human Kachinas dangle the figures on their wrists and elbows in front of Hopi boys and girls.

Hints for Collectors
To identify a kachina, study its costume and markings. The earliest are decorated with earth pigments; later dolls are painted with oil colors, watercolors, and acrylics. The Butterfly Maiden can be recognized easily by the structure of her tablita (the flat wooden headdress attached to her mask) and by brown spots on her cheeks and lines on her chin. This type of kachina is a favorite among collectors because of the haunting beauty of the tablita. The left portion of the tablita on the doll illustrated is damaged, which detracts somewhat from its value.

Hopi kachina

Description

Ho-ó-te kachina. Black case mask with pop eyes, protruding mouth, and curved horns. Painted lozenge-shaped motif with rings covers top of head and descends between eyes. Feather headdress. White crescent on right cheek, white star on left. Painted red torso and yellow shoulders, white kilt with painted geometric border designs, red and gray boots.

Materials, Marks, and Dimensions

Cottonwood root. Height: 12½".

Maker, Origin, and Period

Hopi Pueblo. Arizona. c. 1940–50.

Comment

Kachinas have been divided into different categories by collectors and historians. Often a single one belongs to several categories, the best known of which are Chiefs, Clowns, Runners, Women, Guards, and Animals. The facial features of this Animal kachina are simplified and abstract, and he is covered with symbols that have ritual significance. The various colors with which a kachina is painted may indicate forms in nature, geographic locations, or whether the figure represents a benevolent or fearsome spirit.

Hints for Collectors

Before the expansion of the tourist trade in the 1940s and '50s, the Hopi people did not allow their dollmakers to sign their kachinas. Today restrictions have been relaxed and collectors compete for dolls signed by their favorite Hopi artists. Women, prohibited until recently from making kachinas, are now creating many beautiful figures.

Hopi kachinas

Description
Wolf and Cháveyo kachinas in action poses. Left: Wolf has painted gray mask, white spots on forearms and lower legs, yellow body. Fox skin ruff at neck, feathered kilt, red boots. Carries feathered stick and rattle. Right: Cháveyo has black case mask with protruding snout, teeth, and large red ears. Mark on forehead represents snipe track. Carries knife in one hand, bow and arrow in other. Leather shoulder holster contains axe.

Materials, Marks, and Dimensions
Cottonwood root. Height: 9½″ (left); 10½″ (right).

Maker, Origin, and Period
Hopi Pueblo. Arizona. c. 1950–60.

Comment
The Hopi people believe that Animal kachinas protect them against illness and the malevolent creatures that often appear in their mythology. The wolf figure on the left is a Warrior kachina, who holds a rattle in one hand to scare off monsters and a stick in the other to attack his prey. Cháveyo, the Ogre kachina on the right, is a Hopi "boogie man."

Hints for Collectors
Brightly colored kachina dolls like those shown here have been made for tourists since the late 1950s. They are not true kachinas because they were never used in ceremonies. Nevertheless, these dolls are much sought after by collectors who enjoy modern Indian figures. Early kachinas, on the other hand, are valued by museums, ethnographers, and others for the beauty of their original, stately forms.

Skookum dolls

Description
Indian couple with baby. Molded and painted features, side-glancing brown eyes, sharp noses, closed mouths. Braided wigs of human hair with machine-stitched center parts. Left: Man wears original costume of flannel blanket over fringed felt pants; leather shoes with painted stars, bead necklace. Right: Woman wears original costume of buckskin headband, flannel blanket over cotton dress, leather shoes, glass and wooden beads. Baby wrapped in mother's blanket wears buckskin headband.

Materials, Marks, and Dimensions
Composition heads; stuffed cloth bodies over wooden armatures; wooden legs. Paper labels attached to feet marked "SKOOKUM/ (Bully Good)/Indian/USA." Height: 12¾" (left); 10½" (right).

Maker, Origin, and Period
Designed by Mary McAboy. Missoula, Montana. Manufactured by H. H. Tammen Co. Los Angeles, California. Distributed by Arrow Novelty Co. New York City. c. 1920–30.

Comment
Skookum dolls, with their stereotyped features and dress, are not authentic Indian dolls. They were created by Mary McAboy, who commercially produced apple-head dolls with Indian dress as early as 1913. The dolls' patented trade name, Skookum, is the Siwash word for "bully good." The Siwash people were native to the northwestern United States.

Hints for Collectors
A collector interested in Skookum dolls should look for examples of the entire range, from those with dried apple heads to the last dolls made in the 1950s with composition heads. However, collectors specializing in authentic Indian dolls shun Skookums.

Heubach Indian doll

Description
Character doll of old American Indian woman with bisque
shoulder-head. White mohair wig parted in center and tied in
braid. Realistically modeled wrinkled face, painted half-closed
brown eyes, broad nose, downturned mouth. Original costume of
beige fringed leather cape, skirt, and leggings with turquoise and
multicolored glass beading. Leather moccasins.

Materials, Marks, and Dimensions
Bisque shoulder-head and arms; kid body; cloth feet. "Heubach
Germany" with trademark symbol on shoulder plate. Height:
14½".

Maker, Origin, and Period
Gebrüder Heubach. Germany. c. 1910.

Comment
By the end of the 19th century, the American Indian had become
a favorite subject for novelists and frontier artists. Dollmakers
here and abroad seized upon this interest to create dolls that
would satisfy a growing taste for the exotic, but rarely with the
skill and attention to detail seen in this handsome Indian woman.
Her face has the expressive qualities of Indian portraits painted
by artists of the American West.

Hints for Collectors
The German firm of Heubach also made an Indian chief doll with
the head used here. The company was especially well known for
the fine quality of its bisque character doll heads; bodies were
made of cloth, kid, or jointed composition. The realistic features
and Plains-Indian-style costume of this doll make her quite
valuable.

Cheyenne doll

Description
Female doll with brown horsehair sewn into scalp. Tinted face, bead eyes and mouth, red painted cheeks. Original clothing of fringed, cape-style buckskin dress with elaborately beaded banding and belt, occasional glass beads scattered across dress, leggings, and moccasins. Long, tubular white glass bead earrings and purple bead necklace.

Materials, Marks, and Dimensions
Buckskin. Height: 13¾".

Maker, Origin, and Period
Cheyenne. Southern Plains. c. 1930.

Comment
The Cheyenne Indians decorated both ceremonial and everyday objects with elaborate beadwork. Their dolls, like those of other Plains Indians, were usually made from buckskin and adorned with simplified versions of the intricate beadwork patterns that appeared on adult clothing. During the late 19th century, Plains women covered everything with beads in order "to make them worth much," as one Indian woman remarked.

Hints for Collectors
The age of a Plains doll can often be determined by the size and coloring of its trade beads, the European-made ornaments used as barter by pioneer traders. Large "pony" beads were introduced by traders in the early 1800s, and tiny seed beads in the 1840s. Translucent seed beads appeared in the 1870s, followed shortly by metallic beads in the 1880s. While old-style beadwork was muted in color, brighter hues were fashionable in later years. Plains dolls may also be dated by the type of thread used to stitch them. Sinew was used before 1850 and cotton thread afterwards.

Indian play doll

Description
Doll with applied feathers and black and gray horsehair sewn into scalp. Single red beads for nose and eyes, light red beads for mouth. Single feather attached to crown. Brown plastic earrings hang from painted oilskin headband tied with buckskin strips. Fringed green flannel dress adorned with red, white, and blue beading and 2 brass buttons.

Materials, Marks, and Dimensions
Linen. Height: 6″.

Maker, Origin, and Period
Maker unknown. Found in Kentucky. c. 1920.

Comment
While most Indian dolls were made to teach children about tribal traditions or were produced specifically for tourists, this doll was probably intended solely as a plaything. Indian children practiced the craft of beadwork on their dolls, just as pioneer children practiced sewing skills by making doll quilts.

Hints for Collectors
This doll can be given an approximate date on the basis of her plastic earrings, which clearly place her in the 20th century. Like many Indian items, especially those that were meant to be sold, the doll shown here is decorated with patriotic motifs. Note the brass buttons—embossed with a cannon and flag—and the red, white, and blue beads representing the colors of the American flag. Both motifs suggest a First World War vintage. This doll is moderately priced because she is not skillfully fashioned and lacks identifying tribal marks. She is of historical interest, however, since few such play dolls have survived.

Seminole dolls

Description
Dolls with embroidered eyes and mouths. Noses modeled by stitching. Left: Male doll wears original costume of multicolored patchwork tunic, red cotton kerchief, pink turban with metal band. Right: Female doll in original costume of colorful patchwork cotton dress, green cape. Black cotton bonnet. Several strands of glass beads; one adorned with tin pendants is attached to blouse.

Materials, Marks, and Dimensions
Palmetto fiber. Height: 18½" (left); 16" (right).

Maker, Origin, and Period
Seminole. Florida. c. 1920.

Comment
In the early 19th century, the Seminoles who settled in Florida adopted the cool cotton clothing of the pioneers already living there. By 1870 Seminole Indian women had developed unique patchwork designs for their garments using hand-cranked sewing machines. Strips of fabric were joined together in specific patterns with multiple borders and made into long skirts, poncholike capes, tunics, and shirts. Seminole dolls, whose costumes were fashioned in the same way, were carved from wood or made of bound palmetto fibers. Unlike the male dolls, who wore short tunics that revealed their limbs, the female dolls were generally made without articulated arms and legs, since these would be hidden beneath long skirts and capes. Male dolls usually wear red caps, and women dolls, black bonnets.

Hints for Collectors
Most dolls made for tourists range from 4" to 12" in height. Larger dolls, like those shown here, are more valuable and often have more elaborate costumes.

Seneca dolls

Description
Doll couple with faceless cornhusk heads. Cornhusk bodies. Left: Man wears original costume of beige cotton tunic with blue bead buttons, beaded red woolen belt, hat, and armbands, and black bead-trimmed pants. Beaded buckskin moccasins. Right: Woman with cotton cloth hair parted in center. Original costume of black, rust, and tan cotton tunic decorated with white beads. Black bead-trimmed leggings, bead necklace and earrings. Beaded buckskin moccasins.

Materials, Marks, and Dimensions
Cornhusk. Height: 11¼″ (left); 10½″ (right).

Maker, Origin, and Period
Seneca. Cattaraugus Reservation, New York State. c. 1920.

Comment
Corn was a staple of the Seneca Indians, and a great many of their dolls were made with cornhusk bodies and dried apple heads. Many early dolls represented the benevolent spirit "Loose Feet," who was supposed to grant the wishes of small children. Known as "happy heads" or "wish dolls," they were given to children as good luck symbols. Although the dolls shown here were made in the 20th century, they wear 19th-century-style clothing.

Hints for Collectors
Today many cornhusk dolls are made by the Mohawk Indians, who, like the Seneca, are a branch of the Iroquois Confederacy living in upper New York State. The Mohawk dolls are dressed in tribal clothing and frequently have dried apples for heads. It is becoming increasingly hard to find 19th- and early 20th-century Iroquois dolls, particularly those made from fragile cornhusks.

Navajo dolls

Description
Doll couple with painted features and black hair made of thread.
Left: Man wears original costume of burgundy velveteen shirt
with tin and turquoise bead buttons; striped serape, orange
cotton headband, and brown buckskin boots. Concha belt, bead
earrings and necklace. Right: Woman wears original costume of
blue velveteen shirt with tin and turquoise bead buttons; colorful
striped cotton skirt, white cotton underskirt, and brown
buckskin boots. Concha belt, bead necklace and earrings, tin
and turquoise bracelet.

Materials, Marks, and Dimensions
Cloth. Height: 13″ (left); 12¼″ (right).

Maker, Origin, and Period
Navajo. Southwestern United States. c. 1945.

Comment
When the Navajos were confined to Fort Sumner, New Mexico,
in the 1860s, the women began wearing the long, flowing calico
skirts of the soldiers' wives. Navajo women also favored
velveteen blouses with silver buttons, concha belts, and silver
jewelry. Both male and female Navajo dolls from this period
faithfully mirrored the costumes of their makers and were
adorned with intricate silver jewelry. Women dolls, with their
elaborate hairdos and gay skirts, often seem more interesting
than men dolls.

Hints for Collectors
Most Navajo dolls have large cloth heads, but those with smaller
heads are often more detailed. Navajo dolls made in recent years
are still moderately priced. They may be found in museum shops,
on reservations, and in gift stores throughout the Southwest.

Sioux doll

Description
Female doll with black braided wool hair. Painted brows and
eyes with black glass bead pupils. Nose and mouth modeled by
stitching. Original costume of long red cotton dress cinched at
waist with buckskin belt and sash covered with tin disks. Red
felt underskirt, buckskin leggings decorated with blue and white
beading, leather "high-top" moccasins with green, pink, and
white beads. Braids tied in buckskin strips decorated with clear
beads and tin disks. Colorful beaded awl case with quill-wrapped
pendants hangs from belt. Two tin and bead earrings in each ear,
faceted trade-bead necklace, white beaded breastplate with tin
disks.

Materials, Marks, and Dimensions
Muslin. Height: 13½″.

Maker, Origin, and Period
Sioux. Rosebud Reservation, South Dakota. c. 1889.

Comment
A fine example of early Sioux crafts, the cloth doll shown here
reflects the interchange between Indian and pioneer cultures.
Her accessories, especially the trade-bead necklace, breastplate,
and awl case, are important objects in traditional Sioux life. Her
dress, though designed in an authentic Sioux style, includes
commercially woven fabrics made available by the pioneer
settlers.

Hints for Collectors
It is rare to find an Indian doll with an established provenance.
This particular example, however, is known to have been made
at the Rosebud Reservation in South Dakota about 1889. Such
information adds considerably to the worth of a doll.

Navajo doll

Description
Female doll with painted leather head. Braided silk hair styled in elaborate rolled back knot. Painted features. Stump arms, rudimentary fingers. Original costume of printed cotton blouse and apron with ribbon-trimmed waistband and shoulder straps worn over yellow skirt with print border. Trade-bead earrings.

Materials, Marks, and Dimensions
Leather face; muslin body and limbs. Height: 20½".

Maker, Origin, and Period
Navajo. Southwestern United States. c. 1890.

Comment
The hairstyle and dress of this traditional doll faithfully depict those worn by Navajo women in the late 19th century. While stumplike arms are found on many such dolls, the addition of the tiny fingers seen here is out of the ordinary. This doll is unusually large and was probably made for a child. It may also be an early example of a doll created for the tourist trade, an industry some Indian tribes began to develop when they first moved to reservations. Later Navajo dolls, made entirely of cloth, wear elaborate costumes of velvet shirts, long flowing skirts, concha belts, and jewelry.

Hints for Collectors
Indian dolls made in the late 19th century seldom appear on the market. Most of these early figures were acquired long ago by museums and collectors of Indian dolls. From time to time, however, they will turn up at an Indian-art auction or at a store specializing in Indian artifacts. These dolls are beyond the means of the budget-conscious collector, but once in a great while an unrecognized doll may be found at a flea market.

Cradleboard doll

Description
Indian baby in cradle. Painted features. Limbless cloth body
wrapped in checked wool blanket and hood. Cradle has painted
wooden prong hood; wooden frame partially wrapped in blue and
white homespun cloth, covered with deerskin, and laced with
cotton thread. Red cotton trade-cloth lining.

Materials, Marks, and Dimensions
Cloth doll; wood, cloth, and deerskin cradleboard. Height: 15½″.

Maker, Origin, and Period
Maker unknown. Probably Great Basin area, northwestern
United States. c. 1825–1875.

Comment
The cradleboard shown here, which contains an Indian doll
wrapped in swaddling clothes, is a miniature version of those
traditionally used by many Indian families. Most Indian babies
spent their first year in cradleboards carried on their mothers'
backs or suspended from a tree branch or the rafter of a
dwelling. Constructed of wood or basketry materials,
cradleboards were often decorated with painted or beaded
designs, reflecting the unique craft traditions of various Indian
groups. The dazzling beadwork patterns for which the Plains
Indians are noted distinguished their cradleboards as well as
clothing and other objects. The Salish Indians, a Northwest
tribe, carved one-piece dolls and cradleboards from single
lengths of wood, while Mohave Indians made cradleboards of
juniper fiber for their terra-cotta dolls.

Hints for Collectors
19th-century cradleboard dolls are difficult to find. Many
collectors favor the elaborately beaded examples made by the
Plains Indians.

Eskimo doll

Description
Doll with leather face and embroidered features. Hide body, mitten hands. Original costume of fur parka with wooly hood, matching fur leggings, and boots.

Materials, Marks, and Dimensions
Seal fur and hide. Height: 17½″.

Maker, Origin, and Period
Eskimo. Alaska. Early 20th century.

Comment
The relative geographic isolation of the Eskimos stimulated an extraordinary craft tradition. Dolls were made from such diverse materials as bone, antler, cloth, ivory, and wood. Dolls had great importance as teaching tools in Eskimo culture. Little girls carried dolls in their fur hoods just as their mothers had carried them, and made doll clothes and accessories from the skins of small animals. Some dolls represented motherly figures with infant dolls snuggled in their hoods. Others were made with widely spaced legs that allowed them to fit around the necks of their small owners. Boys played with male dolls equipped with kayaks and harpoons, enacting the hunting and fishing roles they would assume in their adult lives.

Hints for Collectors
Early Eskimo dolls sometimes suffer from deterioration of the fur and from infestation by insects that live on their natural materials. Before acquiring a doll, check its outfit for telltale shedding. Gently shake it to see if there are any loose pieces of fur. If it is in poor condition, its reverse side will resemble a moth-eaten garment.

58 Eskimo dolls

Description
Couple and baby with carved ivory faces attached to leather
heads with pegs. Painted features. Left: Man wears original
costume of fur parka and hood. Hide mittens, sewn hide shoes.
Right: Woman with baby in hood. Original costume of fur parka
with ivory toggle and ulu. Hide mittens, sewn hide shoes.

Materials, Marks, and Dimensions
Seal fur and hide; walrus ivory. Height: 9½″ (left); 9″ (right).

Maker, Origin, and Period
Eskimo. Alaska. c. 1900–10.

Comment
Eskimo dolls were traditionally dressed in miniature versions of
adult clothing and were often made as family projects. Fathers
carved the dolls and mothers stitched their skins. In the
northernmost regions of Alaska, dollmakers favored walrus ivory
and whale teeth for the dolls' bodies. Farther south, however, a
wider choice of materials was available, including wood, skins,
cloth, and bone. Before cotton thread became available, clothing
was sewn with sinew. Today dental floss is often used.

Hints for Collectors
19th- and early 20th-century ivory dolls are difficult to find,
and few ivory dolls are being made today. The skills and the
incentive required for carving them may have been lost among
certain groups. However, some co-ops commission local
craftsmen to create souvenir ivory dolls costumed in machine-
made clothing. Although these figures are produced for tourists,
the workmanship is of a high quality.

National Costume Dolls

 Dolls in foreign costumes are probably the most widely acquired kind of dolls, even though sophisticated collectors usually prefer other types. Most were produced abroad as inexpensive souvenirs. Fine examples with detailed workmanship and authentic period costumes were also available, and these better-quality dolls, particularly ones made prior to the Second World War, are now gaining in popularity. Collectors should distinguish between dolls created specifically for tourists and those rarer types produced chiefly for domestic sale; the latter were meant for display or for ceremonial use.

Far Eastern Dolls

In Japan, the art of dollmaking is a tradition that has been handed down from generation to generation since ancient times. There are more than 300 types of Japanese dolls, some of which were commercially produced as early as the 17th century. Most Japanese dolls originally had a ritual significance. For example, Boys' and Girls' Day Festival dolls, fashioned for hundreds of years, were part of the Japanese cult of chivalry and symbolized bravery and loyalty to country and emperor. While antique Festival dolls are treasured family heirlooms, new versions are popular for their graceful evocation of a long-gone era. Other Japanese dolls were made for export, including the child dolls called *Yamato Ningyo*, which enjoyed wide popularity in Europe in the late 19th century. Dolls were much less prominent in Chinese culture, but some, such as the Door of Hope Mission dolls, were made as souvenirs from the turn of the century until the early 1940s.

Dolls by European Manufacturers

As early as the mid-19th century, lady dolls with bisque, wax, or papier-mâché heads were outfitted in national costumes, though this clothing was not always entirely accurate. Expert knowledge is often required to determine if an outfit is a faithful copy of a regional style or a fanciful creation by the designer of the doll's clothing. From the 1870s to 1920s dolls in national costumes were produced by some of the finest European dollmakers, including Jumeau, Steiner, and Armand Marseille. These usually have bisque heads made from either standard molds or from molds specifically designed to portray the facial features of an ethnic group. Many such dolls, particularly those representing Africans, West Indians, South Sea Islanders, or people of the Middle East, have bisque heads that are tinted brown.

In the late 19th and early 20th centuries, national costume dolls were handcrafted by European artisans, whose skills today have largely died out. Some of these figures could be considered folk dolls. More recently, costume dolls have been created by noted contemporary doll artists.

Description
Chinese gentleman and maidservant (amah) carrying child on
back. Carved and painted wooden heads and hands. Left:
Gentleman has painted black hair and long queue. Original tan
satin jacket with black frogs, ivory brocade robe, blue silk
brocade pants. Black cotton hat and shoes. Right: Woman, with
painted black hair, wearing original blue cotton tunic and pants
and white cotton shirt. Black hat, black cotton shoes. Little
girl carried in printed cotton pouch embroidered with yellow
butterfly and secured with orange cotton straps. Wears original
pink dress and elaborate tasseled silk headdress.

Materials, Marks, and Dimensions
Wooden heads and hands; cloth bodies. Tag inside man's jacket
reads "Gentleman, Shanghai 1912 Henrietta Brewer." Height:
11¾″ (left); 10½″ (right).

Maker, Origin, and Period
Door of Hope Mission. China. c. 1912.

Comment
The Door of Hope Mission was established in Shanghai in 1901 as
a home for rescued slaves and abandoned children. The dolls
shown here were dressed by girls at the mission and carved by
men living in a neighboring city. Clothed in miniature versions of
authentic period costumes, the dolls depict Chinese people of
various ages and social classes.

Hints for Collectors
Door of Hope dolls can be identified by their pearwood heads and
hands; moreover, the spoonlike hands have distinctive stylized
fingers. Made both as tourist souvenirs and as playthings, these
dolls are now attracting collectors, who purchase them at
auctions or from dealers.

Chinese grandparents

Description
Grandfather and grandmother with composition heads. Molded and painted features and white hair. Left: Grandfather has white mustache and beard and open-closed mouth. Wears wire-rimmed glasses and original brown mandarin jacket and tunic, and molded black shoes with green stripes. Molded black hat. Right: Grandmother has closed mouth. Original rust-colored silk coat with embroidered trim; beige silk pants with matching trim. Molded blue and orange shoes. Carries handbag and pipe. Figures mounted on green wooden bases.

Materials, Marks, and Dimensions
Composition heads, hands, and feet; straw, paper, and wire bodies. Height: 14″ (left); 13″ (right).

Maker, Origin, and Period
Maker unknown. China. c. 1891–95.

Comment
Before about 1860, when dolls were first produced commercially in China, only idolmakers were permitted to fashion and sell miniature likenesses of the human form, and children had to be content to play with homemade wooden or rag dolls. The dolls shown here, typical of those made for export at the turn of the century, depict elderly people, who have always been revered in China.

Hints for Collectors
Although the dolls shown here are not marked, identical examples have been found bearing the words "Made in China." This label suggests that they were made for export after 1891, when American customs law began to require foreign products to be stamped with the name of their country of origin.

61 Warrior doll

Description
Boys' Day Festival doll with composition head. Molded and painted features; face painted with gofun. Long black beard. Multicolored silk brocade kimono with white silk obi. Hooded brocade headdress. Holds spear in right hand.

Materials, Marks, and Dimensions
Composition head and hands; paper and straw body and feet. Height: 16″.

Maker, Origin, and Period
Maker unknown. Japan. c. 1875.

Comment
The doll shown here, representing Benkei, a Japanese warrior, was made specifically for display during the traditional Boys' Day Festival (*Musha Ningyo*) celebrated in May in Japan. On this day, banners in the shape of a carp, the fish signifying fortitude, are flown outside the houses of young boys; inside, an array of fierce-looking warrior and hero figurines equipped with miniature armor and weapons are displayed on a tiered cloth-covered stand. Each year a boy receives a new doll to add to his set. Symbolizing bravery, strength, and loyalty to parents, country, and emperor, such dolls are vestiges of the Japanese cult of chivalry and the Samurai.

Hints for Collectors
Boys' Day dolls are usually in good condition, since they are treated with great care and stored when not in use. Antique sets are treasured family heirlooms and are therefore seldom sold. They are particularly hard to find in America, except sometimes at auctions.

62 Emperor and Empress dolls

Description
Girls' Day Festival dolls with composition heads. Molded and
painted features; faces painted with gofun. Silk thread hair.
Seated on wooden platforms. Left: Emperor in original elaborate
robe, obi, and headdress. Right: Empress in original blue and
peach silk kimono with multicolored brocade design. Headdress
not shown.

Materials, Marks, and Dimensions
Composition heads and hands; cloth and straw bodies. Height:
10¾″ (left); 9¾″ (right).

Maker, Origin, and Period
Maker unknown. Japan. c. 1850.

Comment
The Girls' Day, or Dolls' Festival, celebrated as early as the 17th
century, was intended to instill the virtues of patriotism and
domesticity in young girls and to glorify the Imperial family. The
holiday is still celebrated in Japan in March during the height of
the peach blossom season. A few days before the festival,
mothers and daughters take their dolls out of storage and display
them on steps, the *hina dan*, which are covered with red cloth.
A set of these dolls traditionally consists of 15 figures. The
Emperor and Empress are placed on the top step, presiding
over court musicians, ladies-in-waiting, guards, and dancers.
Furniture, flowers, trees, and accessories complete the tableau.

Hints for Collectors
A young girl receives a new festival doll each year to add to her
group. Old dolls, some of which date back several hundred years,
are handed down from one generation to the next and rarely
appear on the market. The best such examples are painted with
gofun and wear luxurious original costumes.

Kestner Oriental baby doll

Description
Oriental baby girl with bisque head. Short brown wig with
bangs. Almond-shaped brown sleep-eyes, thin arched eyebrows,
upturned nose, chubby cheeks, and open mouth showing 2 teeth.
Jointed bent-limb body. Fingernails and toenails outlined in red.
Wears red brocade kimono with gold and blue medallions,
maroon and gold trim, and maroon velvet sash. Lace-trimmed
white cotton underpants.

Materials, Marks, and Dimensions
Bisque head; composition body and limbs. "243 J.D.K." incised
on back of head. Height: 16″.

Maker, Origin, and Period
J. D. Kestner, Jr. Germany. c. 1910.

Comment
The Oriental doll shown here is one of the character baby
dolls produced by J. D. Kestner about 1910, when the term
"character" was commonly used to describe dolls with
naturalistic rather than idealized features. George Borgfeldt,
who distributed some of Kestner's popular character babies,
claimed in an advertisement that "they are so cunning and
lifelike that no little girl is satisfied until she possesses one."

Hints for Collectors
Dolls with Oriental features made by Kestner or other German
firms are very desirable today. Manufacturers produced many
more Oriental child dolls than Oriental babies. Kestner Oriental
baby dolls with the mold number 243, such as the one shown
here, are scarce and especially prized.

Yamato Ningyo

Description
Japanese girl doll with composition head. Molded and painted features; face painted with gofun. Black silk hair, brown inset glass eyes, closed mouth. Original multicolored floral kimono with large obi; purple silk jacket (*haori*) painted with clouds; white stockings (*tabis*). Stick inserted through obi. Carries cloth-covered book.

Materials, Marks, and Dimensions
Composition body, hands, and feet; cloth upper arms and legs. Height: 17″.

Maker, Origin, and Period
Maker unknown. Japan. Late 19th century.

Comment
Like most *Yamato Ningyo*, the figure shown here has a composition head probably modeled after a wooden carving by the dollmaker. Such dolls were designed both as playthings and display objects, and were dressed in children's outfits of the period. This little girl, for example, wears a brightly colored kimono rather than one in the subdued hues that characterize the garments of married women. Dollmakers found it difficult to fashion miniature copies of traditional costumes, since the many layers proved too bulky for small dolls. Some makers simply omitted undergarments, while others created figures that were slender but sturdy enough to wear these elaborate outfits.

Hints for Collectors
Although *Yamato Ningyo* dolls are still produced in Japan, those made nowadays wearing traditional costumes are specifically intended for display. In recent years they have declined in popularity in Japan largely because of a preference for modern play dolls dressed in Western garb.

Yamato Ningyo

Description
Japanese boy doll with composition head painted with gofun.
Painted hair, brown inset glass eyes, closed mouth, large molded
ears. No arms. Molded penis. Wears multicolored brocade
kimono tied with green silk obi.

Materials, Marks, and Dimensions
Composition. Height: 19¾".

Maker, Origin, and Period
Maker unknown. Japan. c. 1875.

Comment
The portrait doll shown here is called *Yamato Ningyo*—a
combination of the ancient Japanese words for "Japan" and
"human form." Such figures were some of the first commercially
produced play dolls in Japan. This example is typical of the early
dolls made as individual portraits. Note that the boy's hair has
been delicately painted with a fine writing brush. The faces of
Japanese dolls, including this one, are often painted with several
layers of gofun, a fine white paste composed of pulverized oyster
shell and glue. Dollmakers sometimes applied as many as 20
coats of this mixture, polishing it to achieve a porcelainlike finish.

Hints for Collectors
Although these dolls were usually sold undressed in Japan, those
made for export wore traditional kimonos. Since *Yamato Ningyo*
dolls were produced in great quantities, they frequently turn up
on the American market; in 1927 alone, about 10,000 examples
were sent to the United.States as part of a good-will exchange.
These dolls depicted children of 6 or 7 years of age dressed in
costumes representing all the regions of Japan.

Simon & Halbig Oriental doll

Description
Japanese girl doll with olive-tinted bisque socket head. Black
mohair wig with cloth apple blossoms surrounding topknot.
Almond-shaped brown glass eyes, open mouth with upper teeth,
pierced ears. Ball-jointed body. Wears purple and gold satin robe
with black brocade insert at back. Underdress of floral brocade
bodice and gold satin skirt with floral motif embroidered at hem
and red satin border. Black stockings.

Materials, Marks, and Dimensions
Bisque head; composition body. "SH 1129 Dep. 8" incised on
head. Height: 20".

Maker, Origin, and Period
Simon & Halbig. Germany. c. 1900–10.

Comment
This Japanese girl is one of the Asian figures created by the
German firm of Simon & Halbig, which also made a Hindu doll
and a Burmese doll. The heads of Simon & Halbig ethnic dolls
were more realistically tinted, with color fired directly into the
bisque, than were those made by other German firms. In 1895
Simon & Halbig introduced the "Dolls of Four Races"—fully
jointed European, African, Chinese, and American Indian dolls
dressed in appropriate costumes—which were sometimes used to
teach children about geography.

Hints for Collectors
The mold numbers on Simon & Halbig dolls usually denote
particular head or facial types. For instance, those ending in 0
are shoulder-heads without swivel necks; those ending in 9, as
this one does, have slightly open mouths showing teeth. Simon &
Halbig Oriental girl dolls of this high quality are most desirable
when they retain their original kimonos.

Steiner bébés

Description
Bébés with brown-tinted bisque heads. Black lamb's-wool hair, brown glass eyes, painted eyelashes. Jointed limbs. Left: Le Petit Parisien with closed mouth. Wears cotton floral print dress and hat; white cotton underskirt and pantaloons. Right: Le Parisien has open mouth with 3 upper teeth. Wears lace-trimmed white cotton dress and underclothes, and cap with red ribbons. White silk stockings; black imitation-leather boots.

Materials, Marks, and Dimensions
Bisque heads; composition bodies and limbs. Left: Back of head marked "J. STEINER/BTE S.G.D.G./PARIS/F1 A7". Body stamped "LE PETIT PARISIEN/BÉBÉ STEINER/MÉDAILLE D'OR/PARIS 1889." Right: Back of head marked "A.3.4 Paris." Body stamped "BÉBÉ ·LE PARISIEN/MÉDAILLE D'OR/PARIS." Height: 14″ (left); 11″ (right).

Maker, Origin, and Period
Jules Nicholas Steiner. France. c. 1889 (left); c. 1892 (right).

Comment
Although black dolls had been produced for most of the 19th century, it was not until the introduction of bébés about 1870 that they were colored in delicate shades of brown. Those meant to represent mulatto children were particularly popular in the French colonies and the United States.

Hints for Collectors
Because few were made, Steiner dolls with the warm brown skin tones seen here fetch higher prices than their white counterparts. The painted composition bodies of Steiner bébés often have a purple underwash visible around the joints. These dolls usually have cardboard pates rather than the cork pates found on other bébés.

Description
Female doll in regional costume with brown-tinted bisque head.
Dark brown mohair wig; brown glass eyes, painted eyelashes and
thick brown brows, closed mouth, pierced ears. Body jointed at
elbows and knees. Original costume of beaded and embroidered
white silk blouse with lace sleeves; gold-trimmed yellow silk
vest; and white silk pantaloons with striped silk sarong and
elaborate sequined belt. Yellow hat with tassels, beads, gold
braid, and coins. Gold coin dowry necklace, coral bead necklace,
rings, earrings, and bracelets. Gold mesh shoes.

Materials, Marks, and Dimensions
Bisque head; kid body and limbs. "Jumeau Médaille d'Or Paris"
stamped on back. Height: 15″.

Maker, Origin, and Period
Jumeau. France. c. 1880–1910.

Comment
The richly detailed, exotic costume of the figure shown here,
probably based on a Middle Eastern outfit, is proof of the
Jumeau firm's unsurpassed attention to doll clothing. Dolls in
national costumes were often specially ordered or created
expressly for foreign markets.

Hints for Collectors
Jumeau produced a number of chocolate-colored and tan-colored
dolls in its many lines, but these seldom turn up on the market
today. Examples on which the skin color was fired into the
bisque, such as this one, are more valuable than those with
painted complexions.

Doña Juanita and Don Pancho

Description
Spanish costume dolls. Leather mask faces with center seam.
Glued-on hair. Molded and painted features including side-
glancing eyes and closed mouths. Applied ears. Bodies jointed at
shoulders and hips. Left: Original red silk dress with black lace
trim; white cotton underskirt edged with lace, and ecru lace
mantilla. Black leather shoes. Carries paper fan. Right: Original
gray cotton suit with metal buttons; pleated white cotton shirt
and gray felt hat. Leather shoes.

Materials, Marks, and Dimensions
Leather. Round stickers on soles of left shoes read "Beristain
Ca/Barcelona"; "F Monereo/Barcelona" hand-signed on right
shoes. Height: 17″ (left); 16″ (right).

Maker, Origin, and Period
F. Monereo. Spain. c. 1924.

Comment
The flamenco dancer and her escort shown here are early
examples of a type of Spanish costume doll that became very
popular in the 1950s. Unlike most, these 2 dolls have extremely
well-made, hand-sewn bodies and finely stitched clothes. It is
unusual that the male wears a suit rather than the traditional
matador's outfit.

Hints for Collectors
American collectors often acquire dolls in national costumes
when traveling abroad. Most such dolls are mass produced today
and sold as tourist items. Because craftsmanship has declined
over the years, early 20th-century costume dolls are generally of
better quality than later examples.

Poured-wax doll

Description
Lady doll with gray beeswax shoulder-head. Inserted brown
hair; blue glass eyes with half-closed lids; closed smiling mouth.
Wears original red satin brocade dress with metal-jeweled collar
and embroidered white satin bodice; metallic belt; gold braid and
green satin band at hem. White organdy and lace apron, lace-
trimmed cotton underskirt and pantaloons. Leather shoes. Black
ribbon headdress.

Materials, Marks, and Dimensions
Wax shoulder-head and hands; cloth body and limbs.
Height: 15½″.

Maker, Origin, and Period
Maker unknown. Probably Germany. c. 1850–75.

Comment
Although English firms were the most famous for fine wax dolls,
the German dollmaking center of Sonneberg was also renowned
for poured-wax figures. Most German wax dolls' heads were
reinforced with plaster or composition, but a few were poured
wax. The head of the doll shown here is made of beeswax, a dark
variety rarely employed in dollmaking. The tilt of her neck
suggests that she was modeled after a statue or figurine. The
doll's inserted hair, more prevalent in England than Germany, is
a mark of fine craftsmanship.

Hints for Collectors
Though this doll is probably German, it is not known which
European country or region her beautiful costume is supposed to
represent. Her finely modeled features and carefully detailed
dress make her far more valuable than similar dolls commonly
produced for tourists.

French peasant doll

Description
Lady doll in French costume. Papier-mâché head with molded and painted features including black pate beneath wig of human hair, thin closed mouth, and pierced nostrils. Glass eyes. Wears original ornate dress with pink and white striped bodice, gold sequins, lace collar trimmed with pink velvet ribbon, elbow-length striped satin sleeves edged with gold metallic decoration, and white lace undersleeves. Orange taffeta skirt. Dark green silk apron with pink ribbon flowers, pink ribbon trim, and black lace edging. Paper petticoat and lace-trimmed cotton pantaloons. Black stockings; high black leather boots. Flower-trimmed straw hat.

Materials, Marks, and Dimensions
Papier-mâché head and hands; cloth body. Height: 18½″.

Maker, Origin, and Period
Maker unknown. France. c. 1845–50.

Comment
Fashioned of delicate and finely sewn materials, this figure's costume may be native to the Provence region in southeastern France. This doll has the painted pate and slender face typical of some 19th-century papier-mâché figures. Though she has a cloth body, other similar dolls have kid bodies with clothes sewn on them. The example shown here was probably produced commercially, which was rare for national costume dolls of this period.

Hints for Collectors
Keep papier-mâché dolls in a cool place, since extreme heat may cause them to crack and peel.

Description
Male and female dolls with composition heads. Carved and painted features including blue eyes and closed mouths. Left: Man with brown hair. Original red and green striped woolen vest, white cotton shirt with high lace-trimmed collar; multicolored scarf. White woolen coat; leather breeches with gold metal buttons. White woolen stockings and black leather shoes. Right: Woman with blond hair. Original appliquéd and embroidered red cotton vest, white satin blouse, and white linen shawl with black embroidery; black woolen skirt, blue apron with red and white braid trim and sash; coarse linen underskirt. White woolen stockings and black leather shoes. Lace-trimmed white satin bonnet.

Materials, Marks, and Dimensions
Composition heads and hands; cloth bodies. Handwritten labels sewn inside coat and in skirt lining read "Made in Sweden." Height: 18½" (left); 19" (right).

Maker, Origin, and Period
Maker unknown. Sweden. c. 1939.

Comment
The doll at left wears the colorful peasant costume of Vastergotland, Sweden, lacking only the peaked woolen hat sometimes worn by the men of that region. The lady wears a Varmland peasant outfit embellished with traditional Swedish needlework designs.

Hints for Collectors
These composition dolls resemble traditional Swedish wooden figures. They were made for exhibition at the New York World's Fair of 1939–40, which accounts for their fine quality.

French peasant dolls

Description
Male and female dolls in French peasant costumes. Molded stockinet faces with embroidered and painted features. White wool hair. Pointed wooden shoes (sabots). Left: Bearded fisherman wears original black felt suit with gray and white striped shirt; brown beret, red neckerchief. Carries fisherman's net. Right: Bretonne woman in original black felt dress with gold braid on bodice and cuffs; white linen apron, white hat.

Materials, Marks, and Dimensions
Cloth heads and hands; straw-filled cloth bodies and limbs. Cloth labels attached to jackets read "Made In France." Height: 10¼" (left); 10½" (right).

Maker, Origin, and Period
Bernard Ravca. France. c. 1930.

Comment
Renowned dollmaker Bernard Ravca won first prize at a Paris exposition in 1937 for a pair of Norman peasant figures much like the dolls shown here, who instead wear clothing native to the Brittany region in western France. Ravca created the unique expressive faces of his dolls by stitching and painting each contour and feature by hand. Many collectors regard his dolls as soft sculpture, a genre that has risen in popularity in recent years.

Hints for Collectors
Contemporary dollmakers influenced by Ravca's work have imitated his style with varying degrees of success. Paper labels were originally affixed to all Ravca dolls, but since tags often get lost, it may be difficult to distinguish copies from originals.

Description
Portrait doll with sculpted porcelain head. Glass eyes, closed mouth. Original Scottish costume of gray woolen jacket, brown rayon vest, white cotton shirt, brown tie. Green plaid woolen kilt with short black pants underneath; leather and fur pouch (sporran), black tam, black cotton socks, and black leather shoes. Holds crooked wire cane in one hand and pipe in the other. Wooden base with inscription.

Materials, Marks, and Dimensions
Porcelain head, hands, and lower legs; cloth body. "Sir Harry Lauder by Fawn Zeller" inscribed on wooden base. Height: 9″.

Maker, Origin, and Period
Fawn Zeller. Inverness, Florida. 1951.

Comment
The doll shown here, a portrait of British music-hall comedian Sir Harry Lauder, was created by Fawn Zeller, a doll artist best known for portraits of famous men such as Winston Churchill, Franklin Roosevelt, and Dwight D. Eisenhower. Zeller, who began designing dolls professionally in 1948, once remarked that she strove to produce not just a doll, but a "human-appearing subject in miniature." Some of her figures have heads modeled in porcelain and bodies made of crepe paper, gauze, or cotton wrapped over wire armatures.

Hints for Collectors
Expect to pay very large sums for dolls as meticulously crafted as this one. Many artists use rare and expensive materials; Zeller, for example, waited 2 years to acquire a certain type of German-made blown-glass eye; and she used real gold thread imported from India on some of her dolls' dresses.

Famous Figures, Families, and Other Dolls

Though quite varied in style, materials, and age, the dolls in this group represent well-known historical figures as well as figures in recognizable occupational or family roles.

Historical and Political Figures

Well-known historical and political figures have long been favorite subjects for doll artists eager for the challenge of recreating the images of these characters down to the most minute detail. Often such dolls were made in limited editions or as one-of-a-kind examples. A few of these, such as the figures of Lee, Lincoln, and Grant seen in this section, were commissioned by museums, while others may have been requested by private collectors. Still other examples, such as the Eleanor of Aquitaine doll included here, reflect the specific historical interests of the artist, who may research a project for months in striving for accuracy, particularly regarding costume design. Photographs, engravings, and other visual sources may be used; Martha Thompson, who captured the regal presence of Henry VIII in doll form, based his likeness and those of his 6 wives on portraits by the 16th-century German painter Hans Holbein.

Role Figures

Dolls that portray various professional, domestic, or military roles reflect social and historical currents. Although they are rarely seen today, chimney sweeps and peddlers were a part of daily life in earlier centuries. Mammy dolls, made as late as the 1950s, depict black women in the much-stereotyped role of caring for white children. Dolls such as Red Cross nurses, G.I. Joes, and WAC and WAVE figures show that toys have been used to illustrate military occupations as well as to instill patriotic feelings in both boys and girls.

Family Figures

Entire families have been created to inhabit dollhouses of all sizes, the more well-to-do of such establishments filled also with retinues of domestic servants. These dolls, ranging from tiny bisque or china miniatures to larger figures fashioned in a variety of materials, often mirror the customs of the period in which they were made. Some occasionally doubled as wedding-cake decorations. Illustrating other aspects of family life are groups like the Dionne Quintuplets, whose birth in 1935 was regarded as an important medical and historical event, inspiring the manufacture of sets of dolls representing all 5 sisters as infants and then as toddlers. Portraying an older subject was Mattel's Barbie, a doll that was extremely popular with young girls throughout the 1960s and '70s because she personified the archetypal teenager they hoped to become—one with a perfect figure, a glamorous wardrobe, and, of course, a boyfriend. The Angela Appleseed dolls created by Dewees Cochran as part of her "Grow-up" series show this artist's more naturalistic, less idealized perception of a young girl on her way to womanhood.

Description
Dolls with bisque heads, molded and painted features. Left: Court lady with dark brown mohair wig. Original costume of pink and white striped cotton dress, green woven shawl, large green and pink bonnet decorated with ribbons and flowers, red satin shoes. Stands on base. Right: Anne of Austria has blond mohair wig. Original costume of maroon velvet gown with ermine bodice and trim, purple velvet train edged in ermine. Elaborate brocade headpiece decorated with seed pearls and glass beads. Silk underskirt. Embroidered purse.

Materials, Marks, and Dimensions
Bisque heads and limbs, cloth bodies. Left: "Court Lady—The Reign of Louis XVI At The Petit Trianon" inscribed on base. Height: 8″ (left); 10″ (right).

Maker, Origin, and Period
Maker unknown. Clothing and wigs made by Mlle. Riera. France. 1908.

Comment
For its 40th Anniversary Exposition in 1908, the Philadelphia department store Strawbridge & Clothier commissioned the French doll designer Mlle. Riera to make a group of 24 costume dolls called portraits of "The Age of Drapery." Among them were the figures illustrated here. Their 18th-century costumes were hand-dyed, and their handmade wigs were styled by using knitting needles as curling irons.

Hints for Collectors
Although Mlle. Riera only outfitted this pair, she did make wax-head dolls early in her career until she found that importing mass-produced German bisque heads was easier. Riera's dolls can be found in private and museum collections.

Eleanor of Aquitaine

Description
Female doll in knight's garb, with hand-carved wooden head and painted features. Blond mohair wig. Cloth body over wire armature. Original costume of silver cloth tunic, chain-mail hood, silk surcoat emblazoned with the Greek cross. The crown of France fitted over plumed silk-gauze helmet. Leather scabbard holds jeweled sword. Mirror and leather purse stamped with gold fleurs-de-lis hang from girdle. Gilded, jeweled boots. Doll holds lance with silk banner of St. Denis, the *oriflamme* of France. Mounted on revolving stand.

Materials, Marks, and Dimensions
Wooden head, lower arms, and hands; cloth body. "Eleanor of Aquitaine/Margaret Finch '80" signed on base. Cloth NIADA label affixed to tunic. Height: 16".

Maker, Origin, and Period
Margaret Finch. New Rochelle, New York. 1980.

Comment
Eleanor of Aquitaine, the 12th-century French queen, is depicted here as a young woman disguised as a knight ready to accompany her first husband, Louis VII, on the Second Crusade in May of 1147. Meticulously researched details such as Eleanor's purse, although hidden from view, received the same treatment as her outer clothing.

Hints for Collectors
Many contemporary doll artists sign or initial their dolls, and those marked with the initials NIADA were made by a member of the National Institute of American Doll Artists. Some dolls are dated and also numbered if made in a limited edition. Most of Margaret Finch's dolls have a semicircular black-edged paper label bearing her signature and the name of the individual doll.

Elizabeth I

Description
Portrait doll with crepe face. Painted features, mohair wig.
Copper wire armature supports body. Original costume of
jeweled crown, ornate velvet dress trimmed with pearl and
jeweled bands, brocade sleeves, and lace ruff collar. Black veil
cape. Gold and green petticoats over white linen underslip.
White silk stockings. White silk shoes with green and orange
embroidery. Wears pearl ropes and jeweled brooch and carries
feathered scepter. White lace gloves.

Materials, Marks, and Dimensions
Cotton crepe head, padded cotton body. Tape on underside of
skirt marked "Dorothy Wendell Heizer." Height: 9¾".

Maker, Origin, and Period
Dorothy Heizer. Chatham, New Jersey. c. 1940–43.

Comment
The late doll designer and NIADA member Dorothy Heizer
designed this regal figure of Queen Elizabeth I. The face is
modeled after a historic portrait of the queen, and the dress is a
replica of an outfit that Elizabeth once actually wore. Another
celebrated doll by Dorothy Heizer represents Queen Elizabeth II
as a bride. Made in 1948, the figure was elaborately adorned with
45,000 pearls, rhinestones, and beads. Exquisite workmanship
and painstaking detail are evident in all of Heizer's dolls.

Hints for Collectors
The National Institute of American Doll Artists (NIADA) is a
small organization with high standards and strict rules for
membership. A doll purchased from an NIADA member is
always accompanied by a certificate of its authenticity and
usually commands a high price.

Henry VIII

Description
Portrait doll with bisque shoulder-head; molded and painted features and beard. Original costume of richly brocaded, gold lamé outfit with cloak of red velvet and fur trimmed in gold braid; jeweled black hat with white feather, gray brocade underdrawers, black garter and white garter, painted white stockings, white molded shoes trimmed with gold. Carries brown kid gloves in right hand. Jeweled rings on both hands, jeweled chain around shoulders, brass chain with pendant around neck.

Materials, Marks, and Dimensions
Bisque head and limbs, cloth body. "Henry VIII MDT 56 B Body: Martha Thompson" imprinted on back of shoulder. Height: 14″.

Maker, Origin, and Period
Martha Thompson. Wellesley, Massachusetts. c. 1956–57.

Comment
A top portrait-doll artist, Martha Thompson specialized in figures of the British royal family, historical personalities, and modern celebrities. She created this doll of Henry VIII as well as sets of Henry and his 6 wives based on Hans Holbein's 16th-century painted portraits. Here Thompson captured perfectly the notorious king's determined gaze and regal stance. Working from her original sketches, the artist first sculpted the doll's head in clay, then made a mold and fired the head herself.

Hints for Collectors
Martha Thompson died in 1964. Her dolls are scarce but can sometimes be obtained at auctions or from antique doll dealers. The doll shown here wears an outfit fashioned by noted costume designer and researcher Susan Sirkis, a fact that makes it especially valuable.

Description
Gentleman and lady dolls with poured-wax shoulder-heads and finely detailed painted features. Left: Powdered wig tied with black ribbon. Original costume of gold brocade silk coat with pink silk lining. Matching breeches and vest, white linen lace-trimmed ascot, white stockings, and gold leather shoes. Right: Powdered mohair wig curled and rolled into a pompadour. Heavily shadowed eyelids, downward-glancing eyes. Original costume of gold brocade and pink silk dress trimmed with lace and gold braid. Replaced underskirt.

Materials, Marks, and Dimensions
Wax shoulder-heads; cloth bodies; bisque hands. Height: 15½″ (left); 14″ (right).

Maker, Origin, and Period
Maker unknown. France. c. 1850–1900.

Comment
The exquisite wax couple shown here, whose clothes and hairstyles were meticulously modeled after those of 18th-century French aristocrats, were probably commissioned and meant for a mantelpiece or for a woman's boudoir.

Hints for Collectors
It is possible that the dolls illustrated originally had wax hands, but their long wax fingers probably broke off, so the hands were replaced with others made of bisque. Such replaced parts would not adversely affect the value of these dolls because the figures are beautifully made and are definitely a pair. Poured-wax dolls may be cleaned by gently rubbing them with a cloth saturated with unsalted butter. Avoid cleaning painted facial features, since the paint may adhere to the rag.

Description
Doll couple with bisque heads and molded and painted features. Long thin noses, closed mouths. Left: Groom with brown glass eyes wears white wig tied by satin bow. Original costume of satin topcoat with lace and pearl button trim, matching pants, painted black shoes. Right: Bride with blue glass eyes wears elaborate white pompadour wig. Original costume of satin and lace gown with pearls, gauze veil. Carries white cloth flowers with streaming satin ribbons. Dolls mounted on cake stand.

Materials, Marks, and Dimensions
Bisque heads, hands, and lower legs; cloth bodies and upper legs. Height: 6¾".

Maker, Origin, and Period
Maker unknown. Germany. c. 1900.

Comment
These turn-of-the-century figures served as both dollhouse dolls and wedding-cake dolls, and were originally sold either clothed or unclothed. Those sold unclothed were outfitted at home by family members. Watch for unusual wedding-cake dolls that were dressed in homemade miniature versions of the clothes worn by an actual bride and groom.

Hints for Collectors
The United Federation of Doll Clubs defines miniatures as dolls less than 8″ tall. Miniature dolls were very rarely marked. It is difficult to determine the maker of an unmarked doll unless it is found in its original box, which sometimes bears the name of the manufacturer. Dollhouse bridal dolls are occasionally found in the catalogues of department stores or toy distributors.

Abraham and Mary Todd Lincoln

Description
Portrait dolls with wax heads, molded and painted features.
Left: Abraham Lincoln has graying hair and beard, blue eyes.
Original costume of black wool coat, pants, and vest. White shirt
and black silk bow tie. Metal watch chain worn on vest. Right:
Mary Todd Lincoln has black hair worn in bun with pink and
green flowers at crown. Brown eyes. Painted pearl necklace.
Original costume of off-shoulder white dress covered with black
lace, paper flowers fastened to bodice. Lace-trimmed pantaloons.

Materials, Marks, and Dimensions
Left: Wax head and neck; cloth body and upper arms; wax-over-
composition lower arms and legs. Right: Wax shoulder-head;
wax-over-composition arms; composition legs. Height: 15½"
(left); 14½" (right).

Maker, Origin, and Period
Lewis Sorensen. Los Angeles, California. 1950.

Comment
The wax dolls shown here belong to one of two complete sets of
United States presidents and their wives created by the noted
doll artist, Lewis Sorensen. These are the first figures he made
from colored wax, which imparts a more lifelike skin tone than
paint. It is Sorensen's work in wax that has brought him the
greatest acclaim.

Hints for Collectors
Since the 1960s doll collectors have actively sought out one-of-a-
kind or limited-edition dolls created by contemporary artists
because high-quality modern dolls can be acquired for far less
than antique examples. It is also especially gratifying to collect
the work of living artists.

Lee, Lincoln, and Grant

Description
Portrait dolls with hand-carved wooden heads and painted
features, cloth hair. Limbs made of stockings stuffed with cloth
over wire armatures. Left: Lee wears gray felt Confederate
uniform with brass buttons; leather belt with brass buckle. Gray
felt hat, brown leather boots, wood and metal sword. Center:
Lincoln wears black satin overcoat, black velvet vest with black
glass buttons and brass watch fob in pocket. Cardboard top hat,
imitation-leather shoes. Right: Grant wears blue woolen Union
uniform with brass buttons over white cotton shirt; matching
hat, black imitation-leather shoes. Holds cigar in left hand.

Materials, Marks, and Dimensions
Wooden heads, torsos, and forearms; wire and cloth limbs; cloth
bodies. Labels on coats read "A Peggy Lenape doll." Height:
16½" (left); 19" (center); 15½" (right).

Maker, Origin, and Period
Margaret Finch. New Rochelle, New York. 1955.

Comment
Margaret Finch created this Civil War group for the Department
of Education of the Brooklyn Children's Museum in New York.
Known for her attention to detail, Finch made use of old
photographs and engravings to achieve accurate likenesses of
these historical figures.

Hints for Collectors
These early dolls by Finch—which are labeled with her
professional name, Peggy Lenape—are not as finely detailed in
modeling and costume as her later figures. Finch's dolls rarely
appear on the market except at an occasional estate sale. At the
present time, she makes dolls only on commission.

Franklin Roosevelt and Winston Churchill

Description
Portrait dolls with composition heads and molded and painted features. Wigs of gray human hair. Limbs supported by wire armatures. Stockinet hands. Left: Churchill, with cigar between his teeth, stands with right hand on hip and pats Roosevelt on shoulder with left hand. Original costume of dark gray cotton serge suit and vest with black and white striped tie. Right: Roosevelt seated, with cigarette holder clenched in teeth. Original costume of gray cotton serge suit and vest with striped silk tie.

Materials, Marks, and Dimensions
Composition heads, cloth bodies and limbs. Tags stamped "RAVCA Original" sewn to vests. Height: 18½" (left); 22" (right).

Maker, Origin, and Period
Bernard Ravca. United States. c. 1940–50.

Comment
The noted European dollmaker Bernard Ravca emigrated to the United States from France during the Second World War. Here he continued to make portrait and character dolls from silk stockinet, chemically treated breadcrumbs, and other more traditional materials. Ravca's unusually lifelike dolls include portraits of Maurice Chevalier, Marguerite from Gounod's *Faust*, and a 3-foot-tall Adolf Hitler.

Hints for Collectors
The dimensions of Ravca dolls vary considerably, ranging from very small to larger than life-size. Although some dolls can still be acquired for moderate prices, collectors often pay substantial amounts for the larger figures.

Uncle Sam dolls

Description
Patriotic dolls with bisque heads, molded and painted features.
Smiling closed mouths, wrinkles outlined in red. Jointed bodies
and limbs. Dolls wear original outfits of blue jackets, blue cotton
vests printed with white stars, white cotton shirts, red bow ties,
red and white striped cotton pants, and black patent leather
shoes. Left: Gray mohair wig and beard, brown glass eyes,
aquiline nose. Gray felt hat. Right: Brown mohair wig, blue glass
eyes. Brown satin hat. Brass watch fob on blue ribbon.

Materials, Marks, and Dimensions
Bisque heads, composition bodies and limbs. Left: "Made in
Germany S 8" marked on head. Right: "S" marked on head.
Height: 18½" (left); 13¼" (right).

Maker, Origin, and Period
Maker unknown. Germany. c. 1890.

Comment
The first known Uncle Sam was Samuel Wilson, a supplier of
beef to American troops during the War of 1812. The familiar
personification may have grown out of cartoons by Thomas Nast
and other political satirists. Uncle Sam was a favorite patriotic
motif during the late 19th and early 20th centuries and appeared
in the Hearst newspapers during the Spanish-American War of
1898. One of the Brownies designed by Palmer Cox in 1892 was
an Uncle Sam figure. His likeness was also among the "All
Nation Indestructible Dolls" advertised in 1905 by Butler
Brothers, a doll manufacturer and distributor.

Hints for Collectors
The doll on the left shows wear—chipped paint on the body, a
finger missing from the right hand, a worn wig, and replaced
clothing. These flaws reduce the figure's overall value.

Ringmaster

Description
Manikin with carved features painted in enamel. Brown hair, mustache, and goatee. Brown eyes. Fully jointed with steel springs. Holes in heels fit over prongs of original stand. Original costume of black cardboard hat, white cotton shirt and pants, yellow felt vest, red felt jacket with brass buttons, and knee-high leather leggings over painted boots. Right hand clasps painted wooden whip.

Materials, Marks, and Dimensions
Wood. Height: 19″.

Maker, Origin, and Period
A. Schoenhut & Co. Philadelphia, Pennsylvania. 1915.

Comment
The Ringmaster is one of approximately 1000 finely crafted manikins made by Schoenhut. While specifically created for older children, they were also used as artists' models and for advertising displays. Schoenhut manikins were originally sold dressed or undressed, and their costumes could be purchased separately. Highly detailed football, baseball, basketball, or circus outfits were available, accompanied by appropriate accessories, such as a ringmaster's whip or a football helmet and noseguard.

Hints for Collectors
All Schoenhut manikins portray young men with pensive expressions. Their facial features are modeled after Schoenhut's first Ringmaster, part of the extraordinary miniature "Humpty Dumpty Circus" of 1903. Manikins can be easily distinguished from other varieties of Schoenhut dolls, since they are the most mature-looking.

Chimney sweep

Description
Penwiper bathing doll with one-piece china body and stationary limbs. Molded and painted hair and features. Blond hair, blue eyes, closed mouth. Original costume of black cotton cap and suit. Wire ladder wrapped with thread. Broom of twigs and wire. Heavy felt penwiper base.

Materials, Marks, and Dimensions
China. Height: 5″.

Maker, Origin, and Period
Maker unknown. Germany. c. 1850–1920.

Comment
In the days before fountain pens were widely used, penwiper dolls performed an important function. Their full skirts or felt bases were used to absorb excess ink from quill pens. These inexpensive dolls were discarded once their bases became saturated. Made in many forms, including the versatile one-piece china bathing doll shown here, they often portrayed popular 19th-century characters, such as stylish ladies or chimney sweeps dressed entirely in black. Many penwiper dolls carried cards with amusing verses. An example made from a wishbone had a note that stated, "Once I was a wishbone and grew upon a hen / Now I am a little slave and made to wipe your pen."

Hints for Collectors
In general, bathing dolls have not risen as dramatically in price as other 19th-century figures. This is partly because collectors prefer dolls with wigs and fanciful clothing to such plain molded figures. The bathing doll shown here is exceptional, because it has been cleverly outfitted and transformed into a utilitarian object. Still moderately priced, it would make an unusual addition to a general collection of dolls.

Peddler doll

Description
Young woman with bisque head; molded and painted features
and blond hair. Blue eyes, closed mouth. Original costume of
print dress and gray shawl decorated with orange appliqué. Tall
black hat trimmed with ribbon and lace tied over white cap.
Holds knitting and umbrella on lap. Sits in ladder-back chair
surrounded by baskets holding wares; feathers attached to back
of wooden chair. Baskets contain shells, flowers, vegetables, and
eggs. Entire ensemble mounted on round wooden base.

Materials, Marks, and Dimensions
Bisque head and hands, cloth body. Height: 10¼″.

Maker, Origin, and Period
Maker unknown. Possibly England. c. 1870–90.

Comment
Early peddler dolls from the 18th century were costumed in the
ragged clothing seen on street hawkers of the period. They had
crude wooden faces and stumplike bodies. In the 19th century
peddler dolls usually depicted old women in black bonnets and
large aprons, although a few young ladies, such as the one shown
here, have been found.

Hints for Collectors
A peddler doll can sometimes be dated by the wares in its
baskets or tray. For example, if a doll carries pins made from 2
pieces of brass wire, one coiled into a head, it was probably made
before pins were commercially produced in the 1820s. On the
other hand, spools of thread on a doll's tray indicate that it was
made after 1820, since before that date thread was available only
in hanks or skeins.

Peddler doll

Description
Woman with parian-type shoulder-head, molded and painted features, and blond molded hair. Blond eyebrows, blue eyes, rosy cheeks, closed mouth. Columnar cloth-covered cardboard base supports lower body. Original costume of black ribbed silk dress, lace-trimmed ecru cotton underskirt, white linen apron. Carries traditional peddler tray with array of wares including miniature bisque dolls, books, silverware, hats, purses, and a chair-shaped pincushion.

Materials, Marks, and Dimensions
Untinted bisque shoulder-head; cloth torso and arms; cardboard base. Height: 12¼".

Maker, Origin, and Period
Maker unknown. England. c. 1860.

Comment
During the Regency and Victorian periods, English peddler dolls were commonly made to resemble the peddlers and vendors who brought decorative items to remote country towns. These dolls sometimes carried as many as 125 tiny items and were made from all types of materials, including cloth, kid, wood, papier-mâché, apples, and wax. Peddler dolls as delicate as the one shown here were designed strictly as ornamental pieces and were kept under glass domes.

Hints for Collectors
Although most peddler dolls appear to be homemade, many were actually fashioned by skilled toymakers. Genuine 18th- and 19th-century peddler dolls are rare and very costly. Beware of modern fakes that bear a few authentic antique items and are sprinkled with dust to deceive the buyer about the doll's true age.

Description
Black man and woman dolls with poured-wax heads; molded and painted features and hair. Inserted glass eyes. Wax over wire-frame bodies mounted on wooden stands. Original cotton clothing dipped in wax. Left: Man wears black suit, red and white polka-dot shirt, oversize top hat. Cord of wood tied onto back by rope. Carries rope with attached iron hook in hands. Right: Woman wears checked bandanna over short hair, red and white polka-dot scarf over striped green floral blouse, green and yellow floral skirt. Right hand holds carrots. Basket of vegetables at doll's feet.

Materials, Marks, and Dimensions
Wax. "VARGAS/New Orleans, La." marked on bottom of both bases. Height: 7″ (left); 6″ (right).

Maker, Origin, and Period
Probably Lucy Rosado. New Orleans, Louisiana. c. 1920.

Comment
The dollmaker Francisco Vargas emigrated from Mexico to New Orleans in the late 19th century. He began his career by modeling statues of saints using a beeswax formula obtained from his parish priest. He subsequently patented this wax technique and used it to make a series of remarkable dolls representing cotton-pickers, vendors, and other tradespeople.

Hints for Collectors
After Vargas died in the 1890s, his heirs, particularly his granddaughter, Lucy Rosado, continued to make dolls until the mid-20th century. The earliest dolls fashioned by Vargas himself were not marked and were so fragile that few if any have survived.

Mammy doll

Description
Mammy doll with composition head, molded and painted
features. Black mohair wig. Brown eyes, broad nose, prominent
cheekbones, open-closed mouth with row of teeth. Oversize
hands and feet. Original costume of red and white print cotton
dress, white cotton apron, red print bandanna. Molded shoes.
Mammy holds baby with composition head, molded and painted
features. Brown hair, side-glancing eyes, closed mouth. Jointed
body wrapped in white flannel blanket and pink satin ribbon.

Materials, Marks, and Dimensions
Mammy: Composition head and limbs, cloth body. Gold tag
pinned on dress reads "Tony Sarg's/Mammy Doll/Sole
Distributor/George Borgfeldt Corp./New York, N.Y." Baby:
Composition. Height: 20″ (mammy); 8″ (baby).

Maker, Origin, and Period
Designed by Tony Sarg for Geo. Borgfeldt & Co. New York
City. c. 1930–39.

Comment
The mammy doll shown here was designed by Tony Sarg, the
noted puppeteer, illustrator, and author of children's books. He
designed puppets for Walt Disney, dolls for Madame Alexander,
and created the original animal balloons for Macy's first
Thanksgiving Day parade.

Hints for Collectors
In most cases, the baby dolls once held in the arms of mammy
figures are missing; this is an unusual example because both dolls
have been preserved. Mammy dolls are seldom made today, so
the older versions are in great demand. Composition heads made
during the 1930s are prone to cracking, as can be seen on the
faces of the dolls shown here.

Gendarme

Description
Male doll with stitched and molded features. Plush velvet face
with center seam, large jutting nose, black button eyes, and red
wool embroidered mouth and nostrils. Body and limbs stuffed
with cork dust. Mitten-type hands with stitched fingers. Wears
felt suit adorned with gold epaulettes, braids, and brass buttons.
Linen scarf, black leather shoes with felt soles.

Materials, Marks, and Dimensions
Velvet head and hands, felt body and limbs. Height: 14″.

Maker, Origin, and Period
Margarete Steiff. Germany. c. 1900.

Comment
The noted dollmaker Margarete Steiff originally made stuffed
animals from remnants discarded by a felt factory near her
home. In 1894 she produced her first dolls with felt heads and by
1903 had expanded her operations throughout Europe. Steiff
character dolls, which include German and American military
figures, a Chinaman, an Irish footman, an Indian, a fashionable
black gentleman, and assorted clowns, are all rather comical and
very appealing.

Hints for Collectors
Steiff character dolls are easily identified by the center seam on
their felt or velvet faces, and by their prominent noses. They
often have very large feet that enable them to stand without
support. Since their cork-dust stuffing makes them brittle and
their velvet faces are easily soiled and damaged, early Steiff dolls
in good condition are rare and command high prices. Steiff dolls
made after 1905 are marked with an identifying button attached
to one ear.

Quebec couple

Description
Male and female dolls with simple embroidered features and hair.
Left: Original costume of woolen overcoat with fur collar, orange
woolen scarf tied around waist. Orange woolen cap, patent
leather boots. Right: Original costume of herringbone woolen
coat with fur collar, woolen dress, cotton checked apron.
Multicolored scarf and mittens, patent leather boots.

Materials, Marks, and Dimensions
Cloth. Cloth labels attached to jackets read "Manoir Richelieu/
Hand Woven/Murray Bay/Homespun/Canada Steamship Lines."
Height: 9½″ (left); 10″ (right).

Maker, Origin, and Period
Manoir Richelieu. Canada. c. 1940–50.

Comment
The dolls illustrated, representing a traditional Quebec
couple, were sold in Canadian craft and souvenir shops and
aboard a Canadian steamship line. Similarly dressed dolls
were distributed in Montreal during the 1940s. Those made
by Manoir Richelieu may be identified by their triangular
embroidered eyes and heavy woolen clothing.

Hints for Collectors
There are a number of ways to obtain information about small,
little-known firms such as Manoir Richelieu. By studying a
variety of dolls made by one firm or dollmaker, it is sometimes
possible to establish stylistic traits that might not be evident
when studying only a single doll. If a dollmaker's place of
residence is known, further information may often be provided
by a local chamber of commerce, historical society, or doll club.

Dollhouse bridal group

Description
Dollhouse dolls with bisque heads, molded and painted features and hair. Blue eyes, closed mouths, rosy cheeks. Original costumes. From left to right: Child wears blue satin dress, woven straw hat, cotton lace-trimmed underpants, black painted-on Mary Jane shoes. Bridegroom wears black felt suit, white cotton shirt with glass buttons, black painted-on shoes. Bride wears white satin dress, white gauze veil, white cotton lace-trimmed underskirt and pantaloons, black painted-on high-heeled shoes. Holds white bouquet. Bridal attendant wears blue satin blouse, pleated beige satin skirt, woven straw hat, lace-trimmed cotton underskirt, blue satin underpants, black painted-on high-heeled shoes.

Materials, Marks, and Dimensions
Bisque heads and limbs, cloth bodies. "461-11/0" inked on cloth shoulders of dolls. Height: 4″ (child); 5¼″ (bridegroom); 5″ (bride and attendant).

Maker, Origin, and Period
Maker unknown. Germany. c. 1920.

Comment
Made in the 18th century of alabaster, wood, wax, or silver, the earliest dollhouse dolls were fragile miniatures created for the amusement of the upper class. In the 19th century they were gradually replaced by dolls of papier-mâché, bisque, china, and other, less precious materials.

Hints for Collectors
The stocky proportions and molded, short bobbed hairstyles on the dolls seen here are characteristic of dollhouse figures made in the 1920s. Female dolls are also found with molded buns at the napes of their necks.

Butler, cook, and housemaid

Description
Dollhouse dolls with molded and painted hair and features. Original costumes. Left: Butler wears black felt tuxedo and white felt vest with glass buttons. Center: Cook wears white cotton chef's hat, white cotton apron over white shirt, and checked trousers. Right: Maid wears lace cap, black satin uniform with lace collar and apron. Molded black pumps.

Materials, Marks, and Dimensions
Composition head, hands, and feet; cloth bodies and limbs over wire armatures. Height: 6″ (left); 6½″ (center); 5¼″ (right).

Maker, Origin, and Period
EFFanBEE (trade name for Fleischaker & Baum). New York City. c. 1950–60.

Comment
Dollhouses are often built to resemble the ordered homes of well-to-do families served by an attentive staff. Since the 18th century, sets of miniature dolls designed for dollhouses have included butlers, maids, and other domestic employees. This modern EFFanBEE dollhouse group may have originally come with parents, grandparents, babies, and even a nanny. In 1952 EFFanBEE produced another group of dolls made of hard plastic and jointed with string. Dolls like those shown here, with flexible wire limbs, are far more popular.

Hints for Collectors
Bisque and celluloid dollhouse dolls made in the late 19th and early 20th centuries are often found reclothed. Children played with them frequently, removed their original clothing, and often replaced it with hand-sewn garments. Dolls found in their original outfits are usually of a finer quality because they were meant for display rather than play.

Red Cross nurse

Description
Red Cross nurse doll with bisque swivel head. Blond mohair wig, brown glass eyes, open-closed mouth showing teeth. Original white cotton uniform and headdress adorned with Red Cross insignia. White cotton underclothing and white kid high-heeled boots.

Materials, Marks, and Dimensions
Bisque head and hands; cloth body; kid lower arms and legs. "L.P./Paris/03" marked on head. Height: 11″.

Maker, Origin, and Period
Maker unknown. France. c. 1920.

Comment
Dolls dressed as Red Cross nurses appeared in Europe and in the United States during and immediately after the First World War. The Galeries Lafayette, a Parisian department store, listed china-head and cloth-head dolls dressed as Red Cross nurses in their catalogues of that period. Patterns for doll-size military uniforms and Red Cross nurses' costumes were printed in *La Semaine de Suzette*, a French periodical, in 1916. From 1916 to 1920 Red Cross dolls were so popular in America that one wholesale catalogue advised retailers to "buy an extra supply of the Red Cross dolls (nurses) with insignia on cap and arm, dressed in white."

Hints for Collectors
Many dolls are found with their original costumes in tatters; others have somehow lost their clothes. What a doll wore when it was made can sometimes be traced through such documentation as the manufacturer's advertisements and catalogues, a photograph of a doll in its vintage costume, or a museum acquisition card that lists a doll's original garment.

Dionne Quintuplets and Dr. Dafoe

Description
Portrait dolls with composition heads and molded and painted features, mohair wigs. Quintuplets: Side-glancing brown eyes and jointed chubby limbs. Each wears original costume of different colored organdy dress and bonnet with metal nameplate pinned to front. White socks and shoes. Dr. Dafoe: Swivel head, jointed limbs. Wears original costume of surgeon's cap and uniform, horn-rimmed glasses, and oilcloth shoes with metal buckles.

Materials, Marks, and Dimensions
Composition. Quintuplets: "Alexander" stamped on bodies, "Dionne Alexander" stamped on heads; cloth labels on dresses read "Dionne Quintuplets Madame Alexander USA." Height: 7½" (quintuplets); 13½" (Dr. Dafoe).

Maker, Origin, and Period
Madame Alexander. New York City. Quintuplets: 1937. Dr. Dafoe: 1936.

Comment
The birth of the Canadian Dionne quintuplets in 1935 generated tremendous excitement among the public. Dollmakers were quick to produce sets of Annette, Yvonne, Marie, Cecile, and Emilie as babies, as toddlers, and as little girls, along with their doctor. Manufactured until 1939, the dolls were often sold with extra sets of clothing and specially designed furniture.

Hints for Collectors
Although many doll companies produced versions of the quintuplets, only Madame Alexander was granted permission to use the Dionne family name in her trademark. Sets complete with Dr. Dafoe may be hard to find, but can sometimes be assembled from dolls found separately.

Description
Dolls depicting same person as adult and child, with latex swivel heads and molded and painted features. Blond wigs, human-hair eyelashes, open-closed mouths with teeth. Jointed limbs. Left: Adult wears original costume of green and black short-sleeved dress with black leather belt and black sandals. Right: Child wears original costume of short-sleeved rosebud print dress with white collar and cuffs, socks, and shoes with metal buckles.

Materials, Marks, and Dimensions
Latex. Left: "AA '58/#7" marked on neck. Right: "DC/AA-52/#24" marked on head. Height: 17½" (left); 12½" (right).

Maker, Origin, and Period
Dewees Cochran. Vermont. Left: 1958. Right: 1952.

Comment
Dewees Cochran is best known for her doll portraits depicting youngsters as they grow from childhood to maturity. She developed the highly regarded "Grow-up" series, in which girls were portrayed at ages 5, 7, 11, 16, and 20; and boys at 5, 14, and 23. Angela Appleseed, illustrated here at ages 5 and 20, was one of 5 dolls modeled by Cochran after real children. Cochran also made doll portraits using one of 6 head molds she called "Look-Alike" heads.

Hints for Collectors
Dewees Cochran designed a group of dolls for EFFanBEE called "America's Children" or "Portrait Dolls." These are not as valuable as the "Grow-up" series and other dolls manufactured in her own studio.

98 Barbie doll

Description
Teenage doll with plastic head, molded and painted features and hair. Blue sleep-eyes, closed mouth. Body jointed at shoulders and hips, bendable knees. Original costume of pink rayon swimsuit with matching cap, pearl earrings. Accompanying box contains 3 wigs, lawn swing, planter, and wire stand.

Materials, Marks, and Dimensions
Plastic head and torso, vinyl arms and legs. Wrist tag reads "Barbie." Base of head marked "© MT," "USA" marked on right buttock. "© 1958/Mattel Inc./U.S. Patented/U.S. Patent Pending" printed on both feet. Height: 12″.

Maker, Origin, and Period
Mattel, Inc. Hawthorne, California. c. 1964.

Comment
Ruth Handler, an official of the Mattel Corporation, originally conceived of Barbie as a plaything for her daughter Barbara. First patented in 1958, Barbie was designed with a fully developed figure and a large wardrobe with optional accessories. Not long after Barbie's debut, companion dolls were introduced, including her boyfriend Ken. Barbie's success inspired numerous imitations, none of which attained her popularity.

Hints for Collectors
Collecting Barbies is big business nowadays, and the first-edition, mint-condition Barbie dolls in original boxes sell for very large sums. Some types of Barbies are still relatively inexpensive, however. Collectors often seek just one category of Barbie dolls, such as celebrities, black dolls, or a Barbie from each year. The *Barbie Bulletin* and *Barbie Gazette* provide up-to-date information about the numerous examples produced from 1958 to the present.

G.I. Joe

Description
Male doll with vinyl head and flocked blond hair, mustache, and beard. Painted features. Brown eyes, closed mouth, scar on right cheek. Fully jointed body, hands designed to grip objects easily. Original clothes of cotton camouflage-print shirt, cotton khaki pants, cotton belt with pockets and plastic cartridge cases.

Materials, Marks, and Dimensions
Vinyl head and plastic body. Lower back embossed "G.I. Joe ®/Copyright 1964/by Hasbro ®/Pat. 3277,602/Made in U.S.A." Height: 11¾".

Maker, Origin, and Period
Hasbro (trade name for Hassenfeld Bros.). Pawtucket, Rhode Island. c. 1974.

Comment
In 1964, when he was first marketed, G.I. Joe was advertised as an "action figure" rather than as a doll so that little boys would not be embarrassed to play with him. He was designed in numerous versions, and a new series was introduced every year. In 1965 the firm produced a black doll, in 1967 a talking doll, in 1974 this doll with its hands in "Kung Fu" position, and in 1975 a doll with well-developed muscles and a molded-on swimsuit. The anti-war sentiment of the late 1960s and early '70s transformed G.I. Joe into a peacetime adventurer who dived, climbed mountains, and went on archaeological expeditions.

Hints for Collectors
While not as popular as the Barbie doll, G.I. Joe has many fans who regard him as a figure of social significance. Collectors of recently made dolls should note that mint-in-box examples are always worth substantially more than those that have been played with.

WAC and WAVE dolls

Description
Dolls with molded and painted caps, hair, and features. One-piece heads and molded torsos. Jointed limbs. Molded breasts. Left: WAC doll wears original costume of khaki uniform and matching hat, white blouse, black tie, green wool stockings, black oilcloth and leather shoes. Right: WAVE doll wears original costume of blue cap with black band, blue cotton uniform with silver metal buttons, and white oilcloth shoes.

Materials, Marks, and Dimensions
Composition. Left: Paper tag on front of uniform reads "W.A.C." Right: Paper label on jacket reads "WAVES/Manufactured by Freundlich Nov. Corp./New York, NY." Height: 15″.

Maker, Origin, and Period
Freundlich Novelty Corp. New York City. c. 1943.

Comment
This WAC and WAVE were some of the first dolls to reflect the changing roles of women in contemporary life. Capitalizing on wartime patriotism, dolls in military uniforms were made in the United States and Europe in the early 1940s. These included a General Douglas MacArthur doll, also designed by the Freundlich Novelty Corporation, and a line of soldier dolls made by Belgian refugees in England for the Horsman Company.

Hints for Collectors
Second World War figures appeal to modern doll fanciers and to those who collect war memorabilia. An interesting collection could be made of officer dolls or of dolls representing each branch of the armed forces.

Storybook, Celebrity, and Cartoon-Character Dolls

 Fictional characters and real-life celebrities have served as models for dolls in every conceivable material. By and large these dolls are a 20th-century phenomenon, though they have antecedents in such 19th-century examples as paper dolls of Little Eva and Topsey from Harriet Beecher Stowe's *Uncle Tom's Cabin.* Children's books have also supplied charming characters for early dolls, including the immediately recognizable Golliwog, based on Bertha and Florence Upton's *The Adventures of Two Dolls—and a Golliwogg,* published in 1895.

Comic-Strip and Cartoon-Character Dolls
In 1895 Richard Outcault drew the first color comic strip, "Hogan's Alley," for the *New York World.* Its hero, a 7-year-old street urchin named the Yellow Kid, proved so popular that he became the subject of Yellow Kid toys, games, and a homely doll with protruding ears and buck teeth. Since then nearly every major comic-book or newspaper comic-strip character has become a doll. Before the age of plastic, Ideal, EFFanBEE, Cameo, and numerous other firms modeled cloth, bisque, composition, rubber, and wooden dolls after the comic characters Little Orphan Annie, Popeye, Nancy and Sluggo, Superman, Ella Cinders, and the Katzenjammer Kids, to name just a few. Walt Disney's animated cartoons inspired dolls of Pinocchio and Jiminy Cricket, Snow White and the Seven Dwarfs, and many other dolls that are reputed to have been more profitable for Disney than the movies themselves. The comic-strip and cartoon characters on which many dolls were based offer a fascinating glimpse into the social history of America. Popeye, for example, was created in 1929; his sustenance, spinach, was a symbolic cure-all for what ailed America during the Depression. The frantic antics of the turn-of-the-century Katzenjammer Kids reflected the struggles between children and adult authority figures.

Celebrity and Fad Dolls
Some dolls that portray celebrities were made for a brief time, capitalizing on the stars' short-lived fame. Dolls depicting individuals with longer careers were often made for decades. The popular ventriloquist's dummy Charlie McCarthy made his debut on radio in the 1930s and appeared on television years later; dolls in his image were made from 1936 to the 1970s. The caricatured faces and stuffed-animal or fairylike bodies of such novelty dolls as Googly, Billiken, and Kewpie made these figures immensely popular in their day. Before being made into dolls, both Kewpie and the Campbell Kids first appeared as illustrations in the *Ladies' Home Journal,* a magazine also noted for its numerous doll advertisements.

Clowns, Cowboys, and Other Figures
Cloth dolls representing such characters as clowns, sailors, and cowboys are popular with collectors because of their imaginative designs, not always evident in other doll types. One-of-a-kind figures and those by unknown makers are desirable because they are often charming, yet inexpensive. On the other hand, the fine characters created by noted manufacturers, including Steiff, Lenci, and Victoria Toy Works, may be costly, but they are probably good investments.

Knitted doll

Description
Male doll knitted entirely from head to toe, stuffed with cotton. Embroidered eyebrows and mouth, button eyes, unraveled brown yarn hair. Dressed in red suit with matching hat; short red cape edged with tatting and tied with yellow silk cord. Embroidered cross-stitching on chest. Brown leggings. Cross-stitched laces on pink shoes.

Materials, Marks, and Dimensions
Wool yarn. Height: 16″.

Maker, Origin, and Period
Maker unknown. United States. c. 1895.

Comment
Harper's Bazaar featured a pattern in its November 19, 1892, issue for a knitted boy doll that looked very much like the jaunty fellow shown here. The instructions advised the reader to use 4 steel knitting needles and guaranteed an "absolutely reliable set of directions." By the turn of the century, these dolls were the rage. Knitters frequently altered the printed instructions to allow for such embellishments as elegant jackets, jabots, elaborate cuffs, and jewelry; many dolls were designed with striped stockings. A very unusual black version of the doll shown here can be found in the Essex Institute in Salem, Massachusetts.

Hints for Collectors
Look for knitted dolls at flea markets and garage sales, where 19th-century figures sometimes turn up and sell for very little money. Be wary of moth-eaten or partially unraveled dolls.

Description
Cowboy doll knitted entirely from head to toe, stuffed with
kapok. Embroidered and molded features, blond knitted hair,
applied ears, mitten-shaped hands. Outfit of red, green, and
black striped shirt, black vest; red kerchief tied with yellow
yarn; tan looped chaps; black shoes. Knitted black cowboy hat.
Holds twine lasso.

Materials, Marks, and Dimensions
Wool yarn. Height: 19″.

Maker, Origin, and Period
Maker unknown. United States. c. 1940–45.

Comment
This colorful yarn doll came with 4 pages of typewritten
instructions calling for both #11 and #13 double-point needles,
kapok, and an assortment of colored yarns. The complicated
directions were either produced by a yarn-goods store or written
by an accomplished knitter to pass along to friends. The cowboy
was originally part of a group that included at least 2 other dolls
—a knitted soldier and sailor dressed in uniforms dating from the
Second World War. The costumes suggest that all 3 dolls were
made in the early 1940s.

Hints for Collectors
Yarn dolls are still being made today, although few are as
detailed as the cowboy shown here. Prior to the 1940s, knitted
dolls were often introduced by patterns published in ladies'
magazines. Since the cowboy's instructions were unpublished, it
is likely that only a few were made—a factor that enhances this
doll's value.

Description
Clown dolls with beige cotton stocking heads. Stuffed with cork dust. Molded and embroidered features, black bead eyes. Left: Black wool hair and mustache. No hands. Original multicolored wool chenille costume sewn to body. Wool bow at neck, peaked hat, faded black linen shoes. Right: Red wool hair. Mitten hands with stitched fingers. Original sewn-on striped knit outfit with large yellow wool buttons. Peaked hat, black cotton stocking shoes.

Materials, Marks, and Dimensions
Cotton, wool, and linen. Height: 14″.

Maker, Origin, and Period
Maker and locale unknown. c. 1900–25.

Comment
The dolls shown here were most likely made in the early 20th century, when the clown Pierrot, a well-known character in French pantomime, was an extremely popular figure with children and adults. Pierrot dolls wore silk costumes with double ruffled collars, large buttons, loose-fitting trousers, and pointed caps with ruffles or bells. Inspired by the popularity of such figures, manufacturers produced other examples of humbler stock, as illustrated by the pair above.

Hints for Collectors
When documentation for a doll is absent, collectors must do some sleuthing to determine its age and origin. For example, the chenille used for the outfit of the doll at left was popular in the early 20th century. Moreover, both dolls are stuffed with cork dust, which suggests that they were produced prior to 1920. Dolls made afterward were usually stuffed with cotton.

Clown

Description
Cloth doll stuffed with cotton batting. Molded nose and chin.
Painted features include red, white, and black eyes, red triangles
on cheeks, red mouth with 2 white teeth. Original sewn-on
costume of pink linen clown outfit printed with Kewpie dolls
swimming, riding, and petting animals; red cotton ruff. Faded
pink flannel shoes. Pointed red hat. Squeak mechanism in
stomach.

Materials, Marks, and Dimensions
Muslin. Height: 22".

Maker, Origin, and Period
Maker unknown. Probably United States. c. 1920–25.

Comment
Without its costume, it would be difficult to determine the age
and origin of this unmarked doll. The doll's outfit is made from
cloth that was produced for children's clothing in the United
States about 1920. The fabric is printed with pictures of Rose
O'Neill's Kewpies, which were so popular at the time that their
images appeared on every imaginable kind of merchandise,
including wallpaper, bottles, toy pianos, and postcards.

Hints for Collectors
This clown's costume is sewn to its body, making it impossible
to clean it without ripping the seams apart to remove it. To clean
a doll with sewn-on clothes, rub it lightly with a soapy cloth,
and be sure not to immerse the doll's body in water. When
contemplating repairs on a doll, consider whether the cost is too
high to justify the effort. For example, it would probably cost
more to fix this doll's broken cry box than to replace the doll.

Harlequin

Description
Felt doll with molded and painted features. Side-glancing brown eyes, black mask. Open-closed mouth displaying teeth. Multicolored felt patches sewn to body to form costume. Flexible limbs, stitched fingers. Black felt hat. Ruffles at neck and wrists. Slippers.

Materials, Marks, and Dimensions
Felt. Height: 17½″.

Maker, Origin, and Period
Lenci (trade name for Elena Scavini). Italy. c. 1920.

Comment
Harlequin, the traditional clown from the *commedia dell'arte*, was one of Lenci's favorite characters, and the firm produced him in several versions. Harlequin appealed especially to adults, who admired his fascinating lineage and decorative clothing.

Hints for Collectors
Older cloth dolls whose bodies were constructed with sewn-on clothing are seldom well preserved, since without the protection afforded by extra removable outfits they became easily soiled. Felt Lenci dolls in good condition, like the one illustrated here, are quite valuable and among the most sought-after cloth examples today. When storing Lenci dolls, avoid wrapping them in plastic, since they tend to become stained with mildew. To remove mildew, lightly rub the affected area with a cloth moistened with dry-cleaning fluid or wool-rug shampoo. Lenci dolls displayed in a dust-free, mothproof environment will last for generations.

Description
Cloth doll couple with mask faces. Molded and painted red hair
and features including side-glancing brown eyes. Felt hands.
Left: Closed mouth, applied felt ears. Sewn-on yellow velvet
jumpsuit, brown velvet jacket, brown felt shoes. Right: Closed
rosebud mouth, dimples. Sewn-on red velvet dress and pants;
brown velvet jacket, brown felt hat, red felt shoes.

Materials, Marks, and Dimensions
Cotton heads, velvet and felt bodies. Neck tags read "I'm one of
Norah Wellings' 'Little Pixie People.' " Labels on soles of feet
marked "Made in England by Norah Wellings." Height: 9¼".

Maker, Origin, and Period
Designed by Norah Wellings for Victoria Toy Works. England.
c. 1940.

Comment
The impish cloth dolls shown here were made by Norah
Wellings, an English doll designer who ran the Victoria Toy
Works with her brother Leonard from 1926 to 1959. The firm's
soft toys and dolls, known for their well-made costumes, were
often sold as mascots aboard British ocean liners. Heads of felt,
velvet, or cotton were stiffened with buckram and plastic wood,
using a technique patented in 1926. Some dolls were made with
inset movable glass eyes.

Hints for Collectors
Norah Wellings designed dolls for Chad Valley for 7 years before
starting her own firm. Not surprisingly, there is a marked
similarity between some Chad Valley dolls and those made by
Victoria Toy Works. When attribution is in doubt, collectors
should look for a label sewn to a doll's hand or foot.

Golliwog

Description
Felt doll stuffed with straw. Black mohair wig, plastic eyes, red and black appliquéd smiling mouth. Mitten hands. Original sewn-on costume includes gray felt jacket and gold velvet vest with brass buttons; red velvet pants. Sewn-on shoes with black tops, yellow soles, and tan spats.

Materials, Marks, and Dimensions
Felt. Marked on bottom of foot "Made in England/Lenart Imports Ltd." Height: 12″.

Maker, Origin, and Period
Maker unknown. England. c. 1910.

Comment
British troops stationed in Egypt during the late 19th century noticed that Egyptian workers called *ghuls* wore armbands initialed W.O.G. "Golliwog," a portmanteau word, was the name given to small black dolls the soldiers brought back with them to England. Not long afterward, Florence and Bertha Upton created the black-faced character Golliwog for their illustrated book, *The Adventures of Two Dolls—and a Golliwogg*, published in 1895. Golliwog's ungainly charm endeared him to countless children. Doll versions of the character were manufactured through the 1920s.

Hints for Collectors
Look for felt and velvet Golliwogs and those stuffed with straw. They were made earlier than all-cloth examples and are considerably more valuable. Although most Golliwogs are unmarked, a 1917 version registered in the United States as a "Gollywog" by Etta Mansfield does have a woven label.

Gold Dust Twins

Description
Advertising dolls of brown cloth stuffed with kapok. Painted features include side-glancing eyes and red smiling mouths. Black string topknots. Gauze skirts.

Materials, Marks, and Dimensions
Stockinet. Height: 5¼″.

Maker, Origin, and Period
Nelke Corp. Philadelphia, Pennsylvania. c. 1920–29.

Comment
Gold Dust, an all-purpose cleanser, was widely advertised in women's magazines in the early part of this century. Prominently displayed on its box were 2 little black children known as the Gold Dust Twins. In the 1920s the twins, called Goldie and Dusty, were produced as cuddly doll premiums by the Nelke Corporation, a firm that had begun making soft toys around 1918. Nelke's first dolls, called Nelke Dollies, were 12″ high. They were dressed in rompers and had waterproof, washable faces. The company also manufactured large numbers of soft Kewpies, clowns, boy and girl dolls, and other toys.

Hints for Collectors
Jean Nelke West, daughter of the founder of the Nelke Corporation, commented that the dolls shown here were the only Gold Dust Twins she had seen in many years. This is surprising, since the dolls were produced in large numbers. It is possible that many of them lost their Nelke trademark ribbons and that they lie unrecognized in attics, toy shops, and flea markets.

Raggedy Ann and Andy

Description
Cloth dolls with reddish-brown hair made of yarn. Painted
features, black plastic button eyes, red triangular noses. Flexible
limbs, mitten hands. Printed red and white striped stockings and
black shoes. "I Love You" inscribed in hearts printed on torsos.
Left: Raggedy Ann in original costume of floral-print cotton
dress and white cotton apron; white pantaloons. Right: Raggedy
Andy in original outfit of one-piece plaid cotton shirt and blue
pants with white buttons. Black ribbon at neck. White sailor cap.

Materials, Marks, and Dimensions
Cloth. Labels inside clothing read "Johnny Gruelle's own
Raggedy Andy [Ann] Doll/Trademark Reg. U.S. Patent Off./
Copyright 1920 by John B. Gruelle/Georgene Novelties, Inc./
New York City." Height: 20".

Maker, Origin, and Period
Designed by John Gruelle for Georgene Novelties, Inc. New
York City. c. 1930–50.

Comment
A long-forgotten rag doll in his mother's attic inspired John
Gruelle to create the beloved Raggedy Ann and Andy dolls. The
earliest versions were very different from the examples most
people know today. They had brown hair, inverted pear-shaped
faces, and red celluloid hearts affixed to their torsos. In 1978
one of the original Raggedy Ann dolls made a notable trip to
Indianapolis, Gruelle's birthplace, where she received a key to
the city from the mayor.

Hints for Collectors
Although the dolls shown here are not expensive, competition
for the earlier versions is keen. Many Raggedy Ann fanciers
have collections of the dolls numbering in the hundreds.

Shrinking Violet

Description
Talking doll with applied and painted features. Blue felt eyes, rouged cheeks, yellow yarn hair tied in pigtails with pink ribbon. Stitched fingers. Arms attached to sleeves of sewn-on lavender dress. Cotton tulle underskirt, white lace-trimmed socks, and black Mary Jane shoes. String on back of doll activates voice box in torso and causes lips and eyelids to flutter simultaneously.

Materials, Marks, and Dimensions
Cloth. Label on hip marked "Mattel Shrinking Violet." Reverse side of label marked "63 by The Funny Company/All Rights Reserved Throughout The World/Pat. [numbers]/Pat. Canada 1962." Height: 12".

Maker, Origin, and Period
Mattel, Inc. Hawthorne, California. c. 1964–65.

Comment
Shrinking Violet was one of several successful talking dolls that Mattel designed for small children. She was capable of uttering 12 phrases, such as "I'm so embarrassed," that youngsters could identify with. Chatty Cathy, Mattel's first talking doll, was introduced in 1960, followed by Mattie, Sister Belle, Charmin' Cathy, Singin' Chatty, Casper the Ghost and, of course, the shy miss shown here.

Hints for Collectors
Quality control and high manufacturing standards cannot prevent the voice mechanism of a talking doll from breaking with repeated usage. Since the distinguishing feature of such a doll is its ability to speak, it would be wise to pass up one whose voice box does not work. The cost of repairs might exceed the price paid for the doll itself.

Description
Cartoon-character dolls with mask faces, molded and painted features. Left: Sluggo wears original costume of yellow shirt with white cuffs, black jacket, blue pants, orange felt cap. Right: Nancy wears black wig, original costume of white cotton blouse, black vest, orange felt skirt, and sewn-on striped socks.

Materials, Marks, and Dimensions
Cloth. Paper tag on left arm of each doll reads "A Georgene/Doll/ Sluggo [Nancy]/by Ernie Bushmiller/United Syndicate/Georgene Novelties, Inc./New York, N.Y./Made in U.S.A." Height: 14½" (left); 14" (right).

Maker, Origin, and Period
Georgene Novelties, Inc. New York City. Left: 1944. Right: 1946.

Comment
The comic strip "Nancy" originally appeared in the 1920s. This little girl's escapades were most widely followed in the 1950s and '60s by fans who loved her cheekiness. Nancy and her friend Sluggo were first made into dolls in the 1940s. An all-rubber Nancy doll, whose manufacturer is unknown, followed the Georgene Novelties version shown here. Nancy and Sluggo dolls were also made by Ideal in the 1950s and most recently by the Knickerbocker Toy Company in 1973.

Hints for Collectors
There are no firm price guides for comic-character dolls because they are a relatively new field of collecting. It is still possible to pick up an important doll at low cost. The most desirable are examples made before the Second World War that are still in their original boxes. Decorated with comic-strip illustrations, the boxes themselves are today collectible.

Katzenjammer Kids

Description
Cartoon-character dolls with applied and painted features. Glass
bug eyes, bulbous noses, grinning mouths. Original costumes.
Left: Hans wears red shirt with white collar and black bow tie,
striped pants, black shoes. Center: Captain has black yarn
whiskers, black coat with gold braid and large pearl buttons,
blue rayon pants, black shoes, and blue and black hat. Right:
Fritz wears black cotton jacket over white shirt, red pants, black
shoes, black felt hat.

Materials, Marks, and Dimensions
Cloth. Paper tags attached to shirts read "Katzenjammer/Kids/
[each doll's name]/Knickerbocker/Toy Co., Inc./New York."
Reverse of tags marked "Manufactured by/Knickerbocker Toy
Co., Inc./New York/Licensed by King Features Syndicate, Inc."
Height: 14″ (left); 18″ (center); 16½″ (right).

Maker, Origin, and Period
Knickerbocker Toy Co., Inc. New York City. c. 1925.

Comment
Created as comic-strip characters by Rudolph Dirks in 1897,
the Katzenjammer Kids were first serialized in the *American
Humorist*. Readers of all ages laughed at the irreverent antics of
the twins Hans and Fritz, who tormented such authority figures
as the Captain, his irascible wife, Mamma, and the Inspector.
As early as 1908, Samstag & Hilder Brothers produced
Katzenjammer Kids dolls, and a printed-cloth Fritz was
manufactured by the Saalfield Publishing Company in 1914.

Hints for Collectors
Since Katzenjammer Kids dolls are based on some of the earliest
comic-strip characters, they are sought avidly not only by doll
fanciers but also by those who collect comic-strip memorabilia.

Description
Cartoon-character doll with lithographed features. Winking eyes attached bulbous nose, uneven ears. Corncob pipe inserted in mouth at side of face. Muscle-bound arms with anchor tattoos. Original costume of white hat with black oilcloth brim, black and red shirt with large white plastic buttons, white cuffed pants, and black shoes.

Materials, Marks, and Dimensions
Cloth head and body, composition feet. Height: 16″.

Maker, Origin, and Period
Maker unknown. Probably United States. c. 1930–50.

Comment
The illustrator Elzie Segar created the character Popeye in 1929 for his comic strip, "Thimble Theater." The unbeatable sailor was so popular that many Popeye artifacts were manufactured, and the sale of the vegetable he ate to give him strength, spinach, is rumored to have increased dramatically during the Depression. Some Popeye dolls that date from the early 1930s were made of brightly painted wood. Other dolls of Popeye and his companions, Olive Oyl and Jeep, were manufactured in cloth, vinyl, rubber, and composition. Popeyes are often marked "K.F.S." or "King Features," a licensing organization from which doll companies obtained the rights to produce dolls modeled after many such fictional celebrities.

Hints for Collectors
Only very specialized collectors try to obtain every version of a cartoon or celebrity doll. When offered a choice of dolls in equally good condition, pick the oldest, since it is probably the rarest.

Fred Flintstone

Description
Cartoon-character doll with vinyl head, molded and painted
features. Black hair styled in flat-top and cowlick. Crossed oval
eyes, arched eyebrows. Bulbous nose and half-moon smile. Cloth
body with large gauntlet hands and oversize feet in brown cloth
shoes. Original costume of blue imitation-fur shirt, red felt tie,
and bright yellow felt collar.

Materials, Marks, and Dimensions
Vinyl and cloth. Back of neck impressed "Hanna Barbera/PROD.
1962 AND T. M. JAPAN." Height: 10½″.

Maker, Origin, and Period
Maker unknown. Japan. c. 1962.

Comment
Since 1960 Fred Flintstone and his gang of relatives and friends
have endeared themselves to young and old alike through the
popular television cartoon series and comic strip. Fred, his wife
Wilma, their lovable neighbor Barney Rubble, the children Bam-
Bam and Pebbles, and even the house cat Sabertooth have all
been made into dolls.

Hints for Collectors
Cartoon-character dolls are growing in popularity among
collectors. Although older dolls are moderately expensive, newer
examples are quite affordable and can sometimes be found for
just a few dollars. There are a number of reasons why these dolls
will probably increase in value over the next decade, among
them the fact that each character is made for only a few years
and in limited quantity. Since the dolls reflect the era of a
cartoon's greatest popularity, they have nostalgic appeal.
Moreover, their comical appearances make them fun to collect.

Description
Dolls with rubber heads, molded and painted features. Squinting
eyes, bulbous noses, large ears, and smiling closed mouths.
Stuffed bodies. Fingernails outlined in black ink. Imitation-
leather and felt shoes. Left: Sailor wears original costume of
blue beret, red and white striped cotton shirt with orange
neckerchief, blue felt trousers. Carries wood and cardboard
accordion. Right: Cowboy wears original costume of battered felt
cowboy hat, brown felt vest with leather tassels over checked
cotton shirt; yellow satin neckerchief, brown felt pants, leather
belt. Wooden gun in leather holster.

Materials, Marks, and Dimensions
Rubber heads, felt bodies and limbs. Yellow and red circular
paper labels attached to shirts. Left: Label reads "Mat/Steiff
Original Marke." Right: Label reads "Boy/Steiff/Original
Marke." Height: 8″ (left); 8½″ (right).

Maker, Origin, and Period
Margarete Steiff. Germany. c. 1950.

Comment
The Steiff company is known for well-made imaginative dolls
whose unusually large feet enable them to stand unsupported.
Founded at the turn of the century by Margarete Steiff, the firm
is still producing dolls and toys in East Germany. Steiff products
are distributed throughout the world.

Hints for Collectors
Everything made by Steiff is collectible. Prices for later dolls,
such as those shown here, are escalating rapidly as the demand
for them grows.

Charlie Chaplin

Description
Celebrity doll with molded and painted features and hair. Body stuffed with straw. Original costume of white shirt with gold metal stickpin, wool jacket with painted wooden buttons, wool pants, gray leather shoes, dark gray derby. Carries cane.

Materials, Marks, and Dimensions
Composition head and hands, cloth body. Cloth label on sleeve depicts Indian chief and reads "CHARLIE CHAPLIN DOLL/WORLD'S GREATEST COMEDIAN/MADE EXCLUSIVELY BY LOUIS AMBERG AND SON, N.Y./BY SPECIAL ARRANGEMENT WITH ESSANAY FILM CO." Height: 14".

Maker, Origin, and Period
Louis Amberg & Son. New York City. 1915.

Comment
Charlie Chaplin was one of the first movie stars to be the inspiration for a doll. The figure shown here is dressed as the famous character Chaplin created for his film of 1914, *The Little Tramp*. Louis Amberg faithfully copied Chaplin's baggy trousers, derby, oversize shoes, bamboo cane, and, of course, celebrated brush mustache. Dolls such as these originally sold from 65¢ to $1, depending on their size.

Hints for Collectors
While the original Charlie Chaplin dolls by Louis Amberg are considered the most desirable, collectors also seek examples produced by other firms. Chaplin dolls have enjoyed such long-lasting popularity that in 1973 Kenner Products Company successfully marketed a lithographed-cloth version with a special walking mechanism that simulated the actor's famous waddle.

Charlie McCarthy

Description
Celebrity doll with ventriloquist's dummy head. Molded and painted features and brown hair, side-glancing eyes. Mitten hands. Original costume of black cotton jacket, white dickey, black bow tie, checked cotton pants, imitation-leather shoes. String at back of head opens lower jaw.

Materials, Marks, and Dimensions
Composition head; cloth body and limbs. "Fleischaker & Baum" marked on back of shoulder. Height: 17½".

Maker, Origin, and Period
EFFanBEE (trade name for Fleischaker & Baum). New York City. c. 1940–41.

Comment
From 1936 through the 1960s, the ventriloquist Edgar Bergen and his dummy Charlie McCarthy entertained millions of Americans through their radio, movie, and television performances. Inspired by the team's popularity, EFFanBEE produced its first Charlie McCarthy doll in 1937. The doll was highly sought after for many years, prompting EFFanBEE to produce a number of other versions, including a vinyl puppet in 1970. The Juro Novelty Company manufactured its own version of the doll, with a plastic head and cloth body, in 1965. Although the doll illustrated has a string at the back of the head to open its jaw, it is not considered a true ventriloquist's dummy because of its small size.

Hints for Collectors
Early Charlie McCarthy dolls with composition heads can be distinguished from newer plastic and vinyl versions by their side-glancing eyes. Recently made dolls are of substantially less value than those that date from the late 1930s and '40s.

W. C. Fields

Description
Celebrity doll with ventriloquist's dummy head. Molded and painted features and hair. Blue eyes. Original costume of black felt coat with gray velvet trim, white dickey, blue glass and brass stickpin affixed to red polka-dot tie, gray and white checked trousers, and white felt spats over black shoes. Pearl-gray beaver hat. Jaw is worked by string that extends from hole in back of neck and terminates in brass ring.

Materials, Marks, and Dimensions
Composition head, hands, and shoes; cloth body. "W. C. FIELDS, AN EFFANBEE PRODUCT" incised on back of shoulder. Height: 18″.

Maker, Origin, and Period
EFFanBEE (trade name for Fleischaker & Baum). New York City. c. 1930.

Comment
Shown here is an outstanding celebrity doll that captures the high spirits and irascible humor of the famous W. C. Fields. The dapper costume, particularly the oversize stickpin and the wonderful velvet collar and cuffs, imparts a rakish air to this doll.

Hints for Collectors
EFFanBEE produced a huge variety of baby and toddler dolls, but the company's puppets, marionettes, and ventriloquist's dolls proved expensive to make; therefore relatively few were issued. Always look for the oddity in a large company's line, since it is likely to appreciate in value because of its rarity. Collectors search avidly for celebrity figures that are as appealing and skillfully rendered as this one.

Mortimer Snerd and Baby Snooks

Description
Celebrity dolls with swivel heads. Molded and painted features and hair. Flexible-spring body construction. Black wooden shoes. Left: Mortimer Snerd has red hair, blue eyes with raised eyebrows. Grinning mouth with 2 large upper teeth. Original costume of white shirt, red and yellow tie, brown felt jacket, brown and white herringbone woolen pants. Right: Baby Snooks has white ribbon inserted through loop in light brown wavy hair. Blue eyes, red open mouth. Original costume of pink floral cotton dress with large white organdy collar; matching pants.

Materials, Marks, and Dimensions
Composition heads and hands; wooden torsos; wire limbs. Left: "Ideal Doll/Made in USA" embossed on back of neck. Tag on waist reads "FLEXY/AN IDEAL DOLL/Edgar Bergen's/MORTIMER SNERD." Right: "Ideal Doll" embossed on back of head. Height: 12¾" (left); 12" (right).

Maker, Origin, and Period
Ideal Novelty & Toy Co. New York City. c. 1939.

Comment
Mortimer Snerd was the well-loved dummy character introduced in the 1930s by ventriloquist Edgar Bergen. Baby Snooks was a character created by Fanny Brice, a radio and stage celebrity of the same era. Dolls of the 2 characters were first made in the 1930s and reissued in the 1970s. The Mortimer Snerd figure shown here, made by Ideal in 1939, does not have a movable jaw and is thus strictly a doll, but in 1974 the Juro Novelty Company created a ventriloquist's dummy version.

Hints for Collectors
Celebrity dolls are still obtainable and may be the basis for an interesting but relatively inexpensive collection.

Googly dolls

Description
Dolls with composition mask faces, molded and painted features. Blue glass googly eyes, closed red mouths. Left: Original costume of white imitation-fur hooded suit fastened with gold metal buttons; white imitation-leather shoes. Right: Light brown mohair wig. Original costume of tan cotton suit with gold metal buttons; white cotton socks, black imitation-leather shoes.

Materials, Marks, and Dimensions
Composition faces, cloth bodies and limbs. Height: 11½″ (left); 8¾″ (right).

Maker, Origin, and Period
Maker unknown. Germany. c. 1920.

Comment
These amusing dolls, which appear to have just stepped out of a cartoon, are distinguished by their mask faces and googly eyes. Mask faces date from the mid-19th century, when they first appeared on English novelty dolls called London Rag Babies. These dolls had faces made of wax and stretched muslin; the backs of their heads were cloth. Dollmakers favored this type of construction because it was lightweight and inexpensive.

Hints for Collectors
In the early 20th century, Googly dolls were manufactured by some of the most prestigious European doll firms, including Armand Marseille, Heubach, Steiner, and Kämmer & Reinhardt. Collectors are drawn to the dolls because of their nostalgic appeal and endearing expressions.

Billiken

Description
Elflike doll with molded and painted features and hair. Slanted brows and eyes, pug nose, impish grin, large pointed ears. Beige plush body with jointed limbs. Brown thread claws on hands and feet. Green and white label sewn to right side of chest.

Materials, Marks, and Dimensions
Composition head, plush body. Label on chest depicts Billiken and reads "Licensed stamp copyright 1909 by The Billiken Company." Height: 11½″.

Maker, Origin, and Period
Designed by Florence Pretz for E. I. Horsman Co. New York City. 1909.

Comment
Billiken was originally created by Florence Pretz of Kansas City, Missouri, who patterned him after Joss, the Chinese god of "things as they ought to be." He was a cross between a good luck charm and a cuddly mascot. The Horsman Company manufactured Billiken dolls for 2 years and sold more than 200,000 of them during the first 6 months of production. They were distributed throughout the world in boxes containing a sentimental poem that read in part: "Be very sure that you are good / and always act just as you should: / I love obedient girls and boys / I am the KING of all the toys." Billiken was a fad doll that initially sold in great quantities but soon declined in popularity.

Hints for Collectors
Billiken dolls usually enjoyed short lives, since children loved them to death. As a result, they are relatively scarce today and in great demand. Many fad dolls disappear quickly, making them great favorites with collectors years later.

Kewpie dolls

Description
Kewpie dolls with molded and painted features and hair in peaked topknot. Side-glancing black eyes. Closed mouths with impish smiles. Blue wings at shoulders. Left: Kewpie stands with outstretched arms jointed at shoulders. Right: "Thinker" Kewpie sits with arms resting on knees, hands cradling chin.

Materials, Marks, and Dimensions
Bisque. Left: "CMU" printed on back in triangle over vertically printed "Fulper"; "Made in USA" below. Right: "O'Neill" and "5" painted on base. Height: 9″ (left); 5″ (right).

Maker, Origin, and Period
Left: Fulper Pottery Co. Flemington, New Jersey. 1920. Right: J. D. Kestner, Jr. Germany. c. 1913.

Comment
Rose O'Neill originally designed Kewpie—the charming combination of a cupid and baby figure—as an illustration for the *Ladies' Home Journal* in 1909. Under her supervision, the Kestner firm produced the first Kewpie dolls in 1913 and found themselves deluged with orders. By the 1920s this little sprite was all the rage. Other firms jumped on the Kewpie bandwagon including the Fulper Pottery Company of New Jersey, which produced the doll illustrated on the left.

Hints for Collectors
Authentic Rose O'Neill Kewpies are usually marked with the designer's name and copyright on the base. In addition to the mark, O'Neill's signature is sometimes inscribed along the side of the body. Unmarked copies of the Kewpie doll are considered collectible, but not as choice as originals. This holds true for the Fulper Kewpie, which is very rare, but still not as valuable as a signed O'Neill example.

Description
Advertising doll with molded and painted features and hair. Side-glancing eyes. Jointed at neck, shoulders, and hips. Chubby legs, dimpled knees, and feet pointing outward. Wears white dress and apron, chef's hat with red letter "C" on front. Painted white socks and black shoes.

Materials, Marks, and Dimensions
Composition. Original tag pinned to apron with picture of Campbell's tomato soup can and the words "Campbell's Kid/ A HORSMAN DOLL/Permission of Campbell Soup Company." "Campbell Soup Co." incised on neck. Height: 12″.

Maker, Origin, and Period
E. I. Horsman Co. New York City. 1948.

Comment
Grace Drayton's original illustrations of the chubby, wide-eyed Campbell Kids appeared in the *Ladies' Home Journal* in 1905. They had such broad appeal that their image was copyrighted by Joseph Campbell about 1910 for use in soup advertisements, and they have been made into dolls ever since (*see* 259).

Hints for Collectors
Most Campbell Kid dolls were manufactured by Horsman under the license of Joseph Campbell. Many of the dolls manufactured from 1910 to 1925 are unmarked, or marked only by cloth labels in the seams of their outfits or stickers on their chests. Some early dolls have sateen bodies and horizontally striped sateen legs. Other companies produced identical dolls without acknowledging Grace Drayton or the Campbell Kids. Be wary of these imitations, which are often passed off as originals.

Description
Advertising dolls with molded and painted features and hair. Painted side-glancing eyes and red smiling mouths. Movable arms. Left: Buddy Lee wears original costume of engineer's striped denim overalls, shirt, and cap sporting company's label. Red and white neckerchief. Right: Black Magic painted black. Original costume of light blue shirt, blue denim overalls, and cap embroidered in red with doll's name.

Materials, Marks, and Dimensions
Composition. Left: Labels on front of cap and overalls read "Lee Union Made." Label on back of overalls reads "Union Made Lee Sanforized Reg. U.S. Pat. Off." Right: Cloth label sewn on back of overalls reads "Union Made Lee Reg. U.S. Pat. Off." Height: 13″ (left); 12¼″ (right).

Maker, Origin, and Period
Maker unknown. Distributed by H. D. Lee Company, Inc. United States. Left: 1925. Right: 1920.

Comment
Buddy Lee and Black Magic dolls were made by an unknown firm for the H. D. Lee Mercantile Company of San Francisco, a manufacturer of denim goods. Buddy Lee was dressed in a new outfit each year and distributed to retailers to display Lee's clothing, and was subsequently sold as a doll. Clothing for all Lee dolls was manufactured in Lee plants.

Hints for Collectors
Buddy Lee first appeared in 1920 and was discontinued in 1962. Early Buddy Lee dolls were made of poor-quality composition that broke easily; in 1949 a new improved doll was manufactured in hard plastic. Most dolls were white, and the very few Black Magic dolls that were produced are rare.

Description

Cartoon-character dolls. Left: Annie with molded and painted features and hair. Fully jointed. Original costume of red cotton dress with white collar and sleeves, white cotton underclothing, white ribbed stockings, leather and paper shoes fastened with silver metal snaps. Right: Sandy has molded and painted features, pupil-less eyes. Hollow body.

Materials, Marks, and Dimensions

Composition. Paper label on Annie's wrist with picture of Annie and Sandy reads "Little Orphan Annie and her pal Sandy." Height: 11¼" (left); 6¾" (right).

Maker, Origin, and Period

Maker unknown. United States. c. 1930–40.

Comment

Little Orphan Annie and her ever-faithful sidekick Sandy made their debut as comic-strip characters in the 1924 edition of the *New York News*. Created by the illustrator Harold Gray, the comic strip ran continuously for 52 years until Gray's death in 1976. The Little Orphan Annie and Sandy dolls shown here were among many versions marketed during the 1920s and '30s. In the 1960s and '70s, Madame Alexander, Remco, and various Japanese companies produced Orphan Annie and Sandy dolls. In response to the Broadway show and movie, *Annie*, new dolls are being made today.

Hints for Collectors

Fads in dolls come and go. Celebrity and cartoon-character dolls are reissued whenever a performer or character reenters the limelight. However, the second or third versions are often not as interesting as the originals, and collectors should be careful to distinguish earlier dolls from later ones.

Ella Cinders

Description
Cartoon-character doll with molded and painted features and hair. Black hair, freckles, rosy cheeks, wide-eyed expression. Swivel head and movable limbs. Original costume of white apron over pink and white checked dress with white collar and cuffs. Black and white socks. Black oilcloth shoes fastened with plastic buttons and leather bows.

Materials, Marks, and Dimensions
Composition head and limbs, cloth body. "C/1925/M.N.S." inscribed on back of head. Tag on dress reads "Ella Cinders/ Trademark Reg. U.S. Pat. Off./Copyright 1925/Metropolitan Newspaper Service." Height: 18".

Maker, Origin, and Period
E. I. Horsman Co. New York City. 1925.

Comment
Ella Cinders was a comic-strip character created by Bill Conselman and Charlie Plumb for the Metropolitan Newspaper Service. A rags-to-riches heroine, she was featured in a 1920 movie and 5 years later was made into the doll pictured here by the Horsman Company of New York City.

Hints for Collectors
Ella Cinders is one of many dolls that has increased dramatically in price as a result of the recent fascination with memorabilia of the 1920s and '30s. Entire exhibitions are devoted to dolls from this period. Although Ella Cinders was a well-loved comic character of her time, this may be the only doll of her that was produced, which makes it especially desirable. A collector seeking a doll of every comic-strip character might be willing to pay a great deal for this rare figure.

Little Red Riding Hood and the Wolf

Description
Topsy-turvy doll. Red and white striped skirt flips to reveal one head at a time. Top: Little Red Riding Hood has molded and painted features, blond wig, blue glass eyes, closed mouth. Original red silk hood trimmed with black velvet and lace, red silk bodice and white cotton apron edged in lace. Brass cross on chain at neck. Bottom: Wolf with brown glass eyes, molded snout with gray nose and red mouth. Original cotton nightcap decorated with lace and velvet ribbon.

Materials, Marks, and Dimensions
Top: Bisque head and arms. Bottom: Imitation-fur head; cloth body. Height: 11½″.

Maker, Origin, and Period
Maker unknown. France. c. 1890.

Comment
Some early topsy-turvy dolls were probably intended to be magical objects. Pennsylvania German hex dolls, for example, were made with one head representing a man's face and the other a pig's—one head was meant to cure warts, and the other to cast spells. Other topsy-turvy dolls were inspired by folk tales. The Little Red Riding Hood and the Wolf figure illustrated here is one of a number of 19th-century dolls made with fine bisque heads. Those produced in the 20th century generally have cloth heads.

Hints for Collectors
The character of Little Red Riding Hood has appeared on many children's items including baby plates, cookie jars, and books. Doll collectors seeking fine 19th-century examples like this one must compete with devoted enthusiasts who will buy any object connected with their favorite character.

Snow White, Sneezy, and Grumpy

Description
Cartoon-character dolls with molded and painted features and hair, swivel heads, jointed limbs. Left: Sneezy has brown eyes and white beard. Original costume of orange velvet hat printed with name; blue velvet jacket, red velvet pants, blue belt. Brown painted shoes. Center: Snow White has painted blue bow in short black hair. Brown eyes. Original costume of white taffeta dress with navy-blue velvet bodice, blue velvet cape lined with red silk, white pantaloons; white socks and shoes. Right: Grumpy with black eyes and white beard. Pink velvet hat printed with name, original pink and tan velvet outfit with green belt in same style as Sneezy's, and brown painted shoes.

Materials, Marks, and Dimensions
Composition. Back of Snow White's head marked "Knickerbocker Toy Company." Each dwarf's back marked "Walt Disney Knickerbocker Toy Co." Height: 9″ (left); 12¼″ (center); 9″ (right).

Maker, Origin, and Period
Knickerbocker Toy Co. New York City. 1938.

Comment
Many doll companies, such as Madame Alexander, Mattel, and Ideal, produced versions of Snow White and the 7 Dwarfs based on Walt Disney's 1937 movie. They were so popular that puppets and such novelty items as colorful chalk figures sprinkled with glitter were manufactured along with more traditional dolls.

Hints for Collectors
The Snow White, Sneezy, and Grumpy dolls shown here are part of a set that originally included the other 5 dwarfs—Happy, Bashful, Dopey, Doc, and Sleepy. Collectors often find one doll and then try to complete the set.

Description
Cartoon-character dolls. Left: Pinocchio has molded and painted features and hair, swivel head, and jointed limbs. Original costume of yellow felt hat with red feather, purple silk bow tie, pink and blue cotton shirt, and light blue short pants with 2 large yellow plastic buttons. Molded yellow gloves and green shoes. Right: Jiminy Cricket with molded and painted features and clothing. Black jacket, yellow pants, original blue top hat with felt brim and yellow painted band. Carries red umbrella.

Materials, Marks, and Dimensions
Composition. Left: Back of head marked "Pinocchio W. Disney Prod. C.T."; back of body marked "W. Disney Made in USA Crown Toy Co. Inc." Tag reads "Walt Disney's" above, and "Pinocchio" below image. Right: Foot marked "Jiminy Cricket/ By Walt Disney/Made by Ideal Novelty & Toy Co." Height: 11" (left); 8¼" (right).

Maker, Origin, and Period
Left: Crown Toy Co. New York City. Right: Ideal Novelty & Toy Co. New York City. c. 1940.

Comment
Numerous American companies manufactured wood, cloth, and composition Pinocchio and Jiminy Cricket dolls based on images from the well-loved Walt Disney movie of 1940. The film's story was derived from the 19th-century novel *Pinocchio* by Italian author Carlo Collodi.

Hints for Collectors
Since many cartoon dolls were cheaply made, collectors should expect them to be peeling and cracked. Dolls that are still in their original boxes may have been stored unused; these will be in mint condition and will thus command top prices.

Betty Boop

Description
Cartoon-character doll. Molded and painted face and hair. Large round side-glancing eyes, painted lashes. Black hair, button nose, closed rosebud mouth, jowly cheeks. Jointed at neck, shoulders, hips, and knees. Molded upper torso. Painted and molded black strapless dress, high-heeled black shoes.

Materials, Marks, and Dimensions
Composition head, hands, and upper torso; turned wooden arms, legs, and lower torso. Height: 12″.

Maker, Origin, and Period
Designed by Joseph Kallus for Cameo Doll Co. Port Allegany, Pennsylvania. c. 1932.

Comment
During the 1930s Betty Boop delighted moviegoers in cartoons produced by Fleischer Studios for Paramount Pictures. Her face was modeled after that of the singer Helen Kane and her figure after Mae West's. Inspired by these cartoons, Joseph Kallus created the Betty Boop doll, which was widely distributed in toy departments of variety stores and at carnivals. Betty Boop appeared in several different versions including a cloth doll and a part-composition doll dressed as a little girl.

Hints for Collectors
Collectors of 1930s memorabilia avidly seek Betty Boop dolls, books, and accessories. The dolls, which were available in great numbers only a few years ago, have become increasingly hard to find. Dolls with their labels still intact are the most desirable. The figure shown here originally came with a label on the front of her dress that read "BETTY BOOP/DES. & COPYRIGHT/by FLEISCHER/STUDIOS."

Description
Doll with molded and painted features and hair. Fully jointed body. Original painted costume in blue, red, and yellow with large "S" on chest. Red cloth cape tacked to back. Painted red boots.

Materials, Marks, and Dimensions
Composition head and upper torso, wooden body and limbs. "Des. & Copyright by Superman, Inc. Made by Ideal Novelty & Toy Co." printed on belt. Height: 13″.

Maker, Origin, and Period
Ideal Novelty & Toy Co. New York City. c. 1945.

Comment
The immense popularity of Superman, the comic-book and, later, television hero, inspired this early doll. Here, Superman's eyes are shut tight as he summons up his superhuman strength for an extraordinary feat. In 1965 Ideal reissued a vinyl Superman doll with a strikingly handsome face and the familiar cowlick. Recent Superman dolls share the limelight with such heroes as Superboy, Superwoman, and Spiderman, and often come with a wide range of accessories.

Hints for Collectors
According to legend, Superman was invulnerable, but the doll shown here bears battle scars—a chipped head and a hole in his shoulder—that challenge the myth. A doll that is in fair or poor condition should be purchased only if its rarity offsets its defects or if it temporarily completes a collection until an example in mint condition becomes available.

Description
Doll with molded and painted features. Orange hair, side-glancing blue eyes, broad nose. Smiling closed mouth, freckles on face, large ears. Fully jointed, segmented body. Red upper torso and arms, yellow hands. Blue lower torso and upper legs, orange lower legs. Black feet.

Materials, Marks, and Dimensions
Wood. Fragment of torn label on upper torso reads "HOWDY DOODY." Height: 13".

Maker, Origin, and Period
Maker unknown. United States. c. 1947–52.

Comment
The Howdy Doody Show, one of the first television programs for children, was broadcast from 1947 to 1960. During that time, its engaging, freckle-faced puppet star with the wide grin was manufactured both in doll and marionette versions by several American companies. EFFanBEE made a Howdy Doody doll with a hard plastic head and cloth body about 1947. In 1950 Ideal manufactured a 20" version with a hard plastic head, gauntlet hands, and freckles scattered all over his smiling face. In 1954 Ideal also produced a Howdy Doody marionette with a vinyl head, blue metal sleep-eyes, and a string-activated mouth.

Hints for Collectors
Interest in Howdy Doody dolls, especially those in puppet form, increases each year. However, it is still possible to find them for reasonable prices at garage sales and flea markets.

Paper Dolls

Paper figures were fashioned in ancient China and medieval Germany, but the creation of paper dolls as playthings began in the 18th century, when paper became widely available. The first may have been *pantins*, or Jumping Jacks—flat paper dolls with movable jointed limbs operated by pull strings. Pantins most often depicted harlequins, but were sometimes made as caricatures of famous politicians or personages. Ladies of that era made another type of doll by painting miniatures of themselves on paper and creating separate up-to-date outfits meant to be laid over them. By 1800 paper figures had become the popular reflections of current fashions and celebrities that they remain today.

The 19th-Century Heyday

The tremendous growth of the publishing industry during the 19th century led to a paper doll boom. These figures were printed on scrap or thin cardboard and sold in sheets, booklets, envelopes, or boxes. At mid-century, commercial publication of paper dolls was widespread, particularly in England, Germany, and the United States. Prior to 1840 most such dolls were printed from engraved copper or steel plates; shortly after 1840 lithography largely replaced engraving, but images continued to be colored or stenciled by hand until color lithography was perfected later in the century.

In America the first commercially produced paper doll was made in the 1850s. Popular early subjects were the opera singer Jenny Lind, dancers, fairy-tale figures, and literary characters. In England, Raphael Tuck began producing numerous paper dolls as a sideline to his highly successful postcard and stationery business. These figures were sold worldwide and are today regarded as perhaps the finest paper dolls. Tuck & Sons created not only girl and lady paper dolls but also paper soldiers, walking figures, rocking animals, and huge folding panoramas. Because paper was the cheapest and easiest way for manufacturers to spread word about their wares to a wide audience, paper dolls became a common form of advertisement beginning in the 1890s and continuing into the 20th century.

Modern Paper Dolls

Pages of paper dolls, often accompanied by verses or stories, began to appear at the turn of the century in women's magazines. One favorite was "Dolly Dingle of Dingle Dell" by Grace Drayton, creator of the famous Campbell Kids. Rose O'Neill's ubiquitous Kewpie also appeared in paper doll form, as did many other popular doll characters.

In the 1920s well-known entertainers were favorite subjects for doll booklets, and in the 1930s movie-star and comic-strip character paper dolls became the rage. Paper dolls reached their peak of popularity in the 1930s, when many families could not afford more expensive toys. Figures like Shirley Temple and Charlie McCarthy were printed on the cardboard covers of booklets filled with paper clothing—a format still used today.

The prosperous postwar generation made television personalities the subjects of paper dolls, but interest and quality were declining. Since the 1950s TV and political figures have predominated, ranging from Ozzie and Harriet and Partridge Family booklets to sets based on Queen Elizabeth's coronation and the marriage of Prince Charles.

The Heavenly Twins

Description
Lithographed paper baby dolls and envelope. Heads, arms, and bottles made of cardboard scrap; bodies formed by long white tissue-paper dresses. Black doll at left wears white tissue hat. Each doll drinks from round green nursing bottle with long tube. Tan envelope printed in blue.

Materials, Marks, and Dimensions
Paper. Palette-and-easel trademark at bottom left corner of envelope. Envelope: 6¼" x 4". Height of dolls with dresses: 5¾".

Maker, Origin, and Period
Raphael Tuck & Sons. England. c. 1893–98.

Comment
Raphael Tuck & Sons, a printing firm established in London in 1866, was famous for fancy stationery, particularly postcards, calendars, and Christmas cards. Tuck is also known to have led the field in the manufacture of fine paper dolls, although the company's production records were largely destroyed by the bombs of the Second World War. Tuck's paper dolls ranged from portraits of popular stage actresses complete with fashionable wardrobes to simple half-figures like the Heavenly Twins.

Hints for Collectors
Though Raphael Tuck paper dolls can be identified by the company's famous palette-and-easel trademark, they are not so easy to date. Patent dates can be misleading because dolls were frequently sold before the patents were applied for and long after they were issued. Neither the lack of a precise date nor the minor tears and stains on the envelope shown here adversely affect the value of the Heavenly Twins, since the dolls themselves are in excellent condition.

Homemade paper doll

Description
Paper doll and 3 costumes with shoulder tabs; all affixed to red paper sheet. Doll has penciled features and hair in ringlets. Penciled necklace, slip with zigzag neckline and hem, penciled shoes. Outfits include white tissue-paper dress with silver foil belt and polka dots, blue tissue-paper dress with paper lace doily bodice, and white oilcloth suit with black paper blouse and trim.

Materials, Marks, and Dimensions
Paper and oilcloth. Height of doll: 4″.

Maker, Origin, and Period
Maker unknown. New England. c. 1930.

Comment
This simple stick figure, with its tight short curls, was probably made by a little girl to represent a child her own age. As is true here, the wardrobes of homemade paper dolls are often more elaborate than the dolls themselves. Note that the white oilcloth suit at right has one sleeve longer than the other and a bent elbow. This may have been the child's simple miscalculation in designing the jacket, but more likely this suit was originally made for a different doll.

Hints for Collectors
Homemade dolls may be dated by the styles of their clothes and accessories, and by additional materials used as trim. Some enthusiastic paper-doll makers created homes for their dolls complete with pets, gardens, and paper furniture; the style of such furnishings may help to date the sets.

Dolly Dingle of Dingle Dell

Description
Little girl paper dolls and 9 outfits on uncut magazine page.
Dolly Dingle has curly blond hair with black bow, chubby cheeks,
and side-glancing eyes. Wears white chemise, bloomers, and
socks. Black strap shoes. Outfits include party, afternoon, and
roller-skating dresses, day suit, rompers, milkmaid costume, and
accessories. Gypsy Jane and her 3 outfits printed on same sheet.

Materials, Marks, and Dimensions
Paper. Copyright date and publisher printed in bottom margin.
Page: 10¾" x 16".

Maker, Origin, and Period
Designed by Grace Drayton for *The Pictorial Review*. New York
City. March 1913.

Comment
Dolly Dingle made her debut in the March 1913 issue of *The
Pictorial Review*. One of the longest running and most popular
paper-doll series, Dolly Dingle of Dingle Dell appeared in the
magazine more than 200 times before publication ceased in 1933.
Shown here is the first version, a chubby-cheeked little girl
resembling one of Grace Drayton's Campbell Kids. Dolly's
friends and relatives, including Cousin Marion, Mama Dingle,
and Denny Sweetie, also appeared periodically.

Hints for Collectors
A complete March 1913 issue of *The Pictorial Review* containing
the first edition of Dolly Dingle is most desired by collectors,
followed by an uncut, mint-condition page, as shown here. The
original renderings of any paper doll, as initially submitted for
publication, are the most valuable collectibles of all, but rarely
appear on the market.

Description
Kewpie paper dolls on uncut magazine page. At top, front and
back views of undressed figure called Careful of his Voice, with
topknot sticking out of striped scarf. At center, front and back
views of Sister Nan wearing red bow in blond hair, white slip
over pantaloons, white stockings, and high brown shoes. Front
and back of long-sleeved red and white plaid dress printed below.

Materials, Marks, and Dimensions
Paper. Page: 10½″ x 16″.

Maker, Origin, and Period
Designed by Rose O'Neill for *Woman's Home Companion*.
January 1913.

Comment
The immediate success of Rose O'Neill's original Kewpie
drawings and verses in the 1909 *Ladies' Home Journal* inspired
cloth and bisque Kewpie dolls and the very popular "Kewpie
Kutouts," a series of paper dolls and stories published in
Woman's Home Companion from 1912 to 1913. Many characters,
including Dotty Darling, Wag the Chief, Stern Irene, and the
Kewpie Gardener, were introduced in the series. Note that these
dolls have front and back views when fully assembled.

Hints for Collectors
Although collectors of Kewpie paper dolls treasure the original
series featured in *Woman's Home Companion*, similar dolls
published in 1914 by the Saalfield Publishing Company are
now even more desirable because fewer are available. Uncut
examples are especially rare. Kewpiemania has lasted more than
50 years, spawning Kewpie paper doll sets as late as 1967 and
still going strong today.

Description
Celebrity paper dolls in uncut booklet format. Front cover
shows Shirley Temple doll clad in chemise, flanked by smaller
faceless figures in various outfits. Second doll on back cover.
8 pages of costumes.

Materials, Marks, and Dimensions
Paper. Copyright date and publisher printed inside cover.
Booklet: 10¾" x 12½".

Maker, Origin, and Period
Designed by Bill and Corinne Bailey for Saalfield Publishing
Co. Akron, Ohio. 1938.

Comment
During the 1930s Shirley Temple became the best-loved child
star of the silver screen, and the toy and publishing industries
eagerly created a wide range of products in her image. In 1933
the Saalfield Publishing Company obtained exclusive rights to
Shirley Temple publications, producing numerous sets of paper
dolls through the 1940s. When Shirley Temple appeared on
television in the late 1950s, Saalfield began to manufacture new
paper dolls of her. One of these sets, #4435, proved so successful
that it was reissued 12 times.

Hints for Collectors
Reissues of paper dolls often vary from first editions; they may
have a new cover or title, fewer pages, or different costumes.
Such a set is not always worth appreciably less than the original,
especially if it is created by a noted illustrator or contains
additional material. Many collectors try to find all the reissues of
an original booklet.

Charlie McCarthy

Description
Celebrity paper doll in uncut booklet format. Doll appears on
front cover wearing monocle, white shirt, black trousers, and
black shoes. Movable mouth, top hat, tuxedo jacket, and
accessories appear below. Set includes 4 dolls with 5 pages of
clothing and accessories.

Materials, Marks, and Dimensions
Paper. Copyright date and publisher printed on inside page.
Booklet: 10½" x 17".

Maker, Origin, and Period
Designed by Queen Holden for Whitman Publishing Co.
Racine, Wisconsin. 1938.

Comment
Ventriloquist Edgar Bergen's dapper dummy, Charlie
McCarthy, became a celebrity in his own right through radio,
movie, and television performances. In 1938 he joined the ranks
of other famous personalities as the subject of a paper doll
booklet. Illustrator Queen Holden, who created paper dolls of
many well-known figures, devised a mouth for Charlie that could
be opened and closed by means of a paper strip inserted through
a slit between his lips.

Hints for Collectors
Paper-doll production declined in the 1960s, and paper dolls
based on characters from popular 1970s television series
attracted considerably less interest than earlier celebrity dolls
had generated. However, their scarcity makes modern
personality paper dolls desirable, and a wise collector will buy
sets while they remain inexpensive. Booklets of Tricia Nixon
(1970) and Princess Diana and Prince Charles (1982) dolls are
already being collected by many enthusiasts.

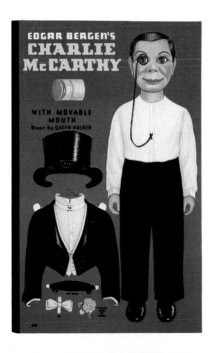

Advertising paper doll

Description
Boy doll lithographed on uncut sheet with 5 costumes and various accessories. Boy has brown hair and wears white shirt with blue yoke and bow tie, blue knickers and stockings, and black shoes. Costumes include green jacket with light blue piping, green sailor suit, green military uniform, Cossack uniform, and tan overcoat with fur collar. Accessories include hobbyhorse, racquet, spade, drum, butterfly net, cane, ball, and kite.

Materials, Marks, and Dimensions
Paper. "Presented by The Willimantic Thread Co." printed across bottom. Sheet: 6¼" x 5¾".

Maker, Origin, and Period
Designed for Willimantic Thread Co. Willimantic, Connecticut. c. 1890.

Comment
The 1890s were known as the Golden Age of paper-doll advertising. Dolls were made as giveaways by such textile manufacturers as Clark's O.N.T., J & P Coates, and the Willimantic Thread Company. These very successful promotional items helped to increase the profits of the firms they advertised. Manufacturers even produced sets of dolls in such elaborate tableaux as dances and wedding parties.

Hints for Collectors
Some advertising sets were sold to merchants without any printing on the dolls themselves so that the store's own message could be stamped on them before distribution. This means it is possible to find identical dolls with different advertising imprints. Collectors try to assemble groups of these.

Description
Little girl and boy paper dolls on uncut magazine page. 12 dolls with 8 additional outfits, 8 hats, 3 accessories.

Materials, Marks, and Dimensions
Paper. Page: 11″ x 16″.

Maker, Origin, and Period
Designed by Sheila Young for *Ladies' Home Journal*. Philadelphia, Pennsylvania. September 1909.

Comment
Lettie Lane first appeared in the October 1908 issue of the *Ladies' Home Journal* and was published intermittently in the magazine through 1915, sometimes in color, sometimes in black and white. No doubt children eager to collect the entire series urged their mothers to continue subscribing to the magazine. During the run of this popular series, Sheila Young created a whole spectrum of friends and relatives for Lettie and portrayed them in various activities and styles of costume, such as the fancy party outfits shown here.

Hints for Collectors
Among the most avidly collected paper dolls are examples that were printed in newspapers and magazines. Paper dolls abounded in the *Delineator*, a women's magazine popular around the turn of the century. Pollykins Pudge, the Nipper series, Alice's Adventures in Wonderland, Betsy McCall, and numerous other choice sets appeared in *McCall's Magazine*. Many magazine paper dolls are still readily available, making it possible to assemble an interesting collection showing not only the progression of period clothing styles but also the evolution of graphic styles.

Description

Lithographed paper doll and 4 outfits, with box. Little girl has blond hair with green bow and wears white chemise, green petticoat, black stockings, and black shoes with green bows. Costumes with matching hats include blue and white print dress with doll at side, brown dress with yellow ribbon trim, green coat with ermine trim and muff, and green dress with white lace trim and bouquet of violets. White box cover printed in brown.

Materials, Marks, and Dimensions

Paper. Palette-and-easel trademark, publisher, and "Printed in Germany" on box cover. Box: 5¾" x 9". Height of doll: 9".

Maker, Origin, and Period

Raphael Tuck & Sons. England. c. 1901–10.

Comment

In the mid-18th century, when paper dolls were first made, costumes were not affixed to a doll's body but were simply laid over it. Later, 2-sided outfits were slipped over the doll's head or slid across the body like an envelope. Tabs were invented in the mid-19th century and have remained the most popular means for attaching clothing to paper dolls.

Hints for Collectors

Sweet Sybel's elaborate costumes are clear examples of Raphael Tuck's imaginative versions of prevailing fashions. Tuck gradually replaced "Dainty Dollies" with sets like "Our Bonnie Series of Dressing Dolls," which were meant for young children and had simpler clothing. These were designed in New York and printed in England. Look for "Bonnie Billy" from this series—boy paper dolls are scarcer than girl dolls and are therefore very desirable.

Description
Lithographed paper doll, stand, and 3 outfits on 4 uncut sheets.
Girl doll with bobbed brown hair wears blue chemise, blue
banded white socks, and black strap shoes. Outfits include pink
dress and matching hat, purple dress with matching hat and
headband, and brown plaid coat with black beret and high-button
shoes. Accessories include fireworks, American flag, Japanese
lantern, toys, books, cat, and sled.

Materials, Marks, and Dimensions
Paper. Each sheet: 3½" x 7¼".

Maker, Origin, and Period
American Colortype Co. Chicago, Illinois. c. 1910.

Comment
By 1910 paper dolls reflected the new image of the American
girl. No longer was she a mere fashion plate for the formal
costumes of the Edwardian era. Instead, her clothes, though
still somewhat fanciful, were designed to accord with an active
lifestyle. Sporting clothes such as tennis whites, riding outfits,
and bicycling costumes were introduced, emphasizing the
pastimes of the modern age. Little Alice Busy-Bee dolls came in
2 sizes, and new costumes, sold separately, were sometimes
designed to fit both.

Hints for Collectors
The rarest paper dolls are sold by specialists in the field,
although lucky finds may turn up elsewhere. Examples that are
torn or scribbled over are worth very little, even if rare. Uncut
sheets usually command at least twice as much as cut versions.
Sometimes complete sets of specific paper dolls and their
wardrobes can be assembled from pieces found separately.

Description
Lithographed paper doll in folding booklet format. At right, front cover shows Topsey in red dress and blue apron. Separate fold-out panels show, from left, cover outfit with red bandanna; long-sleeved maroon blouse and pleated skirt with white apron; and green dress over striped underskirt with red shawl and bonnet. Doll shown on last panel wears slip with dark stockings and boots. Back cover lists company's available series.

Materials, Marks, and Dimensions
Paper. Title and publisher printed on front cover. Unfolded booklet: 11½" x 3".

Maker, Origin, and Period
McLoughlin Bros. New York City. c. 1875–76.

Comment
In 1828 John McLoughlin started a small business in New York publishing children's stories and booklets. His brother had joined the company by 1857, when the firm became one of the first in America to print paper dolls commercially. Shown here is a lithographed doll that was advertised in McLoughlin's 1875–76 catalogue. Topsey was an impish little black girl familiar to readers of *Uncle Tom's Cabin*. Another of the book's popular characters, Eva St. Clair, was also the subject of a paper-doll booklet, reflecting the widespread popularity of Harriet Beecher Stowe's novel.

Hints for Collectors
Early paper dolls were hand-tinted with paints that were not colorfast. To ascertain whether color was applied by hand, moisten a cotton swab and carefully dab a tiny area of the paper's tinted surface. Lithographed color will not rub off.

Description

Lithographed paper doll in folding booklet format. Girl on front cover with wavy hair and bird perched on one hand; wears blue jacket with red buttons and yellow trim, yellow apron over red skirt, and blue spats over black shoes. 3 elaborate outfits with tabs appear on adjoining panels, with doll clad in chemise and necklace on last.

Materials, Marks, and Dimensions

Paper. Title and publisher printed on front cover. Unfolded booklet, with detached cover: 15″ x 4¼″.

Maker, Origin, and Period

McLoughlin Bros. New York City. c. 1875–76.

Comment

Amelia belonged to the Gem series of paper dolls published by the McLoughlin Brothers, which included 5 other figures named Emily, Isabella, Julia, Martha, and Josie. Known as "penny paper dolls," Amelia and her kind were extremely inexpensive and well within the means of any little girl. In the Gem series, none of the extra ensembles repeated the outfit worn by the doll on the booklet's cover, a departure from the company's usual practice.

Hints for Collectors

In recent years the demand for paper dolls and other ephemera has grown, prompting a rise in the number of antiques shows featuring paper collectibles. Specialists in virtually all types of printed matter exhibit at these shows, offering the paper-doll collector exposure to a wide range of items, such as postcards and advertisements, that can be used as comparative material.

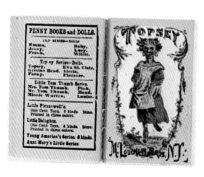

Fate Lady

Description
Paper doll with head and upper body of lithographed paper on cardboard. Lady with curly black hair, brown eyes, and smiling mouth; wears red bandanna, green vest over white blouse, extravagant jewelry. Skirt of colored paper sheets with printed fortunes. Colors correspond to astrological signs on base.

Materials, Marks, and Dimensions
Paper and cardboard. "Patent pending in U.S. and abroad" marked on base and on several sheets. Height: 9¾".

Maker, Origin, and Period
Maker unknown. United States. c. 1900–20.

Comment
In the 19th century, fortune-tellers, also known as Fate Ladies, traveled throughout the English countryside predicting the future for small fees. In 1833 and 1838, *Girl's Own Toy-Maker*, an English book that featured activities and projects for young ladies, published the first known instructions for making a Fate Lady doll. Other books and magazines followed suit with directions for a variety of dolls. Although most fortune-telling dolls were needlework projects, some dolls made of lithographed paper over wood or over cardboard were commercially manufactured.

Hints for Collectors
Very few fortune-teller dolls have survived in good condition. Their paper skirts have dried out with age and individual sheets have been damaged by constant refolding; many of the fortunes are torn or missing. Usually dolls were discarded once their fortunes disappeared. Do not try to restore a damaged paper skirt by substituting new leaves, because this will diminish a doll's value.

Fortune-teller

Description
Peg-wooden doll with carved and painted features. 2-toned
hair with gold tuck comb. Jointed body. Blouse with striped silk
sleeves and replaced gray bodice. Fortunes handwritten on
paper leaves of skirt. Orange and yellow feet painted to resemble
shoes.

Materials, Marks, and Dimensions
Wood and paper. Height: 6¼″.

Maker, Origin, and Period
Maker unknown. Germany. c. 1850.

Comment
Peg-wooden dolls such as the one shown here were perfectly
suited to be fortune-tellers, since they were lightweight and had
small waists to which pages could be fastened. Written in
English, French, German, and Italian, this doll's fortunes, like
those of other early Fate Ladies, offer a fascinating glimpse into
19th-century life. For instance, the young Princess Victoria's
fortune-telling doll came with the prediction, "Happy and blest
with the man you love best." A French bisque fortune-telling doll
recently sold at auction wore a skirt with a variety of messages,
some critical ("you are very naive"), some optimistic ("you will
live to see your great-great grandchildren"), some benevolent
("good news soon"), and others that were disheartening ("you
will triumph over your enemies, but too late").

Hints for Collectors
A fortune-telling doll like this one may turn up only at auction,
where a collector should be prepared to pay a sizable sum for it.

Printed-Cloth Dolls

 The development of inexpensive means of printing on fabric about 1880, largely through the lithographic process, facilitated the commercial production of printed-cloth dolls. These were described at the time as "this century's model of the old-fashioned rag doll that Grannie used to make." Nearly all early printed-cloth dolls were designed to be cut, sewn, and stuffed at home, and had detailed instructions printed on the sheets alongside the figures.

Storybook Characters
Most early printed-cloth dolls were produced in the Northeast, particularly in New England, which was the center for textile manufacturing in America. In 1884 Edward Peck designed one of the first such dolls, a Santa Claus figure reputed to have later inspired Celia and Charity Smith to design similar printed-cloth dolls. In 1889 the Smith sisters-in-law designed dolls for Lawrence & Company, a Boston textile manufacturer in business from 1889 to 1893; this firm distributed dolls to fabric shops and general stores, which sold them by the yard. In the 1890s Celia and Charity Smith designed dolls for Arnold Print Works, a Massachusetts textile producer that made a variety of novelty dolls and dolls based on storybook characters. An ingenious feature of this firm's dolls was the fabric circle under their feet, to which the doll's owner could attach a piece of cardboard, enabling the doll to stand. Art Fabric Mills of New York produced charming character dolls such as Buster Brown, Foxy Grandpa, and Punch and Judy. This manufacturer offered customers the opportunity to purchase dolls through the mail, whereas dolls made by Arnold Print Works were only available at shops. However, both firms' dolls were distributed by Selchow & Righter, the company that took over Art Fabric Mills in 1911.

Advertising Dolls
The early printed-cloth dolls were an enormous success, inspiring various food companies to issue cheap cloth advertising dolls about 1900. Most were premium dolls—figures offered by a company for a small sum or in exchange for proof of purchase of one of its products. Besides Art Fabric Mills and Arnold Print Works, the major producers of printed-cloth advertising dolls included Grinnell Lithographic Company and Niagara Lithographing Company. The early dolls are favorites among collectors because they are reminders of long-gone products and reflect the fashions and customs of their era. Because many such dolls promoted food products, they also provide insights into America's dietary habits. Early dolls were made of muslin, cambric, sateen, or linen, and were often depicted in Kate Greenaway-style clothing. The manufacture of these cloth figures declined in the 1940s, when rubber or plastic advertising dolls became common. Cloth advertising dolls were made again in the 1960s and '70s, primarily by the Chase Bag Company of Reedsville, North Carolina. These recent dolls, always factory-assembled, are becoming increasingly popular with collectors.

Punch and Judy

Description
Lithographed-cloth dolls. Sewn and stuffed. Left: Judy has sharp-featured profile, black hair. Long plaid gown with white collar and lace trim. Red, blue, and white bonnet. Right: Punch has characteristic hooked nose, jutting chin, wide grin, and hunchback. Lace-trimmed plaid jacket, red pants, blue shoes. Blue and red peaked hat.

Materials, Marks, and Dimensions
Cotton. Height: 23″ (left); 23½″ (right).

Maker, Origin, and Period
Art Fabric Mills. New York City. c. 1900.

Comment
The rakish characters Punch and Judy appeared in English puppet theaters in the 17th century and were made as paper dolls as early as 1810. In 1900 Art Fabric Mills printed Punch and Judy on cloth sheets, along with directions that called for complicated cutting and sewing to assemble the dolls. These large, brightly colored figures were among the most ambitious ever produced by the noted firm. Art Fabric Mills advertised their cloth-sheet dolls as "this century's model of the old-fashioned rag doll that Grannie used to make." Among their other well-known characters were Buster Brown and Foxy Grandpa.

Hints for Collectors
The dolls shown here look very much like the Punch and Judy printed-sheet dolls distributed by the little-known Textile Blueing Company of New York. One way to tell them apart is by their fabric. Punch and Judy dolls made by Art Fabric Mills are printed on a very heavy cloth that resembles linen.

Santa Claus

Description
Lithographed-cloth doll made from 2-piece printed fabric
pattern. Sewn and stuffed with cotton batting. Closed eyes, red
nose, white beard, pipe in mouth, sepia suit. Pocket watch peeks
out from under fur-edged jacket. American flag tucked into belt.
Holds armful of toys including Chinese doll, pinwheel,
hobbyhorse, drum, girl doll, ball, stuffed animal, bell, sword,
and wagon.

Materials, Marks, and Dimensions
Cotton. "PATENT APPLIED FOR" printed under hand near flag,
"SANTA CLAUS" printed beneath. Height: 15″.

Maker, Origin, and Period
Designed by Edward Peck for New York Stationery and
Envelope Co. New York City. c. 1884–86.

Comment
Designed and patented by Edward Peck and manufactured by
the New York Stationery and Envelope Company, this stocky
cloth Santa Claus may have been the first commercially made
doll of its kind in America. The toys he carries show which
playthings were popular in the late 19th century, when he was
printed. Peck's Santa was the forerunner of the Santa Claus
character later made by Celia and Charity Smith for the Arnold
Print Works.

Hints for Collectors
The Arnold Print Works and Art Fabric Mills were the largest
producers of printed-cloth dolls. Several small firms and
individual designers came out with interesting examples as well,
including this doll. Look for a patent date when purchasing a
printed figure.

The Brownies

Description
Lithographed-cloth dolls. Uncut. Left: Irishman dressed in yellow peaked hat, green shirt, brown pants, and brown shoes. Center: Indian wears feather in hair, fringed jacket, and brown shoes. Right: Soldier wears blue hat with red pompom, red shirt, buckled belt, blue pants, and brown shoes.

Materials, Marks, and Dimensions
Cotton. Right foot of each figure marked "Copyrighted 1892 by PALMER COX." Company trademark printed at bottom center of sheet. Height of each doll: 8".

Maker, Origin, and Period
Designed by Palmer Cox for Arnold Print Works. North Adams, Massachusetts. c. 1892.

Comment
The Brownies appeared in a number of books for children written and illustrated by Palmer Cox from 1887 to 1913 and in a story by him in *St. Nicholas Magazine* in 1893. These imaginary sprites, who worked and played while mortals slept, may be the descendants of the Brownies of Scottish folk tales. Besides the 3 shown here there were characters named Uncle Sam, Dude, John Bull, Highlander, and others. In 1892 the Arnold Print Works squeezed 12 of them onto one yard of fabric and sold them for 20¢. Among the earliest fictional characters to appear in printed-cloth form, the Brownies had a comic appeal that came from their exaggerated features—large round eyes, downturned or smiling mouths, bowed legs, and stooped postures. They proved so popular that in 1895 the New York Biscuit Company offered a set of 16 paper-doll Brownies.

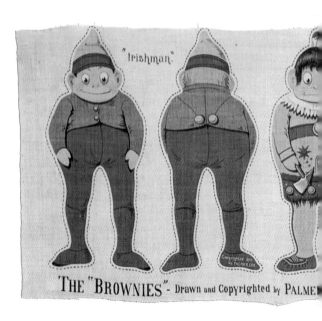

The Thomas and Wylie Litho Company of New York also issued paper-doll Brownies that carried the Arnold Print Works copyright. Other firms made Brownies in leather, cloth, and even papier-mâché, but none were as successful as Arnold's cloth originals. The Brownie camera, designed in 1900 especially for children, is said to have been named after Cox's creations.

Hints for Collectors

Reprints of these dolls appeared in the 1960s. Although paler in color than the originals, they are hard to recognize because many vintage dolls have faded over time to the same light tones, and because the reproductions bear the original 1892 copyright date. Note that original versions measure 8″, while the reprints measure 7″.

Arnold Print Works, which billed itself as "one of the largest manufactories of Prints and Dress Goods in America," did not distribute its own dolls, but made them available through fabric stores. It advertised extensively in newspapers and in such magazines as *The Youth's Companion*. Interested collectors are well advised to seek these ads because they depict the firm's many different dolls in great detail.

Quaker Crackels doll

Description
Lithographed-cloth advertising doll. Uncut. Shoulder-length blond hair, large blue eyes, smiling open mouth. Lavender suit with gold buttons, light green vest, oversize white collar and cuffs. Box of Quaker Crackels cereal appears in back pocket. Brown buckled shoes.

Materials, Marks, and Dimensions
Muslin. Height of doll: 16½".

Maker, Origin, and Period
Designed for Quaker Oats Co. Chicago, Illinois. c. 1924–30.

Comment
Soon after Quaker Oats introduced Crackels cereal in 1924, the Crackels cloth doll was printed as a promotional item. A jovial young man wearing the traditional Quaker hairstyle, he was designed as a plaything for little boys. A hand-grip exerciser was another premium the company offered as part of the ad campaign, which stressed the body-building properties of the cereal, touted by heavyweight boxer Max Baer. Despite these marketing efforts Crackels cereal was not a commercial success, so the doll was issued for only a short time.

Hints for Collectors
Collectors of Quaker Oats dolls may have difficulty finding Crackels. However, the company's newer dolls appear on the market regularly, and these inexpensive advertising figures are already considered collectibles. The 1960s and '70s dolls include plastic and cloth versions of such characters as Cap'n Crunch, Jean La Foote, Quake, and Quisp.

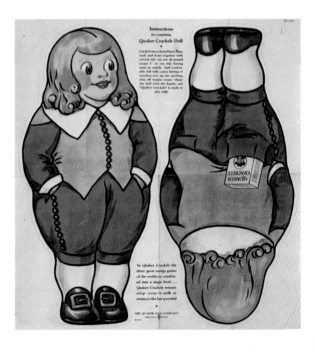

Description
Lithographed-cloth advertising doll. Uncut. Blond corkscrew curls tied with red bow. Wide-open blue eyes and round open mouth; rosy cheeks. White blouse, blue buttoned vest, white skirt with floral border and "Kellogg's" printed in red script below waist. Red belt, white socks, black shoes with red bows.

Materials, Marks, and Dimensions
Cloth. Kellogg's trademark printed in red at top of sheet. Height of doll: 14".

Maker, Origin, and Period
Maker unknown. Distributed by Kellogg Co. Battle Creek, Michigan. c. 1926.

Comment
The first of over 90 premiums issued by the Kellogg Company, Goldilocks and the 3 Bears were printed as sets of cloth dolls in 1925 and 1926. Each of the 4 figures from the charming folk tale was available separately. The 1925 edition included a frightened Goldilocks in a lace-trimmed dress, Papa Bear wearing checked green pants and holding a box of Kellogg's cereal in his paws, a 12" Johnny Bear with a surprised expression on his face, and a 14" bespectacled Mama Bear. Dolls in the 1926 edition differed slightly in clothing style and dimensions.

Hints for Collectors
When first issued, each doll from these editions was sold for 10¢ plus a box top, and the entire set for 30¢ and 4 boxtops. Complete sets are now rare and command high prices. Collectors usually find one doll at a time and group together examples from both the 1925 and 1926 sets in order to assemble a family.

Miss Malto-Rice

Description
Lithographed-cloth advertising doll assembled from 2-piece
fabric pattern. Short brown hair, round eyes, open smiling
mouth. Lace-trimmed chemise with red ribbon at neck and "My
name is/Miss Malto-Rice" printed on body. Applied ribbed cotton
stockings and red oilcloth shoes.

Materials, Marks, and Dimensions
Cloth. Height: 20″.

Maker, Origin, and Period
Maker unknown. Distributed by American Rice Food and
Manufacturing Co. New Jersey. c. 1900.

Comment
Made as a premium, cheerful Miss Malto-Rice proudly displays
her name on her waist. Advertisements in the *Ladies' Home
Journal* of 1901 offered this sheet doll in exchange for coupons
found in boxes of Malto-Rice cereal. An additional 10¢ was
requested to cover mailing costs. Her lithographed face, short
hair, and chemise are typical of many large cloth dolls from the
turn of the century. The distributor also issued a nearly identical
Miss Flaked Rice doll and a Cook's Teddy Bear premium. Sewn
together from a pattern of 15 pieces, the Teddy Bear was
considerably more complicated to assemble than the Miss Malto-
Rice and Miss Flaked Rice dolls.

Hints for Collectors
Some collectors prefer the uncut flat sheets to dolls that have
already been sewn and stuffed. When buying a completed doll,
check its condition carefully. Be sure that it retains most of its
original stuffing, that its seams are intact, and that its outer
fabric is not too worn.

Little Red Riding Hood

Description
Lithographed-cloth doll assembled from 3-piece fabric pattern.
Curly blond hair. Long red cape and hood tied with big red
ribbon, white dress with banded hem, white stockings, brown
shoes with bows. Basket over arm and 2 daisies in hand. Floral
background at feet.

Materials, Marks, and Dimensions
Muslin. Inscription on oval base reads, "Patented July 5, 1892 &
Oct. 4, 1892. Arnold Print Works. North Adams, Mass.
Incorporated 1876." Height: 16″.

Maker, Origin, and Period
Designed by Celia and Charity Smith for Arnold Print Works.
North Adams, Massachusetts. c. 1892.

Comment
Arnold Print Works manufactured thousands of yards of
lithographed cloth to be fashioned into dolls at home. Celia and
Charity Smith of Ithaca, New York, designed many of the firm's
inexpensive and immensely popular doll patterns. Printed on the
disposable parts of the cloth sheets were the instructions, "Cut,
sew, stuff with cotton, bran, or sawdust."

Hints for Collectors
Little Red Riding Hood, Pickaninny, and other popular turn-of-
the-century cloth dolls have recently been reproduced both on
printed sheets and as finished dolls. The fresh, bright colors of
these newer versions distinguish them from older printed dolls,
most of which have faded with time and from exposure to the
sun. Many older printed dolls have acquired a brownish tint.
They are often found in patched condition, and some have lost
the bulk of their filling. Assembled old printed dolls in perfect
condition are hard to find.

Aunt Jemima and Uncle Mose

Description
Lithographed-cloth advertising dolls with brown eyes and broad smiles. Sewn and stuffed. Left: Aunt Jemima wears yellow dress with brown polka dots, red and white striped apron with name printed at hem, red and white polka-dot shawl, and plaid bandanna. Right: Gray-bearded Uncle Mose wears red shirt, yellow polka-dot tie, patched blue jeans with suspenders, brown shoes, and yellow straw hat.

Materials, Marks, and Dimensions
Cloth. Height: 15″ (left); 15½″ (right).

Maker, Origin, and Period
Printed by Grinnell Lithographic Co. New York City. Distributed by Aunt Jemima Mills. St. Joseph, Missouri. c. 1924.

Comment
Around the turn of the century, the R. T. Davis Company acquired the rights to the trade name Aunt Jemima. Launching an ambitious ad campaign to promote its pancake flour, the firm enlisted the aid of Nancy Green of Missouri, who assumed the role of Aunt Jemima at store demonstrations and at the 1893 World's Columbian Exposition in Chicago. In 1905 the company followed the success of its Aunt Jemima Family paper-doll premiums with cloth versions. The R. T. Davis Company, which changed its name to Aunt Jemima Mills in 1914, was acquired by the Quaker Oats Company in 1926.

Hints for Collectors
The features and clothing of this popular couple were modified with each succeeding edition. The early figures looked ragged and were extreme caricatures; later dolls were better dressed and less exaggerated. Collectors often try to obtain a family of dolls or a doll from each set.

Rastus

Description
Lithographed-cloth advertising doll with smiling features. Sewn and stuffed. Holds red and white bowl that reads "Cream of Wheat." White shirt, black and white striped pants, and black shoes. Detachable chef's hat and apron.

Materials, Marks, and Dimensions
Cotton. Height: 18″.

Maker, Origin, and Period
Maker unknown. Distributed by Cream of Wheat Corp. United States. c. 1930.

Comment
Rastus, the smiling Cream of Wheat chef pictured on packages of the cereal since 1899, was first produced as a 16″ printed-cloth doll around 1922. Offered as a premium for a box top and 10¢, Rastus wore the standard chef's uniform with which he became identified. Advertisements claimed that he was printed "in brilliant colors, ready to sew and stuff." In 1930 two new editions of Rastus were produced, a 20″ version and the 18″ doll shown here, both without a cutting line to separate the legs. The doll was reissued in 1949 with the same simple undivided legs.

Hints for Collectors
Although this figure has always been known to doll collectors as Rastus, there is no evidence that he was so named by the Cream of Wheat Corporation. Instructions printed on the original versions say only "Cream of Wheat Doll." It is rare to find a Rastus doll with his original apron and chef's hat intact, since they could be detached and were thus easily lost.

Description
Lithographed-cloth advertising doll. Blond hair, side-glancing eyes, Pinocchio-type nose, smiling open mouth, oversize ears. Wears big chef's hat with "Snap!" printed on brim; red and yellow striped shirt, blue pants, white apron, red shoes.

Materials, Marks, and Dimensions
Cloth. "Copr. 1948 Kellogg Co., Battle Creek, Mich." printed in blue at bottom right. Height of doll: 12½".

Maker, Origin, and Period
Maker unknown. Distributed by Kellogg Co. Battle Creek, Michigan. c. 1948.

Comment
The Kellogg Company attributes its huge success in part to extensive advertising campaigns. The "snap, crackle, and pop" sound of Rice Krispies cereal in milk inspired one of the most effective promotions in advertising history. To millions of Americans, Rice Krispies became synonymous with 3 little elves named Snap, Crackle, and Pop. Although the cereal was introduced in 1928, the first dolls did not appear until 1948. The 12½" printed-sheet dolls were available for 15¢ plus one Rice Krispies boxtop. A slightly larger 16" set was issued in 1954 at the original price.

Hints for Collectors
Snap, Crackle, and Pop dolls are not difficult to find, but some of Kellogg's earlier premium dolls are rare. The 1928 Fairyland Series of Little Bo-Peep, Mary and her Lamb, Little Red Riding Hood, and Tom the Piper's Son are treasured for their charm and fine detailing.

Liberty Belle

Description
Silk-screened cloth doll sewn together with yellow floss. Stuffed with kapok. Brown hair, blue eyes, rosebud mouth. Red and white striped hat with white stars and "LIBERTY BELLE" printed across blue band. Jumper in shape of Liberty Bell with "150 YEARS OF/AMERICAN INDEPENDENCE/1776–1926/SESQUICENTENNIAL" printed on skirt worn over red shirt with star-studded blue collar and cuffs. Red and white striped socks, blue shoes with gold buckles.

Materials, Marks, and Dimensions
Muslin. "Pat. Appl'd for Annin & Co. N.Y." printed on back. Height: 13¾".

Maker, Origin, and Period
Annin & Co. New York City. c. 1926.

Comment
Patriotic dolls, souvenir handkerchiefs, flags, and a myriad of other gift items always crop up during the celebration of national holidays. Miss Liberty Belle, created in 1926 to commemorate this country's sesquicentennial, was originally sold for about one dollar or given away. Her skirt is a detailed replica of the Liberty Bell, complete with crack. The example shown here is distinctive because of the beautiful blanket-stitched outline. Printed-sheet dolls were usually sewn together with ordinary cotton thread.

Hints for Collectors
A limited bicentennial edition of Liberty Belle, based on the original shown here but with the years 1776–1976 printed on her skirt, was recently produced by a Massachusetts firm. Look for both versions.

Topsy-turvy doll

Description
Black-and-white topsy-turvy doll with lithographed faces and
hair. Cloth body and sewn-on clothes. Skirt flips to reveal one
face at a time. Top: Black doll with black hair and brown eyes.
Wears white cotton dress, apron, and cap. Bottom: White doll
with short blond, wavy hair and blue eyes. Wears pink and white
floral print cotton dress with lace collar.

Materials, Marks, and Dimensions
Cloth. Height: 10¼".

Maker, Origin, and Period
Maker unknown. United States. c. 1900.

Comment
Topsy-turvy dolls were made primarily at home during the 19th
century. Spurred by the popularity of these imaginative figures,
mail-order firms and cloth manufacturers began producing their
own versions about 1900. Some had lithographed faces based on
photographic images, as shown here; the faces of others were
taken from artists' drawings.

Hints for Collectors
Among the more common early lithographed dolls that appear on
the market today are Elms & Sellon's "Dolly Double" and a
mask-faced "Double-Ender" manufactured by the Brückner
Company. It is rare to find a stamp or label on these printed
dolls. Many early topsy-turvy figures were clothed in pale prints
and calico dresses. Those that date from the 1920s and '30s were
often crudely made and wear garish prints or bright polka-dot
outfits.

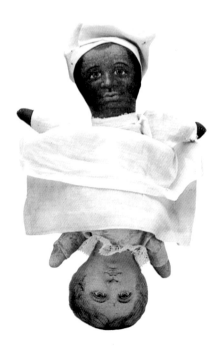

Babyland Rag doll

Description
Cloth girl doll with lithographed face. Blond wavy hair, brown
eyes, closed mouth. Body jointed at shoulders and hips. Wears
pink coat with single button at waist over white cotton dress
with embroidered lace waistband and cuffs. Ruffled pink bonnet
worn over white cotton lace-trimmed bonnet. White cotton lace-
trimmed slip and pantaloons.

Materials, Marks, and Dimensions
Cloth. Height: 14½″.

Maker, Origin, and Period
E. I. Horsman Co. New York City. c. 1907.

Comment
First produced with painted faces in 1904, Babyland Rag dolls
were manufactured with lithographed faces in 1907 as a result of
technological advances in the printing industry. Advertised by
R. H. Macy in 1909, these popular dolls were available in 4 sizes
ranging from 12″ to 18″, and costing from 24¢ to $1.98. From 1910
to 1913 the dolls were issued in both painted and lithographed
versions with such names as Babyland Rag, Babyland Fancy,
and Babyland Beauty. Some were printed with as many as 15
colors. The manufacturer claimed that the faces of all these dolls
could be washed safely with soap and water.

Hints for Collectors
Most Babyland Rag dolls were outfitted with hats, and many
had the type of bonnet worn by the figure shown here. These
dolls can also be identified by their mitten-shaped hands. On
large versions, the hands are stitched to suggest fingers.

Baby Dolls

During the approximately 130 years that baby dolls have been commercially produced, they have undergone a fascinating evolution from solemn-looking, stiff figures made of wax, wood, or papier-mâché, to modern-day synthetic wonders that have soft, correctly proportioned bodies and a wide variety of mechanisms for eating, drinking, talking, and walking. These developments were largely made possible by advances in technology. In the quest for ever more lifelike and durable dolls, dollmakers were some of the first to experiment with such new materials as rubber, gutta-percha, celluloid, biskoline, vinyl, and plastic.

1700–1900

Until the 19th century, dolls were referred to as "poppets" or "babies," yet the vast majority had adult proportions and features. A child who desired a baby doll would merely dress a small figure in an infant gown. In 1857 the German dollmaker Charles Motschmann created one of the first infant dolls, modeling it after a Japanese baby doll. This popular figure, whose body resembled that of a real baby, had a wax-over-composition head and cloth torso. In the 1850s and '60s the renowned English dollmaking firms of Montanari and Pierotti produced baby dolls out of wax, a fragile but malleable material that had been used for centuries to make lifelike figures and religious statues. Baby dolls became increasingly popular in the latter part of the century, when they were made in virtually all the common doll materials. These were not rough-and-tumble toys, but expensive luxury items reserved for display and only periodic supervised handling and dressing.

Character Babies

A breakthrough in dollmaking occurred in Germany between 1900 and 1910 with the creation of increasingly realistic figures, which were called "character" dolls. This change reflected the growth of the behavioral sciences and, in particular, a new understanding of children. French bébés and lady dolls came to be seen as unnaturally pretty and frivolous. Such noted dollmakers as Marion Kaulitz and Käthe Kruse began making child dolls with expressive, lifelike features. The firms of Kestner, Kämmer & Reinhardt, Gebrüder Heubach, Simon & Halbig, and Armand Marseille quickly followed, producing character babies with carefully detailed bodies that had round bellies, rolls of fat, and broad infantile shapes. The introduction of bent limbs around this time was a significant advance that made it possible for dolls to be placed in sitting or crawling positions.

Bye-Lo and Other 20th-Century Babies

Many of the fine European baby dolls were distributed in America by George Borgfeldt, who is also credited with the distribution of the American Bye-Lo Baby, designed by Grace Putnam. This immensely popular doll, supposedly modeled after a 3-day-old infant, was introduced in 1922. Numerous imitations of the Bye-Lo doll were produced, some as late as 1950. After the Second World War the development of synthetics gave new life to the American doll industry. The United States became the major producer of dolls, for the first time outstripping Germany and France.

Lamkin

Description
Baby doll with composition head; molded and painted features and hair. Brown sleep-eyes, red rosebud mouth. Original costume of white cotton lace-trimmed gown, white flannel slip and diaper. Pink satin ribbon binds doll to pillow.

Materials, Marks, and Dimensions
Composition head and limbs, cloth body. "A New Playmate/ Lamkin Trade Mark/An EFFanBEE Durable Doll" marked on inside cover of original oval doll box. Height: 15¾".

Maker, Origin, and Period
EFFanBEE (trade name for Fleischaker & Baum). New York City. c. 1930.

Comment
Founded in 1910 as Fleischaker & Baum, EFFanBEE originally specialized in bisque, cloth, and composition baby and toddler dolls, many of which had mechanical parts. In the 1920s the motto "They Walk, They Talk, They Sleep" was part of the company's trademark, appearing even on dolls with none of these traits. The cherubic doll shown here is a particularly fine example of EFFanBEE craftsmanship. Note its characteristically chubby arms and cheeks and pink-rimmed fingernails.

Hints for Collectors
Collectors of modern dolls rate EFFanBEE products, with their high-quality composition and natural modeling, among the finest. Marked EFFanBEE dolls are usually stamped "EFFanBEE," although a few simply say "F & B." The Lamkin doll shown here can be identified by the way the index finger of the left hand points outward and the rest of the fingers are curved. A painted gold ring is molded on the middle finger of the right hand.

Tee-Wee

Description
Hand puppet baby doll with bisque head; molded and painted
features and hair. Blue glass sleep-eyes, open mouth showing
2 lower teeth. Original costume of white cotton lace-trimmed
gown tied with ribbon, and lace-trimmed white rayon pillow with
large pink bow attached to front. Puppet operated through
sleeve attached to back of pillow.

Materials, Marks, and Dimensions
Bisque head, cloth body, celluloid hands. "AM/Germany"
imprinted on neck. Heart-shaped blue paper label pinned to
bedding reads "U.S. & CANADIAN/PATENTS PENDING/TEE-WEE/
HAND BABE/The Living Doll/MANUF. BY/S & H NOVELTY CO./
ATLANTIC CITY/N.J." Height of head: 3″.

Maker, Origin, and Period
Head by Armand Marseille. Germany. Distributed by S & H
Novelty Co. Atlantic City, New Jersey. c. 1920–25.

Comment
Tee-Wee hand puppets were designed as miniature versions of
the popular Bye-Lo and My Dream Babies. The puppets were
first produced with bisque heads, but after 1928 with composition
heads. While some versions were outfitted with muslin pillows
and plain clothing, most had elaborate, lace-trimmed accessories.

Hints for Collectors
Tee-Wee puppets are rare today because their pillows soiled
easily and many were thrown out. Look for an unusual version
marked "A.M./Germany/341-10," which originally came with a
celluloid rattle embossed with the nursery rhyme, "Mary, Mary,
Quite Contrary."

Gerber Baby

Description
Baby doll in wicker basket. Vinyl head with molded and painted features and hair. Flirty blue eyes, painted lashes, open mouth. Original costume of white eyelet dress; cap tied with white satin ribbon. Lies on matching white cotton pillow decorated with eyelet ruffle and white satin bow.

Materials, Marks, and Dimensions
Vinyl head and limbs, cloth body. Tag attached to wrist reads "Certificate/Atlanta Novelty/Division of Gerber Products Industry." Height: 17″ (doll); 21″ (basket).

Maker, Origin, and Period
Atlanta Novelty Co. Atlanta, Georgia. 1979.

Comment
The 1979 Gerber Baby shown here was made in celebration of the baby-food company's 50th anniversary. The last in a long line of Gerber dolls, it was the only version not designed as a premium. In 1936 Gerber introduced its trademark dolls, silk-screened with the famous Gerber Baby face. Clothed in either pink or blue outfits, these early dolls were sold in color-coordinated boxes for 10¢ plus 3 Gerber labels. Between 1936 and 1979, Gerber issued 27,000 dolls.

Hints for Collectors
All Gerber premium dolls are difficult to find, but the earliest version is extremely rare. In 1977 the *Detroit Free Press* asked its readers to locate examples of the first Gerber Baby for the company's archives. Only one of the original dolls, still in its mailing carton, was submitted.

Bye-Lo Baby

Description
Baby doll with composition head, molded and painted features and hair. Brown sleep-eyes. Bent legs. Original costume of matching white flannel shirt, diaper, and blanket. Pink ribbon trim on blanket and shirt, wide pink sash tied around body.

Materials, Marks, and Dimensions
Composition head and hands, cloth body and legs. Back of neck embossed "Grace Storey Putnam." Height: 12½".

Maker, Origin, and Period
Designed by Grace Storey Putnam. Head manufactured by Cameo Doll Co. Body by K & K Toy Co. Distributed by Geo. Borgfeldt & Co. New York City. c. 1924–25.

Comment
Grace Putnam spent months perfecting what came to be known as "the Million Dollar Baby." Supposedly modeled after a 3-day-old infant, Bye-Lo was a great commercial success in the 1920s, attracting an audience that sought dolls with realistic rather than idealized features. George Borgfeldt & Company, the exclusive distributor of Bye-Lo Babies, commissioned a number of American and German firms to produce the dolls' heads and bodies.

Hints for Collectors
Check that a Bye-Lo Baby's blanket is original—its label should read "Bye-Lo Baby Reg. U.S. Pat. Off. Putnam/George Borgfeldt & Co. N.Y., N.Y." Unfortunately, the print on the label was impermanent and faded upon washing, as seen on the blanket shown here.

Papier-mâché mechanical baby

Description
Character baby doll with papier-mâché head; lying in blue cradle.
Molded and painted features and bonnet. Blue eyes, open mouth
with molded tongue, rosy cheeks. Brown silk print gown, white
cotton bib and pillow. Netting around cradle. Pull cords in lower
torso cause arms and head to move back and forth as doll
squeaks.

Materials, Marks, and Dimensions
Papier-mâché and metal. Height: 9¼".

Maker, Origin, and Period
Maker unknown. Europe. c. 1885–95.

Comment
French automata were so popular in the late 19th century
that copies were mass produced all over Europe. Many were
constructed quite economically. The mechanical baby illustrated
here is operated by an inexpensive pull-cord mechanism—one
cord moves the arms and the other operates the squeak box.
Even so, this doll was considered a superior example in its day
because of its silk outfit and careful detailing.

Hints for Collectors
Regarded as a real toy, a mechanical doll such as this example
was subject to much wear and tear. If its pull cords broke,
however, they were easily fixed from the inside by lifting the
body of the doll out of its cradle. Be sure to consult an expert
before repairing a valuable mechanical figure like one shown
here; by now, its papier-mâché shell is brittle with age and may
require special care.

Pierotti wax baby

Description
Baby doll with pink poured-wax shoulder-head. Inserted blond hair, blue glass eyes, closed mouth. Wax arms and legs attached to body with cotton thread running through sew holes. Doll wrapped in wool binder and yellow wool wrapper with ribbon ties.

Materials, Marks, and Dimensions
Wax shoulder-head and limbs, cloth body. "Charles/Dolls of all kinds repaired in a/few days/388 Oxford Street London, W." printed in oval on front of torso. Height: 14½".

Maker, Origin, and Period
Designed by Henry Pierotti. Distributed by Charles Morrell. England. c. 1870–84.

Comment
The Victorian idealization of children as "little ladies" and "little gentlemen" resulted in baby and child dolls that merely resembled adults with short hair. In the 1850s Henry Pierotti and a few others broke with this convention by introducing baby dolls with chubby bodies and realistically modeled features. The deep pink color of the wax infant shown here is characteristic of Pierotti dolls. The firm used tinted wax, which was poured into molds and allowed to harden before another layer was added. The last pouring was the most heavily tinted.

Hints for Collectors
Since tinted wax fades when exposed to sunlight, be prepared for uneven coloring on many wax dolls. Moreover, the cracks commonly found in wax cannot be repaired. Since it is impossible to match pieces of wax perfectly, restoration is always noticeable.

Black Bye-Lo Baby

Description
Baby doll with black bisque head, molded and painted features and hair. Brown sleep-eyes, closed mouth. Squeaker in stomach. Wears long white lace-trimmed infant gown with pearl and composition buttons; white embroidered slip.

Materials, Marks, and Dimensions
Bisque head; cloth body and limbs; composition hands. "© 1923 by/Grace S. Putnam/Made in Germany" incised on back of neck. Height: 16½".

Maker, Origin, and Period
Designed by Grace Storey Putnam. Distributed by Geo. Borgfeldt & Co. Germany. c. 1923.

Comment
Grace Putnam made over 20 versions of Bye-Lo before she was satisfied with the modeling of the body and legs. The first Bye-Lo had a composition body that was unnaturally hard for a baby doll. In the final cloth version the legs and torso were cut from one piece of fabric and the legs were turned inward in a naturalistic position. Ironically, store owners initially feared that Bye-Lo would not sell because it was too realistic.

Hints for Collectors
Bye-Lo Babies share top billing with Barbie, Kewpie, and Shirley Temple as the biggest money-making dolls of all time. Every conceivable version of Bye-Lo was marketed, including black dolls like this one, and many types of materials were used to make them. (*See* 163 *and* 172.) In 1925 A. Schoenhut & Company introduced a wooden Bye-Lo Baby, considered by collectors the rarest and among the most desirable. Early Bye-Los have delicately painted eyelashes and faint brows. Later examples are more crudely finished and often have heavy brows.

Description
Baby doll with black bisque head, molded and painted features.
Black sleep-eyes, button nose, open red mouth with 2 lower
teeth. Bent limbs. Wears white organdy lace-trimmed gown with
pink ribbon sash. White cotton underclothing and stockings.

Materials, Marks, and Dimensions
Bisque head, composition body and limbs. "AM/Germany/351"
imprinted on neck. Height: 14".

Maker, Origin, and Period
Armand Marseille. Germany. c. 1923.

Comment
The prolific German doll manufacturer Armand Marseille
produced his first black baby dolls at the turn of the century.
Made from standard molds, some of the firm's black doll heads
were merely sprayed or painted with dark color, but a few fine
quality examples, like this one, had pigment mixed directly into
the bisque before firing. Although it was claimed that the painted
dolls could be washed, their color usually came off in water. The
doll shown here is a black version of Marseille's popular My
Dream Baby (see 174).

Hints for Collectors
The body and limbs of the doll shown here have been repainted,
reducing its value somewhat. During the 1920s Armand
Marseille made other infant dolls that resembled My Dream
Baby, including a bisque-head doll named Kiddie Joy with
straight limbs, a cloth body, and celluloid hands. Celluloid was a
material commonly used for dolls' hands during this period.
Unfortunately, the substance is brittle and hands made of it were
easily broken.

Rubber baby

Description
Black baby doll with painted lips and white eyes. One-piece head and body. Unclothed.

Materials, Marks, and Dimensions
Rubber. "Goodyear's/&N. York Rubber Co./Patents 1848–9 & 51" stamped in circular depression on back. Height: 5".

Maker, Origin, and Period
Goodyear Rubber Co. New Haven, Connecticut. c. 1851.

Comment
The doll shown here, with its bright red mouth and white eyes, is an extremely rare black rubber doll, one of the earliest made by the Goodyear Rubber Company. The doll is probably a male, since most female dolls had molded hair. He is dyed black but does not have characteristically black features. Rubber dolls were either painted white or dyed black; black was a more practical color because white paint tended to chip and peel, exposing the natural olive color of the rubber beneath. Lampblack, a carbon product, was probably this doll's coloring agent.

Hints for Collectors
Rubber dolls are extremely vulnerable to changes in weather. Old dolls are usually brittle and cracked, and their heads are often flattened in the back from being stored for long periods of time. Dolls like the one shown here are so rare that they usually change hands only privately or perhaps at auctions. Other rubber dolls, such as shoulder-head lady dolls, are sometimes found in antiques shops or at flea markets, but rarely in good condition.

Bathing dolls

Description
All-china babies with molded and painted features and hair.
Closed mouths, rosy cheeks, clenched fists. One-piece bodies.
Left: Blond hair, dark blue eyes; pink face and white body.
Right: Black hair, blue eyes; pink face and body.

Materials, Marks, and Dimensions
China. Height: 15¾″ (left); 15″ (right).

Maker, Origin, and Period
Maker unknown. Germany. c. 1870–1920.

Comment
"Bathing dolls" are also known as *Badekinder*, pillar dolls, solid-china dolls, and Frozen Charlottes. Made as early as the mid-19th century, the dolls were most popular in the 1870s and continued to be manufactured well into the 20th century. These rather chubby figures have one-piece, unjointed bodies made of china, bisque, or metal, and range in size from 1″ to over 18″. Originally intended as Victorian bath toys, they were made to float in water. In late 19th-century England, the tiny 1″ dolls were often used in teacups to draw the heat of the boiling water away from the porcelain and keep the cup from cracking. The dolls were so cheap—39¢ a dozen for the 4″ size in 1886—that it did not matter if they broke during this procedure.

Hints for Collectors
Most bathing dolls are very plain nude figures with simple molded hairstyles. Look for the more unusual versions, which, although undressed, wear elaborate bonnets or hair ribbons.

Scootles

Description
All-bisque baby doll with molded and painted features including blond hair, side-glancing blue eyes, closed smiling mouth. Jointed shoulders.

Materials, Marks, and Dimensions
Bisque. Left foot marked "Scootles," right foot marked "Rose O'Neill." Heart-shaped red paper shield on chest reads "Scootles Reg. U.S. Pat. Off. Germany." Height: 5½".

Maker, Origin, and Period
Designed by Rose O'Neill. Manufactured and distributed by Geo. Borgfeldt & Co. New York City. c. 1925.

Comment
Scootles was designed by Rose O'Neill and modeled by Joseph Kallus, the same team that created the immensely popular Kewpie doll. Because it was so similar in appearance to Kewpie but not as appealing, Scootles never really caught on. The first Scootles was manufactured in Germany in 1925 and was made of wood-pulp composition. The doll continued to be made into the 1930s. Composition and bisque versions were sold dressed or undressed; the composition dolls came with white cotton socks and white imitation-leather sandals. In 1964 Scootles was reissued by Borgfeldt in an all-vinyl version priced at $10.

Hints for Collectors
Novice collectors may confuse Scootles with Kewpie. Always look for molded blond curly hair on Scootles and a peaked topknot on Kewpie. Watch for rare black Scootles dolls, which, like black Kewpies, command higher prices than white versions.

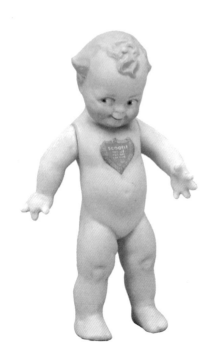

Queue San and Chin-Chin Babies

Description
All-bisque baby dolls with molded and painted Asian features.
Molded hats, shoes, and black queues. Jointed at shoulders;
arms attached with rubber bands. One-piece legs. Left:
Queue San Baby with white and pink cap, replaced arms, blue
shoes. Right: Chin-Chin Baby has yellow hat with black trim,
starfish-shaped hands, yellow shoes. Head tilted to one side.

Materials, Marks, and Dimensions
Bisque. Left: Red diamond-shaped label on chest reads "Queue/
San/Baby/Reg. U.S. Pat. Office." Right: Red and yellow
triangular label reads "Chin/Chin/Baby/[trademark]/Germany."
Height: 4½″ (left); 4¼″ (right).

Maker, Origin, and Period
Left: Designed by Hikozo Arakia for Morimura Bros. New York
City. c. 1915. Right: Gebrüder Heubach. Germany. c. 1916.

Comment
Morimura's Queue San Baby and Gebrüder Heubach's Chin-Chin
Baby are almost identical in appearance, and collectors often
mistake one for the other. They were both inspired by Rose
O'Neill's Kewpies. Their starfish-shaped hands with the second
and third fingers molded together are so distinctive that it is
easy to spot replaced arms, such as those on the doll at left.

Hints for Collectors
Heubach dolls are noted for the fine quality of their bisque.
They bring significantly higher prices than Morimura examples.
Morimura Brothers, a Japanese import house located in New
York City, manufactured dolls from about 1915 to 1922.

Description
Seated baby dolls with bisque heads, molded and painted features. Bodies jointed at hips and shoulders. Left: Blond wig, blue glass eyes, closed mouth, stationary neck. Molded white socks and blue shoes. Center: Painted blond hair, brown glass sleep-eyes, closed mouth, swivel neck. Molded white diapers, white socks, and blue shoes. Right: Painted blond hair, blue glass eyes, closed mouth, stationary neck. Molded white socks and pink shoes.

Materials, Marks, and Dimensions
Bisque. Left: "Copr. By Grace S. Putnam Germany" marked on back of torso. Center: "886-12 Copr. By Grace S. Putnam Germany" marked on back of torso. Paper label on chest reads "Bye-Lo Baby G.S. Putnam Germany." Right: "20-10 Copr. By Grace S. Putnam Germany" marked on back of torso. Height: 4½" (left); 5" (center); 4¼" (right).

Maker, Origin, and Period
Designed by Grace Storey Putnam for J. D. Kestner, Jr. Germany. Distributed by Geo. Borgfeldt & Co. New York City. c. 1925–30.

Comment
Kestner all-bisque Bye-Lo dolls were designed as smaller, inexpensive versions of the original Bye-Lo. A 6" doll cost as little as 67¢ in 1925.

Hints for Collectors
Collectors may choose from a variety of Bye-Lo Babies with painted or glass eyes, painted hair or wigs, and bare feet or molded shoes and socks. Bisque Bye-Los are fragile and must be handled carefully. The strings or elastic cords attaching the limbs to the bodies may break or stretch if pulled too often.

Tynie Baby

Description
Baby doll with bisque head, molded and painted features.
Blond hair, painted lashes, blue paperweight sleep-eyes with red
dots in corners. Closed mouth. Voice box in stomach. Wears
white cotton gown trimmed in eyelet and lace, white cotton slip.

Materials, Marks, and Dimensions
Bisque head; cloth body and legs; composition hands and arms.
Back of head marked "© 1924 by/E. I. Horsman Co. INC./Made
in Germany/u." Height: 13¾".

Maker, Origin, and Period
Designed by Bernard Lipfert. Distributed by E. I. Horsman Co.
New York City. c. 1924.

Comment
Grace Putnam's Bye-Lo Baby was so popular in the 1920s that
numerous companies manufactured their own newborn infant
dolls. Tynie Baby, sometimes called "The Horsman Bye-Lo,"
was produced with bisque or composition heads, soft cloth
bodies, and voice boxes that produced a crying sound when
pressed. These dolls ranged in size from 11″ to 20″ and came in
long white gowns. Full layettes were also available. Tynie Baby
was created by Bernard Lipfert, the noted doll designer, whose
other dolls included such best-sellers as Patsy, Shirley Temple,
and the Dionne Quintuplets.

Hints for Collectors
Infant dolls are so frequently handled that their gowns become
soiled and often need to be replaced. Since baby gowns are not
especially distinctive in style, replacing one will not seriously
detract from a doll's value.

My Dream Baby

Description
Baby doll with bisque head and flange neck. Blond hair, closed rosebud mouth, button nose, brown glass sleep-eyes. Bent legs. Wears white cotton infant gown with blue ribbon bows and lace at neck and cuffs. Matching lace-trimmed cap.

Materials, Marks, and Dimensions
Bisque head, cloth body. "A.M./Germany" incised on neck. Height: 13½".

Maker, Origin, and Period
Armand Marseille. Germany. c. 1923.

Comment
My Dream Baby was Armand Marseille's idealized imitation of Grace Putnam's popular newborn infant doll, the Bye-Lo Baby. The German firm manufactured Dream Babies with bisque heads, cry-voices called squeakers, and cloth bodies. Armand Marseille also produced dolls for the American company Arranbee (which registered the "My Dream Baby" trademark in New York about 1924), using bisque heads with flange necks on its dolls with cloth bodies, and bisque socket heads on those with composition bodies. Flange necks are often seen on dolls with bisque, china, or composition heads and cloth bodies. The flange is a slight lip at the neck edge that secures the head to the body. Cloth is usually gathered over the flange, enabling the head to move from side to side.

Hints for Collectors
Armand Marseille made several variations of My Dream Baby, including a crying Dream Baby with a bisque swivel head, and a pillow Dream Baby; the latter is a bisque-head hand puppet called Tee-Wee (161). Today these dolls are rare and valuable.

Century doll

Description
Baby doll with bisque head and flange neck. Molded and painted features and blond hair with curly forelock. Blue glass eyes with painted lashes, open-closed mouth with molded tongue and 2 upper teeth. Wears white cotton dress with pink embroidery and lace trim; white cotton slip.

Materials, Marks, and Dimensions
Bisque head; cloth body and limbs; composition hands. Back of head marked "Germany/Century Doll & Co." "4" marked on back of neck. Height: 15½".

Maker, Origin, and Period
Manufactured by J. D. Kestner, Jr. Germany. Distributed by Century Doll Co. New York City. c. 1909–25.

Comment
The Century Doll Company was a well-known distributor of a wide variety of baby dolls. Most of the firm's dolls featured the innovative "Mama-type" cloth body, popular with children because of its soft touch and broad infant shape. Its dolls had such realistic features as molded fontanels (the soft spots in a newborn's skull), chubby cheeks, curly forelocks, and facial expressions ranging from cheerful smiles to scowls. The newborn features of the Century doll shown here resemble those seen on Grace Putnam's Bye-Lo Baby (*see* 163).

Hints for Collectors
These dolls were handled constantly by children, so their cloth bodies were easily soiled. Try using a mild cleaning solution or a damp soapy cloth to remove stains from old dolls. Never immerse them in water.

Tantrum baby

Description
Character baby doll with bisque head; molded and painted features including blond hair, blue eyes, open-closed mouth. Wears white cotton gown and diaper.

Materials, Marks, and Dimensions
Bisque head and lower arms, kid body and legs. "Heubach [inscribed in square]/Germany" incised on back. Height: 9½".

Maker, Origin, and Period
Gebrüder Heubach. Germany. c. 1910.

Comment
Character baby dolls whose facial expressions realistically reflected a baby's many moods became popular around the turn of the century. The Heubach tantrum doll illustrated here is a prime example of this genre. Heubach produced its own doll heads, but many of the bodies were manufactured by other companies, and their quality varied greatly. Most larger dolls have well-made composition, cloth, or kid bodies; smaller dolls, however, are often attached to crude torsos. Some are simply pieces of cardboard with glued-on arms and legs. Heubach sent identical heads to its various distributors, each of which used whatever type of torso and limbs it favored.

Hints for Collectors
The majority of Heubach dolls are babies and toddlers with idealized faces. Tantrum dolls, large "pouties," and molded-bonnet dolls are rarest and considered most desirable. The tantrum doll was sold with molded hair, as shown here, or with a wig. While the example illustrated does not have a mold number, dolls with this head sometimes bear the numbers 7843 and 7761.

Kaiser Baby

Description
Character baby doll with bisque head, molded and painted features and hair. Blue eyes, open-closed mouth. Body jointed at shoulders and hips. Bent limbs. Wears long white linen gown with lace trim at collar and cuffs.

Materials, Marks, and Dimensions
Bisque head, composition body and limbs. Back of neck marked "28 K [star trademark] R/100." Height: 11″.

Maker, Origin, and Period
Kämmer & Reinhardt. Germany. c. 1910.

Comment
Collectors sometimes refer to the infant shown here, marked with the mold number 100, as the Kaiser Baby, because it was believed to have been modeled after the son of Kaiser Wilhelm II. Actually, the doll is a likeness of the designer's son. One of the earliest, perhaps even the first, of the bent-limb dolls, the Kaiser Baby was manufactured by Kämmer & Reinhardt, a firm known for its technical innovations. The company was the first to design dolls' mouths with visible teeth, to use wooden character heads of the type later favored by Schoenhut, and to make bathing dolls with movable arms. In addition to the petulant infant shown here, K & R produced another baby doll, bearing mold number 126, with a more cheerful expression.

Hints for Collectors
This Kämmer & Reinhardt baby proved so successful that other companies, such as France's SFBJ, copied the doll. Dolls made by K & R are usually of a finer quality than the imitations and bring substantially higher prices.

Bubbles

Description
Baby doll with composition shoulder-head, molded and painted features including blond hair, blue sleep-eyes with painted eyelashes, open mouth showing 2 upper teeth and molded tongue. Bent limbs. Jointed at shoulders and hips. Finger in mouth. Original costume of white dotted swiss gown with smocked yoke and lace trim, white cotton underskirt, pantaloons, white kid moccasins.

Materials, Marks, and Dimensions
Composition shoulder-head and limbs, cloth body. "FB 3" marked on head. Height: 24½″.

Maker, Origin, and Period
Designed by Bernard Lipfert for EFFanBEE (trade name for Fleischaker & Baum). New York City. c. 1927.

Comment
The earliest of many successful Bubbles dolls was produced during the height of the Bye-Lo Baby craze in 1924, although most examples date from after 1925. Bubbles became one of the most widely advertised baby dolls of the 1920s. As Montgomery Ward's catalogue claimed, "You know some real baby just like her—some year-old baby with twinkling roguish eyes and one wet little finger that must always be pulled out of her rosy mouth before you can give her a kiss." The forefinger on Bubbles' left hand just fits into her slightly open mouth.

Hints for Collectors
Although many Bubbles dolls are readily available on the market, a few models are quite scarce. The rarest of all is a black Baby Bubbles, a special-order doll with molded and painted black hair, deep brown skin coloring, brown tin eyes, and composition lower legs attached to muslin upper legs.

Lil' Darlin

Description
Baby doll with vinyl head and flange neck. Molded and painted features including brown hair, slitlike blue eyes with underlying pouches, wrinkled brow, pug nose, open-closed mouth, molded tongue. Bent limbs. Voice box in stomach. Reclothed in white cotton flannel shirt, diapers, and robe with satin ties.

Materials, Marks, and Dimensions
Vinyl head and limbs, cloth body. "EFFanBEE" marked on head. Height: 20″.

Maker, Origin, and Period
EFFanBEE (trade name for Fleischaker & Baum). New York City. c. 1947–50.

Comment
Lil' Darlin has the features of a newborn infant, showing the lasting influence of the 1920s Bye-Lo Baby. First introduced in 1947, Lil' Darlin was popular for only a few years because children didn't like the feel of its vinyl skin. Early vinyl dolls were marred by an unpleasant stickiness that grew worse with age. They soiled easily, and attempts to clean them often resulted in paint loss. EFFanBEE also produced a 16″ sleep-eyed version of Lil' Darlin that portrayed a slightly older baby.

Hints for Collectors
Nail-polish remover may be used to clean early vinyl dolls, but the treatment must be repeated every few months. These dolls should be stored in a cool, dry environment, and their heads should not touch anything that will adhere to them. Despite special care requirements, such dolls are well worth collecting because they were among the first figures to be made of the new material.

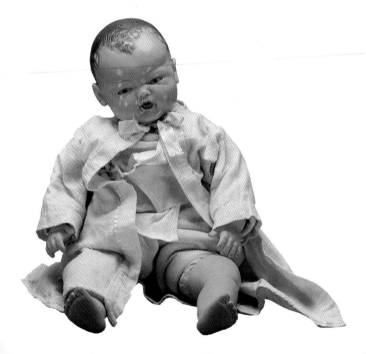

Bonnie Babe

Description
Baby doll with bisque head and flange neck. Molded and painted features and brown hair. Brown glass sleep-eyes, open mouth with 2 lower teeth. Body jointed at shoulders and hips. Voice box in lower back. Wears pink cotton gown with white pleated yoke and lace trim. Lace cap tied with satin ribbon. Crocheted cotton booties.

Materials, Marks, and Dimensions
Bisque head; cloth body; rubber limbs. "Copr't by Georgene Averill/1093/3652/Germany" imprinted on back of neck. Height: 20″.

Maker, Origin, and Period
Designed by Georgene Averill for Averill Manufacturing Co. New York City. c. 1920.

Comment
Until 1923 the Averill Manufacturing Company was run by the husband-and-wife team of James and Georgene Averill; afterwards it was headed by Georgene's brother, Rudolph Hopf. The firm manufactured a wide range of character, little girl, and baby dolls. Bonnie Babe, shown here, was produced in several sizes with a bisque, celluloid, or composition head.

Hints for Collectors
In selecting a doll from a prestigious line, the collector should consider several factors. Widely known examples sometimes attract more interest than a rare, but less familiar doll. A well-known doll in an unusual size—the very largest or smallest in a company's particular line—will bring a greater return on one's investment. The 20″ Bonnie Babe illustrated here is especially desirable because of her size.

Baby Grumpy

Description
Character baby doll with composition head, molded and painted features and hair. Light brown ringlets, side-glancing eyes, knitted brow, scowling closed mouth. Wears long white dotted swiss gown, lace cap tied with blue satin ribbon, white lace-trimmed cotton slip, flannel diaper, and socks.

Materials, Marks, and Dimensions
Composition head and lower arms, cloth body and limbs. "176" marked on back of neck. "8" penciled on back of torso. Height: 14½".

Maker, Origin, and Period
EFFanBEE (trade name for Fleischaker & Baum). New York City. c. 1914–23.

Comment
Produced between 1914 and 1939, Baby Grumpy was one of EFFanBEE's most endearing dolls. "Couldn't you just love Baby Grumpy with the petulant little frown caught from life by our artist," read a 1916 advertisement in the *Ladies' Home Journal*. Living up to its name, Baby Grumpy was always on the verge of tears, crying whenever its voice box was pressed. EFFanBEE manufactured several versions over the years, and Baby Grumpy got grumpier, its pout turning to an angry scowl. By 1921 the dolls were waterproof, unbreakable, and had almost doubled in price from the initial 50¢ of 1914.

Hints for Collectors
The rarest Baby Grumpy dolls are the few black examples and a version originally dressed as a nun. Some early dolls are stamped "DECO," which may have been the trademark of Otto Ernst Denivelle, who invented a formula for composition used by EFFanBEE.

Patsy Baby in hamper

Description
Baby doll with layette in wicker hamper. Composition head with molded and painted features. Synthetic blond wig, brown sleep-eyes, closed mouth. Bent limbs. Original costume of white cotton polka-dot dress trimmed with blue smocking; lace cap. Original hamper lined in blue silk and lace contains coat and hat, snowsuit, additional dress, comb, rattle, brush, face cloth, towel, and soap.

Materials, Marks, and Dimensions
Composition. "EFFanBEE/Patsy Baby" marked on back of head. Metal bracelet with heart-shaped metal tag on left wrist reads "EFFanBEE Patsy Baby-Kin." Height: 12".

Maker, Origin, and Period
EFFanBEE (trade name for Fleischaker & Baum). New York City. c. 1932.

Comment
Patsy Baby was one of many immensely popular Patsy dolls produced by EFFanBEE in the 1930s. These baby dolls came in several versions, with molded hair or synthetic wigs, brown, blue, or green eyes, and composition or cloth bodies. They were so well liked that the firm successfully issued such variations as twin dolls and male Patsy Babies. In 1936 a black Patsy Baby was named Amosandra (*see* 254) after the child supposedly born to the characters Amos and Ruby of the popular radio show, "Amos 'n' Andy."

Hints for Collectors
Although the mark on the back of her head reads "Patsy Baby," the doll shown here was advertised as "Patsy Baby-Kin." Dolls with their original wardrobes appear only occasionally on the market.

All-wax baby in basket

Description
Baby doll with wax head, blue glass eyes, painted eyelashes, eyebrows, and closed mouth. Lies in woven reed basket. Jointed limbs. Wears white cotton lace-trimmed gown, cape, and cap.

Materials, Marks, and Dimensions
Wax. Paper label on basket reads "542/0." Height: 6″.

Maker, Origin, and Period
Maker unknown. Probably Germany. c. 1850–60.

Comment
It was only in the mid-19th century that dollmakers first attempted to create baby dolls with realistic bodies. Some of these early dolls were made of wax, a substance that had been used to create lifelike figures for hundreds of years. Such naturalistic details as dimples, fingernails, and molded elbow joints reflected a growing trend toward realism that culminated in the character dolls of the early 20th century.

Hints for Collectors
Wax baby dolls are so fragile that few have survived. Those that have wax heads as well as limbs are likely to be composed of their original parts, since restoring or replacing wax components was too difficult to be worthwhile. Instead, readily available china and bisque limbs were quite often substituted. Although German wax dolls are not considered to be as fine as those made by the English, they can be quite appealing. All but the very finest are moderately priced. The figure shown here is unusual because it is made of poured wax rather than the wax-over-composition typical of German dolls.

Multi-face doll

Description
Doll with 3-faced bisque head inside papier-mâché hood. Crying
face illustrated. Red mohair wig, blue glass eyes, open-closed
mouth, molded tears. Wears long-sleeved white cotton gown
trimmed with lace, matching bonnet with large white bow, white
cotton underskirt, and long black cotton stockings. Brass knob at
top of hood turns the faces, which revolve on rod attached to
torso. Pull strings attached to left side of doll activate voice box
inside torso.

Materials, Marks, and Dimensions
Bisque head; composition shoulders, arms, and lower legs;
cloth-over-cardboard body. "CB" stamped on back of shoulder.
Height: 13½".

Maker, Origin, and Period
Probably Carl Bergner. Germany. c. 1904–5.

Comment
Although it has never been proven conclusively, it is widely held
that the "CB" mark found on many multi-face dolls stands for
Carl Bergner. Examples with this mark have similar facial
features and body construction. In 1904 and 1905, Bergner
registered patents for multi-face dolls that, like the example
shown here, cried, laughed, and slept. One interesting version
had a white sleeping face, a mulatto smiling face, and a black
crying face.

Hints for Collectors
Multi-face dolls were produced commercially as early as the mid-
19th century, but most date from about 1900. In general, heads
were of a better quality than the durable but poorly made bodies.

Japanese baby doll

Description
Baby doll with bisque head, molded and painted features.
Curly blond mohair wig, brown glass sleep-eyes, open mouth
with 2 upper teeth. Wears embroidered white voile gown with
lace cuffs, white eyelet-edged bonnet tied with satin ribbon,
embroidered white cotton underskirt, white cotton diapers,
white woolen booties.

Materials, Marks, and Dimensions
Bisque head, composition body and limbs. "B 8 [in diamond
shape] R E/Made in Nippon" marked on back of shoulder.
Height: 18¼".

Maker, Origin, and Period
Maker unknown. Japan. Early 20th century.

Comment
In the early 20th century, Japanese and American dollmakers
ventured into the European doll market with copies of German
and other European dolls that were unobtainable during the
First World War. Some Japanese-made dolls bear an uncanny
resemblance to the German originals. Others are slipshod copies
made from poor-quality bisque with florid coloring.

Hints for Collectors
Although the manufacturer of this baby doll is unknown, other
dolls with similar Nippon markings turn up from time to time. A
mark that reads "Nippon"—the Japanese word for Japan—
suggests that a doll was made prior to the Second World War.
These dolls are becoming increasingly more valuable along with
other Nippon collectibles.

Little Bright Eyes and Peero

Description
Googly dolls with bisque heads and molded and painted features. Googly eyes, closed smiling mouths. Pink oilcloth shoes. Left: Little Bright Eyes has molded and painted brown topknot, blue intaglio eyes, bent limbs. Wears white dress with floral trim. Right: Peero has short blond wig, blue glass sleep-eyes. Original costume of pink bonnet, bib trimmed in red and yellow, yellow and white dress with red plastic buttons and pink stockings.

Materials, Marks, and Dimensions
Left: Bisque head, composition body and limbs. "GB252/German A3/0M/DRMR" imprinted on neck. Right: Bisque head; composition body; wood and composition limbs. "GB/253/Germany/A310M" imprinted on head. Height: 12″ (left); 10½″ (right).

Maker, Origin, and Period
Armand Marseille. Germany. Left: c. 1915. Right: c. 1920.

Comment
Googly dolls are characterized by their sweet impish faces, toddler-shaped bodies, and side-glancing eyes. Also known as "goo-goo eyes," "goggle eyes," "roguish eyes," and "eccentric eyes," this amusing feature appears on many dolls made between 1910 and 1925 and was the trademark of the well-loved comic-strip character Barney Google. He was featured in "Married Life," a comic-strip published by the *Chicago Herald*, and was the subject of the 1920 Billy Rose hit song, "Barney Google with the Goo-Goo-Googly Eyes."

Hints for Collectors
Googly dolls were produced in many versions, with painted glass eyes, wigs, or molded hair. They are very desirable collectibles that bring high prices.

German character baby

Description
Baby doll with bisque head and blond mohair wig. Blue glass sleep-eyes, open mouth showing 2 teeth. Ball-jointed body. Starfish-shaped hands. Original costume of lavender and white checked cotton romper with embroidered lavender flowers. Lavender piping on white collar; white cuffs and belt. Matching lace-trimmed cap.

Materials, Marks, and Dimensions
Bisque head, composition body and limbs. "K [star trademark] R Simon & Halbig 126 Germany" marked on back of head. Height: 8¾".

Maker, Origin, and Period
Head by Simon & Halbig. Body manufactured and distributed by Kämmer & Reinhardt. Germany. c. 1910–20.

Comment
Simon & Halbig manufactured many of the heads for Kämmer & Reinhardt's baby dolls. Collectors sometimes mistakenly attribute these dolls to only Simon & Halbig because the K & R mark is often obscured by a wig, while the S & H mark is usually visible at the base of the head. On this doll, however, both marks are imprinted on the back of the head.

Hints for Collectors
Look for the rare Simon & Halbig/Kämmer & Reinhardt character baby that could lower and raise its arms while crying "Mama." Some of these dolls had metal devices that locked the eyes in an open position when the babies were laid to one side. Eyes were released when the dolls were tilted in the opposite direction. Always check the working order of eye mechanisms; repairing a faulty device can be expensive and time-consuming.

Biskoline baby

Description
Character baby doll with blue eyes and open-closed mouth. Fully jointed body with bent limbs. Wears pink cotton romper. Molded pink socks, black shoes with orange soles.

Materials, Marks, and Dimensions
Biskoline. Stork trademark embossed on head. "T.M./The Parsons-Jackson Co./Cleveland Ohio" embossed on back. Height: 13¾".

Maker, Origin, and Period
Parsons-Jackson Co. Cleveland, Ohio. c. 1910–19.

Comment
In the late 19th and early 20th centuries, many dollmakers experimented with such new materials as gutta-percha, rubber, and celluloid in the hope of producing an unbreakable doll. However, most of the substances proved more perishable than the porcelain products they were supposed to replace. The Parsons-Jackson Company is reputed to have spent 8 years developing the material biskoline. Their advertisements claimed, it "has no surface color to wear off, will never crack, break, surface chip or peel, one year guarantee." Although time has proven these claims extravagant, the firm's first dolls were marketed successfully in 1910. By 1913 Parsons-Jackson was producing 56 versions of fully jointed, straight-limb, and bent-limb biskoline dolls.

Hints for Collectors
Other registered trademarks for Parsons-Jackson dolls are "K K K" and "Biskoline." Molded shoes and socks, like those pictured here, are rare and increase a doll's value.

Description
Infant dolls with molded and painted features. Toddler-type
bodies. Left: Walking doll has painted hair, curved arms.
Legs swing from hips. Right: Doll has bald head; jointed limbs.

Materials, Marks, and Dimensions
All-wood with steel springs. Left: Schoenhut circle marked on
back of head. Large "C" inscribed in center, "Schoenhut 1919"
printed on rim. "Schoenhut doll pat. Jan. 17th 1911 U.S.A."
marked on shoulder. Blue stamp beneath says "patent applied
for." Right: "Schoenhut Doll" marked on back of shoulder.
Height: 11″ (left); 10½″ (right).

Maker, Origin, and Period
A. Schoenhut & Co. Philadelphia, Pennsylvania. Left: c. 1919–
25. Right: c. 1913.

Comment
Note that the heads of the dolls illustrated are almost identical
except for painted hair on the doll at left. Such naturalistic baby
heads were designed and copyrighted by the Italian artist
Adolph Graziana; Harry Schoenhut obtained the copyright in
1913 and sold them bald, with a wig, or with painted hair. The
curved arms of the walking doll on the left were made by fitting 2
pieces of wood together at the elbow, a technique perfected by
Schoenhut in 1913. Schoenhut often put infant doll heads on
toddler-type bodies.

Hints for Collectors
The walking doll was one of the few Schoenhut figures made
without holes in the soles of the feet. The soles of its shoes were
angled so that the doll could walk easily.

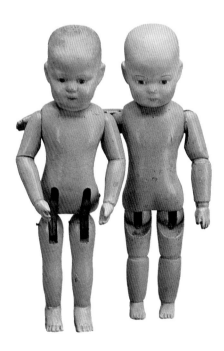

Boy and Girl Dolls: China and Bisque

 Just as 19th-century writers and artists idealized children in their works, so too did European dollmakers. The bébé, introduced in France about 1870, and the character child doll, developed in Germany at the turn of the century, represent some of the finest bisque products of that era.

Manufacture of Bisque Heads

Bisque is an unglazed, mat-finished porcelain made from kaolin clay tinted in various shades. Its quality ranges from the very smooth, translucent grade seen in the heads of the finest dolls to the coarse, grainy variety used in cheaper examples. Either of 2 standard methods was used to form the heads. In one, bisque paste was kneaded, rolled out, cut in squares, and pressed into plaster molds. In the other, a liquid bisque mixture was poured into the molds. When the heads were removed from the molds, sockets for glass eyes were cut, and ears, unless molded, were applied. The heads were stacked in a kiln and fired for about 27 hours; once cool, they were sanded smooth. Next, facial details were painted and then fired at a low temperature. (China heads were made in similar fashion but glazed in an additional firing.) Finally, the eyes, if glass, were inserted, some with patented mechanisms to control their movement. In France cork pates were placed over the open crowns, while in Germany cardboard or plaster ones were often used; these were covered by wigs of human hair, mohair, or lamb's wool.

French Dollmakers

At its peak in the 1870s and '80s, the French dollmaking industry was dominated by such distinguished firms as Jumeau, Bru, Huret, and Steiner, and the expertly crafted, stylishly dressed bébé epitomized the era. Made to represent a young child between the ages of about 6 and 12, the bébé usually had a bisque head and a composition, kid, or wooden body with childlike proportions. By the end of the 19th century French dollmakers were overshadowed by their competitors in Germany. In an effort to regain a share of the market they had lost, the Société Française de Fabrication de Bébés & Jouets (SFBJ), a syndicate of French manufacturers, was formed in 1899. Though many fine dolls continued to be made, quality on the whole was sacrificed once cheaper materials and mass production were adopted in the interest of keeping costs down.

German Dollmakers

The centers of the German doll industry were located primarily in the regions of Thuringia and Bavaria. Among the most respected companies were Simon & Halbig, Kämmer & Reinhardt, J. D. Kestner, Armand Marseille, and Gebrüder Heubach. Perhaps their greatest contribution was the so-called character doll, noted for expressive facial features modeled after real children.

20th-Century Bisque Dolls

During the First World War, when German manufacture of bisque dolls was curtailed, a few English and American firms attempted to fill the gap. The Fulper Pottery in New Jersey, for instance, briefly created bisque heads based on popular German examples. European production resumed after the war, but as the 20th century advanced, bisque was eventually replaced by inexpensive, unbreakable materials.

Gesland bébés

Description
Girl dolls with bisque socket heads and swivel necks. Wigs of human hair. Brown glass paperweight eyes. Heavy brows, closed red mouths. Stockinet-covered bodies over jointed metal frameworks. Left: Dark brown hair. Right: Auburn hair, pierced ears with clear glass bead earrings.

Materials, Marks, and Dimensions
Bisque heads; cloth bodies and upper arms over metal frames; composition shoulder plates, lower arms, and legs. Left: "FG/8" within ribbon design incised on back of head. "E Gesland S.P.D.E. 5 Rue Beranger 5 Paris" printed on body. Right: "Bébé E Gesland Brev S.G.D.G. 5 Rue Beranger 5 Paris" printed on back of body; mark on head identical to that on doll at left. Height: 19¼" (left); 15" (right).

Maker, Origin, and Period
Heads: Possibly by François Gauthier or Fernard Gaultier. Bodies made in Germany for E. Gesland. France. c. 1880–90.

Comment
The bodies of these dolls are jointed in such a way that, as advertisements claimed, "knees and elbows move exactly like those of the human body." According to a recently discovered document, their unique jointed metal framework was patented in Germany, suggesting that the bodies were imported by Gesland and stamped with that company's trademark.

Hints for Collectors
There is some question about the attribution of the heads of these dolls, which are marked "FG." Characterized by plump cheeks and full, outlined lips, they were long thought to be the work of Fernand Gaultier, but are now ascribed to a François Gauthier.

Huret bébé

Description
Bébé with bisque socket head and wig of auburn human hair.
Blue painted eyes with shadowed lids, rouged cheeks, closed
mouth. Body jointed at waist with kid strip. Wears beige silk
dress with silk sash and lace overskirt. 2 underskirts, white
cotton pantaloons. Silk socks, brown leather shoes.

Materials, Marks, and Dimensions
Bisque head; wooden torso jointed with kid; wooden limbs; metal
hands. "HURET/68 RUE DE LA BOÉTIE" incised on doll's back.
Height: 18½".

Maker, Origin, and Period
Maison Huret. France. c. 1870–80.

Comment
Beginning in the 1860s and '70s, French doll companies competed
vigorously to produce bisque- and china-head dolls with the most
naturalistic heads and jointed bodies. The French firm of Maison
Huret experimented with many materials and patented several
designs for finely constructed, lifelike figures. Huret's wooden
doll bodies were well known for their excellent tongue-and-
groove joints. The round-faced bébé shown here has a 2-piece
torso jointed at the waist with kid, enabling her to sit down.
Other Huret innovations were not so successful; for instance, the
firm manufactured dolls of a rubberlike substance known as
gutta-percha, which had to be abandoned because it became
brittle and cracked with age.

Hints for Collectors
Although this doll's body was repainted, the surface is showing
signs of wear. While an unretouched example is, of course,
preferable, this doll's desirable qualities, particularly her fine
body construction, more than compensate for her restoration.

Description

Girl dolls with bisque heads and ball-jointed bodies. Left: Flange neck. Blond mohair wig, blue glass paperweight eyes, closed mouth, pierced ears with white glass and gilt-metal earrings. Wears white cotton smock and pantaloons, white socks, and black imitation-leather shoes. Right: Socket head. Reddish-blond wig of human hair, brown glass paperweight eyes, closed mouth, pierced ears with pink glass and gilt-metal earrings. Wears white cotton dress with pink satin sash. White cotton underskirt, stockings, and cloth slippers.

Materials, Marks, and Dimensions

Bisque heads, composition bodies and limbs. Left: "O/B [illegible mark] S.G.D.G." on back of head, Schmitt trademark on buttock. Paper store label on stomach reads "AU NAIN BLEU/E. CHAUVIÈRE/Boul'd des Capucines, 27/PARIS." Right: "5/[Schmitt trademark]" on back of neck. "JUMEAU/MÉDAILLE D'OR/PARIS" on torso. Height: 14½" (left); 13½" (right).

Maker, Origin, and Period

Schmitt & Fils. France. c. 1875–90.

Comment

The French firm of Schmitt & Fils received patents for many improvements in its dolls' bisque and wax-over-composition heads, which are beautifully modeled, and have deep paperweight eyes set off by eyeshadow.

Hints for Collectors

The trademark Schmitt & Fils used both on the heads and lower torsos of its dolls consisted of a pair of crossed hammers and the initials "SCH" within a shield; however, not all Schmitt dolls were so marked. The body of the doll at right was made by Jumeau.

Jumeau bébé

Description
Girl doll with bisque head. Reddish-brown wig of human hair,
blue glass paperweight eyes, closed mouth. Ball-jointed body.
Wears tan cloak with rust brocade trim; pale blue ruffled silk and
lace dress tied at waist with white satin ribbon. Large straw hat.
Lace-trimmed cotton underskirt and pantaloons, white silk
stockings, and pale blue leather shoes with composition buttons
and white silk tassels. Strings at torso terminate in pink and blue
glass knobs and operate cry mechanism when pulled.

Materials, Marks, and Dimensions
Bisque head, composition body and limbs. "JUMEAU/MÉDAILLE
D'OR/PARIS" marked on back. Height: 16½".

Maker, Origin, and Period
Jumeau. France. c. 1870–80.

Comment
As a means of advertising, Emile Jumeau sometimes enclosed
small illustrated pamphlets in his dolls' boxes. The text extolled
the virtues of Jumeau bébés, while describing German dolls in
the most contemptuous terms. In one of these booklets, a doll
says, "I am unbreakable, a priceless quality, which I inherit from
my father, M. Jumeau, the best of fathers and the most famous
of manufacturers. . . . I am the happiest of babies to have as my
little mother a girl so nice as you."

Hints for Collectors
Experienced collectors sometimes knowingly buy copies of
Jumeau bébés made by reputable dollmakers as examples of top-
quality doll manufacture. These interesting facsimiles, which are
incised with the dollmakers' names, are, of course, much less
costly than originals.

Bru bébé

Description

Girl doll with bisque shoulder-head and swivel neck. Original blond mohair wig has been cut short. Blue blown-glass eyes, closed mouth, pierced ears. Molded bosom. Original wine-colored satin dress with ivory satin and lace trim. White cotton underslip and pantaloons trimmed with lace. Ivory satin bonnet with lace and ribbon trim, red glass and metal drop earrings. Red net stockings, dark brown leather shoes with metal buckles.

Materials, Marks, and Dimensions

Bisque shoulder-head, lower arms, and hands; kid over wood upper arms; kid body and legs. "6" marked on head and right shoulder, "BRU JNE" on left shoulder, "BRU JNE Paris" marked on soles of shoes. Height: 18½".

Maker, Origin, and Period

Bru Jne & Cie. France. After 1883.

Comment

Founded by Casimir Bru in 1866, the French firm of Bru Jne & Cie won several gold medals for its dolls under the skillful direction of H. Chevrot, who ran the company from 1883 to 1889. The finest Bru dolls have heads that fit into shoulder plates with well-modeled breasts. Painted with great delicacy, their faces often have a wistful beauty.

Hints for Collectors

Casimir Bru and his successors aimed for the highest quality by limiting production, and thus made fewer dolls than their rival firm, Jumeau. Bru dolls are relatively scarce and, because of their fine craftsmanship, bring the highest prices. They can often be distinguished from Jumeau dolls by their molded shoulder plates and bosoms as well as bisque arms and hands.

Jumeau bébé

Description
Girl doll with bisque head and original blond mohair wig. Large blue blown-glass eyes, applied pierced ears, open-closed mouth in laughing smile showing molded upper teeth. Jointed body with swivel wrists. Original costume of pale green floral brocade coat and dress with pink insert at skirt; embroidered red velvet trim and cuffs. Large gold-colored gathered fabric hat with upturned brim trimmed in coral piping. Pink socks and satin shoes with leather soles.

Materials, Marks, and Dimensions
Bisque head, composition body and limbs. Back of head stamped "DÉPOSÉ/TÊTE JUMEAU/Bte. S.G.D.G./12"; body stamped "JUMEAU/MÉDAILLE D'OR/PARIS"; soles of shoes marked "BÉBÉ/JUMEAU/MÉD. D'OR 1878 [within rectangle]/PARIS/DÉPOSÉ." Height: 22″.

Maker, Origin, and Period
Jumeau. France. c. 1878–1900.

Comment
During the prosperous 1870s and '80s, men and women of the growing upper middle class dressed in the very latest fashions. Children, too, were stylishly attired, and so were their dolls. The great success of Jumeau's dolls derived in part from their elaborate outfits, which appealed to the prevalent taste for display and finery.

Hints for Collectors
When choosing a Jumeau doll, beware of altered marks, unmarked reproductions, and Jumeau bodies that are joined to heads made by less distinguished French manufacturers. Beginning collectors are advised to buy rare, expensive dolls only from established dealers who will guarantee that their dolls are authentic.

Jumeau bébé

Description
Girl doll with bisque swivel head and short blond mohair wig.
Blue glass paperweight eyes, open-closed mouth with teeth,
pierced ears. Ball-jointed body, one-piece wrists and ankles. Doll
reclothed in authentic period outfit of brown felt hat, brown and
tan wool and satin suit with ceramic buttons, white cotton
underskirt and pantaloons, striped cotton socks, and leather
boots with brass buttons and silk tassels.

Materials, Marks, and Dimensions
Bisque head, composition body and limbs. "E.7 J." incised on
back of head, "JUMEAU/MÉDAILLE D'OR/PARIS" on back of body.
Height: 16½".

Maker, Origin, and Period
Jumeau. France. c. 1880.

Comment
Emile Jumeau claimed to have invented the bébé, and this
exquisite doll is typical of his early examples. The eyes, made of
the same blown glass used for paperweights, are unusually
detailed and luminous. Jumeau described these features in his
advertisements as "human." Perhaps this is why collectors refer
to early dolls of this type as "portrait dolls," although they were
not modeled after specific individuals.

Hints for Collectors
Collectors should not assume that a Jumeau doll with the date
1878 on its back was made in that year. The mark refers to the
gold medal won by Jumeau at the Paris Exposition of 1878 and
was used on his dolls for many years afterward. Though in
matted condition, the original wig on this doll is still an asset. A
badly matted wig can sometimes be untangled by a professional
at a doll hospital.

Belton-type bébé

Description
Girl doll with bisque head; 2 holes in crown. Blond wig of human hair, blue glass eyes, closed mouth, pierced ears. Ball-jointed body and limbs. Original costume of burgundy satin jumper over lace-trimmed pink cotton blouse, matching hat, 2 white cotton underskirts, lace-trimmed white cotton pantaloons, white cotton socks, and brown leather shoes with green cotton ribbon ties.

Materials, Marks, and Dimensions
Bisque head; composition body and limbs; wooden joints. Height: 10″.

Maker, Origin, and Period
Maker unknown. France or Germany. c. 1875–90.

Comment
Though unmarked, this doll has facial features that are typical of Belton-type examples, as well as the characteristic holes in the flattened area of the crown. These holes were designed for stringing the head to the body, and sometimes as many as 4 were used. The heads of some similar dolls are marked with the letter "B," but there is no further evidence that Belton—briefly in partnership with Jumeau in the 1840s—made them. The doll shown here is one of very few Belton-types still dressed in its original clothing.

Hints for Collectors
This doll's head is badly cracked, but given the rarity of Belton-type dolls, a collector may nonetheless wish to buy such a damaged figure in order to complete a collection. If a perfect example is later found, the collector then faces the challenge of trying to sell the damaged doll.

Description
Girl doll with bisque head. Wig of golden brown human hair in long corkscrew curls. Blue glass paperweight eyes. Painted lashes and heavy brows, closed mouth. Jointed body. Wears ecru satin and lace dress with red velvet belt and mother-of-pearl buttons in back. Lace-trimmed white cotton underskirt and pantaloons. Straw hat lined in satin and covered with silk flowers and ribbons. Beige silk stockings and white leather shoes with silver metal buckles.

Materials, Marks, and Dimensions
Bisque head, composition body. Height: 22½″.

Maker, Origin, and Period
Jumeau. France. c. 1880–1900.

Comment
Collectors refer to the Jumeau doll pictured here as a "long-face" type because her face is more elongated than those of other bébés the firm produced. The doll is also known as a "Cody" Jumeau because of a persistent but unproven story that Buffalo Bill Cody purchased such a doll during a trip to Paris in 1889. "Long-face" or "Cody" Jumeaus are generally unmarked.

Hints for Collectors
Trademarks used by French dollmakers were first registered in 1885, though doll patents began to be issued several decades earlier. In the absence of makers' marks, energetic collectors often try to identify the manufacturers of their dolls by examining the materials and construction, and then researching when those particular methods of construction were invented. However, manufacturers did not always register their innovations right away.

Belton-type bébé

Description
Girl doll with bisque head and blond mohair wig. Solid crown
with several small holes. Large blue glass paperweight eyes.
Heavy brows, mouth with lips slightly parted; pierced ears with
blue glass earrings. Ball-jointed body. Wears beige satin dress
with ecru lace overskirt and blue ribbon trim, matching hat
adorned with flowers. Lace-trimmed white cotton underskirt and
pantaloons. Beige silk stockings, green imitation-leather shoes.

Materials, Marks, and Dimensions
Bisque head, composition body and limbs. "137/14" inscribed on
back of neck. Height: 24″.

Maker, Origin, and Period
Maker unknown. Probably France or Germany. c. 1885.

Comment
Belton-type dolls have long puzzled researchers. They have been
associated with M. Belton, the French dollmaker who worked
with Jumeau during the 1840s and is thought to have originated a
way of stringing dolls' heads through 1 to 4 small holes in the
pate. However, it has not been proven that Belton was
responsible for this invention; many French and German firms
produced such heads, which are either unmarked or bear only a
mold or size number. Belton-type dolls are rarely marked on the
body.

Hints for Collectors
Belton-type dolls are best identified by the holes in the tops of
their heads. Like the example illustrated here, a number of them
have mouths with slightly parted lips. Most inexpensive Belton-
type dolls made after 1900 have bisque heads with crude
composition bodies and straight unjointed limbs.

Description

Girl dolls. Large seated doll has bisque shoulder-head and swivel neck. Blond mohair wig with bangs and corkscrew curls. Blue blown-glass eyes, closed mouth, pierced ears. Wears white dress with elaborate embroidery on skirt, and white satin sash. 3 underskirts, white socks, and brown leather shoes with metal buckles. Small doll held in lap has bisque head with blond lamb's-wool wig. Blue blown-glass eyes, closed mouth, pierced ears. Wears white dotted swiss dress, lace underskirt and pantaloons, white silk socks, and brown leather shoes.

Materials, Marks, and Dimensions

Large doll: Bisque shoulder-head, lower arms, and hands; kid body and legs. "A 10 T" incised on back of head, "AT" on shoulder. Small doll: Bisque head, composition body and limbs. "A 2 T" incised on back of head. Height: 22″ (large doll); 9½″ (small doll).

Maker, Origin, and Period

Probably A. Thuillier. France. c. 1880.

Comment

Although it has never been proven that the mark "AT" refers to A. Thuillier, it is generally accepted that dolls bearing these initials were his creations. Thuillier worked in Paris from 1875 to 1890, producing bébés with bisque heads attached to jointed bodies that were made of kid, composition, or wood. The best of his dolls are as fine as those by Bru.

Hints for Collectors

Dolls attributed to Thuillier are marked on their heads with the initials "AT," and sometimes with numerals that represent size. These range from approximately 2 to 14, corresponding to about 12″ to 29″. A few Thuillier examples are initialed on their shoes.

Lanternier bébé

Description
Girl doll with bisque swivel head. Blond mohair wig, blue glass eyes, open-closed mouth showing teeth. Jointed body and limbs. Wears white cotton dress and white bonnet with gauze trim; white cotton underskirt and pantaloons. Pink cotton socks, tan suede moccasins with blue ribbon ties.

Materials, Marks, and Dimensions
Bisque head, composition body and limbs. "Déposé/Fabrication/Francaise [in block]/Caprice/No 12/A.L. & Cie/Limoges" marked on back of head. Height: 25½".

Maker, Origin, and Period
A. Lanternier & Cie. France. c. 1921–30.

Comment
The highly colored coarse bisque of the 20th-century bébé shown here does not compare with the smooth pale bisque of fine older French examples. Although this doll is attractive and well made, the House of Lanternier turned out many that were less desirable, as did other firms in the Limoges region. This may surprise those collectors familiar with the famous china produced in Limoges. Lanternier studied the pottery and porcelain business at the firm of Wedgwood, but his bisque rarely met the standard set by that well-known English company.

Hints for Collectors
Dolls made by Lanternier and other Limoges firms bring high prices because many people want to own a French doll, regardless of its quality. A Lanternier example would be a good addition to a collection focusing primarily on the history of French dollmaking.

Le Parisien

Description
Girl doll with bisque head and long blond wig. Blue glass sleep-eyes. Painted lashes and heavy brows, closed mouth. Wears white cotton gown with eyelet embroidery, bone buttons, and scalloped hem. Lace bonnet tied with pink satin ribbon. 2 lace-trimmed white cotton underskirts and pantaloons. White silk socks, blue imitation-leather shoes with metal buckles and pale blue ribbon ties.

Materials, Marks, and Dimensions
Bisque head, composition body and limbs. Back of head marked "A5 Le Parisien." "BÉBÉ 'LE PARISIEN'/MÉDAILLE D'OR/PARIS" stamped on body. Height: 12¼".

Maker, Origin, and Period
Jules Nicholas Steiner. France. c. 1892.

Comment
In 1892 Amédée Lafosse succeeded Jules Steiner as head of the well-known Steiner doll firm. He advertised the company's diversified line of bébés, including walking, talking, and mechanical dolls, and registered patents for "Le Parisien," shown here, and for "Premier Pas," a walking bébé. Both have unusually heavy bisque heads, which Lafosse claimed were unbreakable. Unfortunately, these dolls turned out to be just as fragile as any other bisque examples.

Hints for Collectors
The marks "Le Parisien" and "Le Petit Parisien, Bébé Steiner" were occasionally used respectively on the heads and bodies of these dolls. Steiner mechanical dolls, however, are marked only on the mechanisms inside their torsos. Like this example, most Steiner dolls have each big toe separated from the rest, and fingers of equal length except for the thumbs.

Fulper doll

Description
Girl doll with bisque shoulder-head. Blond mohair wig with pink bow, blue glass eyes, open mouth showing tongue and 2 large upper teeth. Jointed body. Wears white cotton dress trimmed with embroidered ruffles, embroidered white cotton slip, lace-trimmed drawers, ribbed socks, and oilcloth shoes.

Materials, Marks, and Dimensions
Bisque shoulder-head, lower arms, and hands; kid body. "FULPER" incised vertically within outline on back of head, "S-10" appears beneath. Height: 19¼".

Maker, Origin, and Period
Fulper Pottery Co. Flemington, New Jersey. c. 1920.

Comment
German bisque dolls were unobtainable in this country during the First World War. In an attempt to capture the wartime market, Fulper, an American firm known chiefly for its art pottery, produced bisque dolls' heads by using the molds of Armand Marseille and of other German firms. A variety of dolls were manufactured in collaboration with the Horsman Company of New York; these sometimes bear both firms' marks. In 1919 Fulper's first bisque dolls were advertised in the trade magazine *Playthings*, and numerous models were available by 1920. When German dolls were imported again in 1921, the demand for Fulper examples dwindled and the company stopped producing them.

Hints for Collectors
Although Fulper dolls are not as fine as German bisque figures, they are sought after for their historical value and rarity. Dolls with intaglio eyes and molded hair are more in demand than traditional versions with glass eyes and wigs.

Girl doll

Description
Girl doll with bisque swivel head. Long blond wig of human hair, blue glass sleep-eyes with lashes of human hair, open-closed mouth with 4 upper teeth, and pierced ears. Ball-jointed body and limbs. Wears low-waisted pale blue silk dress with pearl buttons and pleated flounce; cotton petticoat and challis slip. High cotton socks and white leather shoes with metal buckles.

Materials, Marks, and Dimensions
Bisque head, composition body and limbs. "46" incised on back of head, "W" on forehead under wig. Height: 18″.

Maker, Origin, and Period
Head: Simon & Halbig. Body: Kämmer & Reinhardt. Germany. c. 1900.

Comment
Simon & Halbig made exquisitely modeled bisque dolls' heads for many companies, including Kämmer & Reinhardt, which produced the body of the doll shown here. The firm was also known for making beautiful eyes. Eye materials and movements have always been important in dollmaking, and more patents were recorded for these than for any other doll-related innovations. Simon & Halbig registered numerous eye patents, including one in 1890 for the first "flirting eyes." In succeeding years they developed many improvements in sleep-eyes, among them innovations in the mechanisms for opening and shutting and for side-to-side movements.

Hints for Collectors
When possible, collectors should examine a doll's eyes to make sure that they are in working order. Some old dolls have sleep-eyes that no longer move because their control mechanisms were considered too costly or troublesome to repair.

Florodora

Description
Girl doll with bisque shoulder-head. Long curly brown wig
with side part and red satin bow. Blue glass eyes, rosy chubby
cheeks, 4 upper teeth in open mouth. Wears lace-trimmed white
dress with flounced yoke, sleeves, and hem, and red satin sash.
Lace-trimmed white pantaloons and underslip, long white
stockings. Red oilcloth shoes with pink bows and gold metal
buttons.

Materials, Marks, and Dimensions
Bisque shoulder-head and hands; kid body and arms; cloth lower
legs. Mark on shoulder reads "A0M/Florodora/Armand Marseille/
Made in Germany." Height: 21¼".

Maker, Origin, and Period
Armand Marseille. Germany c. 1901.

Comment
"Florodora" was a trademark registered in Germany for dolls
with kid bodies and bisque heads manufactured by Armand
Marseille from 1901 to about 1909 and exported mainly to
America. These dolls appealed to the public because of their
large pretty eyes and gentle expressions. Most were sold in
cheap clothing or in a simple chemise.

Hints for Collectors
Armand Marseille produced numerous dolls' heads for other
firms. Collectors have found more early 20th-century Armand
Marseille heads than those of any other manufacturer. The most
common mold numbers are 370 for shoulder-heads and 390 for
socket heads. Florodora shoulder-heads were combined with the
kid bodies usually reserved for finer dolls, while the more
plentiful Florodora socket heads were mounted on jointed
composition or wooden bodies.

Dolly Dimple

Description
Girl doll with bisque head. Brown mohair wig with center part and long corkscrew curls. Blue glass eyes, open mouth showing 4 upper teeth. Prominent dimples in chin and cheeks. Jointed body. Wears cotton floral print dress with ruffled neckline and yoke, lace trim, and blue satin sash. Lace-trimmed white cotton underskirt and pantaloons. Tan cotton stockings and brown leather shoes with cloth laces.

Materials, Marks, and Dimensions
Bisque head; composition body and hands; wooden arms. "Dolly Dimple/H/Germany/14" incised on head. Height: 26½".

Maker, Origin, and Period
Hamburger & Co. Germany. c. 1907–13.

Comment
Dolly Dimple typifies some of the character dolls that became popular in the first decades of the 20th century. Her open mouth, deeply molded dimples, slightly furrowed brow, and expressively articulated hands create the animated quality that German dollmakers in particular strove for during this period.

Hints for Collectors
Hamburger & Company, a Berlin doll manufacturer and distributor, responded to the growing character-doll trend with Dolly Dimple, for which it registered a trademark in Germany in 1907. Dolly Dimple represented quite a departure from the company's 1903 Marguerite doll, a popular decorative bisque-head lady with a molded floral hat (see 308). Such diversity indicates that business-minded dollmakers aimed to create products that would appeal to a variety of tastes.

Kestner girl doll

Description
Girl doll with bisque socket head and long blond mohair wig. Blond fur eyebrows, blue glass eyes with dark eyelashes, open mouth with 4 upper teeth. Fully jointed body. Original light blue satin dress with lace collar and cuffs; lace-trimmed bib and apron with blue satin bow at waist. 2 white cotton slips, blue satin underskirt, and lace-trimmed white cotton pantaloons. Leather shoes with metal buckles and satin laces.

Materials, Marks, and Dimensions
Bisque head, composition body. "F ½ made in Germany 10½/196" incised on back of head. "Germany 3" stamped on body in red. Height: 23".

Maker, Origin, and Period
J. D. Kestner, Jr. Germany. c. 1910.

Comment
In 1910 Kestner patented eyebrows, called "fur brows," made of mohair or human hair. As a realistic touch, hair was inserted at the brow line through slits incised in the bisque head. This emphasis on naturalism was also evident in the company's line of character baby dolls produced about the same time.

Hints for Collectors
The marks on Kestner dolls may be confusing. Many of the heads are incised with the initials "JDK" and with a letter and a number that indicate the approximate circumference of the head. An additional 3-digit number generally represents the mold or model used. Some dolls that vary slightly in appearance—one, for instance, may have an extra molded curl, another an extra dimple—bear the identical number because it refers to the model on which the doll was based rather than to the mold in which it was cast.

Bleuette

Description
Girl doll with bisque head. Blond mohair wig with braids, blue glass side-glancing eyes, painted lashes, open mouth showing upper row of teeth. Jointed body. Original costume of white organdy dress and pale blue organdy apron trimmed in lace. White cotton underskirt and pantaloons. Pale blue imitation-leather shoes tied with ribbons.

Materials, Marks, and Dimensions
Bisque head, composition body and limbs. "UNIS FRANCE 301" marked on head. Paper label attached to apron reads "Marque/Déposée/BLEUETTE/18 Rue Jacob/PARIS VIe." Height: 11½".

Maker, Origin, and Period
SFBJ. (Société Française de Fabrication de Bébés & Jouets). France. c. 1910.

Comment
In 1912, SFBJ advertised that it was manufacturing 5 million dolls a year at its Vincennes factory alone. The undressed dolls were sent from there to Paris, where they were costumed in fashionable outfits that were often more beautiful than the dolls themselves. SFBJ dolls range from extremely fine to quite mediocre. Bleuette, shown here, is an average example. Her mouth, awkwardly shaped and boldly painted in a dark shade of red, detracts somewhat from her overall appearance.

Hints for Collectors
Some SFBJ dolls are marked "UNIS FRANCE," which probably stands for "Union Nationale Inter-Syndicale." Bleuette dolls are quite common, but very few still possess their original labels. One such doll, with marks and face identical to the example shown here, has sleep-eyes and an outfit from the Alsace region in France.

Armand Marseille girl doll

Description
Girl doll with bisque socket head. Blond wig, blue sleep-eyes
with lashes, 4 upper teeth in open mouth. Fully jointed body.
Wears pink and white dress with lace trim. Ribbed pink cotton
stockings and white shoes with gold metal buckles.

Materials, Marks, and Dimensions
Bisque head; composition body and limbs; wooden joints.
"Armand Marseille/Germany/390/A 2½ M" incised on head.
Height: 20″.

Maker, Origin, and Period
Armand Marseille. Germany. c. 1910.

Comment
Dolls by Armand Marseille are in plentiful supply. At one time,
the firm issued more than 1000 of them a week. The company
specialized in the manufacture of dolls that were pretty enough
to please most little girls and cheap enough to suit their parents'
pocketbooks. While some outstanding dolls were made, the firm's
output varied greatly in quality. Many of the large, jointed
examples had poorly made bodies, amateurish detailing, and
crude coloring. The figure pictured here was produced in great
numbers and is thus commonly found today. Her bisque head is
of fine quality, but the "dolly" facial features are not especially
noteworthy.

Hints for Collectors
Armand Marseille incised a variety of names and marks on its
dolls' heads, using the initials AM to denote the firm. Dolls
marked "A & M," however, were made by M. J. Moehling,
another German manufacturer active at the time. Collectors
should be careful not to confuse the trademarks of these 2 firms.

Gretchen

Description
Girl doll with bisque head. Blond mohair wig. Incised blue
eyes, rosy cheeks, and closed pouting mouth. Fully jointed body.
Wears low-waisted pink cotton dress trimmed with panels of lace
and blue satin ribbon. Lace collar and lace-trimmed sleeves; blue
satin bows at neck and waist. Lace-trimmed white slip and
pantaloons. Large floppy pink cotton hat trimmed with lace and
cloth flowers. Ribbed white stockings and white leather shoes
with ribbon bows and brass buttons.

Materials, Marks, and Dimensions
Bisque head, composition body and limbs. "K [star trademark] R
114" incised on head. Height: 16½".

Maker, Origin, and Period
Kämmer & Reinhardt. Germany. c. 1910–28.

Comment
The firm Kämmer & Reinhardt was well known for fine quality
dolls whose faces reflected the full range of children's moods.
The company called these gay or sulky figures "character dolls,"
a term that has been retained by collectors. Gretchen, the
exquisite doll shown here, with chubby cheeks, a cute little nose,
and pouting expression, was orginally modeled after Reinhardt's
nephew and was also sold dressed as a little boy called Hans.
These dolls wore clothing in the styles of their period, a feature
that further enhanced their popularity.

Hints for Collectors
All of Kämmer & Reinhardt's character dolls are in great
demand, but the little children with sulky expressions,
occasionally referred to as "pouties," are the most treasured.

Kämmer & Reinhardt boy doll

Description
Boy doll with bisque shoulder-head. Short blond wig. Incised
blue eyes and blond raised eyebrows. Turned-up nose, rosy
cheeks, and closed mouth. Wears red velvet jacket with pearl
buttons, long-sleeved white cotton shirt with large flounced
collar, and yellow cotton trousers. Straw hat with black satin
ribbon band. Shoes missing.

Materials, Marks, and Dimensions
Bisque shoulder-head, lower arms, and hands; kid body and legs.
"K [star trademark] R 201" incised on back of head. Height: 20″.

Maker, Origin, and Period
Kämmer & Reinhardt. Germany. c. 1910–20.

Comment
The cherubic little boy shown here has a pensive expression
typical of many character dolls. Modeled after young children,
Kämmer & Reinhardt character dolls were frequently sold
bearing either a boy's or girl's name, depending on the type of
wig worn. Character boy dolls are less numerous than girls.

Hints for Collectors
Highly regarded by collectors, Kämmer & Reinhardt's beautiful
character children are among the most expensive German bisque
dolls. However, many are priced lower than French bisque dolls
of similar quality. German bisque figures are the only group of
prestigious antique dolls that are still relatively affordable,
although there are exceptions, such as some Kestner character
examples, which may sell for several thousand dollars.

Simon & Halbig girl doll

Description
Black girl doll with bisque head. Short black mohair wig, large brown glass sleep-eyes, broad nose; full red lips parted to show 6 tiny teeth in open mouth. Pierced ears have gold loop earrings. Fully jointed body painted black. Wears red and yellow floral print cotton dress trimmed with yellow ribbon at waist and hem, pearl button in back. White cotton slip edged in lace.

Materials, Marks, and Dimensions
Bisque head, enameled composition body. Back of head incised "1358 Germany Simon & Halbig S & H 6." Height: 18″.

Maker, Origin, and Period
Simon & Halbig. Germany. c. 1900–10.

Comment
Simon & Halbig captured the natural beauty of a black child in the realistically modeled features of this rare doll. Her tiny teeth resemble those of the best French dolls. The mold number 1358 is unusual, since most of the company's black dolls were made from molds numbered 739 or 759. A similar Simon & Halbig doll, known as "Willie Lee," bears the same mark but no mold number. It was common practice among German dollmakers to use carefully crafted heads on standard mass-produced bodies; thus the painted composition body of this doll is not of the same fine quality as the delicate baked-color bisque head.

Hints for Collectors
It is rare to find a bisque-head doll made during this period that has such realistic black features. Simon & Halbig black dolls are prized for their historical merit and beauty and are therefore expensive when available.

Just Me dolls

Description
Girl dolls with bisque swivel heads. Jointed bodies, bent limbs.
Left: Blond mohair wig with blue ribbon; blue glass sleep-eyes,
closed mouth. Original ruffled blue organdy dress, white cotton
underskirt and pantaloons, white socks and imitation-leather
shoes. Right: Brown mohair wig with bangs; blue glass side-
glancing sleep-eyes, closed mouth. Wears gold satin dress
decorated with lace and ribbon, 2 white cotton half-skirts, and
pantaloons. Painted brown Mary Jane shoes.

Materials, Marks, and Dimensions
Bisque heads, composition bodies and limbs. Left: "Just Me/
Reg./Germany/310/A 7/0 M" incised on head. Right: "Just Me/
Registered/Germany/310/A 11/0 M" incised on neck. Height: 10″
(left); 7″ (right).

Maker, Origin, and Period
Armand Marseille. Germany. c. 1928.

Comment
Armand Marseille character dolls are among the finest products
of this prolific firm. Collectors especially prize the "Just Me"
dolls, which were popular in their day and are now rare.

Hints for Collectors
Most Armand Marseille dolls are marked with the company's
name or initials, the mold number, head size number, and
sometimes a patent number, as well as with the name of the
distributing firm. Marseille made character dolls from the same
molds for years, but by dressing them or painting their features
differently, or by interchanging heads and bodies, the firm varied
its output. When considering the purchase of a doll, it is usually
acceptable to carefully remove the wig or clothing in order to
inspect the marks.

Poulbots

Description
Girl and boy dolls with bisque heads; jointed bodies and limbs.
Left: Orange mohair wig, brown glass eyes, closed mouth.
Original costume of blue woolen blouse, dark blue short pants,
blue and white checked cotton apron, and brown leather shoes.
Right: Light brown mohair wig, brown glass eyes, closed mouth.
Original costume of red and white woolen polo shirt, gray
herringbone knickers with patch, suspenders, gray herringbone
cap, brown silk socks, and brown leather shoes.

Materials, Marks, and Dimensions
Bisque heads, composition bodies and limbs. Back of both heads
inscribed "SFBJ/239/PARIS/POULBOT." Height: 13″ (left); 13¾″
(right).

Maker, Origin, and Period
SFBJ. (Société Française de Fabrication de Bébés & Jouets).
France. c. 1913.

Comment
Modeled after Parisian street waifs, Poulbots were inexpensive
dolls designed to compete with German character dolls. Gone are
the elaborate outfits and detailed facial modeling of the French
bébés. The tattered clothing and garish wigs of these urchins
endow them with the characteristic appeal of forlorn children.
These dolls were often advertised in pairs, the boy as "un
poulbot" and the girl as "une poulbotte."

Hints for Collectors
Although generally less expensive than 19th-century versions, a
few SFBJ character dolls are rare and thus usually fetch large
sums. Among the rarest are "Laughing Jumeau" (mold #236);
"Twirp" (#237); and "Poulbot" dolls (#239).

SFBJ bébé

Description
Girl doll with bisque head. Blond mohair wig, blue glass eyes, and closed pouting mouth. Wears blue cotton romper suit with large white collar, belt, and cuffs; mother-of-pearl buttons. White cotton undershirt, pants, and socks; white leather sandals with composition buttons.

Materials, Marks, and Dimensions
Bisque head, composition body and limbs. "21 SFBJ 252 Paris 11" marked on back of head. Height: 24½″.

Maker, Origin, and Period
SFBJ (Société Française de Fabrication de Bébés & Jouets). France. c. 1900–25.

Comment
Although the French corporation SFBJ occasionally used German-made dolls' heads and other parts, it did not advertise this fact, and customers assumed that they were buying all-French dolls. Most heads on SFBJ dolls were indeed made in France, but this did not guarantee good quality, since the heads were sometimes mass-produced from inferior bisque and were carelessly modeled.

Hints for Collectors
A large number of SFBJ dolls' heads bear the mold numbers 60 or 301. Character dolls, such as the pouting toddler shown here, usually have numbers from 203 to 252. Collectors consider the character bébés among the best of SFBJ's output and are therefore willing to pay high prices for them.

Century doll

Description
Girl doll. Bisque head with flange neck and molded and painted reddish-blond hair. Blue glass sleep-eyes, closed mouth. Wears red and white cotton print dress over playsuit of same material. Black leather shoes with black cotton laces.

Materials, Marks, and Dimensions
Bisque head; cloth body; composition limbs. "Copr. by Grace C. Rockwell Germany" incised on back of head. Height: 18″.

Maker, Origin, and Period
Designed by Grace Corry (Rockwell). Head probably made by J. D. Kestner, Jr. Germany. Distributed by Century Doll Co. New York City. c. 1925.

Comment
Though they distributed a wide range of dolls, the Century Doll Company specialized in baby dolls, which they called "Century Babies." In 1921 Grace Corry designed Fiji Wiji rag dolls, her first line of dolls for Century, and went on to create a number of child dolls for the firm. These have composition or bisque heads, painted or glass sleep-eyes, cloth bodies, and composition limbs. She also created dolls for the Averill Manufacturing Company, including "Little Brother" and "Little Sister" (*see* 264).

Hints for Collectors
The doll shown here is the most valuable of those designed by Grace Corry for the Century Doll Company. Its skillfully modeled bisque head was probably made by Kestner, since Century was known to have used that company's parts. Collector interest in Kestner products enhances the value of this doll, as does Grace Corry's mark.

Whistling boy doll

Description
Boy doll with bisque shoulder-head. Molded and painted blond hair and blue eyes; open mouth with lips pursed as if whistling. Wears black velvet jacket with lace collar and cuffs, matching pants, white cotton shirt, and purple velvet cap. Black imitation-leather shoes with brass buttons and black cotton laces. Bellows behind wooden block in center of chest causes whistling noise when block is pressed.

Materials, Marks, and Dimensions
Bisque shoulder-head and lower arms; cloth body, upper arms, and legs; wooden mechanism. "4 Germany [square Heubach trademark]/[undecipherable word]" imprinted on back. Height: 11¾".

Maker, Origin, and Period
Gebrüder Heubach. Germany. c. 1914–28.

Comment
This doll whistles through pursed lips when his chest is pressed. Other whistling dolls marketed by various companies at the time included a version made in 1913 by Samstag & Hilder that was almost identical to this one. Another, "Whistling Joe," produced by an unknown German firm, emitted a 2-tone whistle when his stomach was squeezed. In America, Louis Amberg manufactured "Whistling Willie." After suspending production during the First World War, Heubach reissued its whistling doll in 1924, calling him "Whistling Tom."

Hints for Collectors
This whistling boy doll, regarded as one of Heubach's most appealing designs, has lost the identifying paper tag that was originally attached to his clothes, a common occurrence with old dolls.

SFBJ boy doll

Description
Boy doll with bisque head. Blond molded and flocked hair, blue glass eyes, open-closed mouth with 2 molded upper teeth. Jointed body. Wears brown corduroy suit with tan sailor's collar and dickey trimmed in brown braid. Ribbed tan socks and brown leather shoes.

Materials, Marks, and Dimensions
Bisque head; composition body and limbs. "SFBJ 235 Paris" incised on back of head. Height: 17".

Maker, Origin, and Period
SFBJ (Société Française de Fabrication de Bébés & Jouets). France. c. 1910.

Comment
Founded in 1899, SFBJ was a group of French dollmakers that included such notable firms as Jumeau, Bru, Fleischmann & Blödel, and Danel & Cie. These and other makers banded together to compete with the formidable German doll industry, which had captured a large portion of the toy markets in Europe and America.

Hints for Collectors
Almost all SFBJ dolls have bisque heads, jointed composition bodies, and glass eyes rather than painted ones. Wigs were more commonly used than molded hair, except on boy dolls, such as the example shown here. Though open-closed mouths cost more to produce, manufacturers made them to satisfy turn-of-the-century taste; subsequently dolls with closed mouths became less common. Because of their scarcity, late 19th- and early 20th-century closed-mouth examples command a premium today.

Description
Boy dolls with bisque swivel heads and jointed bodies and limbs.
Left: Molded and painted blond hair, blue glass eyes, open mouth
with 2 upper teeth. Wears black cotton suit, white cotton shirt,
red crepe bow tie, black silk stockings, and imitation-leather
shoes. Right: Walking doll with blond flocked hair. Brown glass
eyes; open mouth showing 4 teeth. Wears white shirt, black wool
pants, black cotton socks, and leather shoes. Legs swing forward
and head moves back and forth when pressure is applied to
shoulders.

Materials, Marks, and Dimensions
Bisque heads, composition bodies and limbs. Left: "SFBJ 235
Paris" incised on back of head. Right: "SFBJ 237 Paris" incised
on back of head. Height: 15″ (left); 15¼″ (right).

Maker, Origin, and Period
SFBJ. (Société Française de Fabrication de Bébés & Jouets).
France. c. 1900.

Comment
SFBJ dolls with character faces bear mold numbers between 203
and 252. The dolls shown here, marked 235 and 237, have faces of
fine, delicately colored bisque. Walking figures such as the one
illustrated are rare today.

Hints for Collectors
Some member firms of SFBJ retained their own trademarks,
which usually appeared alongside an SFBJ mark, though
sometimes they appeared alone. Thus, a doll marked Jumeau
may be mistaken for a product of that firm rather than of SFBJ.
A knowledge of the conglomerate's history and an eye for telltale
characteristics—cheaper construction and materials—will help
collectors to distinguish an SFBJ doll.

Heubach boy dolls

Description
Boy dolls with bisque swivel heads and molded and painted blond hair. Blue intaglio eyes with white highlights on lids. Left: Open-closed mouth with molded tongue. Wears white cotton shirt with large lace-trimmed collar, brown faille jacket with brass buttons and cloth ties, brown woolen pants, white cotton socks, and brown leather boots with wooden buttons. Right: Open-closed mouth with 2 lower teeth. Fully jointed body. Wears formal black woolen pinstripe suit, white cotton vest, pleated cotton dress shirt, black satin tie, black cotton socks, and black patent leather shoes with metal buckles.

Materials, Marks, and Dimensions
Left: Bisque head and hands, kid body. "Germany/[square Heubach trademark]" incised on shoulder. Right: Bisque head; composition body; composition and wood limbs. Height: 23″ (left); 19″ (right).

Maker, Origin, and Period
Gebrüder Heubach. Germany. c. 1910.

Comment
Among Heubach's best-selling dolls were those of children with toothy grins and intaglio eyes. The rims around the eyes were usually painted, and white dots were added as highlights on the lids.

Hints for Collectors
Many smiling Heubach character dolls bear mold numbers from 5000 to 8000, with or without the company's sunburst or square trademark. These numbers, easily overlooked, are incised at the bottom of the shoulder plate or, on dolls wearing wigs, at the edge of the crown.

Parian-type male dolls

Description
Male dolls with untinted bisque shoulder-heads; molded and
painted hair with comb marks; rosy cheeks, closed mouths. Left:
Curly black hair, painted blue eyes. Molded white shirtfront with
bow tie. Wears black velvet suit, brown and black brocade vest
with pearl buttons, and black leather shoes with metal buckles.
Right: Blond hair, blue blown-glass eyes. Wears brown wool suit
with velvet trim and black glass buttons; beige silk shirt and
black leather shoes with cloth bows.

Materials, Marks, and Dimensions
Left: Bisque shoulder-head; cloth body and legs; wooden lower
arms. Right: Bisque shoulder-head, arms, and hands; kid body
and legs. Height: 16″ (left); 14½″ (right).

Maker, Origin, and Period
Maker unknown. Probably Germany. c. 1860–70.

Comment
Some male dolls from the 1860s have molded wavy black hair
parted on the side. Blonds, such as the one shown at right, were
less common; his glass eyes make him even rarer. The same
molds were sometimes used for dolls with glass eyes and for
those with painted eyes.

Hints for Collectors
Male dolls of any kind have always constituted a minority and
consequently are rare finds today. Early male china and bisque
dolls seldom have features that distinguish them either as boys
or men; identical dolls are sometimes dressed in boys' or men's
outfits. Many boy dolls became girl dolls through a simple change
in clothing. Girl or lady dolls whose wigs had been cut short by
their mischievous owners were sometimes reclothed as men.

Betsy Sheffield and Little Brother

Description
Girl and boy dolls with bisque shoulder-heads. Left: Betsy Sheffield has blue glass eyes and molded brown hair with bangs, braids, and pink ribbons. Original costume of white pinafore over pink floral print dress. White underclothes. Straw hat. Molded white stockings and black high button shoes. Right: Little Brother has brown glass eyes and molded brown hair. Original 2-piece sailor suit with navy blue collar and black tie and belt. Navy blue hat. Molded black stockings and high button shoes.

Materials, Marks, and Dimensions
Bisque shoulder-heads, lower arms, hands, and legs; cloth bodies. Left: Back of shoulder marked "MDT '53 Betsy." Right: Back of shoulder marked "M. Thompson 1954." Height: 15" (left); 13½" (right).

Maker, Origin, and Period
Martha Thompson. Wellesley, Massachusetts. Left: 1953. Right: 1954.

Comment
The late Martha Thompson, a charter member of the National Institute of American Doll Artists (NIADA), created these dolls for the community church her sister and brother-in-law belonged to in Sheffield, Alabama. Church members costumed the figures in the style of the early 20th century and then sold them at a church function.

Hints for Collectors
Martha Thompson was acclaimed for her outstanding fashion and portrait dolls, including beautiful renditions of Grace Kelly, Princess Caroline of Monaco at age 2, Queen Elizabeth, and Princess Margaret. Many of her dolls are in museums; they rarely appear on the market.

Description
Boy and girl dolls with molded and painted features, hair, and
clothes. Jointed at shoulders with wire. Left: Boy with long curly
blond hair, blue eyes, and closed mouth. White sailor suit with
purple collar, tie, and cuffs. White sailor cap with purple brim.
White socks and purple boots. Right: Girl has wavy blond hair
with pink bow, side-glancing blue eyes, closed mouth. White
dress trimmed in blue. Pink shoes with green bows.

Materials, Marks, and Dimensions
Bisque. Height: 7½″ (left); 7″ (right).

Maker, Origin, and Period
Maker unknown. Germany. c. 1910.

Comment
Dolls such as the pair shown here are sometimes called "fancy
bisques" by collectors. They resemble figurines except that they
are jointed—with pegs, pins, or elastic. Children in particular
collected them because they could be purchased for just a few
pennies, and it was fun trying to obtain many different examples.
All-bisque dolls enjoyed a long reign of popularity. First
introduced in the 1870s, they were made in great numbers and
variety and were still selling well in the 1940s. Quite a few
porcelain and doll manufacturers, including Kestner in Germany,
produced all-bisques, but for unknown reasons many of these are
unmarked. Aside from pictures in toy catalogues, there is still
relatively little information about them.

Hints for Collectors
All-bisque dolls that have swivel heads are the rarest. Those
with molded and painted clothes are also in demand, especially
the older figures in one-piece white underwear with blue or
pink ruffles.

Description
One-piece all-bisque figurines with molded and painted features and clothes. Left: Girl, seated on sled, with arm raised. Blond hair and rosy cheeks. Textured white hood and long-sleeved coat; white mittens and black shoes. Right: Boy with textured hood and snowsuit; white mittens and gray boots.

Materials, Marks, and Dimensions
Bisque. Height: 3½″ (left); 3¼″ (right).

Maker, Origin, and Period
Hertwig & Co. Germany. c. 1920.

Comment
Snow Babies probably evolved from the early 19th-century German candy toys called *Tannenbaumkonfekte*, which were made as Christmas-tree decorations. In imitation of these sugar-coated marzipan dolls, Hertwig & Company created small figurines dressed in hooded snowsuits made of bisque grout—a rough, granular type of porcelain—and sprinkled with glitter sand. Introduced during the 1880s, Hertwig Snow Babies were immediately successful, though mainly as cake decorations, not as dolls. They were so popular between 1906 and 1910 that many German factories copied them. As sales increased, Hertwig also produced figures in pastel colors and in various active poses. The last German-made Snow Babies, along with inferior Japanese copies, appeared in the 1930s.

Hints for Collectors
Snow Babies made before the 1930s do not have any marks. Figures imported to America before 1891 were not required to bear marks of origin, and later dolls were often identified only by the information stamped on their boxes. Depression-era Snow Babies sometimes have "Germany" stamped on their bases.

Dressed bathing dolls

Description
One-piece, all-china dolls with molded and painted features, hair, and clothes. Left: White girl doll with black hair. Rose-sprigged white dress with red outlining at neck and sleeves. Center: Chinese boy with pink-luster head and hands. Asian features, rosy cheeks, long black queue down back. Blue skullcap with black border, blue tunic over white robe, black shoes. Right: Black doll in white short-sleeved dress.

Materials, Marks, and Dimensions
China. Height: 4″ (left); 5″ (center); 4″ (right).

Maker, Origin, and Period
Maker unknown. Germany. c. 1880–1920.

Comment
Early bathing dolls, also known as Frozen Charlottes, were made in simple 2-part molds, with arms molded to their sides or crossed over their chests. Later dolls had arms bent at the elbows, and flexed fingers. Those made with molded clothing were often used as dollhouse figures in the Victorian era and provided interesting variations to the rather plain, commonplace nude Frozen Charlottes (see 169).

Hints for Collectors
The left foot of the doll on the left was broken off and then reglued, diminishing the figure's value. Collectors looking for vintage all-china dolls should note that many large-size versions are reproductions and usually not marked as such. The most interesting Frozen Charlottes are, like the the ones shown here, those with molded clothing or out-of-the-ordinary detailing. In this group, the Chinese boy is the most unusual and therefore the most desirable.

Boy and Girl Dolls: Wax and Wood

 The child dolls in this section range from mature-looking figures with metal or wax-over-composition heads and cloth bodies to lively, youthful figures with jointed all-wooden bodies capable of being placed in any position. Their varied appearances reveal how society's attitudes toward children changed between the 1850s and 1920s, when these dolls were produced. For centuries dollmakers had depicted children as miniature adults. By the late 1860s, they came to be portrayed distinctly as children, but always with a sweet and innocent look. The best-known child dolls of the period were wide-eyed, pink-cheeked bébés, created in France and imitated elsewhere. By the first decade of the 20th century, a greater understanding of a child's psychological development resulted in dolls that were considerably more naturalistic. These figures were dressed in informal clothes and had realistically curved, expertly jointed limbs.

Materials
Most commercially made 19th-century child dolls were fashioned from wax, china, bisque, or composition. Metal was occasionally used for dolls' heads in the 19th and 20th centuries in an effort to produce unbreakable figures. Some metal dolls were expertly painted so that they would resemble finer bisque examples. Yet these dolls never caught on.

Schoenhut Dolls
Albert Schoenhut, a third-generation German toymaker, emigrated to America as a young man and in 1872 established a wooden toy- and dollmaking firm, A. Schoenhut & Company. In 1911 he received a patent for wooden dolls, which had lathe-turned, ball-jointed bodies. These were ingeniously strung with metal springs in such a way that when the joints were pulled, the springs were compressed rather than stretched, making it nearly impossible for the separate limb segments to loosen or come apart. Schoenhut was undoubtedly influenced by the centuries-old German tradition of making jointed wooden dolls, and by mid-19th-century American jointed wooden dolls, particularly those produced in Springfield, Vermont. The naturalistic features of many of Schoenhut's dolls suggest that he was also inspired by the turn-of-the-century German movement to create lifelike character dolls. Schoenhut was one of the first American makers to produce new doll models every year and to advertise them widely. In the mid-1920s, during his firm's declining years, figures were strung with cheaper elastic rather than metal springs, and some had cloth rather than wooden bodies. Today, among the rarest and most desirable Schoenhut dolls are the wooden Bye-Lo Babies, which are copies of Grace Putnam's original doll, and the manikins; it is thought that only 1000 of the latter were produced.

Multi-face doll

Description
Multi-face doll shown with 3 different wax-over-composition masks backed with fabric; masks attached to dummy head with cloth ties. Masks have blue glass eyes and closed mouths. Left to right: Elderly face has wrinkles and inserted black hair parted in center. Infant has wisp of blond hair. Youth has separate blond mohair wig (not shown). Wears long-sleeved white dotted swiss dress with blue ribbon sash and blue satin bows; 2 cotton underskirts and pantaloons. Embroidered lace bonnet. Molded blue boots with red trim.

Materials, Marks, and Dimensions
Wax-over-composition heads and limbs; cloth body. Height: 20½″ (entire doll); 3½″ (heads).

Maker, Origin, and Period
Maker unknown. Probably Germany. c. 1880.

Comment
Depicted here are 3 views of a single wax-over-composition multi-face doll whose dummy head is covered by masks representing old age, infancy, and youth. Another popular type of 19th-century multi-face doll came with a single head that turned on a vertical axis to reveal faces on the front and back. Patents for multi-face dolls were issued in the 1860s and '70s and again at the turn of the century, suggesting that these novelty items had cycles of popularity.

Hints for Collectors
Because their materials were fragile, very few wax-mask multi-face dolls have survived, and those that do appear on the market are rarely found in good condition. Moderate damage on such rare dolls, however, does not significantly lower their value.

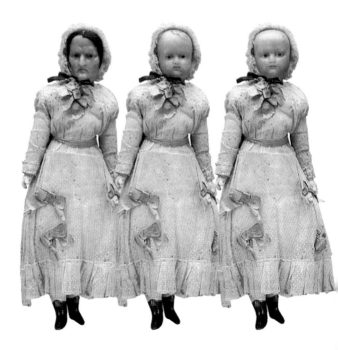

Motschmann-type doll

Description
Child doll with wax-over-composition shoulder-head and swivel neck. Hair inserted into slit in bald head. Blue glass sleep-eyes; open mouth with 2 upper and 2 lower teeth. Cloth torso has bellows-type voice box that cries "mama" and "papa" when lever is pushed. Limbs joined to body with cotton strips. Joints stuffed with cotton. Molded white socks decorated with blue bands; molded blue shoes.

Materials, Marks, and Dimensions
Wax-over-composition shoulder-head and limbs; cloth torso; composition pelvis. Height: 19″.

Maker, Origin, and Period
Maker unknown. Germany. Mid-19th century.

Comment
Charles Motschmann, the Sonneberg dollmaker, was so inspired by the Japanese baby dolls he saw at the 1855 Paris World's Fair that 2 years later he copied and patented several of their essential features. Motschmann's dolls are historically significant because they were some of the earliest to accurately represent a child's or infant's features. These commercially made dolls have joints stuffed with cloth to make them sturdy yet flexible. Variations produced by other firms throughout the 19th century are commonly called Motschmann-type dolls.

Hints for Collectors
Early Motschmann-type dolls can often be identified by their wax-over-composition or papier-mâché heads and shoulder plates. Later versions have china, wax, or even wooden heads. While the original Motschmann dolls are usually stamped with the maker's oval trademark on the leg, Motschmann-type dolls are rarely marked.

Wax-over-composition doll

Description
Young lady doll with wax-over-composition shoulder-head.
Glued-on blond wig, blue glass eyes, open mouth showing teeth.
Pierced ears with blue glass and gilt metal earrings. Head
slightly tilted. Wears plaid cotton dress with blue shawl collar,
cuffs, and satin ribbon sash. Lace-trimmed cotton underskirts
and pantaloons; multicolored striped stockings. Blue molded and
painted high-heeled boots. Blue hair ribbon and straw bonnet.

Materials, Marks, and Dimensions
Wax-over-composition shoulder-head, lower arms and hands;
cloth body; composition legs. "Kyte & Harris/Kindergarten Dolls
& Toys/Fancy Goods/10 East St. Brighton" marked on front and
back of torso. "Holz-Masse" printed in oval of Dressel trademark
on right leg. Adjacent paper label reads "Gegen Nachahmung/
Gesetzlich Geschützt." Height: 18¾".

Maker, Origin, and Period
Cuno & Otto Dressel. Germany. Distributed by Kyte & Harris.
England. c. 1863–95.

Comment
Cuno & Otto Dressel was the oldest doll firm in Europe, having
been established in the great dollmaking center of Sonneberg,
Germany, about 1700. Collectors are most familiar with Dressel's
19th-century dolls, which have wax or composition heads often
attached to finely made, gusseted kid bodies.

Hints for Collectors
The Dressel trademark found on many of the firm's 19th-century
dolls is a winged Roman helmet with a caduceus—a herald's staff
with 2 snakes twined around it and 2 wings at the top. Collectors
often call this a Mercury mark, named after the Roman god.

Minerva doll

Description
Girl doll with metal shoulder-head. Brown mohair wig with white bow. Blue glass eyes; open mouth showing upper teeth. Pink body, upper arms, and upper legs. Black linen stockings and black imitation-leather shoes with metal buckles.

Materials, Marks, and Dimensions
Metal shoulder-head; cloth body, upper arms, and legs; wooden lower arms and hands. "MINERVA" embossed over helmet trademark on front of shoulder plate. "Germany 3" embossed on back. "Wearwell/Unbreakable Doll/Hairstuffed/Made in Germany" stamped in purple ink on torso. Height: 17½″.

Maker, Origin, and Period
Buschow & Beck. Germany. Distributed by Sears, Roebuck & Co. Chicago, Illinois. c. 1922.

Comment
Silver and other precious metals were used to make dolls for the aristocracy as far back as the Middle Ages. Common metals such as brass, tin, and zinc were first employed for mass-produced dolls in the second half of the 19th century. Because they are heavy and cold to the touch, however, these later metal dolls never achieved the popularity of bisque or composition ones. The figure shown here, one of the more attractive metal-head dolls, is called a white metal Minerva or "Wearwell Brand" doll and is coated with a combination of celluloid and enamel paint.

Hints for Collectors
While most metal dolls are unmarked except for a mold number, the Minerva dolls have their name embossed on the shoulder plate. These figures appeal to collectors who specialize in dolls made of unusual materials. They fall into a middle price range.

Description
Girl dolls with molded wooden heads. Fully jointed bodies. Left: Bonnet doll has brown hair and molded white cap with red and green floral design. Brown eyes, closed mouth. Original lace-trimmed cotton underclothing with blue bow. 2 holes in each sole fit over prongs of original stand. Right: Back view of molded-hair doll with braids drawn over ears and tied with molded pink bow. Original cotton underclothing with lace trim and pink satin ribbon. Black cotton stockings and black imitation-leather shoes.

Materials, Marks, and Dimensions
Wood with metal springs. Left: Paper label on back reads "SCHOENHUT DOLL/PAT. JAN. 17TH 1911/U.S.A." Right: "SCHOENHUT DOLL/PAT. JAN. 17, '11, U.S.A./& FOREIGN COUNTRIES" marked on back of shoulder. Height: 14½" (left); 14" (right).

Maker, Origin, and Period
A. Schoenhut & Co. Philadelphia, Pennsylvania. c. 1912–15.

Comment
While many Schoenhut dolls have Germanic features that reflect the heritage of their maker, they also possess the carefree bounciness typical of 20th-century American dolls. Schoenhut dolls were often promoted for their realism. For example, an advertisement for one of them claimed that the doll's head was "artistically modeled in real character style, more natural and life-like than anything ever attempted."

Hints for Collectors
A Schoenhut bonnet doll, as shown on the left, is rarer and commands a higher price than a doll with carved hair, such as the one illustrated on the right.

Wooden girl doll

Description
Girl doll with hand-carved wooden head. Deeply carved hair
styled with center part and short braids framing face. Painted
blue eyes and closed red mouth. Jointed with elastic at shoulders
and hips. Original lace-trimmed white cotton blouse and red
rayon skirt with green rickrack trim; floral print ruffle edged in
lace; red cotton underskirt and lace-trimmed pantaloons.

Materials, Marks, and Dimensions
Wooden head, shoulder plate, and lower limbs; cloth body and
upper limbs. Height: 12″.

Maker, Origin, and Period
Maker unknown. Switzerland. c. 1915–25.

Comment
Swiss dollmakers are known for beautiful hand-carved dolls
whose costumes reflect regional dress styles—either miniature
versions of simple everyday garments or festive holiday clothing.
The gentle expressive faces and soft cloth bodies of 20th-century
Swiss dolls are generally more appealing to children than the
rigid wooden bodies of 19th-century examples.

Hints for Collectors
Compared to the huge number of dolls produced in France and
Germany, Switzerland's output was small. Beginning collectors
sometimes mistake French and German dolls dressed in Swiss
costumes for Swiss dolls. Since few dolls made in Switzerland are
so marked, other documentation is necessary for a definitive
attribution. A doll's age can sometimes be based on the fabric
and style of its original clothing. For example, this doll wears a
skirt of rayon, a material that became popular about 1920,
suggesting that the doll was made at that time.

Description
Child doll with molded wooden head and brown wavy hair. Brown eyes, smiling open mouth showing 2 upper and 2 lower teeth. Body jointed at neck, shoulders, elbows, and hips. Legs swing from hips. Bent arms. Wears red and white check cotton romper. White stockings and white tie shoes.

Materials, Marks, and Dimensions
Wood with metal springs. "C" inscribed in center of circle stamped on head, with "H.E. SCHOENHUT 1919" on outer rim. "SCHOENHUT DOLL/PAT. JAN. 17th 1911/U.S.A." marked on shoulder above blue stamp reading "PATENT APPLIED FOR." Height: 11".

Maker, Origin, and Period
A. Schoenhut & Co. Philadelphia, Pennsylvania. c. 1919–25.

Comment
A. Schoenhut was one of many companies that produced interchangeable heads and bodies for its dolls, a practice that greatly increased the variety of the figures it issued. The head of the doll shown here, introduced in 1911, was among the first of the firm's molded-hair types. Named Schnickel-Fritz, it was made of solid wood that was first carved and then molded under pressure. Its expressive lifelike features proved quite popular, and about 1920 the head appeared on the Schoenhut "walkable" doll body illustrated here. Introduced in 1919, this body type has legs that swing from the hips in a walking movement.

Hints for Collectors
While all Schoenhut dolls made prior to the mid-1920s are in demand, those with carved hair bring higher prices than those with wigs.

Description
Child doll with molded wooden head and short brown hair.
Painted eyes and open-closed mouth. Body jointed at neck,
shoulders, and hips. Legs swing from hips. Wears blue and white
check cotton romper, white cotton socks, and brown and white
saddle shoes.

Materials, Marks, and Dimensions
Wood with metal springs. Height: 13¾".

Maker, Origin, and Period
A. Schoenhut & Co. Philadelphia, Pennsylvania. c. 1920.

Comment
Along with Schnickel-Fritz, the Tootsie-Wootsie doll shown here
has one of Schoenhut's first heads designed with molded hair.
The charming head, originally issued in 1911, was most likely
attached later to this body, which Schoenhut introduced in 1919
and advertised as "walkable" (see 232). A. Schoenhut & Company
was a highly innovative firm; its doll bodies, constructed with
metal springs and swivel joints, were considered an advance over
the common ball-jointed bodies of the period.

Hints for Collectors
This doll is of interest to collectors because of its unusual
combination of a Tootsie-Wootsie head and "walkable" body.
While early Schoenhut dolls are considered to be among the
finest American dolls, those manufactured after the mid-1920s,
when Schoenhut was phasing out its production of dolls in favor
of wooden toys, are not as well made, and thus less desirable.
Dolls produced in the 1920s are often jointed with elastic instead
of metal springs, and have cloth rather than wooden bodies.

Doll-face doll

Description
Girl doll with molded wooden head. Blond mohair wig styled with center part and curls. Brown eyes painted to resemble glass; open mouth has 4 teeth. Fully jointed body. Original lace-trimmed white cotton dress and pink sash tied in bow at back. Matching pink bow in hair. Cotton underwear. Tan cotton stockings and white leather shoes with metal buckles. Shoes and feet have 2 holes in each sole to fit over prongs of accompanying stand.

Materials, Marks, and Dimensions
Wood with metal springs. Inverted mark incised on back reads "SCHOENHUT/DOLL PAT. JAN. 17 '11, U.S.A./& FOREIGN COUNTRIES." Height: 15″.

Maker, Origin, and Period
A. Schoenhut & Co. Philadelphia, Pennsylvania. After 1915.

Comment
Schoenhut called the figure shown here, introduced in 1915, a "doll-face" doll because its pretty, idealized features resemble those of European dolls from the same period. Doll-face types were advertised as having "faces to imitate the finest bisque-head dolls." This distinguishes them from the firm's more naturalistic character dolls (*see* 232 and 233).

Hints for Collectors
For quick identification of Schoenhut dolls, check the hands and feet. With the exception of the manikins (*see* 85), all the hands have a recognizable wedge shape and separated fingers. Most Schoenhut dolls have holes in their feet and shoes to enable them to be set on stands, many of which are now lost; the walking dolls, however, have no holes in their feet.

Description
Child dolls with molded wooden heads. Left: Light brown mohair wig, blue eyes. Jointed at neck, shoulders, and hips. Bent limbs. Wears white cotton dress with eyelet embroidery at neck and cuffs, white cotton undershirt and diaper, and white knitted booties. Right: Hollow swivel head. Blond mohair wig and blue eyes. Voice box in torso. Original white cotton romper suit, socks, and oilcloth shoes.

Materials, Marks, and Dimensions
Left: Wood with metal springs. Oval paper label on back reads "SCHOENHUT DOLL/PAT. JAN. 17TH 1911/U.S.A. " Torn round paper label on neck printed with "C" inscribed in center of circle and "H.E. SCHOENHUT" on outer rim. Right: Wooden head and hands; cloth body and arms. Illegible stamp on back of head. Height: 14″ (left); 16″ (right).

Maker, Origin, and Period
A. Schoenhut & Co. Philadelphia, Pennsylvania. Left: c. 1915. Right: c. 1924.

Comment
About 1913 Schoenhut produced its first doll with bent limbs by fitting together 2 pieces of wood at the elbows and at the knees, as illustrated by the doll at left. In 1924 Schoenhut created a lightweight version of the same doll, shown at right, by hollowing out the head and substituting a cloth body for the wooden one. These later dolls were equipped with voice boxes.

Hints for Collectors
Schoenhut advertised extensively and produced many catalogues. Collectors look for reprints of these publications to determine whether the outfit worn by a Schoenhut doll is original, or a later addition made at home by a previous owner.

Boy and Girl Dolls: Cloth

Throughout history pieces of cloth were either rolled into shapes or were cut, stuffed, and sewn to make rudimentary playthings for children. While some small figures were rough semblances of a human shape, others, created with skill and patience and often composed of many pieces of homespun cloth, accurately depicted men and women. Because they were so perishable, the earliest cloth dolls rarely survived. Exceptions are the unusually well preserved dolls found in ancient Egyptian tombs. Dating from about 2000 B.C., these figures are made of braided papyrus covered with handwoven linen and have embroidered facial features and hair.

19th-Century Dolls

Most cloth dolls available to collectors today are types that have been made since the mid-19th century, when homemade dolls usually had 2-piece torsos and unjointed arms and legs. Stuffing for homemade dolls included cotton, straw, feathers, bran, wood chips, and cork dust. While some seamstresses carefully stitched tiny fingers, occasionally adding a thumb, most were content with mittenlike fists. By stitching the knees and elbows, dollmakers added mobility to their figures. Creative touches such as embroidered or painted fingernails, shoes, and stockings enlivened many cloth dolls, but it was primarily in the rendering of the faces that dollmakers displayed their imagination. Wild wooly wigs, elegant human hair, or delicate silk thread are just a few materials used for doll coiffures.

American Dolls

19th-century American dollmakers strove to create sturdy playthings that would withstand rough handling by young children and the rigors of country life. Unlike the fine European dolls, American dolls had molded-cloth construction and simple faces and bodies that suited local tastes and lifestyles. Many doll types were originally made in homes and later developed commercially. Each dollmaker devised a unique method for fabricating her dolls. Among the best-known makers was Izannah Walker, who may have created dolls as early as 1855, although she received a patent for them only in the 1870s. Inspired by a Walker doll she owned, Martha Chase began designing dolls around 1880. These were followed by the cloth dolls of Julia Beecher, the Adams sisters, Ella Smith, and, in the early 20th century, Gertrude Rollinson and Louise Kampes. Cloth dolls representing fictional characters were produced by Madame Alexander as early as the 1920s.

European Dolls

Sturdy cloth figures were popular in Germany in the early 20th century, in part because they were believed to aid in the psychological development of young children. The noted dollmaker Käthe Kruse remarked that dolls were meant to be "an education toward motherliness," so that soft cuddly cloth dolls were seen as preferable to those made of harder materials. Kruse's pensive-faced dolls were banned during the Third Reich, a time when all German children were supposed to have happy expressions. During the 1930s and '40s, English and Italian manufacturers made cloth dolls of imaginary characters, such as children from the South Seas or those playing sports. Figures by Victoria Toy Works and Lenci were often dressed in extraordinary outfits.

Description
Girl doll with hand-painted features. Short brown hair, blue eyes, heart-shaped nostrils, rosebud mouth, rosy cheeks. Head and body stuffed with cotton around a sawdust core. Painted lower limbs. Stitched at shoulders, hips, and knees. Stitched fingers and toes.

Materials, Marks, and Dimensions
Muslin. "Columbian Doll/EMMA E. ADAMS/OSWEGO CENTRE/N.Y." stamped on back. Height: 29¾".

Maker, Origin, and Period
Emma and Marietta Adams. Oswego, New York. c. 1891–1906.

Comment
Columbian dolls were named for the Columbian Exposition, a world's fair held in Chicago in 1893, where they were exhibited. One of them, called "Miss Columbia," traveled around the world as an ambassador of good will and in 1902 was presented to William Howard Taft, then president of the United States. Designed by Emma Adams and outfitted by her sister Marietta, Columbian dolls wore simple cotton dresses, bonnets or caps, and hand-sewn kidskin slippers or booties. They were priced from $1.50 to $5. Emma Adams hand-painted her dolls' faces with considerable finesse, but after she died in 1900 the work was done by less skillful commercial artists.

Hints for Collectors
Dolls made after 1906 are stamped "THE COLUMBIAN DOLL/ MANUFACTURED BY/MARIETTA ADAMS RUTTAN/OSWEGO, N.Y." All Columbian dolls are rare and very much in demand. A few black versions were produced.

Missionary Ragbaby

Description
Baby doll with molded and painted features. Blue eyes with
brown lashes; nose and mouth outlined in red. Looped yellow
wool hair. Fist-shaped hands, stitched fingers and toes. Wears
long-sleeved white dress trimmed in lace, cotton underclothing,
and white cotton bonnet with tatting.

Materials, Marks, and Dimensions
Silk jersey. Height: 24½".

Maker, Origin, and Period
Julia Beecher. Elmira, New York. c. 1893–1910.

Comment
This handmade doll was called a Missionary Ragbaby because
its sale was meant to benefit a missionary fund sponsored by
the Park Congregational Church of Elmira, New York. Julia
Beecher also made and sold her dolls commercially; she offered a
50¢ discount to people who supplied their own cloth for individual
orders. Beecher's dolls were made out of old silk underwear and
were originally available in 3 sizes priced from $2 to $8. A doll
that sold for $8 was quite costly in 1893, since this is the
equivalent of about $85 today.

Hints for Collectors
All of Julia Beecher's Ragbabies are rare, but the rarest of all
are the black versions. Since the dolls are unmarked, they are
sometimes mistaken for one-of-a-kind homemade figures. To
identify a Beecher doll, look for yarn ringlets, fistlike hands,
and finely detailed features, such as the eyelashes, nostrils,
and dimples seen on the example illustrated.

Martha Chase hospital doll

Description
Baby doll with molded and painted features and blond molded hair. Blue eyes, cherry-red mouth and nostrils, applied ears. Holes in nostrils and ears. Stitched fingers and toes, separately attached thumbs. Washable painted limbs and torso, rubberized interior. Wears white cotton hospital gown.

Materials, Marks, and Dimensions
Cloth and rubber. Chase hospital doll-face trademark under left arm. Height: 22½".

Maker, Origin, and Period
Martha Chase. Pawtucket, Rhode Island. c. 1910.

Comment
This homely life-size doll was specifically designed as a teaching aid with which nurses and other hospital personnel could practice routine child-care procedures. Its special features include a rubberized interior, immersible body, and holes in the nostrils and ears. Hospital dolls were made in various infant and toddler sizes. Although a few of them eventually found their way into children's doll collections, they were not originally intended as playthings.

Hints for Collectors
Martha Chase made a great variety of dolls, including mammies and figures representing literary characters. Most are hard to find today. Her hospital dolls can be recognized by their unusual weight. They were designed to be as heavy as children of the same size and are thus extremely awkward to hold.

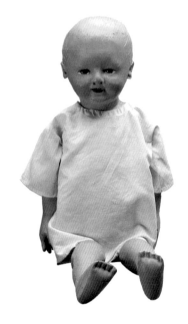

Käthe Kruse toddler

Description
Toddler girl doll with pouting expression. Molded and painted features. Brown hair. Molded ears. Arms jointed at shoulders allowing a to-and-fro motion. Stitched fingers with separately attached thumbs; stitched toes. Original costume of red cotton chambray dress with cross-stitched belt and pockets, lace collar and cuffs, white lace-trimmed pantaloons and slip. White and pink socks, brown leather shoes.

Materials, Marks, and Dimensions
Muslin. "Käthe Kruse/P 73/Germany" marked on sole of foot. Height: 17″.

Maker, Origin, and Period
Käthe Kruse. Germany. c. 1922.

Comment
Käthe Kruse spent years developing a soft and very lifelike cloth doll that she described as "indestructible" and as "an education toward motherliness" when it was first marketed in 1912. Many of Kruse's dolls have poignant expressions based on the faces of her own children or on the faces of cherubs by Renaissance painters. The doll shown here has a head made from several pieces of chemically treated muslin sewn together.

Hints for Collectors
Käthe Kruse's dolls are often marked with 2 adjoining K's or a signature inked on the soles of their feet. Kruse's early dolls usually had painted hair instead of wigs. Since the early dolls' faces tended to fade with time and repeated washings, they were often repainted. Repainting, however, lessens a doll's value considerably.

Alabama Indestructible Doll

Description
Girl doll with oil-painted features and short brown hair. Blue
eyes with lashes, feathered eyebrows, painted nostrils, dark lip
line on red mouth. Applied ears. Stitched mitten-shaped hands
and stitched toes with pink nails. Wears red dress with black
polka dots and pearl button closure.

Materials, Marks, and Dimensions
Cloth. "Mrs. S. S. Smith/Manufactured/Ala." printed on front of
body. Height: 12".

Maker, Origin, and Period
Ella Smith. Roanoke, Alabama. c. 1904–24.

Comment
Ella Smith's small factory is reported to have made as many
as 8000 dolls in a single year. Smith's career began when she
repaired a bisque doll for a neighbor's child and recognized the
need for a doll that was unbreakable. Her firm's advertisements
always emphasized the indestructibility of its dolls. According to
legend, a factory worker claimed that a truck ran over one of
them without even cracking the paint. Ella Smith continually
sought to improve her dolls and took out 5 patents, the last 3 in
1924, the year of her death.

Hints for Collectors
Collectors often refer to Ella Smith's dolls as "Alabama Babies."
Most were originally marked on the stomach with the firm's
name and a date or number, but the print has worn off on many
of them. These dolls were stuffed from the top of the head, so
they can be easily recognized by their stitched circular crowns.
Other distinguishing details include hand-painted heads, short,
simple hairdos, and stitched hands and toes. Black "Alabama
Babies" are rare and extremely valuable.

Philadelphia Baby

Description
Baby doll with molded and painted features. Brown hair. Applied ears. Painted shoulder-head, lower arms and hands, lower legs and feet. Stitched at shoulders, hips, elbows, and knees. Stitched fingers and toes. Seam stitched up back of neck and head.

Materials, Marks, and Dimensions
Stockinet. Height: 22″.

Maker, Origin, and Period
Maker unknown. Distributed by J. B. Sheppard & Co. Philadelphia, Pennsylvania. c. 1900–24.

Comment
The Philadelphia Baby was originally designed about 1900 for J. B. Sheppard & Company, a Philadelphia department store founded in 1860. This simple unadorned doll resembles the famous Chase stockinet doll, although there are significant differences between the two. The Chase doll is usually covered with pink sateen, while the Sheppard body is covered with a rough, off-white stockinet fabric. The Chase doll has a short neck rather than the Sheppard funnel-shaped neck, and is hinged at the elbows while the Sheppard doll is not. Also, the face and ears of the Sheppard doll are not as well articulated as the features on the Chase doll. Philadelphia Babies were produced in 18″ and 22″ sizes.

Hints for Collectors
Sheppard dolls are occasionally found with feet stained by the excess dye applied to their original buttoned boots. Collectors can sometimes use these stains to authenticate unmarked dolls.

Izannah Walker doll

Description
Girl doll with molded and painted features and short brown hair.
Brown eyes, closed mouth. Body covered with brown fabric.
Painted arms and legs. Individually stitched fingers and toes,
separate thumbs.

Materials, Marks, and Dimensions
Cloth. Height: 13¾″.

Maker, Origin, and Period
Izannah Walker. Central Falls, Rhode Island. c. 1870–80.

Comment
Izannah Walker first registered a patent for her dolls in 1873.
She used various molds for the faces, each of which produced
slightly different features. Nevertheless, the resulting heads are
strikingly similar in appearance. All Walker dolls have either
painted corkscrew curls or the short straight hair painted with
fine brushstrokes seen here. In addition, the dolls have applied
ears or, on rare occasions, molded ears; carefully stitched fingers
and either painted bare feet with sewn toes or feet that have
laced shoes painted on them. Most examples wear homemade
clothes, and a few are dressed as boys.

Hints for Collectors
The primitive beauty of Izannah Walker dolls has so endeared
them to collectors that their cost has increased dramatically
over the years. The dolls' distinctive features make them
easy to recognize, even though most examples are unmarked.
Occasionally a doll is marked "Patented Nov. 4th 1873" on the
back of its head.

Izannah Walker doll

Description
Girl doll with molded and painted features and brown hair. Soft
wisps and tiny curls frame face. Large luminous eyes, applied
ears. Individually stitched fingers. Wears pink and white printed
cotton dress with lace-trimmed sleeves. White cotton petticoat
and drawers. Side-buttoned brown leather shoes.

Materials, Marks, and Dimensions
Cloth. Height: 18″.

Maker, Origin, and Period
Izannah Walker. Central Falls, Rhode Island. c. 1870–80.

Comment
In a letter to the *Providence Bulletin*, a grandniece of Izannah
Walker wrote: "Family tradition tells of her struggle to perfect
her work and of the long wrestling with one problem, how to
obtain a resistant surface to the stockinet heads, arms, and legs
without cracking or peeling. With this problem on her mind,
Aunt Izannah suddenly sat up in bed one night to hear a voice
say, 'Use paste.' " Izannah Walker obtained a patent for her
complicated process in 1873. It involved layering and pressing
cloth treated with glue or paste in a 2-part mold, then stuffing,
sewing, and gluing the 2 halves of the figure together around a
wooden armature. Hands and feet were hand-sewn, and the
completed doll was then hand-painted in oil colors.

Hints for Collectors
Possibly made as early as 1855, Izannah Walker's cloth figures
are considered by many to be the first notable American dolls.
Walker's early examples may often be identified by their unusual
size; some are almost as large as a small child. Her black dolls
with wool hair are rare and especially prized.

Description
Boy and girl dolls with molded and painted hair and features,
applied ears, individually stitched fingers. Left: Boy has blond
hair parted on the side, blue eyes, red lips. Wears white cotton
shirt with lace-trimmed collar and cuffs, blue and white striped
cotton pants, white cotton socks, and leather shoes. Right: Girl
has blond bob. Sateen-covered torso. Wears blue and pink
printed cotton bonnet and dress with white lace-trimmed collar
and cuffs. White petticoat and pantaloons. White kid shoes.

Materials, Marks, and Dimensions
Cloth. Right: Chase trademark imprinted on upper left leg.
Height: 16″ (left); 17″ (right).

Maker, Origin, and Period
Martha Chase. Pawtucket, Rhode Island. Left: c. 1925–35.
Right: c. 1922.

Comment
From the 1880s through the 1930s, Martha Chase made sturdy,
washable cloth dolls in a factory behind her house. Inspired by a
beloved Izannah Walker doll she owned as a child, she devised a
complicated method for manufacturing unbreakable dolls. The
heads were made by stretching stockinet over a mask with raised
features, stiffening the material with glue or paste, and then
painting the face with oils.

Hints for Collectors
Chase dolls made during the firm's early years have sateen
torsos. Dolls made later have rough stockinet bodies with a
waterproof finish. The boy doll shown here, acquired from the
Chase family, is unfinished because he lacks the special
waterproof coating. An example as unusual and valuable as this
one is likely to be sold privately.

Rollinson doll

Description
Boy doll with cloth shoulder-head and painted features. Brown hair, blue side-glancing eyes, cherry-red closed mouth. Applied ears. Protective sateen covering over torso and upper arms and legs. Head, lower arms, and legs coated with several layers of paint.

Materials, Marks, and Dimensions
Cloth. Trademark picture of doll and "Rollinson/Doll/Holyoke Mass." stamped on front of torso in diamond shape. Height: 20″.

Maker, Origin, and Period
Designed by Gertrude Rollinson for Utley Co. Holyoke, Massachusetts. c. 1916–17.

Comment
Gertrude Rollinson originally designed cloth dolls for children confined to hospitals. She disliked the flat-faced rag dolls commonly made during the early 20th century, and after much experimentation succeeded in creating a cloth figure that had 3-dimensional features. Sometimes modeled after real children, her appealing dolls ranged in size from 14″ to 28″ and were available with painted hair or with 3 different wig styles—short curls, long curls, or Buster Brown bangs. Baby dolls wore lace-trimmed white gowns, boys sported suits, and girls appeared in white dresses with colored trim.

Hints for Collectors
Rollinson dolls are rare and very valuable. Some of them are almost identical in appearance to those made by Martha Chase. However, the distinctive Rollinson trademark, always stamped on her dolls' stomachs, will prevent any possible misattribution.

Description
Little girl doll with molded and painted features. Rosy cheeks, brown flirty eyes. 2 blue ribbons adorn blond mohair wig. Original cotton floral print dress with lace-trimmed white yoke, matching print bonnet, white lace pantalettes, and pink felt shoes. Carries nosegay of felt flowers.

Materials, Marks, and Dimensions
Felt. Paper tag around neck reads "A1/TOYS/ARE/HYGIENIC/Priscilla/MADE IN ENGLAND/BY/DEAN'S RAG/BOOK CO./LTD." Height: 14".

Maker, Origin, and Period
Dean's Rag Book Co., Ltd. England. c. 1920–30.

Comment
Dean's Rag Book Company printed its first doll on a sheet of linen in 1903. Samuel Dean claimed that he founded the company for "children who wear their food and eat their clothes." The firm's early printed dolls were meant to be cut out and stuffed at home; in later years, factory-stuffed dolls were also produced. In 1920 Dean's introduced a line of "Tru-to-Life" dolls, including the Priscilla doll shown here, whose mask faces were stiffened with buckram backing by means of a hot press. Advertisements extolled the dolls' "indestructibility, washability, and hygienic merit."

Hints for Collectors
The dolls in the "Tru-to-Life" series were available in printed-sheet form, a type in which some collectors specialize. Other collectors find the molded, factory-assembled dolls more interesting. "Tru-to-Life" dolls are marked only with a tie-on label. They can be distinguished from Lenci dolls, which they closely resemble, by their chubby and ill-proportioned limbs.

Tyrolean couple

Description
National costume dolls with molded and painted features. Side-glancing brown eyes, blond mohair wigs, applied ears. Movable necks and limbs. Original costumes. Left: Girl in tall green felt hat with edelweiss flowers and feathers. Green felt vest over white lace-collared blouse. Maroon taffeta apron with yellow border over black felt skirt. Multicolored satin sash. Red stockings, black felt shoes. Right: Boy in green felt hat, green felt vest embroidered with Lamb of God symbol, and red undervest. White cotton shirt with pearl buttons. Brown felt pants and shoes.

Materials, Marks, and Dimensions
Felt. Left: Paper label on petticoat reads "Bambola-Italia Lenci Torino Made in Italy." Right: Paper label on back of shoulder reads same as label on girl's petticoat. Cloth label under paper label reads "Lenci Made in Italy." Height: 14″.

Maker, Origin, and Period
Lenci (trade name for Elena Scavini). Italy. c. 1939–41.

Comment
Some of Lenci's best-known dolls are those dressed in national costumes. Lenci put its efforts into designing elaborate, high-quality outfits, occasionally at the expense of the dolls' other features.

Hints for Collectors
Recent catalogues, articles, and books about Lenci dolls have generated tremendous interest in these figures, which consequently have skyrocketed in value. However, not all Lenci dolls are exorbitantly priced. Smaller figures made during the firm's later years can still be purchased for far less than the large "pouty" children, flappers, or dolls in national costumes.

Description

Little boy doll with molded and painted features. Curly blond wig, side-glancing eyes, applied ears. Original green felt sweater with geometric design; white felt shirt, black tie. Black and white checked knickers, white knit socks with multicolored cuffs, brown leather shoes with fringed tongues.

Materials, Marks, and Dimensions

Felt. Faded blue stamp on left foot. Height: 17″.

Maker, Origin, and Period

Lenci (trade name for Elena Scavini). Italy. c. 1927.

Comment

The Golfer shown here is one of a series of Lenci dolls dressed in the outfits of various sports that were popular in the 1920s. Some of these figures even came with sporting equipment. This little boy's pouting expression and hands-in-pockets pose reflect the maker's familiarity with young children.

Hints for Collectors

Lenci dolls can be recognized by their seamless, pressed-felt construction and by their various marks. Occasionally cloth or cardboard tags inscribed "Lenci Made in Italy" are sewn directly onto the doll's clothing. Sometimes a metal button marked "Lenci" is affixed to a doll, or else numbers or the words "Lenci Turin" are stamped on the bottom of a foot. The faded blue mark on the bottom of the golfer's left foot probably once read "Lenci Turin," but since the felt did not readily absorb ink, the letters of the mark have all but disappeared with time. Because this doll is in excellent condition, the fact that his golf cap and club are missing would not appreciably affect his value.

South Sea Islander

Description
Little boy doll with swivel head and brown curly mohair wig.
Brown glass eyes, molded nose with painted red nostrils, smiling
red lips, and painted teeth. Stitched fingers and toes. Original
red velvet overalls with pearl buttons on pants and suspenders.

Materials, Marks, and Dimensions
Velvet. Label on suspenders reads "MADE IN ENGLAND/BY/NORAH
WELLINGS." Height: 18″.

Maker, Origin, and Period
Designed by Norah Wellings for Victoria Toy Works. England.
c. 1940.

Comment
Norah Wellings designed her cloth dolls for the Victoria Toy
Works from 1926 to 1959. They were distributed in England, and
many were exported for sale in America as well. The brown
plush South Sea Islander pictured here was one of her most
popular characters. Others included a Little Bo Peep, Scot,
Cowboy, and Mountie. She designed a special parachute doll,
Harry the Hawk, as a mascot for the Royal Air Force during the
Second World War and donated part of the proceeds of its sale
to the RAF fund. Her sailors and Britannia dolls were sold as
mascots aboard ocean liners. Wellings was granted a patent in
1926 for the process she used to coat her dolls' fabric heads with
plastic wood—a wood putty—and back them with buckram. The
fabric she used was usually plush velvet, although some cotton
and felt dolls can be found.

Hints for Collectors
Most Norah Wellings dolls have a label stitched securely to
the wrist, foot, or clothing. Be wary of unmarked imitations.

Description

Little girl doll with molded buckram face and painted features. Long curly brown floss wig. Round side-glancing eyes, rosebud mouth. Wired body and limbs. Original costume of fuchsia taffeta bodice and lime-green organdy skirt trimmed with velvet ribbon. Matching purse, lace gloves, and veiled hat adorned with pink floral bouquet. Black velvet shoes sewn to feet.

Materials, Marks, and Dimensions

Buckram face, stockinet body. Tag on dress reads "Little Shaver/Madame Alexander/New York/All Rights Reserved." Height: 14½".

Maker, Origin, and Period

Madame Alexander. New York City. c. 1941.

Comment

Illustrator and dollmaker Elsie Shaver was noted for her drawings of Victorian children. After admiring her pictures at an art exhibit, Madame Alexander bought the reproduction rights to them from the artist in 1919. The Alexander dolls modeled after Shaver's illustrations proved very popular, and versions of them were produced for more than 20 years. Little Shaver graced the cover of the 1942 Christmas catalogue published by the well-known department store Neiman-Marcus.

Hints for Collectors

Madame Alexander dolls were usually marked only by the labels sewn on their clothes. Cloth dolls that are unmarked or that have lost their original clothing are especially hard to identify. Alexander's composition dolls from the 1930s and '40s, however, can sometimes be recognized by their stylized features and distinctive wigs.

Kamkins

Description
Little girl doll with molded mask face. Curly wig of brown
human hair with center part and red ribbon. Painted features.
Deep blue eyes with dot pupils, pencil-thin arched eyebrows,
pug nose, closed red mouth with full lower lip. Body has seams
running down legs and arms. Flexible limbs, stitched fingers.
Doll reclothed in red and white print cotton dress, red cuffs and
bodice, lace collar, belt trimmed in red. Ribbed red socks, white
oilcloth shoes adorned with metal buckles.

Materials, Marks, and Dimensions
Cloth. "KAMKINS/A DOLLY MADE TO LOVE/PATENTED BY L. R.
KAMPES/ATLANTIC CITY, N.J." incised on back of head under wig.
Height: 18″.

Maker, Origin, and Period
Louise Kampes. Atlantic City, New Jersey. c. 1919–25.

Comment
Kamkins, easily recognized by her bright blue eyes and thin
eyebrows, was designed by Louise Kampes, manufactured at her
studio in Atlantic City, and sold at a shop on the boardwalk there
from 1919 to 1925. This adorable doll was made as either a girl or
boy and in sizes that ranged from 16″ to 19″; it originally cost $10
to $15. New outfits were created for Kamkins each season.

Hints for Collectors
Since Kamkins was made for only a relatively short period of
time and was not produced in great numbers, it is considered
rare and brings high prices. Collectors who specialize in cloth
dolls seek out Kamkins, along with the Philadelphia Baby, the
Columbian doll, and dolls made by Izannah Walker and Martha
Chase.

Cloth girl doll

Description
Little girl doll with mask face and painted features. Blond
mohair wig with bangs. Raised eyebrows, side-glancing blue
eyes with red dots in the corners, closed mouth. Swivel head.
Original costume of white cotton coat with red piping and large
red plastic buttons, matching white hat, white cotton
underpants, white rayon knit socks. Red imitation-leather Mary
Jane shoes fastened with metal buckles.

Materials, Marks, and Dimensions
Cotton. Tag on wrist reads "Created by Madame Alexander,
New York" on front; on reverse, "An Alexander Product/
Supreme Quality/And Design." Height: 19½".

Maker, Origin, and Period
Madame Alexander. New York City. c. 1930–40.

Comment
Madame Alexander went into business in 1923. Originally
founded as the Alexander Doll Company in the 1920s and '30s,
her firm made cloth dolls that had hand-painted mask faces and
pink bodies like the example shown here. Many of the early dolls'
faces were painted by Madame Alexander herself, with the
assistance of her 3 younger sisters.

Hints for Collectors
Madame Alexander's early cloth dolls are rare and valuable finds
today because they were produced in smaller quantities than
later composition or plastic dolls, and because they soiled
easily and were thus frequently discarded. Collectors interested
in Madame Alexander dolls should subscribe to one of the
newsletters published by the several clubs devoted exclusively to
them.

Princess Elizabeth and Princess Margaret Rose

Description
Portrait dolls with blond wigs, felt mask faces with blue glass eyes, swivel heads. Original costumes. Left: Princess Elizabeth wears blue felt double-breasted coat over blue cotton print dress, blue felt hat trimmed with daisies, and blue felt shoes fastened with pearl buttons. Right: Princess Margaret Rose wears cotton print dress, pink felt coat, and matching hat and shoes with pearl buttons.

Materials, Marks, and Dimensions
Felt faces, plush velvet bodies. Left: Paper label on coat reads "The Genuine/Princess Elizabeth/British Made Doll." Right: Paper label on coat reads "HRH Princess/Margaret Rose/British Made Doll/By Permission of Her Majesty/The Queen." Cloth labels on both coats read "Made in England." On both dolls, bottom of one shoe reads "The Chad Valley Co Ltd/British Seal by Appointment/Toy Makers to/HM the Queen"; bottom of other shoe reads "Hygienic Toys/Made in England by/Chad Valley Co. Ltd." Height: 18½" (left); 17" (right).

Maker, Origin, and Period
Chad Valley Co. England. c. 1938.

Comment
The Chad Valley Company, originally established in 1860 as Johnson Brothers Ltd., manufactured cloth dolls exclusively. These had heads of buckram, canvas, or felt.

Hints for Collectors
Although numerous Chad Valley dolls were produced over the years, today they are quite difficult to find. Because their cloth faces became dirty and discolored, the dolls were often thrown away. A pair of these very accurate childhood portraits of Princess Elizabeth and Princess Margaret Rose is quite a find.

Boy and Girl Dolls: Miscellaneous Materials

Dolls of the 20th century reflect modern man's striving to perfect an indestructible, inexpensive material that would withstand rough play. In addition, modern dolls are evidence of continued attempts to design figures with which children could easily identify, or at least toys that would capture their attention.

Materials

The traditional dollmaking material, composition, was favored through the 1940s, though substances such as rubber, celluloid, and the newly invented vinyl began to be used extensively for doll manufacture. Because they were malleable, durable, and cheap, these materials were hailed as remarkable advances. Their undesirable qualities—rubber dried and cracked, celluloid was highly flammable, and early vinyls became sticky with age— led to the continued search for yet other materials, eventually resulting in the vinyls and plastics that are still used today. Dolls made of materials that were found to be unsuitable and that were quickly abandoned are very collectible today, not only because relatively few are available, but also because they are important evidence of some of this century's technological trials and errors.

Modern Innovations

While late 19th-century dolls were often equipped with talking devices and with apparatuses that simulated bodily functions, the 20th century has been the heyday for such features. There are modern dolls that walk, talk, cry, squeak, sing, or grow, dolls with interchangeable heads, or with faces that change at the turn of a knob, and dolls with rooted hair that can be brushed, washed, and curled. Many dolls, such as Amosandra, were created merely as novelties or fads and appeared and disappeared from the market rapidly. Others, including Madame Alexander's Scarlett O'Hara, remained popular for decades. Some mass-produced examples were shoddily designed, while others, such as Joseph Kallus's Margie doll, were well crafted in spite of being manufactured by the thousands for maximum sale.

20th-Century Successes

Shirley Temple dolls, particularly composition examples from the 1930s and '40s, have long been favorites, partly because they represent a much-loved character. Many dolls, such as Vogue's Ginny, that were popular commercial successes when introduced in the 1950s have only recently been gaining collectors' notice as more attention is focused on the products of that era. On the other hand, Madame Alexander dolls from almost any decade have always had a solid following. Among the most desirable plastic figures crafted today are Käthe Kruse dolls, which are made in Germany and have the same careful construction and appealing features as the original cloth versions of the 1910s and '20s. The very successful Sasha dolls, produced in England in limited editions, are evidence that well-made, thoughtfully designed figures will always have a place in the competitive doll market, even when their initial cost is relatively high. Experienced collectors are certain that the value of such dolls will increase.

Description
All-rubber black baby doll with molded features; painted hair and eyes. Hole in mouth for bottle. Movable arms and legs. Squeaker in stomach. Wears red cotton print dress with white ruffles.

Materials, Marks, and Dimensions
Rubber. Back of torso marked "Amosandra Columbia Broadcasting System. Designed by Ruth E. Newton/ Mfd. by The Sun Rubber Co. Barberton O. USA Pat 2118682 Pat 2160739." Height: 10".

Maker, Origin, and Period
Designed by Ruth E. Newton for Sun Rubber Co. Barberton, Ohio. c. 1949.

Comment
Amosandra, Amos's daughter on the Amos 'n' Andy radio program, was named in a contest sponsored by the Columbia Broadcasting System. The rubber baby doll shown here, made in her image, was manufactured at the peak of the show's popularity, and was distributed by CBS. This doll was easy to market because of its appealing face, but like most examples based on famous personalities or favorite shows, it was issued for only a brief time, capitalizing on a short-lived fame.

Hints for Collectors
Because it tended to warp or dry out, rubber was not widely used in dollmaking until after the Second World War, when the material was perfected. This doll was made about 1949, long before the "baby boom" of black dolls that occurred in the 1960s. Amosandra dolls are sought by a wide range of doll collectors, particularly those fond of black Americana, and are relatively rare but still affordable.

Rubber doll

Description
All-rubber boy doll with large molded and painted swivel head. Blond hair, side-glancing eyes, open-closed mouth. Stationary arms and legs. Molded and painted blue shorts and shirt with pale blue collar and belt. Pale blue socks, dark blue shoes. Plastic squeaker in left leg.

Materials, Marks, and Dimensions
Rubber. "Newton/The Sun Rubber Co." impressed on head and back. Height: 8¼".

Maker, Origin, and Period
Designed by Ruth E. Newton for Sun Rubber Co. Barberton, Ohio. c. 1938.

Comment
Rubber dolls rose in popularity during the 1930s and '40s largely because of the efforts of such mail-order merchandisers as Montgomery Ward and Butler Brothers, which featured large selections of inexpensive rubber toys in their catalogues. Many dolls were produced by the Sun Rubber Company. Unlike their 19th-century predecessors, these rubber dolls were extremely durable and painted in bright primary colors that would not flake off when the dolls were immersed in water, so the small versions were ideal bathtub toys. Many dolls in all sizes had squeak mechanisms.

Hints for Collectors
In addition to the small boy shown here, Ruth Newton designed other dolls for Sun Rubber, such as Happy Kappy, Bonnie Bear, and Wiggy Wags. Rubber dolls are easy to find and are still inexpensive, but because children sometimes treated them roughly, many such toys show signs of wear.

Description
Multi-face toddler doll with composition head. 3 faces are switched by twisting knob on top of head. Painted features; blond mohair wig. Original fleecy pink and blue rayon hooded snowsuit.

Materials, Marks, and Dimensions
Composition head; cloth body. Height: 14½".

Maker, Origin, and Period
Designed by Elsie Gilbert for Three-In-One Doll Corp. New York City. c. 1946.

Comment
Introduced in 1946, Trudy is a doll with several personalities because she has a knob on top of her head that changes her face from "Sleepy" to "Weepy" or "Smiley." Trudy came in different sizes and outfits. The 14½" Trudy shown here was also available wearing a "fetching party print dress with gay bonnet to match," an outfit in which she was advertised as "a heart snatcher." The 20" Big Sister Trudy wore a party frock and bonnet, and the 16" doll also had a matching hat and dress. Another version had a peaked felt hat and play suit.

Hints for Collectors
Collectors are constantly on the lookout for Trudy because she was one of the last composition dolls made. Occasionally she turns up at yard sales, flea markets, or thrift shops. Check the turning mechanism to see that it works properly. Look for the related paper-doll set entitled "Trudy, Queen of the Paper Doll World," issued in 1947.

Description
Little girl doll with composition head and swivel neck. Molded and painted blond hair and features including side-glancing blue eyes and smiling open-closed mouth showing 4 teeth. Fully jointed, segmented body.

Materials, Marks, and Dimensions
Composition head; wooden body. Red heart-shaped label on chest reads "MARGIE/DES. & COPYRIGHT/BY JOS. KALLUS." Height: 9¼".

Maker, Origin, and Period
Designed by Joseph Kallus for Cameo Doll Co. New York City. c. 1929.

Comment
Joseph Kallus, one of the most innovative doll designers of the 1920s, created Margie as an inexpensive (98¢) answer to German bisque dolls. Margie's construction featured a separate neck component and a well-balanced, 18-piece wooden body strung with elastic so that it could stand erect or assume any pose. Kallus declared in his patent that the unique neck construction not only sped up production, but also made the doll more sturdy. Several hundred thousand Margies were sold in England and America. In 1958 Cameo issued a fully jointed, all-vinyl Margie doll with sleep-eyes and rooted saran hair.

Hints for Collectors
Copies of Cameo's 1929 Margie were made by another firm, but these had fewer segments than the originals. These copies lack the heart-shaped label of the authentic dolls. In 1932 Kallus came out with a Joy doll, which was very similar to Margie.

Description
Identical all-celluloid child dolls in original Swiss regional costumes. Molded and painted features, including blond hair, blue eyes, and closed mouths. Jointed bodies. Left: Wears Vaud-style costume of straw hat, linen blouse, black velvet vest, green satin skirt, and oilcloth shoes. Right: Wears Geneva-style costume of pink satin dress with net scarf.

Materials, Marks, and Dimensions
Celluloid. Crowned mermaid trademark in shield on upper backs. Height: 9¾" (left); 9½" (right).

Maker, Origin, and Period
Cellba Works. Germany. c. 1920–30.

Comment
During the 1920s and '30s, celluloid dolls were exported to America in large quantities, mostly from Germany. The best known of these were made by the Rheinische Gummi und Celluloid Fabrik of Bavaria; collectors call them "turtle-mark dolls" because of that company's turtle trademark. The celluloid "mermaid" dolls pictured here, less familiar but quite similar in style to turtle-mark dolls, were manufactured in Germany by the Cellba Works, which used a mermaid trademark and produced such dolls as late as 1952. Celluloid, a compound of cellulose nitrate and camphor, was introduced in 1870 as a water-resistant doll material that could be easily tinted, shaped, and painted. Highly flammable, it is no longer used for toys.

Hints for Collectors
Celluloid objects must be stored in a cool dark place because this substance begins to melt at 120° F and discolors when exposed to strong light. Celluloid dolls are also easily crushed and are nearly impossible to restore.

Description
Girl and boy dolls with composition heads; molded and painted hair and features. Left: Girl has brown hair and blue eyes. Cry box in body. Wears red silk bow in hair; brown and white print dress. Right: Little boy with brown side-glancing eyes; jointed limbs. Wears pink and blue striped shirt and short pink pants with suspenders. Painted white socks and black shoes.

Materials, Marks, and Dimensions
Left: Composition head and lower arms; cloth body. "© G.G. Drayton" embossed on back of shoulder. Right: Composition. Height: 16″ (left); 12½″ (right).

Maker, Origin, and Period
Left: Maker unknown. United States. c. 1912–16. Right: E. I. Horsman Co. New York City. c. 1948.

Comment
The original Campbell Kid dolls were introduced by E. I. Horsman in 1910, based on drawings by the noted illustrator Grace Drayton. The Campbell's Soup Company popularized the Campbell Kids in its advertisements and between 1910 and 1925 commissioned numerous doll versions of these figures. Drayton designed other dolls, such as Gee Gee and Peek-a-boo, all closely resembling the Campbell Kids, but none achieving their fame.

Hints for Collectors
Manufacture of these dolls halted during the Depression. With the advent of television in the late 1940s, the Campbell Kids were featured in a series of TV-cartoon commercials for Campbell's soups, and the dolls were reissued. The doll shown at right (*see also* 123) was made during this period. Campbell Kid dolls were made as late as 1976; the earliest examples, such as the one at left, are most valuable.

Description

Doll with set of interchangeable molded and painted composition heads and original hats and costumes. Jointed body. Assembled doll shown here has short brown hair, blue eyes, closed mouth. Wears white cotton sailor suit with matching hat and black patent leather shoes with metal buckles. Additional heads in sectioned box are, clockwise from upper left: Head with painted Asian features, including almond-shaped side-glancing eyes, arched brows, tan skin, closed red mouth; black and gold hat. Little girl with blond wig, blue glass sleep-eyes, closed mouth; pink and white polka-dot hat. Girl with blond wig, painted blue eyes, closed mouth; white cotton sailor cap. Baby with painted blue eyes, closed mouth; pleated blue cotton gauze bonnet. Outfits matching hats include Chinese-style black and gold cotton jumpsuit; pink and white polka-dot cotton dress; blue cotton dress with white apron; and white jumper.

Materials, Marks, and Dimensions

Composition. Cardboard box labeled "Famlee Doll" with names and photographs of heads. Height: 16″ (assembled).

Maker, Origin, and Period

Berwick Doll Co. New York City. c. 1921.

Comment

Each head in the Famlee Doll set has a socket that fits over the threaded plug neck of the doll's body, so that a child can easily screw it on.

Hints for Collectors

Sets of this doll originally came with as many as 12 heads and ranged in price from $6 to $20, depending on the number of heads. Today complete sets rarely appear on the market and are quite valuable.

Uneeda Biscuit Boy

Description
Advertising doll with molded and painted features including light brown hair and blue eyes. Original costume of yellow sateen hat and slicker over red and white striped rompers. Black molded rain boots. Miniature wooden replica of Uneeda Biscuit box tied to wrist.

Materials, Marks, and Dimensions
Composition head, lower arms, and feet; cloth body, upper arms, and legs. Label on cuff of raincoat reads "Uneeda Biscuit/pat'd Dec. 8, 1914/Mfd. by Ideal Novelty & Toy Co." Height: 15″.

Maker, Origin, and Period
Designed by Morris Michtom for National Biscuit Co. Manufactured by Ideal Novelty & Toy Co. New York City. c. 1914.

Comment
The Uneeda Biscuit Boy's appealing likeness—modeled after the 5-year-old nephew of the copywriter assigned to the National Biscuit Company's advertising campaign—appeared on many of that firm's products. The first Uneeda Biscuit Boy doll, shown here, was manufactured by Ideal in 1914; 2 other versions were made in 1916. One had jointed legs and was almost identical to the original. The other, 11½″ tall, was made entirely of molded and painted composition, including its clothing.

Hints for Collectors
The face of the doll shown here has been repainted in order to restore it. Opinions differ about repainting; some collectors prefer a doll with original paint, even if it is peeling and chipped, while others like a better-looking, touched-up doll.

Description
Little girl doll with composition swivel head. Molded and painted
features including red hair with bangs, upturned nose, and
rosebud mouth. Green sleep-eyes with lashes. Fully jointed
body. Original white cotton dress with openwork detail and 2
pink bows. White socks with blue and red bands. Black oilcloth
shoes with gold metal buckles and ties. Wears metal bracelet
with charm at wrist.

Materials, Marks, and Dimensions
Composition. "EFFanBEE/Patsy Lou" marked on back.
"EFFanBEE/DurableDolls" printed on dress label. Label on
bracelet reads "EFFanBEE/Patsy Lou." Height: 22″.

Maker, Origin, and Period
Designed by Bernard Lipfert for EFFanBEE (trade name for
Fleischaker & Baum). New York City. c. 1929.

Comment
The Patsy series was the all-time favorite line of EFFanBEE
dolls. First produced in composition in 1927, Patsy dolls were
issued in vinyl as late as the 1970s. In the 1930s EFFanBEE
designed Patsy wardrobes and established a Patsy Doll Club,
which eventually claimed over 270,000 members. Other versions
of Patsy were manufactured over the years, including Patsy
Babykin (182) and a rare 9″ black Patsyette.

Hints for Collectors
Collectors look for Patsy Lou, Patsy Joan, and Patsy Ann dolls
with colorless celluloid fingernails that could be polished and
repolished; these were first introduced in 1936. Some Patricia,
Patsy Babykin, and Patsy Joan dolls of 1949 had "magic" or
"magnetic" hands, which enabled them to hold metal objects.

My Darling's Baby Naughty

Description
Character doll with celluloid head. Blond mohair wig; blue
sleep-eyes with eyelashes; open mouth with movable tongue.
Undressed.

Materials, Marks, and Dimensions
Celluloid head and limbs; kid body. "K [star trademark] R/728/7/
Germany/43–46" marked on back of head. Height: 15".

Maker, Origin, and Period
Head by Rheinische Gummi und Celluloid Fabrik; body by
Kämmer & Reinhardt. Germany. c. 1927.

Comment
This doll is pictured in the 1927 Kämmer & Reinhardt catalogue,
which was originally printed in English, German, French, and
Spanish—evidence of Kämmer & Reinhardt's huge output and
worldwide distribution. This publication featured the "My
Darling" dolls, which the company had manufactured since 1901,
and the "Naughty" dolls, added to that line in 1919. The
catalogue provides clues to the marks K & R used to identify its
dolls; for example, the mark #728/7 on the baby shown here was
used on dolls with celluloid heads and wigs.

Hints for Collectors
Most K & R dolls were assembled from parts produced by other
firms. For instance, K & R sometimes used bisque heads made
by Simon & Halbig, while the elastic for stringing and the mohair
for wigs was supplied by English firms. When celluloid gained
favor in the 1920s, the Rheinische Gummi und Celluloid Fabrik
company manufactured heads in this material for Kämmer &
Reinhardt, based on K & R's earlier bisque versions. These
often bear both the Rheinische Gummi turtle and the "K [star]
R" mark.

Little Sister

Description
Little girl doll with composition head; molded and painted features including blue eyes and closed mouth. Long blond braids made of cotton thread. Original red felt hat, tan blouse, and green skirt; ribbed cotton stockings and pointed wooden shoes.

Materials, Marks, and Dimensions
Composition head and arms; cloth body and legs. Paper label attached to sleeve reads "Little Sister/Trade Mark/Registered/ Copyright by Grace Corry/Made in U.S.A."; "Genuine Madame Hendren/Doll" marked in circle on label. Height: 14".

Maker, Origin, and Period
Designed by Grace Corry for Averill Manufacturing Co. New York City. c. 1925.

Comment
Grace Corry was a prolific doll designer who created dolls both for the Century Doll Company and Averill Manufacturing, which sometimes used the trade name "Madame Hendren." Corry's first successful dolls, the "Fiji Wijis," were manufactured and distributed by Century. Little Sister and her counterpart, Little Brother, manufactured by Averill, were among Corry's most popular dolls. They appeared in rompers and other clothing, including national costumes such as the Dutch outfit shown here.

Hints for Collectors
Check labels and marks on a doll to see if a designer is indicated. Talented designers were in great demand by doll manufacturers during the expansion of the American dollmaking industry that took place from about 1910 to 1930. Because many designers worked for more than one company, keeping track of them sometimes confounds even the experts.

Gretel and Yerri

Description
Girl and boy dolls in original Tyrolean costumes. Celluloid heads
with molded and painted hair and features including blue eyes,
closed mouths, and rosy cheeks. Jointed arms. Left: Gretel
wears red and green plaid dress with black ribbon trim, white
cotton apron and slip, green felt hat with feather, woolen socks,
and black patent leather shoes. Right: Yerri wears lederhosen,
green felt suspenders, and white cotton shirt. Matching green
felt hat with feather. Thick striped socks; black patent leather
shoes.

Materials, Marks, and Dimensions
Celluloid heads; composition arms; stuffed cloth bodies and legs.
"2/0/Hansi/W.Z." marked on necks. Height: 7½″ (left); 8″ (right).

Maker, Origin, and Period
L'Oncle Hansi. France. c. 1917.

Comment
Gretel and Yerri were made by the little-known French firm
L'Oncle Hansi, which specialized in small character and souvenir
dolls with celluloid heads, cloth bodies, and regional costumes.

Hints for Collectors
Although the examples illustrated are dressed as typical
schoolchildren, dollmakers often clothe their dolls in holiday
costumes instead of everyday garments, and take liberties
with details and accessories. Regional costumes do not
always accurately replicate the clothes worn by the people
of a specific country or province. Some collectors specialize in
dolls dressed in variations of a particular regional outfit.

Description
All-composition boy and girl dolls with molded and painted
features including side-glancing eyes, pointed chins, and pug
noses. Blond wigs. One-piece heads and bodies; jointed limbs.
Left: David Copperfield with wig tied back in ponytail. Original
black jacket, white collar, and purple and white striped pants;
molded white socks and black shoes. Right: Tiny Betty in
original gray velvet dress with yarn trim at cuffs and hem, red
felt bonnet with yarn trim, red stockinet mittens. Molded white
socks and black Mary Jane shoes.

Materials, Marks, and Dimensions
Composition. "MME ALEXANDER" embossed on backs. Height: 7".

Maker, Origin, and Period
Madame Alexander. New York City. c. 1935–43.

Comment
These are among the first composition dolls Madame Alexander
produced. Over the years the company featured dolls of more
than 50 characters from children's and classic literature,
including Dickens's *David Copperfield*. Such subject matter
reflected Madame Alexander's belief that dolls should be
educational. Tiny Betty is a miniature figure from the firm's
line of Betty-type dolls, which came in various sizes.

Hints for Collectors
Like many manufacturers, Madame Alexander created several
basic doll types—including Princess Elizabeth, Wendy-Ann,
Margaret, and Cissy—which, through a change of clothing or
hairstyle, could portray any number of characters. The specific
character may be identified by a cloth label sewn inside the
clothing.

Fern Deutsch dolls

Description
Girl and boy dolls with composition heads and molded and painted features. Original costumes based on 19th-century styles. Left: Girl with long black hair wears lace-trimmed pink taffeta dress, 2 white slips, and white lace pantaloons. Picture hat. White stockings and white leather boots. Small doll held in arms wears blue taffeta dress, green taffeta diaper, and white satin booties. Right: Boy with blond hair holds hoop in left hand and stick in right. Wears white cotton shirt with lace-trimmed collar and cuffs; black velvet suit, tie, and hat. White stockings and spats and black leather shoes.

Materials, Marks, and Dimensions
Composition heads and hands; cloth bodies over wire armatures. Height: 13¾″ (left); 13½″ (right).

Maker, Origin, and Period
Fern Deutsch and Besse McGee. San Antonio, Texas. Left: c. 1967. Right: c. 1964.

Comment
Fern Deutsch learned about doll construction from her mother, a noted designer of display figures for New York City department stores. Commissioned by collectors and museums, Deutsch began making dolls in the 1940s. She concentrated on the design and modeling of heads and hands, while her aunt, Besse McGee, specialized in the body construction. Each item of clothing was researched to ensure its authenticity.

Hints for Collectors
Deutsch dolls have bodies made of padded fabric or chamois built over wire armatures. The heads and hands are made from specially formulated composition, then covered with kidskin and painted in oil. Few, if any, are on the market today.

Little Women

Description
Marmee and daughters with molded and painted hard plastic heads, sleep-eyes, and synthetic floss wigs. Bodies jointed at shoulders and hips. Original costumes. Left to right: Jo has long brown hair and red satin dress. Meg has dark blond hair and blue and white satin gown. Marmee has long dark brown hair and green cotton print dress with dark green satin apron. Beth has brown hair and green and white satin dress. Amy has long blond hair and pink and white print cotton gown.

Materials, Marks, and Dimensions
Hard plastic. "ALEX" marked on bases of heads. Cloth labels on dresses read "Louisa M. Alcott's/Little Women/[name of doll]/By Madame Alexander N.Y. USA/All Rights Reserved." Height: 14–16".

Maker, Origin, and Period
Madame Alexander. New York City. c. 1950–51.

Comment
Based on the characters from Louisa May Alcott's novel *Little Women*, the dolls shown here are one of several successful editions of these figures produced by Madame Alexander in various materials since 1933. Marmee did not appear in the first hard plastic set that came out in 1948. In the 1950 series, Marmee, Amy, and Meg have the straight nose characteristic of a Madame Alexander facial type known as Margaret, while Jo and Beth have a Maggie-type face with a pug nose. Dolls from the 1950–51 series have large hands with separated fingers.

Hints for Collectors
Complete sets of Madame Alexander's Little Women are nearly as rare as the company's Dionne Quintuplets, so collectors are often willing to pay a premium for characters they are missing.

Scarlett O'Hara

Description
Girl doll with composition swivel head. Molded and painted features including upturned nose and closed rosebud mouth. Black wig of human hair; green sleep-eyes with lashes. Original brown satin gown with ruffled white organdy collar and green ribbon sash. White flower in hair.

Materials, Marks, and Dimensions
Composition. Paper tag pinned to front of dress reads "Madame Alexander's/SCARLETT O'HARA Doll" with picture of character and Tara. Back of tag reads "Scarlett O'Hara from Gone with the Wind by Madame Alexander. By Special Permission of the Copyright Owners. All Rights Reserved." Height: 10½".

Maker, Origin, and Period
Madame Alexander. New York City. c. 1941.

Comment
Madame Alexander's line of Scarlett O'Hara dolls achieved a popularity almost unsurpassed in the company's history. Composition, hard plastic, and vinyl versions of the heroine of Margaret Mitchell's novel have been made since 1937, and vinyl examples are still being produced today. Many of their costumes are based on the more than 36 that Vivien Leigh wore as Scarlett in the 1939 film.

Hints for Collectors
From 1937 to 1942 Scarlett O'Hara dolls were made of composition and had a standard Madame Alexander face known as Wendy-Ann. From 1949 to 1950 they were made of hard plastic with the Margaret face; from 1955 to 1963 the hard plastic dolls had a variety of faces. After 1963, vinyl and hard plastic versions had Jacqueline, Mary Ann, and Cissette faces.

Late Jumeau bébé

Description
Girl doll with pressed cardboard head. Synthetic blond wig with
corkscrew curls. Blue sleep-eyes; open mouth showing teeth.
Jointed body. Original green felt vest, skirt, and hat and pink
silk blouse. Pink satin underskirt, white cotton underpants and
socks, and white leather shoes. Doll says "mama, papa" when
voice box in torso is activated by pull strings at side.

Materials, Marks, and Dimensions
Pressed cardboard head; composition body, hands, legs, and feet;
wooden arms. "UNIS PARIS/301" incised on head. Paper tag
attached to skirt reads "Fabrication/JUMEAU/PARIS/MADE IN
FRANCE." Height: 20½".

Maker, Origin, and Period
Jumeau in association with SFBJ (Société Française de
Fabrication de Bébés & Jouets). France. c. 1920.

Comment
Late Jumeau dolls cannot compare in quality or aesthetic appeal
to the lovely, smooth, pale bisque bébés that firm made before
1900. German competition pressured the French industry to
produce inexpensive dolls. To cut costs, Jumeau, in association
with SFBJ, mass produced dolls made of cheaper materials, such
as coarse, highly colored bisque or the pressed cardboard from
which this doll's head is made.

Hints for Collectors
Some collectors who cannot afford early, museum-quality bisque
Jumeau dolls buy the company's much-inferior 20th-century
examples simply for the illustrious name. Many experienced
collectors, however, prefer outstanding dolls made by less
famous companies to poorly made examples by well-known firms.

My Rosy Darling

Description
Girl doll with celluloid head. Molded and painted features including open rosebud mouth. Pageboy wig of brown human hair; blue flirty sleep-eyes. Fully jointed body. Fingernails and toenails outlined in red. Original white chemise with china buttons; ruffled pink underpants, white rayon socks, and white oilcloth shoes.

Materials, Marks, and Dimensions
Celluloid head; composition body. "K[star trademark]R 50/717/ Germany" embossed on head. Paper label on dress reads "My/ Rosy Darling/K[star trademark]R Made in Germany." Height: 19½".

Maker, Origin, and Period
Head by Simon & Halbig; body by Kämmer & Reinhardt. Germany. c. 1927.

Comment
As early as the late 19th century, German firms were manufacturing dolls from celluloid, one of the first manmade plastics. The red outlined fingernails and toenails characteristic of My Rosy Darling appear on many Kämmer & Reinhardt dolls. This figure's tall slim body is jointed well above the knees to allow for the shorter skirt styles of the 1920s.

Hints for Collectors
The heads of Kämmer & Reinhardt dolls were often made to order by the firm of Simon & Halbig and are usually so marked. If possible, before buying a doll remove its wig to examine the head for marks. The doll shown here was recently restrung, but this has little effect on its value.

Munich Art doll

Description
Girl character doll with composition head and curly brown wig of human hair. Molded and painted features including brown eyes, rosy cheeks, and closed mouth. Jointed body. Wears tiered white cotton dress with lace collar, cuffs, and hem. Clusters of white cloth flowers on purple ribbons attached to dress. Silklike purple cape. Brown cotton knit stockings; black and brown leather shoes.

Materials, Marks, and Dimensions
Composition. "K III" stamped on back of head under wig. Height: 18″.

Maker, Origin, and Period
Marion Bertha Kaulitz. Germany. c. 1908–12.

Comment
Marion Kaulitz designed lifelike dolls meant to appeal to children. Known as Munich Art dolls, these figures have heads modeled by Kaulitz's associate, Paul Vogelsanger. At an awards ceremony in 1910, Kaulitz was credited with spearheading Germany's *Puppenreform* movement, the aim of which was to produce realistic dolls and toys. These efforts attracted great attention in artistic as well as commercial circles. She inspired Kämmer & Reinhardt to manufacture character dolls under the name *Charakterpuppen* in 1909.

Hints for Collectors
Not all Munich Art dolls are labeled. Some have "Kaulitz" or "K III" stamped on the back of the head; others are stamped "V 3," the mark of Paul Vogelsanger. Kaulitz dolls are collected not only because of their appealing naturalism, but also because they are important in the history of dollmaking.

Sonja Henie

Description
Celebrity doll with composition swivel head and curly blond wig.
Brown sleep-eyes with lashes; open mouth with 4 upper teeth.
Original black velvet sequin-trimmed dress with matching bow
in hair. Ice skates made of gold foil with metal runners and
cotton laces.

Materials, Marks, and Dimensions
Composition. Paper tag around wrist has picture of Sonja Henie
above her name. Reverse side reads "A Madame Alexander
Product/All Rights Reserved/New York." Height: 14″.

Maker, Origin, and Period
Madame Alexander. New York City. c. 1941.

Comment
Sonja Henie dolls, patterned after the well-known Olympic figure
skater who later starred in several movies, were produced from
1939 until 1943. These range in size from 13″ to 21″, and the
smaller versions often have Alexander's Wendy-Ann-type body
with a swivel waist. The wigs come in several shades of blond
and are made of mohair or human hair. Though most are dressed
in winter sports outfits, some dolls wear bridal attire. In 1951
Madame Alexander issued a new edition of 15″, 18″, and 23″
Henie dolls to coincide with the star's popular "Ice Review."

Hints for Collectors
All of Madame Alexander's Sonja Henie dolls have the skater's
dimples and blond hair, but there are some differences between
the 1939–43 and 1951 versions. The later dolls have vinyl heads,
hard plastic bodies, and white ice skates; their mouths are open
but toothless. Early ones are harder to find and more valuable.

Description
Little girl doll with composition head and wavy brown mohair wig. Brown sleep-eyes with lashes and tiny closed red mouth. Jointed limbs. Original multicolored plaid dress and blue tam-o'-shanter cap. Lace-trimmed panties and petticoat; rayon stockings and black Mary Jane shoes. Pin through hips and lower torso allows swinging movement of legs when doll is led by the hand.

Materials, Marks, and Dimensions
Composition. "ALEXANDER/PAT. NO 2171281" embossed on back. Height: 14".

Maker, Origin, and Period
Madame Alexander. New York City. c. 1943.

Comment
Jeannie Walker is the only walking doll Madame Alexander ever made. Introduced as "first-of-its-kind," the figure has a unique walking mechanism that the company patented in 1943. Madame Alexander's advertisements described Jeannie Walker as "the doll that Sits, Stands, and WALKS Like a Perfect Little Lady. Take her by the hand and she walks as easily and gracefully as the little girl she depicts."

Hints for Collectors
The popular Jeannie Walker doll was made in 14" and 18" sizes from 1939 to 1943. The 14" doll has slim legs, while the 18" doll has chubby legs and is pigeon-toed. Most Jeannie Walkers have brown hair; blonds are rarer and are therefore more desirable. Collectors prize examples that wear original outfits.

Toni

Description
Girl doll with original box and toy permanent-wave set. Hard
plastic molded and painted head with glued-on brown nylon wig.
Brown sleep-eyes; closed mouth. Jointed at hips and shoulders.
Original blue rayon dress with lace-trimmed collar and belt.
White rayon hair ribbon. White cotton underclothes and ribbed
rayon socks; pink imitation-leather shoes.

Materials, Marks, and Dimensions
Hard plastic. "P90 Ideal Doll Made in USA" embossed on head,
"Ideal Doll P90 B" on back. Label on back of dress reads
"Genuine Toni Doll with nylon wig made by Ideal Novelty
& Toy Co." Height: 14″.

Maker, Origin, and Period
Designed by Bernard Lipfert for Ideal Novelty & Toy Co. New
York City. c. 1949.

Comment
Introduced during the 1949 Christmas season, Ideal's Toni doll
was an instant success, thanks to the rage for the do-it-yourself
permanent waves invented by the Toni Company, a division of
Gillette. Little girls loved the Toni doll because they could
endlessly wash, set, and curl her durable nylon hair. The doll,
sold in a striped box, came with shampoo, sugar-water wave
solution, curlers, wrapping papers, and a comb.

Hints for Collectors
Ideal made Toni dolls that ranged from 14″ to 20″; the 20″ models
are walkers and are rare. In the mid-1950s the American
Character Doll Company produced vinyl Toni dolls in 4 sizes, but
these are not nearly as well known.

Shirley Temple

Description
Celebrity doll with composition swivel head. Blond wig with red ribbon. Brown sleep-eyes; open mouth with upper teeth. Jointed body. Original costume of red and white polka-dot dress with red trim and red ribbon sash. White socks and shoes. Shirley Temple button at waist displays her picture and inscription.

Materials, Marks, and Dimensions
Composition. Button reads "The World's Darling Genuine Shirley Temple/An Ideal." "Shirley Temple/13" embossed on head and body. Label on dress reads "Genuine/Shirley Temple/Doll Dress/Ideal." Height: 13".

Maker, Origin, and Period
Designed by Molly Goldman for Ideal Novelty & Toy Co. New York City. c. 1934.

Comment
This doll was introduced in 1934 dressed like Shirley Temple in her first movie, *Stand Up and Cheer*. Produced until 1939 and accompanied by ever-changing clothing and accessories, she became America's most popular doll. In 1957 the doll was reissued in hard plastic or vinyl, with flirty sleep-eyes, the famous dimples, rooted saran hair, and a copy of the original red and white polka-dot dress.

Hints for Collectors
The early dolls are often labeled on the head, although some unmarked dolls have been found. Those with marks are, of course, more valuable. Beware of older dolls that have cracked eyes and skin, which may lower their value substantially.

Description
Celebrity doll with composition swivel head and blond mohair
wig. Brown sleep-eyes; open mouth with upper teeth. Jointed
body. Original cowboy suit of brown leather vest and chaps, red
plaid shirt, and rayon neckerchief. Holster and pistol; black felt
cowboy hat. Brown cotton socks; brown imitation-leather boots.

Materials, Marks, and Dimensions
Composition. "Shirley Temple/II" embossed on back. Height:
13¾".

Maker, Origin, and Period
Designed by Molly Goldman for Ideal Novelty & Toy Co. New
York City. c. 1936.

Comment
Ideal's Shirley Temple dolls grossed more than $6 million in sales
for the company. In 1937 Shirley Temple was rated the most
popular movie star—adult or child—the world over, and by then
countless dolls had already been modeled in her image by many
firms, including a cloth version by England's Chad Valley
Company. The Saalfield Publishing Company sold more than a
million paper Shirley Temple dolls in 1934 alone (*see* 137). Of the
composition Shirleys, the Ideal and EFFanBEE examples are
considered the best because of the high quality of their materials
and paint. But like most composition dolls, they too in time
cracked.

Hints for Collectors
Crazing and cracking, as on the face of the doll shown here,
result when composition ages and dries out. When cracks are
small, they may be disguised by an application of pancake
makeup. A little paste wax can help preserve composition.

Terri Lee cowgirl

Description
Girl doll with composition head. Molded and painted features including large brown eyes and lashes, pug nose, and closed red lips. Curly blond synthetic wig. Jointed body. Original fringed white leather vest and skirt, yellow cotton print blouse, and tan imitation-leather boots. Cowgirl hat missing.

Materials, Marks, and Dimensions
Composition. "Terri Lee/Pat. Pending" embossed on back. Height: 16½".

Maker, Origin, and Period
Terri Lee Sales Corp. Lincoln, Nebraska. c. 1946–48.

Comment
Violet Lee Gradwohl, founder of the Terri Lee Sales Corporation, wanted to make unbreakable dolls that children could think of as playmates, and so fashioned them with sturdy toddler-type bodies. Terri Lee dolls had extensive wardrobes, including a full-length made-to-order mink coat that could be bought for about $250. From 1946 until some time after 1962, many versions of Terri Lee were manufactured. One unique talking type had a head fitted with a speaker that could be connected to a record player. Advertised as "Terri Lee, the National Baby Sitter," it could sing songs and tell stories.

Hints for Collectors
Most Terri Lee dolls had hair that could be washed and curled; the talking version was the exception, since contact with water ruined its mechanism. The heads of talking dolls should be cleaned only with a damp cloth. Terri Lee dolls, particularly the talking version, may be hard to find, but they remain relatively inexpensive because collectors have not yet shown great interest in them.

Description
Girl doll with hard plastic head. Blond synthetic wig, blue glass eyes, pug nose, and closed rosebud mouth. Jointed body. Original lace-trimmed white organdy dress with satin ribbon sash; matching bonnet and white piqué underclothes. Green imitation-leather shoes with white ribbons.

Materials, Marks, and Dimensions
Hard plastic. "VOGUE DOLL" marked on back. Height: 8″.

Maker, Origin, and Period
Vogue Dolls, Inc. Medford, Massachusetts. c. 1950–53.

Comment
Vogue's Ginny doll, still selling well after 4 decades, qualifies as an all-time favorite. Ginny was created by Jennie Graves, who got her start during the 1930s by designing and producing dolls' clothes for the Boston department store, Jordan Marsh. The early composition Ginnys were dressed in foreign costumes, play clothing, and "make-believe" character outfits. The hard plastic dolls introduced about 1950 wore imaginative outfits that reflected the fashions of the day.

Hints for Collectors
Composition Ginny dolls are more valuable than the later, hard plastic versions. The earliest composition examples have a bent right elbow and are marked "VOGUE" on the head, "DOLL CO." on the back, and "VOGUE" on a paper label; however, few such labels have survived. Later composition versions have straight arms and only the "VOGUE" mark on the back; in addition, they have a cloth tag.

Description
Girl doll with hard plastic head. Blond glued-on saran wig, blue glass sleep-eyes with lashes, painted eyebrows, closed red mouth. Jointed body. Hands have middle 2 fingers molded together in curled position. Original embroidered white cotton blouse with green rickrack trim, green and white striped rayon skirt, and white organdy half-slip and underpants. Straw bonnet with red silk flowers, tied with black velvet ribbon. White rayon socks; black imitation-leather shoes. Legs swing in walking motion when doll is led by the arm.

Materials, Marks, and Dimensions
Hard plastic. Marked "R & B" on head, "Made in U.S.A." on back. Tag tied around wrist reads "R & B Nanette/WALKS/SITS/STANDS/TURNS HER HEAD/NO WINDING—NO MECHANISM/Wash, Wave, Comb and Curl SARAN HAIR/R & B DOLL COMPANY. NEW YORK CITY." Height: 14¾".

Maker, Origin, and Period
Arranbee Doll Co. New York City. c. 1953–58.

Comment
The Arranbee Doll Company, founded in 1922, was taken over by Vogue Dolls about 1960, after which time the name Arranbee and its initials R & B were no longer used. During the 1950s Arranbee specialized in good-quality, hard plastic dolls such as Nanette shown here; others included Nancy, Angel Face, Dream Baby, Little Angel, and Angel Skin.

Hints for Collectors
The 1950s have recently been acknowledged as an important era in the history of dollmaking. Nanette and other products of that decade are sought nowadays because these dolls reflect the period's innovative use of plastics and other synthetic materials.

Helene and Karlchen

Description
Boy and girl dolls with plastic heads. Molded and painted features; blond human hair. Bodies jointed at legs. Stitched fingers. Identical original white satin shirts and red plush sweaters; plaid cotton pants on boy, skirt on girl; white cotton socks and red imitation-leather shoes.

Materials, Marks, and Dimensions
Plastic heads; cloth bodies. Left: "Käthe Kruse/554322 [right: 553180]/Made in Germany" printed on foot. Paper tag around neck reads "Original/Käthe Kruse/Stoffpuppe/handgeknüpft [right: Echte Haare tressiert]." Paper tag at wrist reads "ORIGINAL/Käthe Kruse [signature]/PUPPE" with doll's name and number. Height: 14½".

Maker, Origin, and Period
Käthe Kruse. Germany. c. 1969.

Comment
Käthe Kruse's daughter Hannah took over the dollmaking business after her mother's death in 1968. Collectors prize the firm's modern, plastic-head dolls, which have the same solemn faces as their cloth precursors of the 1920s and '30s (*see* 239). Other modern Kruse dolls sought by collectors are the rare celluloid dolls made in 1955 and the 9" foam-rubber dolls manufactured in 1957.

Hints for Collectors
The price of a Käthe Kruse doll depends on its age, which can be determined to some extent by the materials used. Before the Second World War most of the dolls were all-cloth. Throughout the 1940s they were felt and cloth, during the 1950s, celluloid and cloth, and since the 1960s, plastic and cloth.

Monica

Description
Girl doll with composition swivel head. Rooted blond human hair. Molded and painted features including blue eyes and closed mouth. Body jointed at shoulders and hips. Original white cotton blouse, red print skirt and vest trimmed with blue and yellow rickrack, and white cotton underpants. White and blue rayon socks and white leather shoes.

Materials, Marks, and Dimensions
Composition. Height: 20″.

Maker, Origin, and Period
Hansi Share, Monica Studios. Hollywood, California. 1943.

Comment
As a child, Hansi Share had wanted a doll with hair she could comb, so she designed one with human hair firmly embedded in the scalp so that it would withstand even the most vigorous brushing. Share produced her first such dolls in 1942, naming these 17″ figures Veronica, Rosalind, and Joan. By 1943, 20″ versions were introduced. In 1949 a hard plastic doll named Marion was offered in 14″ and 18″ sizes with a choice of platinum blond, golden blond, or auburn hair; this model was the company's last, as the firm ceased operations in 1951. An idea ahead of its time, rooted hair did not become a common feature on dolls until the 1960s, when inexpensive synthetic saran was first widely used.

Hints for Collectors
Although Share's dolls were never labeled, they are easy to identify because of their distinctive hair. Composition versions have mature faces with painted eyes, while hard plastic examples have little-girl faces with sleep-eyes. All are hard to find.

Description
Boy and girl dolls with vinyl heads and rooted hair. Painted brown eyes and closed mouths. Fully jointed bodies. Left: Gregor has dark brown hair. Original ribbed black woolen turtleneck sweater, gray flannel pants with leather belt, and white sandals. Right: Sasha has long blond hair. Original gray overalls, white short-sleeved shirt, and white sandals.

Materials, Marks, and Dimensions
Vinyl. Height: 16½″ (left); 16¼″ (right).

Maker, Origin, and Period
Sasha Dolls. England. c. 1970.

Comment
Originated by the Swiss designer Sasha Morgenthaler, Sasha dolls are strikingly contemporary in their realism, which allows children to easily identify with them. In 1980 a limited edition of 5000 Sasha dolls was distributed worldwide, the United States receiving 2500. These were so well liked that the line was quickly sold out. While Sasha does make figures representing specific races, most of the dolls have a fairly dark, uniform complexion that is supposed to represent the average skin color of all the children of the world.

Hints for Collectors
Although most Sasha dolls portray children, a few adult figures have been made. Some have identifying tags attached to their wrists; however, like the examples shown here, many Sasha dolls are not labeled. Experienced collectors know that Sasha dolls, like Madame Alexander and other well-made contemporary dolls, will undoubtedly appreciate in value in years to come.

Lady and Gentleman Dolls: China and Bisque

Used for dolls as long ago as the 18th century, porcelain became one of the most important dollmaking materials by about 1840. Included in this section are dolls made of the 2 basic types: china, a generic term for any glazed porcelain; and bisque, an unglazed porcelain usually tinted in a variety of flesh tones.

China Dolls

The great porcelain-making tradition that began at Meissen in 1710 helped make Germany the world's leading producer of china dolls' heads during the 19th century. Developed primarily in Bavaria and Thuringia, the china-doll industry flourished in the towns of Nuremberg, Coburg, and Sonneberg. Few of the manufacturers are known today because most china dolls left the factories unmarked.

Most early china dolls' heads were made of a translucent porcelain body composed of kaolin clay, feldspar, and silica. Two manufacturing methods were employed: In press molding, clay was rolled in squares and pressed into 2-part plaster molds; in slip casting, a liquid clay mixture was poured into the molds. Examining the hollow interior of a china head will reveal which technique was used. Pressed examples have an uneven inner surface; poured ones, smooth. Heads were dried in the molds in large, centrally heated rooms, and then removed, assembled, fired, and painted. Next a feldspathic glaze was applied, and another firing took place. (Bisque and parian heads were manufactured in similar fashion, but left unglazed.) Produced in many sizes, heads were usually sold separately to be joined to various types of bodies—often cloth or wood—made commercially or at home.

Most china dolls are quite formal-looking and not at all toylike. The majority represent women, and the few male and child figures are distinguished primarily by shorter hairstyles. Figures with black molded hair and blue eyes predominated until the 1880s, when blue-eyed blonds became more common. Bald dolls, meant to be covered by wigs, are some of the rarer china-head types. Glass eyes in china dolls are also rare. The finest china heads have long, slender necks and delicate, detailed features. Although china dolls were less in demand by the turn of the century, they continued into the 20th century in the form of "Pet Name" lady figures, which had china heads and limbs attached to bodies of printed cloth.

Bisque and Parian-Type Dolls

France excelled in the creation of bisque dolls, which gained favor over china ones in the 1860s. This was the era of the exquisitely crafted lady doll, made with luminous glass eyes, stylish wigs of human hair or mohair, and well-shaped kid or cloth bodies designed to show off the latest in fashionable Parisian attire. The firms of Rohmer, Huret, Bru, and Jumeau came to dominate the French dollmaking industry during this period, introducing and patenting many improvements in construction and design. Parian, an untinted bisque, was often used for dolls' heads during the 1870s and '80s, particularly in Germany. By the mid-1870s lady dolls were supplanted by bébés, then enjoying great popularity.

Bald-head china doll

Description
Lady doll with china shoulder-head. Molded and painted features including blue pate, blue eyes, and closed mouth. Wears cotton print dress in purple and white, with low-cut ruffled neckline and tiered skirt; white cotton underskirt and pantaloons. Blue suede shoes with gilded-cloth floral decoration.

Materials, Marks, and Dimensions
China shoulder-head, kid body and limbs. Height: 23¼″.

Maker, Origin, and Period
Maker unknown. Germany. c. 1830–50.

Comment
This doll's long thin face, oval eyes, high uncovered forehead, and gracefully proportioned shoulders and neck are characteristic of china dolls made in the first half of the 19th century. Her sloping shoulders were designed to show off the low-cut or off-the-shoulder gowns then in vogue.

Hints for Collectors
Many 19th-century china dolls have a painted pate, which is either the glue spot for a wig or a dollmaker's finishing mark. This doll's blue pate is extremely unusual, since most were painted black. Dolls with bald heads and painted pates are generally rarer and therefore more desirable than those with molded hairstyles. Look for tiny black spots, caused by impurities in the clay, on the china heads or limbs of many 18th- or early 19th-century dolls. While not all early china figures have these spots, their presence helps to verify that a doll is not a reproduction.

China-head doll

Description
Doll with pink-tinted china shoulder-head. Molded and painted
features including short dark brown hair; brushstrokes visible at
forehead. Pink body and limbs. Elongated arms sewn on at
shoulders; hands have separately stitched fingers. Unclothed.

Materials, Marks, and Dimensions
China shoulder-head, kid body and limbs. "J P" marked in blue
inside head. "PAR BREVET" marked on shoulder. Height: 12½".

Maker, Origin, and Period
Jacob Petit. France. c. 1840–60.

Comment
Jacob Petit was one of the few French doll manufacturers who
produced his own fine china doll heads instead of importing them
from Germany, which was a common practice among French
firms. He received a French patent for porcelain heads in 1843
and an English patent for improved porcelain manufacture in
1853. Petit's china shoulder-head dolls, such as the one shown
here, are usually characterized by delicately modeled faces and 8
sew holes in their shoulder plates. This unclothed figure has the
low-waisted, elongated body proportions that were fashionable in
mid-19th-century dolls.

Hints for Collectors
Marked Jacob Petit dolls are extremely scarce and are therefore
valuable. Most are found only in museums and important private
collections. This doll's painted crown may have been meant to be
covered by a fancy wig; without a wig, the delicate wisps of hair
framing the face suggest a coiffure for a child or male doll.
Collectors should not confuse a short stylized hairdo like this
with the painted caplike pate, never intended to represent hair,
seen on some 19th-century china-head dolls.

Description

Lady dolls with china shoulder-heads. Molded and painted features including black molded hair. Left: Hair styled in sausage curls. Hole in clenched right fist. Red-orange shoes. Center: Brush marks visible on hair. Pink-tinted shoulder-head and forearms. Green shoes. Right: Hair drawn into bun. Orange shoes.

Materials, Marks, and Dimensions

China shoulder-heads, lower arms, and lower legs; wooden torsos, upper arms, and upper legs. Height: 7″ (left); 6¾″ (center); 6″ (right).

Maker, Origin, and Period

Maker unknown. Germany. c. 1845–60.

Comment

China-head dolls with china limbs and wooden bodies are known for their high-quality, fully jointed construction. Wooden pegs were pushed through holes in their jointed elbows and knees, and also inserted through sew holes in their shoulders to connect the china head to the wooden torso. Almost always made in Germany, these dolls usually have black molded hair. The doll on the left has a hole in her right fist into which sewing equipment or a fortune-telling wand may have been inserted, suggesting that she was either a vendor or an ornamental doll.

Hints for Collectors

Dolls with china limbs and wooden bodies are generally more valuable than those with cloth bodies; those with elaborate hairstyles are particularly sought after. Most china shoulder-heads are unmarked except for a mold number and are therefore unattributable to a particular firm.

China-head doll

Description
Lady doll with china shoulder-head. Molded and painted features including black hair with center part, wraparound braid, and fine brush marks at temples. Spoon hands. Wears long-sleeved gold silk taffeta dress with buttoned bodice and brown trim at waist, cuffs, and hem; lace-trimmed collar. White lace-trimmed petticoat. Thin metal necklace. Small pink flat shoes.

Materials, Marks, and Dimensions
China shoulder-head and limbs, cloth body. Height: 15″.

Maker, Origin, and Period
Maker unknown. Germany. Mid-19th century.

Comment
Produced in Germany as early as the 1750s, china dolls reached their height of popularity in the mid-19th century. Examples made prior to 1860 often have 3 or more sew holes in their shoulder plates rather than the 2 seen on later dolls, and have spoonlike rather than cupped hands. Shoes with flat soles instead of heels are another sign of pre-1860 manufacture. By the 1870s and '80s, bisque lady dolls and bébés were favored over china-head dolls, partly because the texture of bisque was softer, more lifelike, and thus more appealing than that of china. The term "china" refers to glazed porcelain, which has a shiny finish, whereas "bisque" refers to unglazed porcelain, which has a mat surface.

Hints for Collectors
The quality and rarity of its china head largely determines the value of a doll. When a china-head doll has replaced parts, it should be dated by the style of its head; however, such a doll is usually worth less than one with its original body and limbs intact.

Description
Lady doll with china shoulder-head. Molded and painted features including short black hair with brush marks framing face. Pink-tinted head and arms. Wears black silk brocade dress with white collar and cuffs.

Materials, Marks, and Dimensions
China shoulder-head and limbs, pink kid body. Height: 11″.

Maker, Origin, and Period
Maker unknown. Germany. c. 1850.

Comment
Although this demure-looking doll wears a somber dress appropriate for an older woman, her short pixielike hairdo gives her a youthful appearance. Similar coiffures were also used on male and child dolls. The pink tint on this doll's head and limbs imparts a delicate glow that was achieved by mixing color into the porcelain before it was fired, rather than painting it on afterwards. Pink-tinted china dolls are not as common as untinted examples and are therefore more desirable.

Hints for Collectors
One of the easiest ways to distinguish an original costume from a replacement is by its fit. For example, this doll's dress is somewhat large for her body, suggesting that it was not made for her. Among the common types of 19th-century china dolls are those with round, plump faces and short necks, as illustrated here. Such dolls are more likely to have glass eyes than are examples with long, slender faces. In general, china dolls with glass eyes are rare and well worth purchasing.

China-head doll

Description
Lady doll with china shoulder-head. Molded and painted features including curly black hair. Blue eyes, elongated nose, red lips, and unusually large molded ears with pierced pearl earrings. Long slender neck. Wears pink silk dress with rose print and beige silk overskirt.

Materials, Marks, and Dimensions
China shoulder-head; cloth body; wooden arms. Height: 16″.

Maker, Origin, and Period
Maker unknown. Germany. c. 1850–75.

Comment
While 19th-century china dolls can often be dated within 20 years by their hairstyle, it is important to keep in mind that some popular dolls continued to be made for decades and thus featured out-of-date coiffures. In general, dolls produced in the 1830s and '40s have long hair parted in the center, draped below the ears, and swept back into a bun or twist in the style supposedly worn by the young Queen Victoria. Mid-19th-century dolls often have snoods or other ornaments in the hair. The doll shown here has fine brush marks on her forehead, indicating detailed craftsmanship. Her hairstyle, with a stand-up braid in front and a group of soft curls behind the head, was popular in the third quarter of the century. This style was followed in the late 19th and early 20th centuries by the "low-brow" hairdo, so named for the wavy curls that fall low on the forehead.

Hints for Collectors
This figure has pierced ears, a rare feature for a china-head doll that makes her quite desirable. Although china-head dolls are usually unmarked and unattributable, it is believed that most were made in Germany, some in Austria, and a few in Denmark.

290 China-head doll

Description
Lady doll with china shoulder-head. Molded and painted
features. Blond hair in black snood decorated with ornate blue
and gold band and small blue bows. Wears striped yellow silk
gown with black velvet band at waist and above hem. Ruffled
cuffs and hem.

Materials, Marks, and Dimensions
China shoulder-head and limbs, cloth body. Height: 11".

Maker, Origin, and Period
Maker unknown. Germany. c. 1850–60.

Comment
The delicate figure shown here is a rare example of a mid-19th-
century china-head doll with blond hair. Blond dolls were seldom
seen before 1880, but gradually became more popular around the
turn of the century. The snood, a net or cloth used to confine hair
at the back of the head, was fashionable about 1860, and had
many variations.

Hints for Collectors
A snood enhances the desirability and value of a china doll, and
the elaborate example worn by this doll makes her particularly
noteworthy. Since china dolls were frequently reclothed by their
successive owners, it is rare to find them on the market wearing
their original costumes. Collectors spend considerable time
searching for suitable outfits in which to reclothe newly acquired
dolls. An outfit should be as much like its original as possible.
Identical clothing can be obtained only if the original garment
was commercially made. While some museums keep a variety
of early doll clothing on hand, most collectors cannot afford
such a luxury and must be content to dress their dolls in less
appropriate costumes or in reproductions of original outfits.

Parian-type doll

Description

Lady doll with untinted bisque shoulder-head. Molded and painted features including blond hair swept into coronet braid topped by gold and black comb. Blue eyes, closed mouth, and pierced ears. Bisque shoulder plate painted as white blouse front with stand-up collar and ruff. Shoulder plate secured to body by cloth tape threaded through 4 sew holes. Wears cream-colored lace dress with blue and white glass beadwork; 2 lace-trimmed white cotton underskirts. Feet painted and glazed to resemble black high-laced shoes.

Materials, Marks, and Dimensions

Bisque shoulder-head, lower arms, and lower legs; cloth body. "5 a & 11" incised on back of shoulder plate. Height: 25¼".

Maker, Origin, and Period

Maker unknown. Germany. c. 1862–75.

Comment

Untinted bisque, commonly called parian by doll collectors, was often used in combination with glazed or painted porcelain for 19th-century decorative objects. Similarly, the beautiful doll shown here has an elegantly coiffed parian-type shoulder-head set in a bisque shoulder plate that was painted before firing to imitate a blouse front. Such rich detailing is found on many parian-type dolls.

Hints for Collectors

Collectors sometimes purchase a separate parian-type head and then seek a kid or cloth body of the proper size and style to attach to it. Such bodies may be found at doll hospitals.

China-head doll

Description
Lady doll with china shoulder-head. Molded and painted features including rosy cheeks and blue eyes. Painted black pate under wig of light brown human hair. Silver and tortoiseshell comb fastens braids at back of head. Wears brown print apron over beige and blue check cotton percale dress trimmed with black braid. White cotton undersleeves. White cotton slip and underpants. Black lace stockings and black leather shoes.

Materials, Marks, and Dimensions
China shoulder-head; leather lower arms; cloth body; china legs. Height: 22″.

Maker, Origin, and Period
Maker unknown. Germany. c. 1840–50.

Comment
Mid-19th-century china dolls usually have cloth bodies, leather lower arms, and china legs. Leather and kid were not commonly used for dolls' bodies until the third quarter of the century. The presence of china hands and feet instead of leather or cloth ones are signs of a better-than-average doll. Since china extremities broke easily, they were often replaced with cast-off parts from other dolls, or with new china hands and feet purchased at a general store. Unless a doll's parts are disproportionate to the rest of the body, it is difficult to distinguish replacements from originals.

Hints for Collectors
The doll shown here is wearing a typical Victorian-style braided wig. Collectors who wish to know everything about an acquisition will gently remove a wig to see if a doll has a bald head and painted pate, as illustrated here, or a short, painted hairstyle beneath the wig.

Description
Lady doll with china shoulder-head and swivel neck. Blond mohair wig with center part. Molded and painted features including blue eyes and rosy cheeks. Pink-tinted lower arms and lower legs. Jointed at shoulders and knees. Crimson satin pull strings at abdomen. Unclothed.

Materials, Marks, and Dimensions
China shoulder-head, lower arms, and lower legs; kid body; wooden upper arms, shoulders, and knee joints. "MME ROHMER/ BREVETE S.G.D.G. PARIS" stamped in oval on stomach. Height: 18″.

Maker, Origin, and Period
Rohmer. France. c. 1857–80.

Comment
Rohmer was one of several highly regarded French doll manufacturers that continually sought to improve the appearance and movement of its dolls. In 1857 Marie Rohmer obtained 2 patents: for gutta-percha or rubber arms and for the articulated joints used to attach wooden or china limbs to kid bodies. In 1858 she received a patent for the type of doll shown here, which has satin pull strings that move the head.

Hints for Collectors
Although many Rohmer dolls have painted eyes, some are found with glass eyes, a rare and valuable feature in china heads. All Rohmer dolls are highly prized; however, a marked figure is considerably more valuable than an unmarked one. For instance, even with glass eyes, an unmarked Rohmer china shoulder-head doll may sell for one-half to one-third the price of a comparable signed example with painted eyes.

Description
Dolls with china shoulder-heads. Molded and painted features including black pates, blue eyes with red eyelids, and rosy cheeks. Left: Man has red dots in corners of eyes. Wears woolen tweed suit with brown piping. White cotton shirt, black crepe bow tie. White cotton socks and brown leather shoes. Right: Lady has trace of red dot in corner of one eye. Black and gold painted boot on right foot; left foot broken off. Wears black long-sleeved silk dress with lace undercuffs; white cotton underskirt and pantaloons.

Materials, Marks, and Dimensions
China shoulder-heads, cloth bodies. Left: Cloth upper arms and legs; kid lower arms with kid hands and individually stitched fingers. "40 Y W" inked on left upper arm. Right: Cloth upper arms and legs; bisque lower arms and legs. Height: 14½″ (left); 11¾″ (right).

Maker, Origin, and Period
Maker unknown. Germany. c. 1850–1900.

Comment
In the past, collectors incorrectly called china dolls with bald heads and black painted pates "Biedermeier" dolls. This term actually refers to the German adaptation of French Empire-style furniture. The painted pates may vary considerably in size.

Hints for Collectors
Because of their nonspecific features and bald heads, the dolls shown here could be ladies or gentlemen, depending on their clothing. China dolls with distinctively male features and molded hairstyles are very unusual. Both of these dolls have blue eyes, which are quite common. A painted-pate doll with brown eyes would be a rare find.

China-head doll

Description
Male doll with china shoulder-head. Molded and painted features including black hair with side part, pink cheeks, and blue eyes. Wears black silk morning coat; black and blue striped silk trousers, floral brocade vest with gold buttons; white shirt and cravat. Red socks and black patent leather shoes.

Materials, Marks, and Dimensions
China shoulder-head and hands; cloth body and limbs. Height: 14¼″.

Maker, Origin, and Period
Maker unknown. Germany. c. 1860.

Comment
The doll shown here, wearing a fashionable hand-stitched silk morning suit, was assembled from a homemade body and a German shoulder-head—one of the few designed with a male hairstyle. Some male dolls, including this one, have exposed ears and wavy hair with a side part. Others have comb-marked hair, so named for its painted swirls, while still others have elaborate curls framing the face. Because male doll heads were available in such limited variety and because the same few types of heads continued to be made long after they were first issued, they are of little help in determining a doll's age.

Hints for Collectors
The value of a china doll is determined by the quality of its head, although a well-made body or elegant original outfit might increase its worth a bit. Fine china heads can be recognized by delicate modeling and glazing, and by such details as light brushstrokes simulating a natural hairline around the face. Many fine china heads have red eyelids and a red dot in the corner of each eye.

Parian-type doll

Description
Lady doll with untinted bisque shoulder-head. Molded and painted features including blond hair set in black snood adorned with blue bows; blue eyes, rosy cheeks, and closed mouth. Replaced arms. Wears floral print satin dress with off-the-shoulder neckline edged in lace. Lace-trimmed sleeves; blue satin sash and large bow at waist. White cotton underskirt and pantaloons edged in lace.

Materials, Marks, and Dimensions
Bisque shoulder-head, arms, and lower legs; cloth body and upper legs. Height: 25¼".

Maker, Origin, and Period
Maker unknown. Germany. c. 1870.

Comment
Nearly all parian-type dolls were made in Germany, the majority in the 1870s. Their unusually elaborate molded hairstyles, often adorned with snoods, ribbons, jewels, and hats, make them quite desirable. While all parian-type dolls are costly and hard to find, a few are especially in demand. These include dolls whose features were supposedly modeled after such aristocratic 19th-century tastemakers as Empress Eugénie, Princess Alexandra, and Countess Dagmar. Also in demand are dolls with fancy coiffures, including high-piled hair, wraparound braids, and curls framing a center part.

Hints for Collectors
Collectors can sometimes determine the date of a porcelain-head doll by the type of stitching on its cloth body. Prior to 1870 most commercially made cloth bodies were fashioned by hand; afterwards, they were sewn by machine and thus have uniform stitching.

Parian-type doll

Description
Lady doll with untinted bisque shoulder-head. Molded and painted features including blond hair in braided coronet with brush marks, blue eyes, rosy cheeks. Pierced ears with crystal earrings. Wears long gold velvet gown and yellow satin slip. High black painted shoes.

Materials, Marks, and Dimensions
Bisque shoulder-head, lower arms, and legs; cloth body. "46" impressed in C of the word "Clear" on back of shoulder. Height: 17¾".

Maker, Origin, and Period
Emma C. Clear. Los Angeles, California. 1946.

Comment
The late Emma Clear was known for her faithful reproductions of fine 19th-century bisque and china dolls. The founder of a doll hospital in the early 20th century, she quickly became dismayed by the expense and unavailability of antique dolls and was inspired to make and sell reproductions. Clear was knowledgeable about glazing and painting, and was also a skilled designer of dolls' clothes. Even though the doll shown here has a 19th-century hairstyle and dress, Emma Clear called her an "Antoinette-style" doll, probably referring to the 18th-century queen, Marie Antoinette. Other Clear dolls named after illustrious women include one of the great soprano, Jenny Lind.

Hints for Collectors
Emma Clear's dolls are marked with her name and their date of manufacture. However, unmarked reproductions of antique dolls are sometimes unwittingly or deliberately sold as originals. Collectors should purchase dolls only from reputable dealers who will testify to their dolls' authenticity.

Description
Lady dolls with untinted bisque shoulder-heads. Molded and painted features including blond wavy hair with center parts and sausage curls. Left: Blue glass eyes. Wears faded pink and white check silk dress with large lace collar and cuffs, pink satin bows at elbows. Lace-trimmed white cotton underskirt and pantaloons. Lace socks and brown leather shoes fastened by glass and brass buttons. Doll sits in orange velvet chair with pine frame. Right: Painted blue eyes. Wears beige brocade dress with red rickrack trim; lace collar, lace overskirt. Painted gold-trimmed stockings and gold luster boots.

Materials, Marks, and Dimensions
Bisque heads, cloth bodies. Left: Kid arms, cloth legs. Right: Bisque arms and legs. Height: 27¾″ (left); 12″ (right).

Maker, Origin, and Period
Maker unknown. Germany. Left: c. 1860–70. Right: c. 1880.

Comment
Parian, an untinted white bisque, was a material generally reserved for high-priced, elegantly fashioned dolls. Parian-type dolls were made in Germany from the 1850s through the 1880s. While many such dolls have elaborate molded hairstyles and slender aristocratic features, the examples shown here have unusually simple coiffures and plain broad faces.

Hints for Collectors
Parian-type dolls usually have painted eyes. The figure on the left has glass eyes, which make her rare and highly prized. Such dolls are generally unmarked.

Dolls with printed-cloth bodies

Description
Lady dolls with china shoulder-heads. Molded and painted features including low-brow hairstyle and blue eyes. Left: Black hair. Printed-cloth body depicts Kate Greenaway design. Painted brown shoes. Center: Blond hair. Shoulder plate with gold collar, bow, and name "Ethel" embossed on front. Alphabet-print cloth body. Painted white stockings; brown shoes. Right: Blond hair. Bald eagle-and-shield emblem of U.S. printed on cloth body; names of states printed on limbs. Painted white stockings; brown shoes.

Materials, Marks, and Dimensions
China shoulder-heads, lower arms, and lower legs; cloth bodies. Left: "D M Germany: 2G" marked on back of head. Right: Paper label on back of shoulder reads "Germany." Height: 12½" (left); 10½" (center); 11" (right).

Maker, Origin, and Period
Maker unknown. Germany. Center: Distributed by Butler Bros. New York City. c. 1900–25.

Comment
Although these figures and others like them have bodies made of cloth printed with charming designs, their china heads with "low-brow" hairstyles are generally run-of-the-mill.

Hints for Collectors
"Ethel," shown at center, was one of many "Pet Name" dolls distributed by Butler Brothers. The dolls were advertised as having molded necklaces, though these were actually collars with bows. Collectors should remember that the descriptions of dolls in catalogues may be misleading because manufacturers tended to exaggerate the qualities of their dolls.

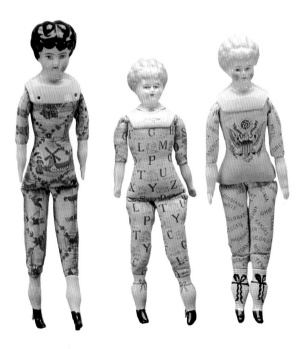

300 Bisque-head doll with trunk

Description

Lady doll with bisque shoulder-head and swivel neck.
Light brown mohair wig with blue ribbon, painted brows
and eyelashes, blue paperweight eyes, closed mouth. Torso
covered with heavy cotton, concealing wooden joints.
Accompanying cardboard trunk contains clothes, accessories, and
a small doll. Clothing, from left to right: Fur muff, shoes, boots,
blue hand-knitted booties, crocheted shawl, cotton petticoat, blue
cotton corset, red and white print dress for smaller doll, long-
sleeved pink dress, brown dress, and white cotton nightgown.
Accessories include white box for muff, wooden case with leather
handle, and 7-piece ivory dresser set with combs, hand mirror,
soapbox, and opera glasses. Smaller doll has bald china head and
wig of human hair. Wears light green dress.

Materials, Marks, and Dimensions

Lady doll: Bisque shoulder-head and lower limbs; wood and
composition torso and upper limbs. Small doll: China head and
limbs, cloth body. Height: 13½″ (large doll); 4″ (small doll); 8″
(trunk).

Maker, Origin, and Period
Maker unknown. France. c. 1850–75.

Comment
In the mid-19th century, the French passion for opulent display was quite evident in upper-middle-class society. Even young girls dressed in clothes of extreme elegance, and their dolls, often more splendidly attired, were accompanied by trousseaus arranged in beautiful little trunks. Department stores carried large selections of dolls' clothes and related items available for separate purchase so that a doll's wardrobe could be enlarged at any time.

Hints for Collectors
The trunk, clothes, and vanity items shown here did not originally accompany this doll. Since doll owners commonly add or discard accessories at will, it is impossible to determine whether such materials initially came with a doll unless documented by an original inventory slip.

Bisque-head doll

Description
Lady doll with bisque shoulder-head and swivel neck. Human
hair inserted into wax crown. Hair adorned with pink silk
flowered band. Molded and painted features including brown
lashes and brows. Blue glass eyes. Molded pierced ears with
amethyst and metal pendant earrings. Necklace of mother-of-
pearl set in gold on lavender velvet band. Original costume of
pink and beige silk gown with silk front panel and pleated ruffles
at hem and wrists. Knit stockings and leather shoes. Carries
woven willow basket filled with silk flowers.

Materials, Marks, and Dimensions
Bisque shoulder-head, kid body and limbs. Back of neck marked
"6 BTE S.G.D.G." Height: 22".

Maker, Origin, and Period
Maker unknown. Probably France. c. 1885.

Comment
The doll shown here, probably made in France, has a fine kid
body and delicately shaped kid hands with long fingers. Her
human hair was inserted into the crown by means of a process
patented by the Austrian designer Josef Kubelka. The procedure
entailed pouring wax over an indentation in the scalp and
then inserting the hair. While there is no proof that Kubelka
manufactured dolls, his patents for hair insertion are on record
in Germany, France, and Austria.

Hints for Collectors
In the 19th century it was common for dollmakers to use one
another's patents. For instance, the Kubelka process was
employed on some Huret bébés, on numerous unmarked dolls,
and on life-size manikins as well.

Bisque-head doll

Description
Lady doll with bisque shoulder-head and swivel neck. Original blond mohair wig has ringlets and long corkscrew curls tied with blue ribbon. Molded and painted features including pierced ears and closed mouth. Blue glass paperweight eyes. Wears pink taffeta dress with bustle, trimmed with blue ribbon. Lace and organdy undersleeves and collar. White cotton underclothes edged in lace. Gold cross on necklace. White cotton socks and brown leather low-heeled shoes fastened with brass buttons.

Materials, Marks, and Dimensions
Bisque head; kid body and limbs. "CC" inscribed in circle on shoes. Height: 17".

Maker, Origin, and Period
Maker unknown. France. c. 1870.

Comment
Fine French lady dolls dressed in stylish clothing are sometimes called fashion dolls. They were designed to be both playthings and manikins on which dressmakers could show off costumes to prospective clients. These figures used to be known as "Parisiennes," a term coined by Jumeau and other French firms for their dolls with bisque heads and kid bodies.

Hints for Collectors
This 19th-century lady doll is particularly fine because of her large paperweight eyes, soft pink complexion, and high-quality mohair wig. Antique mohair wigs can easily be identified because they are softer and more lustrous than new ones. Although this doll's dress was not originally made for her, it is an excellent example of 19th-century craftsmanship. Collectors consider styling and fabric as well as such details as linings and stitching when evaluating the quality of antique doll clothing.

Black bisque-head doll

Description
Lady doll with dark brown bisque shoulder-head and swivel neck. Short wig of curly black mohair. Molded and painted features including upturned nose, open mouth with upper and lower molded teeth. Brown glass eyes. Wears original orange silk gown with 2-tiered skirt; green, orange, and gold brocade bodice with black lace trim and glass buttons; brocade and black lace trim at hem. White lace-trimmed underclothes. Matching pearl earrings and necklace, flower-trimmed straw hat lined with orange velvet. White stockings and high black shoes fastened with wooden buttons.

Materials, Marks, and Dimensions
Bisque shoulder-head, lower arms, and hands; kid body. Height: 18″.

Maker, Origin, and Period
Maker unknown. Probably France. c. 1890–1900.

Comment
In the 1890s bisque dolls of all races were being produced in Europe. Many of these popular dolls represented black people. Although some were painted, the best of them, like this example had color mixed directly into the slip of the bisque before firing. Note the exceptionally fine, realistic modeling of this doll's face.

Hints for Collectors
Black lady dolls, rarer than white ones, are of great interest to collectors and thus command high prices. This doll is particularly unusual not only because of her individualistic features but also because of her open mouth and visible teeth. Lady dolls generally have closed mouths.

Bisque-head doll

Description
Lady doll with bisque head. Wig of brown human hair. Molded and painted features including thickly painted eyelashes and brows and closed red mouth. Large brown glass paperweight eyes. Spring-jointed body, swivel waist. Wears pink silk 2-piece dress adorned with lace, pink fringe at hem. Brocade and straw hat. White cotton half-skirt and pantaloons. White cotton stockings and brown leather shoes with wooden buttons.

Materials, Marks, and Dimensions
Bisque head; wooden body and limbs; metal hands. "Huret" marked on back of head. "Huret 68 Rue de la Boétie" incised on back of body. Height: 17¾".

Maker, Origin, and Period
Maison Huret. France. c. 1870–1900.

Comment
Although the body of the doll shown here, finely crafted from lightweight wood, dates from the 1870s, the head, made from cheap coarse-textured bisque, is probably from about 1900. The head and body may have been assembled at the turn of the century, when Huret temporarily ceased production and made dolls from leftover parts. Huret's invention of the socket swivel head, patented in 1861, enabled the dolls' heads to be turned or tilted in lifelike poses.

Hints for Collectors
Like this figure, most Huret dolls with wooden bodies and metal hands are marked with the address "68 Rue de la Boétie." Bisque dolls usually have wigs of mohair, lamb's wool, or human hair, which are generally of equal value. Look for dolls with finely detailed paperweight eyes and smooth, well-modeled heads, since these are indications of high quality.

Bisque-head doll

Description
Lady doll with bisque shoulder-head and swivel neck. Wig of brown human hair. Molded and painted features. Blue glass eyes, closed mouth. Jointed body. Undressed.

Materials, Marks, and Dimensions
Bisque shoulder-head, lower arms, and lower legs. Torso, upper arms, and upper legs made of kid over wood. "No. 1 à 15" within oval Simonne trademark stamped in turquoise ink on front of torso. Height: 18".

Maker, Origin, and Period
F. Simonne. France. c. 1875.

Comment
Founded in 1847, the French firm of Simonne was famous for its kid-bodied lady dolls, and later, for its bébés—the French term for dolls representing young children. Some of the company's doll torsos were made by gluing kid over wood or over wood and cloth; others were fashioned by stuffing kid with hair, cork, or sawdust. Unfortunately, many dolls stuffed with sawdust lost the ability to stand because the sawdust tended to leak through the joints, causing the dolls to become limp. Examples with all-kid bodies often have remarkably detailed fingers and toes. The invention of gussets—insets at the joints—in the mid-19th century allowed for greater flexibility of the limbs. Lady dolls of this period were often sold unclothed, like this example. Some wore only a simple beaded necklace or hair ribbon.

Hints for Collectors
Known for their exquisitely shaped bodies, Simonne dolls are highly prized by collectors. They can be easily identified by the turquoise stamp on the front of their torsos.

Bisque-head doll

Description
Lady doll with bisque head and blond lamb's-wool wig. Molded
and painted features including blue eyes and closed mouth. Fully
jointed body with swivel waist. Wears rose-colored silk faille
dress with pink trim and lace undersleeves. Matching hat and
train. Lace-trimmed white underclothes. High leather boots with
small heels and gold metal buttons.

Materials, Marks, and Dimensions
Bisque head; wooden body and limbs jointed with metal springs;
metal hands. "Huret 68 Rue de la Boétie" incised on back
between shoulder blades. Height: 18″.

Maker, Origin, and Period
Maison Huret. France. c. 1870–80.

Comment
Maison Huret was a Parisian doll company that made beautiful,
gusseted kid bodies as well as articulated wooden ones. The
firm's numerous patented innovations contributed to the greater
realism of lady dolls after the mid-19th century. The faces of
Huret's early lady dolls, including the one shown here, are fuller
and more youthful than those by other French firms. Maison
Huret manufactured dolls until 1920; some of their lady dolls
made after 1900 have slender, more mature-looking faces.

Hints for Collectors
Huret dolls can sometimes be dated by their marks. Those made
in the 1850s are incised with the address "2 Boulevard des
Italiens"; those from the mid- to late 1860s are marked "22
Boulevard Montmartre"; and those produced after 1870 are
marked "68 Rue de la Boétie." While the firm's address often
appears both on the head and body of a doll, the Huret name
sometimes appears alone, and only on the head.

Half-dolls

Description
Grandfather and grandmother half-dolls with bisque heads.
Molded and painted features including blue eyes, facial wrinkles,
and closed mouths. Legs jointed at hips. Left: Grandfather has
molded brown hat and white hair. Molded white shirt, gray vest,
yellow shoes. Wears original black velvet sleeves and pants.
Right: Grandmother wears molded pale gray kerchief over head.
Molded orange vest over white blouse; blue shoes. Wears
original brown velvet skirt and sleeves, beige cuffs. Lace-
trimmed white cotton half-skirt and pantaloons.

Materials, Marks, and Dimensions
Bisque heads, upper torsos, and lower arms and legs. Cloth
lower torsos and upper arms and legs. "Germany" imprinted on
back of waists. Height: 6½".

Maker, Origin, and Period
Possibly Hertwig & Co. Germany. c. 1911.

Comment
Figures such as these are called "half-dolls" because of their
molded bisque upper torsos and cloth lower torsos. Usually made
in Germany, they were often produced in sets of 6 that included a
boy and a girl, their parents, and 2 grandparents. Many were
small enough to be used in dollhouses. Although the origin of the
half-dolls shown here was a mystery for a number of years, it is
now believed that Hertwig & Company manufactured them,
since they are illustrated in one of the firm's newspaper
advertisements dated 1911.

Hints for Collectors
Do not confuse half-dolls with "half-figures." The latter,
decorative objects made of one-piece heads and upper torsos,
were attached to pincushions and other household items.

Description
Dolls with bisque hats and shoulder-heads. Molded and painted
features. Left: Marguerite has pink flower-shaped hat, blond
curly hair, and necklace of leaves. Wears pink and white check
cotton dress trimmed with rickrack. Organdy collar, apron, and
cuffs; white lace-edged underskirt and pantaloons. Right: Doll
with blond low-brow hairstyle; white hat with blue ribbon.
Wears long-sleeved white dress with blue and white polka-dot
collar; ruffle at hem. 2 white cotton underskirts; white cotton
pantaloons. Leather shoes with cotton tassels.

Materials, Marks, and Dimensions
Bisque shoulder-heads; cloth bodies, upper arms, and legs. Left:
Bisque lower arms and legs. Right: Kid lower arms, bisque lower
legs. Height: 16″ (left); 14½″ (right).

Maker, Origin, and Period
Maker unknown. Germany. c. 1900.

Comment
Figures such as these decorative ladies were produced by
German dollmakers, who dressed them in bonnets and stylish
dresses, some of which were inspired by the storybook
illustrations of Kate Greenaway. Ruffles and trimmings could not
camouflage the poor quality of the stone bisque of which they
were generally made. The doll on the left, known as Marguerite,
was one of a type made about 1900 that sported curious hats
shaped like flowers, butterflies, or clovers.

Hints for Collectors
Collectors also refer to these figures as hooded, bonnet, or fancy-
hatted dolls. Although this Marguerite doll is unmarked, it was
probably made by Hamburger & Company of Berlin, which
registered a trademark for Marguerite dolls in 1903.

Bisque-head doll

Description
Lady doll with bisque shoulder-head, molded and painted features. Brown mohair wig tied in braids. Blue glass eyes. Pierced earrings of blue glass and wire. Wears ornate pink silk dress with train and gathered long sleeves. Gold lamé bodice with gold braid and stitched floral design; intricate floral motif on skirt. Matching hat trimmed with braid and flowers. Long black stockings; black oilcloth shoes with silver metal buckles.

Materials, Marks, and Dimensions
Bisque shoulder-head, lower arms, and lower legs; kid body, upper arms, and upper legs. "S & H 1160 3" imprinted on back of shoulder. Height: 17".

Maker, Origin, and Period
Simon & Halbig. Germany. c. 1905–16.

Comment
Founded in 1870, the Simon & Halbig company became one of the largest makers of dolls' heads in Germany at the turn of the century. The firm had such high standards of workmanship, particularly in its early years, that its products were sometimes mistaken for fine French dolls.

Hints for Collectors
The particular S & H trademark found on the doll shown here was registered in 1905 and does not appear on earlier dolls. Over the years the firm used at least 22 other trademarks. The mold number, 1160, imprinted on this figure is found on the company's shoulder-head dolls with swivel necks that were made from 1905 to 1916. Since many of these dolls had Louis XIV-style wigs, the wig seen here is probably a replacement.

Bisque-head Gibson Girl doll

Description
Lady doll with bisque shoulder-head and blond mohair wig.
Molded and painted features including arched eyebrows, sharply
upturned nose, and closed mouth. Blue glass sleep-eyes. Body
jointed at knees, elbows, and shoulders. Original costume of
purple silk gown with white polka dots. Purple velvet bow
adorned with paste diamond at neck. Large purple velvet hat.
Black lace stockings and black leather shoes.

Materials, Marks, and Dimensions
Bisque shoulder-head and lower arms; kid body, upper arms, and
legs. "7 17 U" marked on head. Kestner crown trademark
imprinted on front of body. "Kerr, Pittsburgh Pa." marked inside
hat lining. Height: 22¾".

Maker, Origin, and Period
Manufactured by J. D. Kestner, Jr. Germany. Distributed by
Geo. Borgfeldt. New York City. c. 1900.

Comment
The illustrious German doll firm of J. D. Kestner based its
Gibson Girl dolls on images by the American illustrator, Charles
Dana Gibson. The dolls have fine white kid bodies and bisque
heads with open crowns over which are placed human-hair or
mohair wigs. Advertised in the *Ladies' Home Journal* in 1910,
these dolls can be recognized by their slightly closed eyes,
upswept hairdos, Edwardian-style clothing, and enormous hats.

Hints for Collectors
Some of these dolls have the word "Gibson Girl" stamped in blue
on their chests. Others, such as the figure pictured here, are
marked with the Kestner symbol of a crown and streamers. This
trademark can be used for dating, since it is only seen on Gibson
Girl dolls made after 1894.

Lady and Gentleman Dolls: Wood

Because of its ready availability, wood has been used to make dolls throughout history. In ancient Egypt, Greece, and Rome, children played with wooden dolls, as they also did during the late Middle Ages in Germany. Jointed wooden dolls were made in England as far back as the 17th century and possibly earlier. The poet Alexander Pope made reference to such a doll in 1721, calling it a "jointed baby," "baby" being one of the common names for dolls during that period. Since then wooden dolls have ranged from rudimentary whittled or lathe-turned human forms to intricately carved miniature sculptures.

English Wooden Lady Dolls

Wooden dolls made in England from the late 17th century until the 1840s are today commonly referred to as Queen Anne dolls, though this term is misleading because the dolls continued to be made long after both the actual reign of Queen Anne (1702–1714) and what is commonly called the Queen Anne period in the decorative arts. These dolls are characterized by one-piece heads and torsos, high foreheads, close-set features, and glass, porcelain, or carved pupil-less eyes. Except for the very earliest, most English wooden dolls were turned on a lathe, a furnituremaker's device on which a piece of wood is rotated about a horizontal axis and shaped with a cutting tool.

Peg-Wooden Dolls

The term "peg-wooden" refers to articulated wooden dolls made in the Grödner Tal in the southern Alps from the late 18th to early 20th centuries. The origin of the peg-wooden doll can be traced to wooden manikins and religious statues produced as far back as the Renaissance. Large peg-wooden dolls have joints in which a ball moves within a socket to allow rotary motion; small examples have joints in which a peg is inserted into a slot to allow for a hingelike, back-and-forth motion. The popularity of peg-wooden dolls in the mid- to late 19th century spurred their makers to mass produce them, sometimes resulting in crudely carved and hastily painted examples.

American Wooden Dolls

In 19th-century America, wooden dolls were whittled and carved and also made from discarded household objects such as spoons, clothespins, and bedpost finials. Beginning in the 1870s the manufacture of wooden dolls benefited from new production techniques borrowed from furnituremaking. For example, Joel Ellis, one of the first commercial dollmakers, patented a doll that was steam-molded by a hydraulic machine and articulated with mortise-and-tenon joints; his patent reads in part: "In the manufacture of dolls it is important to secure sufficient friction at the joints of the limbs to hold the limbs and body in any desired position."

Wood is a favored material among contemporary American doll artists, who are inclined to use traditional methods to fashion their one-of-a-kind figures, and who sometimes spend months carving a single doll.

Description
Lady dolls with one-piece heads and torsos, pupil-less glass eyes.
Left: Carved and painted features. Jointed with wooden pegs at
shoulders, elbows, knees, and thighs. Fork-type hands. Original
costume, sewn directly onto body, of pink silk brocade dress with
green fringe at bodice, white cotton undersleeves, quilted
petticoat. Matching pink hat, white cotton undercap trimmed in
lace. White leather gloves, white silk shoes. Right: Carved nose,
lathe-turned torso with 2 slots in bottom for missing legs.

Materials, Marks, and Dimensions
Wood. Height: 17″ (left); 14″ (right).

Maker, Origin, and Period
Maker unknown. England. Left: c. 1750–1800. Right: c. 1750.

Comment
Jointed wooden lady dolls that date from the late 17th century
until about 1840 are often called Queen Anne dolls. The earliest
of them have torsos with rectangular bottoms, as seen on the
primitive-looking figure at right. Dolls with torsos that narrow
to a point at the bottom were made somewhat later. The doll at
right was originally primed with gesso before being painted, and
may once have resembled the doll on the left. Both of the
examples shown here have flat backs, which may have resulted
from their being modeled from rectangular blocks of wood placed
off-center on a lathe.

Hints for Collectors
Queen Anne dolls may be easily identified by their high
foreheads, carved close-set features, glass or porcelain pupil-less
eyes, and one-piece heads and torsos. Costumed figures in good
condition are rarely seen outside museums, but unclothed dolls
may still sometimes be found on the market.

Description
Lady doll with wooden head and blue hemp hair. Large inset
blue glass eyes, carved nose, painted mouth. Jointed lathe-
turned body, spoon hands. Original costume of blue and silver
floral-patterned silk brocade dress with ornate silver trim at
collar, cuffs, waist, and hem. Blue satin underskirt, white cotton
pantaloons with silk thread fringe. Pearl necklace, brass and
glass hair ornaments. Feet painted black to resemble shoes.

Materials, Marks, and Dimensions
Wood. Height: 19½″.

Maker, Origin, and Period
Maker unknown. England. c. 1930.

Comment
Until recently the doll shown here was mistakenly attributed to
Madame Bourget, a French milliner living in England during the
18th century. It is one of a group of dolls thought to represent
characters from Richard Sheridan's 18th-century comedy of
manners, *The School for Scandal*. These figures are so well made
that several museums included examples of them in their 18th-
century doll collections. However, it is now known that the dolls
are fakes, since their glass paperweight eyes, their fabric, and
the patina of their wood indicate a 20th-century date.

Hints for Collectors
The mystery surrounding the origin of these finely crafted dolls
makes them very desirable. They can be seen in the collections of
the Strong Museum in Rochester, New York, and in London at
the Bethnal Green and Victoria & Albert museums. However, it
is unlikely that any such dolls will reach the marketplace, since
so few exist.

Joel Ellis doll

Description
Lady doll with wooden head. Pressed and painted features and brown hair. Body jointed with metal pegs. Painted bust and hands. Painted high-heeled, side-buttoned black metal boots.

Materials, Marks, and Dimensions
Rock maple head and body, metal hands. Height: 18″.

Maker, Origin, and Period
Designed by Joel Ellis for Co-operative Manufacturing Co. at Vermont Novelty Works. Springfield, Vermont. c. 1873.

Comment
Joel Ellis, a Yankee inventor, manufactured furniture and toys before making wooden dolls. This early Ellis doll is considered one of the first commercial American dolls. It embodies many technical innovations, including the mortise-and-tenon construction (patented May 20, 1873) that permits complete mobility of the limbs. Metal hands fit into the wooden arms midway between wrists and elbows; paint conceals this juncture. The wood used for the doll's body was first pressed under steam to make it malleable, and then turned on a lathe to form the torso and limbs. Ellis dolls came in 12″, 15″, and 18″ sizes; a few were painted black, and all were sold undressed. The prim 1860s hairstyle worn by blonds and brunettes alike gave them a mature, ladylike appearance.

Hints for Collectors
The paint on most Joel Ellis dolls has not withstood the test of time. Peeling and flaking are common, and many dolls are repainted, as is the doll shown here. A well-preserved Ellis doll would be a lucky find.

Peg-wooden doll

Description
Lady doll with wooden head. Carved and painted features. Hair painted in translucent and opaque tones and adorned with carved yellow wooden comb. Black eyes, rosy cheeks, closed mouth. Peg-jointed body, spoon hands. Feet painted orange and tied with silk thread to resemble shoes. Wears pink satin off-shoulder dress trimmed with gray silk, lace, and velvet. Cameo brooch at neckline.

Materials, Marks, and Dimensions
Wood. Height: 6½″.

Maker, Origin, and Period
Maker unknown. Grödner Tal region, southern Alps. c. 1815–30.

Comment
The wooden figure shown here represents a lady of the Empire period, with her upswept hair and high-waisted dress. Such features, along with delicately articulated joints and expressive faces, are characteristic of the 19th-century peg-wooden dolls that were produced by more than 350 dollmakers in the Grödner Tal, the Dolomite Valley of the southern Alps. These dolls can often be dated by the style of their dresses and hair. Some of the early peg-wooden figures, made between 1800 and 1815, have short, windblown hairdos. By the 1830s dollmakers began to eliminate the tuck comb seen on this doll, and by the 1840s her high-waisted dress was no longer in fashion.

Hints for Collectors
Collectors seek Grödner Tal dolls that are more than 12″ tall because these are usually the most carefully carved and painted. However, this tiny lady is very finely constructed for her size. She is also quite valuable because of her age and excellent state of preservation.

Peg-wooden doll

Description
Lady doll with wooden head. Carved and painted features. Hair painted in translucent and opaque tones. Black eyes, closed mouth. Jointed body, carved hands with separate thumbs. Feet painted red to resemble shoes. Wears red cotton calico print dress trimmed in black velvet, lace collar, and ecru linen apron with velvet-trimmed pocket and paisley border. Matching paisley bonnet tied with black velvet ribbon.

Materials, Marks, and Dimensions
Wood. Height: 17¼″.

Maker, Origin, and Period
Maker unknown. Grödner Tal region, southern Alps. c. 1840–50.

Comment
The large size of this peg-wooden figure indicates that she was an important doll, one worth taking the time to fully carve. Her hairstyle, which is painted with translucent color on the front and sides and opaque color on the crown, is characteristic of many Grödner Tal dolls made in the mid-19th century. Although less elaborate than the coiffures of earlier dolls, it is still more carefully designed than the plain black cap hairdo that came later. After 1850, in an effort to compete with the manufacturers of less expensive papier-mâché and china dolls, Grödner Tal dollmakers streamlined their operations by eliminating what they considered superfluous and costly details.

Hints for Collectors
It is especially difficult to determine if the clothing found on peg-wooden dolls is original to them. Much of it is homemade, and the few commercially produced costumes that are found are usually unmarked. Without documentation, the most that can be said of any one of these early outfits is that it is "of the period."

Peg-wooden doll

Description
Lady doll with wooden head. Carved and painted close-set
features. Wavy black hair, rosy cheeks. Painted lower arms and
legs. Body jointed with wooden pegs.

Materials, Marks, and Dimensions
Wood. Height: 10″.

Maker, Origin, and Period
Maker unknown. Grödner Tal region, southern Alps. Late 19th
century.

Comment
Late 19th-century peg-wooden dolls were often hastily made and
delivered to European distributors who shipped millions of them
overseas. In countries all over the world the dolls came to be
known as "Dutch"—a corruption of the word *Deutsch*, meaning
German. The doll shown here is obviously not as well made as
earlier peg-wooden examples. Note that her features are simply
carved in relief rather than fully carved in the round, that her
feet are not applied but are formed by notches at the ends of her
legs, and that her hands are without fingers.

Hints for Collectors
Dolls like this were mass-produced on an assembly line. Young
Tyrolean women painted as many as 1200 of them a week, so it is
understandable that a few of the faces occasionally received an
extra eyebrow or a misplaced eye. Examine late peg-wooden
dolls carefully to be sure that their features are correct, their
pegs are adequately fitted, and they are properly carved and
finished. While these late figures are not nearly as valuable as
earlier, more intricately carved examples, they can be desirable
acquisitions for budget-conscious collectors interested in 19th-
century dolls.

Ship's prow doll

Description
Female doll with wooden head. Carved and painted features. Brown hair styled in sausage roll with center part. Brushstrokes delineate individual strands of hair and wispy curls at brow. Blue eyes, finely chiseled nose, closed mouth. Wears red calico print dress belted at waist with striped brown lining turned up at cuffs. White eyelet-trimmed cotton underskirt.

Materials, Marks, and Dimensions
Wooden head; cloth body and limbs; bisque hands. Height: 33″.

Maker, Origin, and Period
Maker unknown. New England. c. 1850–60.

Comment
This homemade doll, found in a New England town, may have been made by a seafarer for his child. It is currently in the collection of the Brooklyn Children's Museum in New York, where it is affectionately known as a "ship's prow doll" because its face closely resembles figureheads on 19th-century sailing vessels. While the doll's features are finely carved and delicately painted, her cloth body is rather ungainly. Her bisque hands, possibly taken from a commercially made bisque doll, seem curiously out of place with her simple cloth feet.

Hints for Collectors
The dress worn by this doll appears to date from the mid-19th century and may be her original garment. Its simple lines and red calico print are typical of ladies' and children's homemade clothing made from about 1850 to 1875. The same red calico cloth is frequently seen on quilts of that period.

Scottish folk doll

Description
Male doll with one-piece wooden head and torso. Hand-carved and painted features. Brown hair, blue eyes, closed mouth. Flexible red leather upper arms attached to wooden lower arms. Flexible red leather knees join wooden upper and lower legs. Carved fingers and toes.

Materials, Marks, and Dimensions
Wooden head, body, and limbs; leather joints. Height: 21½″.

Maker, Origin, and Period
W. Tapp. Montrose, Scotland. c. 1860.

Comment
This doll's provenance, like that of many folk objects, was discovered by chance. The doll was originally thought to be American, since several versions exist in collections here. After acquiring one such doll at auction in 1978, its owner came across 2 others like it at the Folk Art Museum in Glen Esk, Scotland. These were attributed to W. Tapp, a 19th-century Scottish cabinetmaker from the town of Montrose. The doll's owner passed this information on to the Strong Museum in Rochester, New York, which now attributes its example to Tapp as well. Although it was common at one time for cabinetmakers to create miniature furniture and wooden toys for their clients' children, they rarely made dolls. Note especially that this doll's head resembles the finial of a bedpost.

Hints for Collectors
Although its leather joints have been replaced and its face repainted, this doll is considered an outstanding piece of folk art because its provenance is known, and because its hand-carved body is unusual.

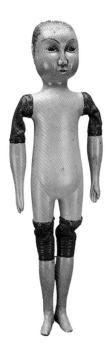

Footman

Description
Black male doll with wooden head. Carved and painted features. Black pupil-less glass eyes, broad nose, full mouth. Original costume of red woolen jacket trimmed with gold braid and brass buttons. White silk vest over white cotton shirt with pearl button closure; red silk cummerbund, and black velvet pants. Painted pewter hands. Wooden feet painted brown to resemble boots.

Materials, Marks, and Dimensions
Cloth body; wooden limbs; pewter hands. Height: 21½".

Maker, Origin, and Period
Maker unknown. France. c. 1850–75.

Comment
During the 19th century, fine black dolls were often dressed as elegant servants, or clad in vivid ethnic costumes reflecting the European fascination with the exotic origins of black people. The footman shown here is unusual because such dolls usually have bisque rather than hand-carved wooden heads. This doll has a sculptural presence that suggests he was made to order by a skilled cabinetmaker or artisan. His hand-sewn clothes are of a professional quality and were probably specially designed for him.

Hints for Collectors
A black wooden doll of this period is extremely rare and valuable, especially one so beautifully costumed. This doll's toes have been broken off, but such minor damage does not affect his value. Pewter hands on a 19th-century wooden doll are unusual. This doll's pewter hands were early replacements and enhance the figure's desirability.

Theodosia Burr

Description
Lady doll with hand-carved and painted features. Brown mohair wig. Fully jointed, hand-carved body. Undressed.

Materials, Marks, and Dimensions
Wood. "MFK 81" signed on base of foot. Height: 16″.

Maker, Origin, and Period
Marta Finch-Kozlosky. Chicago, Illinois. 1981.

Comment
The doll shown here is a portrait of Theodosia Burr, daughter of the famous American political figure Aaron Burr, whose staunch belief in women's equality prompted him to teach her Greek and Latin while she was still a child. Theodosia is depicted here with her arm raised in a gesture of affirmation. This doll was originally clothed in a simple, late 18th-century-style outfit that has been temporarily removed to reveal her expertly made, jointed body. NIADA doll artist Finch-Kozlosky carves her dolls from high-quality, finely grained wood; she does not rely on preliminary drawings or models. Except for the use of a power tool to drill holes for their joints, the dolls are produced entirely by hand. They wear wigs made of antique mohair, which the artist prefers to the synthetic fibers or new mohair commonly used by contemporary dollmakers.

Hints for Collectors
From 1978 to 1982 Marta Finch-Kozlosky completed 10 dolls, including figures of Scarlett O'Hara, Priscilla Alden, and Rebecca of Sunnybrook Farm. Only recently has she begun selling her dolls. They all bear a resemblance to the artist herself and, unlike most dolls, have realistically proportioned hands and feet.

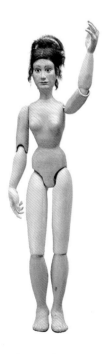

Gertrude Stein

Description
Female doll with carved, painted, and varnished wooden head
and body. Brown hair, brown eyes. Padded wire upper arms,
painted black feet. Original costume of rust-colored long-sleeved
silk blouse and woven tan and rust striped vest. Metallic beaded
brooch at neck. Holds white cloth rose in hands.

Materials, Marks, and Dimensions
Horse-chestnut wood. "Helen Bullard/1966" on lower back.
"Gertrude Stein hb '76" signed in ink on base of skirt. Height: 8".

Maker, Origin, and Period
Helen Bullard. Ozone, Tennessee. 1976.

Comment
Helen Bullard carves her dolls from light-colored hardwoods and
delicately varnishes the wood to develop a mellow patina. Her
commitment to women's rights inspired her to create this figure
of Gertrude Stein, the American author and patron of the arts.
An expatriate who lived in Paris from the early 20th century
until her death in 1946, Stein encouraged the work of numerous
artists and literary figures, including Picasso, Matisse,
Hemingway, and Fitzgerald. She was highly regarded in her own
right for her experimental prose style. Among her best known
works are *Three Lives*, *The Making of Americans*, and *The
Autobiography of Alice B. Toklas*. Stein's famous phrase, "Rose

is a rose is a rose," probably inspired Bullard to depict her holding this flower. Bullard has carved 2 other versions of Gertrude Stein—the latest, made in 1981, appears in a group called *The Real Mentors of Restless Women*, along with such other eminent figures as George Sand, Virginia Woolf, and Lady Ottoline Morrel. Bullard frequently assembles her dolls in pairs and groups reflecting her interest in history. One procession of 9 dolls depicts 9 generations of an American family. Another group of 23 dolls is entitled "Appalachian Farm Family Portrait, 1904."

Hints for Collectors
Helen Bullard is one of the 11 charter members of NIADA. Her dolls can be found in exhibitions throughout the country. It is possible to acquire one by writing directly to the artist, but expect to be put on a long waiting list.

Lady and Gentleman Dolls: Miscellaneous Materials

 Most of the dolls in this section were mass produced in the 19th or early 20th century and made from such common materials as papier-mâché, wax, or rubber.

Papier-Mâché Dolls

Although papier-mâché was referred to as a dollmaking material in 16th-century France, it was not widely used until the beginning of the 19th century, when a mechanical means for pressing the material into molds was invented. This process allowed papier-mâché doll heads to be mass produced, a development that contributed to the success of the German doll industry in the 19th century. Collectors frequently confuse papier-mâché with composition because the 2 materials are made of similar ingredients. A 19th-century dictionary defined papier-mâché as "a tough plastic material made from paper pulp containing an admixture of size, paste, oil, resin or other substances or from sheets of paper glued and pressed to-gether." Composition, essentially a papier-mâché compound to which sawdust or plaster has been added, is a term generally reserved for dolls made after the mid-19th century. Dolls with papier-mâché heads usually have kid or cloth bodies.

Wax Dolls

In 18th-century Europe, wax was used to make a great variety of figures including religious statues, portrait busts, and dolls, most of which were modeled by hand from solid wax. This laborious technique went out of favor by the mid-19th century, when most wax doll heads came to be made of poured wax or wax-over-composition. Poured-wax doll heads were made by pouring tinted liquid wax into metal, wooden, plaster, or clay molds, allowing it to harden, and subsequently repeating the process to build up layers of wax. The resulting wax shell was removed from the mold and its edges smoothed; eye sockets were hollowed out and glass eyes inserted in them. Although English firms produced the majority of poured-wax dolls, they were also made in France, Germany, and the United States. Dolls made by dipping prefabricated composition heads into wax are called waxed, or wax-over-composition, dolls. This technique, which yielded a lustrous, lifelike finish, was also used to coat wooden, papier-mâché, and metal heads. Wax-over-composition dolls were generally manufactured in Germany. Poured-wax and wax-over-composition dolls sometimes have mohair or human-hair wigs glued to the crown; others have hair inserted in a slit forming a center part in the crown. The finest wax dolls have clusters or individual strands of hair inserted into small slits made throughout the scalp with a warm knife. Many dolls with wax heads have cloth or kid bodies.

Rubber

In 1839 Charles Goodyear invented a process that transformed rubber from a sticky, amorphous substance into a firm, unbreakable material that was lightweight and capable of being molded into any form, including dolls. Goodyear's process, called vulcanization, was patented in 1844 and was used to make dolls throughout the 19th century by such firms as Benjamin F. Lee, New York Rubber, Bru, Jules Steiner, and many others. Dolls by these companies are either all-rubber or have rubber heads and cloth bodies.

Papier-mâché doll

Description
Lady doll with papier-mâché shoulder-head. Molded and painted features including brown hair in elaborate Apollo knot adorned with gold tuck comb. Blue eyes, closed mouth. Pearl necklace. Gusseted white kid body. Individually stitched fingers. Left leg replaced. Original costume of gold silk gown with gathered sleeves over rose-colored underdress; lace-trimmed white cotton pantaloons. Red leather shoes with silk bows.

Materials, Marks, and Dimensions
Papier-mâché shoulder-head; kid body and arms; wooden legs. Height: 19".

Maker, Origin, and Period
Maker unknown. Probably France. c. 1825–50.

Comment
This elegantly coiffed papier-mâché lady doll wears the Apollo knot hairstyle favored by women in the 1830s and '40s. Although this coiffure went out of fashion about mid-century, it continued to appear on papier-mâché dolls—whose hair was often made in as many as 8 or 10 separate molds—well into the 1860s. The doll's legs are disproportionately large, perhaps because the dollmaker carved them hastily, knowing they would be covered by a costume. Her feet, however, are properly demure in size.

Hints for Collectors
This doll's delicately painted eyes and mouth suggest French rather than German manufacture, since the features of German dolls were usually more boldly executed. Her gusseted body, made of fine white kid, is also typically French, and does not resemble the stiff and unjointed German doll bodies of the same period. In general, French dolls from the early 19th century cost more than their German counterparts.

Pre-Greiner doll

Description
Lady doll with papier-mâché shoulder-head. Molded and painted
features including black hair with center part and corkscrew
curls. Brown eyes, rosy cheeks, closed mouth. Spoon hands.
Green paper bands cover junctions between legs and body.
Wears off-the-shoulder burgundy and black satin gown, cotton
bloomers, and lace-trimmed cotton underskirt. Painted blue
check stockings and black shoes.

Materials, Marks, and Dimensions
Papier-mâché shoulder-head; kid body; carved wooden limbs.
Height: 13¾".

Maker, Origin, and Period
Maker unknown. Germany. c. 1850–60.

Comment
German dolls that date from the mid-19th century are
characterized by broad plain faces and are easily distinguished
from French dolls, which usually have delicate aristocratic
features. German papier-mâché dolls such as the one shown here
are sometimes referred to as Pre-Greiner dolls, because they are
similar to figures later created by the noted American dollmaker,
Ludwig Greiner, who worked from about 1858 through the 1880s
(see 325 and 327).

Hints for Collectors
Pre-Greiner dolls, most of which are unmarked, may be
identified by their plain hairdos, round faces, kid or cloth bodies,
wooden or kid arms, and painted boots on wooden feet. Dolls
made with kid bodies and wooden limbs often had their joints
reinforced with green or red paper bands. A figure with its
original bands is an unusual find and well worth acquiring.

Wax-over-composition doll

Description
Lady doll with wax-over-composition shoulder-head. Molded and painted features including brown hair in upswept sausage roll. Pupil-less black glass eyes, closed mouth. Spoon hands. Wears pink calico dress with square neck and white rickrack trim. 2 lace-trimmed cotton slips and pantaloons. Painted stockings and flat, high-buttoned black shoes.

Materials, Marks, and Dimensions
Wax-over-composition shoulder-head; cloth body; wooden lower arms and lower legs. Height: 27½".

Maker, Origin, and Period
Maker unknown. Germany. c. 1850.

Comment
Wax-over-composition dolls are so named for the method of dipping their composition-shell heads in wax to make them appear more lifelike, a technique that probably originated in Germany. The doll shown here has inset pupil-less glass eyes and a sophisticated hairstyle, indicating that she was an above-average example. Her flat-heeled shoes suggest a pre-1860 date of manufacture. Until the last quarter of the 19th century, there was no established network for distributing and selling European dolls in America; most were imported independently by businessmen who sold them to shops primarily in New York, Boston, and Philadelphia.

Hints for Collectors
It is rare to find 19th-century wax dolls in good condition, since they have usually been damaged by temperature changes; cold cracks them, while heat softens and misshapes them. Well-preserved wax dolls such as this one, of course, fetch considerably higher sums than disfigured examples.

Greiner doll

Description
Lady doll with composition head. Molded and painted features including black hair parted in center and drawn back to expose ears; black eyes, closed mouth. Wears black and red check dress with white lace collar. Lace-trimmed white cotton underskirt and pantaloons. Brown oilcloth shoes with white stitching.

Materials, Marks, and Dimensions
Composition head; cloth body and legs; kid arms. Paper label on back reads "GREINER IMPROVED PATENT HEADS Pat. March 30th '58." Height: 29".

Maker, Origin, and Period
Ludwig Greiner. Philadelphia, Pennsylvania. c. 1858–72.

Comment
In 1858 Ludwig Greiner received the first known United States patent for dolls' heads. These were made from linen-reinforced papier-mâché, a substance collectors and experts frequently call composition. Composition is a catchall term for paper or wood compounds pressed in molds and used for doll parts. Greiner's original formula called for Spanish whiting (a gessolike product), white paper, rye flour, and glue. In his patent application, Greiner stated that the finished dolls' heads were "painted with oiled paint so that children may not suck off the paint."

Hints for Collectors
Although Greiner advertised his products as "Greiner Everlasting Doll Heads," the paint on their noses and chins frequently wore off from washing or handling. Nevertheless, because Greiner dolls are in great demand, collectors are rarely deterred by such minor flaws.

Papier-mâché doll

Description
Lady doll with papier-mâché shoulder-head. Molded and painted features including short black hair styled in ringlets with wisps framing face. Black glass pupil-less eyes. Jointed body. Individually stitched fingers and toes. Wears red cotton gown with lace-trimmed collar and cuffs. White cotton undervest.

Materials, Marks, and Dimensions
Papier-mâché shoulder-head; kid body and limbs. Height: 20″.

Maker, Origin, and Period
Maker unknown. Head: Germany. Body: probably France. c. 1870.

Comment
Papier-mâché dolls were produced as early as the 18th century in Germany, where they were made from paper-pulp waste, the by-product of the burgeoning book industry. By the last third of the 19th century, however, the demand for them had waned, and they were largely superseded by china, bisque, and wax dolls. The papier-mâché dolls that continued to be produced had much simpler hairdos than the coiffures seen on their mid-19th-century predecessors. French firms often imported German doll heads like this one, which they attached to kid bodies. For example, this doll has a plain but well-made head atop an exquisite, characteristically French kid body, the kind usually reserved for a much finer head. The body has graceful proportions, a pulled-in and swaddled waist, and ample hips. Sewn together from 4 or more pieces of leather, it is probably filled with sawdust.

Hints for Collectors
Dolls with German heads and French bodies may be acquired for less than all-German or all-French dolls of comparable quality.

Greiner dolls

Description
Lady dolls with composition heads. Molded and painted hair and features including blue eyes and closed mouths. Left: Blond hair with center part. Wears red calico dress with white cotton apron. Right: Black hair with center part. Wears 2-piece outfit of light brown moiré.

Materials, Marks, and Dimensions
Composition heads; cloth bodies; kid arms. Paper label on back of each doll's shoulder reads "GREINERS PATENT DOLL HEADS, No 7 [or 5] Pat. Mar. 30, '58, Ext '72." Height: 25" (left); 19" (right).

Maker, Origin, and Period
Ludwig Greiner. Philadelphia, Pennsylvania. After 1872.

Comment
As early as 1840, German-born Ludwig Greiner was listed as a "Toy Man" in the Philadelphia directory. It is surmised that he made dolls for some time before registering his first patent for a doll's head in 1858. Strongly influenced by European traditions, Greiner produced dolls that had full solemn faces and wavy, center-parted molded hair and that resembled German china figures of the period. Early Greiners have black hair, but many that were made after 1872 are blond.

Hints for Collectors
Greiner doll heads were sometimes mounted on cloth bodies made by Jacob Lacmann of Philadelphia, a combination collectors consider desirable. One way to approximate a Greiner doll's age is by checking the patent date on its label; those marked "Ext '72" were made after 1872, when Greiner's patent was renewed.

Rubber lady doll

Description
Lady doll with rubber shoulder-head. Molded and painted
features including blond hair. Brown glass eyes, closed mouth.
Shoulder plate molded as blouse front with blue-trimmed collar
and bow; attached to body with cotton strips inserted through
sew holes. Wears white cotton slip with ruffled hem; lace-
trimmed white cotton pantaloons. Flannel stockings. Sewn-on
brown leather shoes with blue trim.

Materials, Marks, and Dimensions
Rubber shoulder-head; muslin body and legs; kid arms. "N.Y.
Rubber Co. Patent" marked on back of shoulder. Height: 15¾".

Maker, Origin, and Period
New York Rubber Co. New York City. c. 1868–69.

Comment
The New York Rubber Company was granted permission to use
the Goodyear patent for vulcanized rubber, which it employed in
the manufacture of dolls from 1851 until 1917. In 1876 the firm
displayed some of these dolls at the Philadelphia Centennial
exhibition. By 1897 it was producing a variety of all-rubber black
dolls and white dolls that were clothed in knitted wool dresses.
The doll shown here, with her delicate features, glass eyes, and
molded and painted shoulder plate, is obviously patterned after a
fashionable china shoulder-head doll.

Hints for Collectors
Rubber lady dolls were never as popular as china or bisque lady
dolls, so fewer were made, and fewer survive today in good
condition. Their modeling was less detailed than that of porcelain
dolls, and paint did not adhere as well to their rubber heads.
Look for the New York Rubber Company's unusual bathing dolls
wearing knitted outfits rather than molded clothes.

Goodyear rubber doll

Description
Lady doll with rubber shoulder-head. Molded and painted
features including blond hair and blue eyes. Wears light brown
and rose-colored silk dress. 2 white lace-trimmed slips,
pantaloons, and leather shoes.

Materials, Marks, and Dimensions
Rubber shoulder-head; cloth body and feet; kid arms and hands.
Back of shoulder marked "GOODYEAR'S PAT. MAY 6, 1851 EXT 1865."
Height: 24″.

Maker, Origin, and Period
Goodyear Rubber Co. New Haven, Connecticut. c. 1865–90.

Comment
In 1844 Charles Goodyear patented his technique for making
hard rubber, which made possible the large-scale production of
rubber dolls. This process, called vulcanization, consisted of
heating natural rubber with sulphur. Like other rubber
products, doll heads were manufactured by pressing soft rubber
into metal molds and placing the molds in a so-called vulcanizing
bath to harden them.

Hints for Collectors
Goodyear dolls can sometimes be recognized by their round
faces, painted rather than glass eyes, and dark green-colored
rubber visible beneath cracks in their paint. All early rubber
dolls, particularly those in good condition, are avidly sought.
Before purchasing an old rubber doll, examine a variety of
unrestored dolls in museums to see how they compare to the
possible acquisition. Occasionally, repainted dolls do appear on
the market; these should not be confused with well-preserved,
unretouched dolls, which are rare.

Description

Lady doll with rawhide shoulder-head. Molded and painted features including brown hair styled in center part. Wears 2-piece gray and white leaf-print dress with lace collar and black buttons. Black velvet bow at neck and cuffs; matching belt at waist. Original red and white striped cotton stockings. Leather shoes with brass buttons and tiny heels.

Materials, Marks, and Dimensions

Rawhide shoulder-head; cloth body; kid arms and feet. Height: 16″.

Maker, Origin, and Period

Darrow Manufacturing Co. Bristol, Connecticut. c. 1866–77.

Comment

Darrow dolls can be easily recognized by their unique rawhide heads, which were pressed into molds, hand-painted, and often combined with cloth bodies and kid arms and feet. Rawhide lady dolls were not particularly popular, however. The paint on their heads flaked easily, and their rather homely faces and simple suits were no match for elegant china or bisque lady dolls.

Hints for Collectors

Because their rawhide heads are quite perishable, few Darrow dolls survived. Look for the oval green and gold paper sticker on the chests of such dolls; its black print reads "F. E. Darrows Patent May 1st 1866." Since these labels were easily removed, however, many Darrow dolls, including the one shown here, no longer have them.

Springfield doll

Description
Lady doll with wooden swivel head coated with composition.
Blond molded hair styled with bangs. Wears purple and white
print dress trimmed with purple ribbon. Lace slip and lace-
trimmed underpants. Gold bead necklace, gold brooch. Painted
blue hands. Feet painted blue to resemble boots.

Materials, Marks, and Dimensions
Composition-over-wood head; wooden torso, arms and legs;
metal hands and feet. "Mason & Taylor Patent Head May 31,
1881 #242, 210" printed on paper band at waist. Height: 11¾".

Maker, Origin, and Period
D. M. Smith & Co. Springfield, Vermont. After 1881.

Comment
This solemn lady doll was one of many figures produced by
D. M. Smith & Company in the 1870s and '80s. These dolls are
characterized by a painted wooden or composition head, wooden
body, and metal or wooden hands and feet. Feet were usually
painted blue, and heads and shoulders dipped in flesh-colored
paint. The type of swivel head seen here was a new feature
patented in 1881 by Mason and Taylor, a firm whose owners
were closely associated with D. M. Smith & Company.

Hints for Collectors
Springfield, Vermont, a dollmaking center in the mid- to late
19th century, produced some of the first commercial dolls in
America. Each firm in Springfield gave its dolls a distinctive
feature by which they could be identified. For instance, the Co-
operative Manufacturing Company's figures have painted black
feet, while those by D. M. Smith & Company have bright
blue feet.

Composition doll

Description
Lady doll with composition shoulder-head. Molded and painted features including blond hair, blue eyes, and closed mouth. Wears blue and white paisley cotton dress with lace collar and ruffle at hem. Lace-trimmed white cotton apron and underskirt. White cotton stockings with pink bands; red leather and pink satin slippers adorned with pink satin bows.

Materials, Marks, and Dimensions
Composition shoulder-head; cloth body and legs; kid arms. Label on back reads "M & S/Superior/2015." Height: 14¼".

Maker, Origin, and Period
Possibly J. F. Müller & Strassburger. Germany. c. 1865–90.

Comment
German papier-mâché dolls reached the peak of popularity in the mid-19th century, when the simple doll shown here was made. This doll bears a "Superior" label that has also been found on the heads of other German dolls produced by various little-known manufacturers. It can only be speculated that the "M & S" mark that appears alongside the word Superior on this doll's label refers to J. F. Müller & Strassburger, a doll company located in Sonneberg, Germany.

Hints for Collectors
Collectors often mistakenly use the words papier-mâché and composition interchangeably when referring to 19th-century dolls. Strictly speaking, papier-mâché is made from wet laminated sheets of paper that are glued together and pressed into molds, or from a mixture of paper pulp, glue, and other materials; composition is produced by adding plaster or sawdust to this compound.

Bonnet doll

Description
Lady doll with wax-over-composition shoulder-head. Blond hair
glued under multicolored wax bonnet, which is molded to the
head. Black pupil-less eyes; closed mouth. Carved spoon hands
and carved legs with painted black boots. Original costume of
lace-trimmed, off-white linen dress and underskirts.

Materials, Marks, and Dimensions
Wax-over-composition shoulder-head; cloth body; wooden limbs.
Height: 8½".

Maker, Origin, and Period
Maker unknown. Germany. c. 1865–75.

Comment
Bonnet dolls, also called hatted dolls by collectors, were made
during the third quarter of the 19th century by German firms,
which found a ready market for these inexpensive mass-produced
figures. By designing a wide variety of wax hats, some with
imbedded flowers and feathers, dollmakers sought to divert
attention from the dolls' vaguely defined faces and crudely
constructed bodies. Such figures were made with molded hair or
with mohair glued to the heads under the wax hats. The large
versions were of a higher quality than the small ones; the latter
sold for pennies in toy stores and at open-air markets.

Hints for Collectors
Although some collectors do not consider them fine dolls, bonnet
dolls do appeal to those connoisseurs who try to assemble
groupings with different hats, hair ornaments, and hairstyles.
They most often have bisque or china heads. Bonnet dolls with
wax-over-composition or wax-over-wood heads are less common
because few have survived.

Slit-head doll

Description
Lady doll with wax-over-composition shoulder-head. Human hair inserted into crown, styled with center part and corkscrew curls. Brown glass pupil-less eyes, closed mouth. Jointed at shoulders, hips, and knees. Wears white cotton off-the-shoulder dress with red velvet sash; white cotton underskirt and pantaloons. Original red leather shoes adorned with black beads.

Materials, Marks, and Dimensions
Wax-over-composition shoulder-head; cloth body, upper arms, and legs; kid lower arms. Pencil inscription on back of torso reads "August 18, 1860/Mary Mayer." Height: 22½″.

Maker, Origin, and Period
Maker unknown. England. c. 1850–60.

Comment
Wax-over-composition dolls, such as this one, frequently had their hair attached through a long slit incised in the crown. The hair was pulled into the slit, pasted in place inside the head, styled with a center part, and curled into long ringlets with heated tongs. The term "slit-head" derives from this manner of attaching the hair.

Hints for Collectors
This robust-looking doll has a documented provenance, which makes her more valuable than a comparable example whose history is unknown. Purchased in New York in 1860, its first owner was a young girl named Mary Mayer. In 1910, she gave the doll to her cousin Helen Wilcoxson of Lisbon, Ohio, who named it "Mary Louise" and eventually donated it to the Brooklyn Children's Museum in New York.

Pierotti wax doll

Description
Young lady doll with poured-wax shoulder-head. Strands of blond mohair inserted into scalp. Blue glass eyes; closed mouth. Wears twisted silver-foil crown covered with wax flowers. Beige satin wedding gown with pleated skirt, lace collar and cuffs, bustle, and long velvet train. Lace-trimmed white cotton half-skirt, corset, and pantaloons. Lace stockings; satin shoes.

Materials, Marks, and Dimensions
Wax shoulder-head and lower limbs; cloth body and upper limbs. "DOLL TOYS & GAMES/F. ALDIS/11 & 13/BELGRAVE MANSIONS SW" stamped on body. Height: 21″.

Maker, Origin, and Period
Head by Pierotti. Doll distributed by Frederic Aldis. England. c. 1875.

Comment
Pierotti lady dolls are characterized by slim well-modeled bodies, finely detailed poured-wax heads that tilt slightly to one side, and elaborate wigs created by inserting clusters of hair into the wax scalp. The firm also produced fine portrait dolls, soliciting commissions with the phrase, "Likenesses modell'd and casts taken." By "sending their own hair" young ladies could have it implanted to form the doll's wig.

Hints for Collectors
Pierotti dolls often bear a retailer's or distributor's mark on their torsos. Only rarely is "Pierotti" incised on the back of the neck. Since the Pierotti family manufactured dolls from the 1850s to the 1920s, the name of the retailer may help to date them. Variations in style and materials may also indicate the age of a figure; for example, dolls were stuffed with cow hair before 1900, and with kapok afterwards.

Poured-wax doll

Description
Lady doll with poured-wax shoulder-head. Blond mohair inserted in scalp and designed in upswept style with thick wraparound braid. Blue glass eyes, painted lashes and brows; closed mouth and pierced ears. Red shoes painted on feet. Original costume of pale rose and ecru off-the-shoulder gown with pleats, paneling, silk floral bouquets, lace, and silk embroidery. Matching bouquet in hair. Cotton underskirt and lace-trimmed pantaloons.

Materials, Marks, and Dimensions
Wax head and arms; cloth body and legs. Height: 17½″.

Maker, Origin, and Period
Maker unknown. England. c. 1850–75.

Comment
The wax lady doll shown here is one of many fine examples made in England in the mid- to late 19th century. More than 16 makers of wax dolls were listed in the London directory during this period. This doll is exceptional because of its translucent surface, its delicate tinting, and the naturalistic modeling of its head and neck. Judging from its distinctive features, it was probably a portrait of a fashionable woman. The elaborate hairstyle was created by inserting small clusters of mohair into slits made in the scalp with a warm knife.

Hints for Collectors
It is important to distinguish between poured-wax and solid wax dolls' heads. Both types were made in molds, but the former were built up of successive layers of wax poured repeatedly into the mold, while the latter were made by a single casting. Although extensive cracking detracts from the value of poured-wax dolls, some small cracks, such as those seen on this example, are acceptable signs of aging.

Gibson Girl

Description
Lady doll with composition head and wig of dark brown human hair. Blue eyes, closed mouth. Original Gibson Girl costume of peplum jacket with cloth-covered buttons and leg-of-mutton sleeves, and matching long skirt decorated with white braid. Lace-trimmed jabot and lace cuffs. White ribbed socks; white leather shoes with white ribbons and metal buckles.

Materials, Marks, and Dimensions
Composition. "EFFanBEE Anne-Shirley" marked on back of torso. Height: 20″.

Maker, Origin, and Period
Head designed by Dewees Cochran for EFFanBEE (trade name for Fleischaker & Baum). New York City. c. 1938.

Comment
This doll's upswept hair and elaborate costume—which originally included a hat, muff, and parasol—is in the style of Charles Dana Gibson's drawings of fashionable women. The doll itself is an Anne-Shirley type first issued by EFFanBEE in 1935 and advertised in the September 26, 1938, edition of *The Herald Tribune*. It was so named to compete with the Shirley Temple dolls that were all the rage at the time. EFFanBEE used the best grade of composition to eliminate crazing and claimed that Anne-Shirley's complexion was "satin-smooth." The doll was also prized for its finely modeled hands.

Hints for Collectors
The Anne-Shirley Gibson Girl was one of EFFanBEE's top-of-the-line dolls. This figure is particularly desirable because its head was created by the noted NIADA (National Institute of American Doll Artists) dollmaker Dewees Cochran, who was under contract with EFFanBEE during the 1930s.

Metal doll

Description
Male doll with composition head. Molded and painted features including brown hair and brows, prominent nose, red mouth. Ball-jointed body and limbs.

Materials, Marks, and Dimensions
Composition head, hands, and feet; metal body and limbs. "Made in/Switzerland/Patents/Applied for" incised on torso. Height: 8″.

Maker, Origin, and Period
A. Bucherer. Switzerland. c. 1921.

Comment
Though virtually indestructible, metal dolls seldom appealed to children. Neither beautiful like wax or porcelain dolls, nor soft and cuddly like cloth dolls, metal dolls were essentially a novelty that never caught on. Superbly constructed, figures manufactured by the firm A. Bucherer have realistic character heads that seem incongruous atop their well-engineered but robotlike bodies. Their segmented, ball-jointed limbs permit the dolls to assume many poses, and their large feet allow them to stand. The unusual bodies of Bucherer dolls were generally hidden beneath elaborate clothing, such as national costumes or baseball uniforms.

Hints for Collectors
Bucherer dolls were manufactured for only a brief time, so they seldom appear on the market today. Because such dolls, like most unusual designs, are rarely encountered, their prices vary widely. Dolls like these may stump even an experienced collector or dealer and thus may sell considerably below their market value.

Wax lady doll

Description
Lady doll with solid wax shoulder-head and brown mohair wig.
Brown eyes, closed mouth. Original costume of brown silk suit
decorated with black glass buttons. White silk and lace ascot
adorned with silk rose; matching lace cuffs. Large white feather
adorns bronze-colored silk hat. Feet painted black to resemble
shoes. Carries umbrella of beige silk and lace, and metallic-
beaded purse. Wooden stand covered with felt.

Materials, Marks, and Dimensions
Wax head; cloth body; kid limbs. Height: 13¼″.

Maker, Origin, and Period
Lafitte & Desirat. France. c. 1912.

Comment
Lafitte & Desirat lavished attention on this doll's clothing,
faithfully portraying an Edwardian outfit in great detail. The
doll's idealized features suggest that she was strictly a fashion
doll. Numerous other wax figures, on the other hand, were made
as portraits. Stylish women of the 19th and early 20th centuries
often commissioned portrait dolls along with paintings and
sculptures of themselves. Queen Victoria, an avid doll collector,
was the subject of many such dolls.

Hints for Collectors
A doll like this, striking a pose that may have been copied from a
fashion plate, is valued more for her costume than for her head
and body. Such dolls were intended for decorative display. Since
their clothes are easily soiled, fashion dolls should be kept under
glass domes for protection.

Lenci flapper doll

Description
Lady doll with felt head and curly blond mohair wig. Side-glancing eyes, closed mouth. Slender body and legs. Original costume of tall red felt hat, white organdy 3-tiered dress with appliquéd red felt flowers and black leaves; white organdy underclothes. Red leather high-heeled shoes. Gold metal bead necklace. Carries small plush bulldog under arm.

Materials, Marks, and Dimensions
Pressed felt. Height: 26¼″.

Maker, Origin, and Period
Lenci (trade name for Elena Scavini). Italy. c. 1927–30.

Comment
Dolls dressed in flapper-style clothing were quite popular in the 1920s and '30s and were made by a number of firms. Lenci's flapper dolls can be identified by their side-glancing eyes, pensive expressions, well-made heads and bodies, and exquisite clothing. The hands of Lenci dolls are designed either with separated fingers, as seen here, or with fingers articulated only by topstitching. The company was run by the husband-and-wife team of Enrico and Elena Scavini; Lenci was Elena's pet name. The Lenci trademark was registered in Europe in 1922 and in the United States in 1924.

Hints for Collectors
Some flapper dolls were designed to nestle in oversize pillows and were known variously as bed, boudoir, or sitting dolls. These usually have soft bodies and floppy legs and should not be confused with fashion-type flapper dolls such as this one.

Aunt Connie

Description
Lady doll with stockinet over foam-rubber head, seen at 2
angles. Black synthetic hair. Stitched and painted features,
sequin eyes, full red mouth. Original costume of elaborately
beaded and sequined black velvet evening dress, fur boa, and
black sequined hat with fur trim and feathers. Black wooden
base.

Materials, Marks, and Dimensions
Stockinet over foam-rubber head; cardboard and foam-rubber
body. Height: 11½″.

Maker, Origin, and Period
Faith Ringgold. New York City. 1977.

Comment
The Aunt Connie doll shown here was created by the
contemporary artist Faith Ringgold as a portrait of a friend's
aunt. This is one of the first dolls for whose face Ringgold used
foam rubber covered with stockinet instead of padded gauze.
Today's dollmakers favor stockinet as a medium because it can be
molded easily to form expressive facial features. Ringgold
considers her dolls to be both soft sculptures and models for
large-scale figures. She also sees them as statements about
cultural prejudice. Ringgold once remarked that "they are made
by a black woman artist for children—both of whom are
neglected persons in our culture. Besides, the doll figure itself is
usually considered to be a less important object than traditional
art forms in our society."

Hints for Collectors
Collectors are always seeking unusual dolls by new dollmakers.
These individualistic modern creations are good investments
because interest in them is bound to continue growing.

Mechanical Dolls

 In 16th-century Nuremberg and Augsburg, 2 major German clockmaking centers, large town clocks captivated the public with their animated statues that struck the hour. These figures may be considered predecessors of the mechanical dolls of the late 17th century. The latter, also called automata, were operated by clockwork mechanisms and were created for the amusement of the upper class.

18th-Century Mechanical Dolls

Throughout the 18th century, clockwork automata performed their movements accompanied by music produced by bellows, pipes, cranks, and other mechanical devices. Some automata were so expensive and elaborate, incorporating vignettes of life-size figures, that audiences paid to see them. Artisans competed vigorously in creating more and more ingenious figures. One mechanical doll of a dulcimer player, produced in 1780, was so extraordinary that Marie Antoinette acquired it, and the composer Christoph Willibald Gluck wrote music especially for it. Jacquet Droz invented dolls that wrote actual sentences with a pen and moved their heads and eyes simultaneously. Vaucanson, a well-known maker of automata, was a skilled musician who applied his knowledge of music and mechanics to inventions that included a 6-foot-high flute player whose fingers covered the flute's holes while he blew into it.

19th-Century Mechanical Dolls

The Swiss clockmaker Antoine Favre is credited with the invention of a music box that worked by means of a revolving cylinder with a series of small pins that struck against the teeth of a metal comb. This invention, along with the perfection of the clockwork mechanism and improvement of manufacturing methods, led to increased production of luxurious small automata during the 19th century. By the third quarter of the century, makers of musical automata found it profitable to market simplified dolls that performed only a few movements. Mechanisms were usually concealed inside the figure or in the base of these dolls. While a few of these costly figures were designed as children's playthings, most were meant for adult entertainment. Among the best-known 19th-century producers of automata were Jean Rousselot, Fleischmann & Blödel, Phalibois, Léopold Lambert, and Roullet & Decamps, a firm still in business today. Automata by these makers frequently had fine bisque heads by Jumeau or Simon & Halbig.

Walking Dolls

Some of the first walking dolls had wheels or rollers concealed under their skirts. These included a guitar player made by Gautier in 1794 and walking dolls on wheels produced by Nicholas Théroude in the 1840s and '50s. In 1862 Enoch Morrison patented the famous walking doll he called "autoperipatetikos." Jules Steiner developed a walking doll operated by a clockwork mechanism in mid-century; he introduced a perfected version of the doll in 1890 under the name Bébé Premier Pas (or, Baby First Step).

Luxurious mechanical dolls continued to be made until the beginning of the First World War. At the same time cheap copies of French automata—many of which used pull cords instead of clockwork mechanisms—were mass produced all over Europe, particularly in Germany. Automata are still being made as novelty items today. Naturally, these dolls are not as widely collected or as valuable as early examples.

Black banjo player

Description
Musical mechanical doll with bisque head and black Persian wool wig. Molded and painted features, black glass eyes. Wears red satin jacket over white satin shirt. Original black velvet trousers, black cotton stockings, and black velvet shoes. Banjo made of wood, string, and skin. Doll mounted on red velour base that conceals clockwork mechanism and music box. When activated, figure strums banjo and turns head as music plays.

Materials, Marks, and Dimensions
Bisque head and arms; papier-mâché body and legs; metal hands. "3 D" imprinted on back of head. Height: 14″.

Maker, Origin, and Period
Maker unknown. France or Germany. c. 1885.

Comment
As the turn of the century approached, large numbers of extravagant musical automata were produced for the amusement of an increasingly jaded public. Elaborately costumed figures of porcelain or papier-mâché stood atop music boxes and strummed their instruments as the music played. The figures frequently represented picturesque characters, such as organ grinders and circus performers. Black automata were fairly common during this period. Silber & Fleming, a London-based wholesale toy distributor, advertised 3 different black mechanical dolls in 1880 —one played the flute, another sold vegetables, and a third smoked a pipe.

Hints for Collectors
Among the most unusual mechanical dolls were those that satirically portrayed cabaret and stage stars of the 1880s and '90s, several of whom were the subjects of Toulouse-Lautrec's artwork. These automata are rare and highly prized.

Clown mandolin player

Description
Musical mechanical doll with papier-mâché head and red and
gray mohair wig. Molded and painted features. White clown face,
open mouth displaying tongue. Original silk paisley print outfit
adorned with sequins and lace. Yellow collar, beige felt hat.
Yellow shoes. Painted wooden mandolin with metal strings. Doll
seated on stool mounted on wooden base containing clockwork
mechanism and music box. When key activates mechanism,
clown's head turns from side to side, tongue moves in and out,
and left leg crosses over right and raises up and down as one
hand plucks mandolin.

Materials, Marks, and Dimensions
Papier-mâché head and legs; cardboard body; bisque hands.
Illegible inscription on paper label attached to base. Initials "LB"
on key. Height: 23¼".

Maker, Origin, and Period
Possibly Léopold Lambert. France. c. 1870.

Comment
Some of the most popular subjects for musical automata were
circus figures, whose limbs moved as they played their
instruments. These dolls were prized as much for the complexity
of their movement as for the materials used in their construction.
Papier-mâché was often employed as a protective housing for the
dolls' mechanisms, which were usually made of metal.

Hints for Collectors
This clown has the minor flaws of a soiled wig and a chipped face,
which are best left untouched. Should such a doll require
extensive repairs, take it to a restorer experienced in handling
19th-century automata. Even then, collectors find that
mechanical parts for old dolls are sometimes unobtainable.

Boy and girl in boat

Description
Pull-toy dolls with bisque shoulder-heads and blond mohair wigs.
Molded and painted features, blue glass eyes, open-closed
mouths showing teeth. Original costumes. Left: Girl wears pink
silk brocade dress with lace collar, cuffs, and apron. Straw
picture hat. Right: Boy wears Venetian-style blue and white
striped cotton suit with red collar, cuffs, and sash trimmed in
gold fringe. Red silk hat. Holds wooden oar adorned with red
velvet ribbon and brass bells. Red, white, and blue painted
wooden boat mounted on painted platform with metal wheels.
Gears attached to wheels cause boy to row boat when
conveyance is pulled or pushed.

Materials, Marks, and Dimensions
Bisque heads; wood and metal bodies; wooden limbs. "S&H"
imprinted on backs of heads. Height: 5″ (left, seated); 9″ (right).

Maker, Origin, and Period
Simon & Halbig. Germany. c. 1910.

Comment
In the early 20th century, German dollmakers simplified the
elaborate designs of French automata in order to make more
moderately priced versions that would be suitable for a mass
audience. Pull toys like this one were designed for children and
were operated simply by pulling the toy along the floor.

Hints for Collectors
Many 19th-century pull toys did not survive the battering
children gave them. Consequently, the few that are found on the
market nowadays are rare and eagerly sought after. The toy
illustrated here is particularly valuable because the dolls have
Simon & Halbig heads and exquisite costumes, and because the
entire ensemble is in excellent condition.

Bébé with puppet show

Description
Musical mechanical doll with bisque swivel head and blond
mohair wig. Molded and painted features, glass eyes, closed
mouth. Wears gray satin dress with glass buttons and lace trim,
white cotton underskirt and pantaloons edged in lace. Brown
cotton stockings, brown leather shoes. Doll stands behind puppet
theater on wooden box covered with velvet and leather, holds
wand in right hand and string in left. When wound, bébé raises
curtain to show a series of revolving heads. Disk inside theater
rotates so that 5 heads are aligned sequentially atop single
puppet's body while music plays.

Materials, Marks, and Dimensions
Doll: Bisque head and hands; wooden body and legs; metal arms.
"FID" inscribed on head. Puppet heads and body: Composition.
Height: 15¾".

Maker, Origin, and Period
Maker unknown. France. c. 1898–1911.

Comment
The bébé pictured here directs an amusing puppet show in her
own little theater. The pleasure of watching a show-within-a-
show—an idea borrowed from the stage—appealed to 19th-
century collectors of automata.

Hints for Collectors
The marks on this doll cannot be traced to any known
manufacturer. Should an interesting doll with an unknown mark
become available, check 19th- and early 20th-century doll and toy
catalogues for descriptions of similar examples. Such catalogues
are invaluable sources of information.

Boy blowing bubbles

Description
Musical mechanical doll with bisque head and blond mohair wig.
Molded and painted features; blue glass paperweight eyes,
painted lashes, and open mouth showing upper teeth. Holds
brass pipe and pewter bowl. Original costume of blue velvet
suit, matching hat, white blouse with lace collar, black cotton
stockings, brown leather shoes. Wooden base covered with red
velvet conceals music box, bellows, and clockwork mechanism.
Bellows pumps air through tube into boy's mouth while
clockwork mechanism raises and lowers pipe into bowl of soapy
water, causing boy to blow bubbles.

Materials, Marks, and Dimensions
Bisque head, composition body. "Déposé Tête Jumeau" stamped
in red on back of neck. Height: 17″.

Maker, Origin, and Period
Head: Jumeau. Body: possibly Roullet & Decamps. France.
c. 1875–1900.

Comment
The charming image of a boy blowing bubbles appeared in
paintings and illustrations for centuries before it was adapted by
makers of automata. In 1912, the noted mechanical-doll maker
Decamps advertised a male figure wearing an 18th-century
French court costume and blowing bubbles from a pipe.

Hints for Collectors
Most mechanical dolls were made from about 1840 until the onset
of the First World War. They sometimes appear to be older than
their true age because dollmakers tried to enhance their appeal
by dressing them in costumes of earlier periods. Authentic 18th-
century automata are extremely rare and are unlikely to be seen
outside of museums or private collections.

Description
Musical dolls with bisque heads. Molded and painted features.
Blue glass eyes. Torsos encase music boxes; dolls are held from
below by handles. Left: Blond mohair wig, closed mouth.
Original costume of silver lamé tunic with lace-trimmed collar
and lace hem. Bells hang from red and silver lamé ribbons
attached to collar. Silver lamé hat decorated with red ribbon.
Right: Curly white wig, open mouth showing 2 teeth. Original
costume of pink satin tunic adorned with pointed satin strips
ending in yarn balls. Plumed pink satin hat.

Materials, Marks, and Dimensions
Bisque heads, cardboard bodies. Left: Ivory handle. Right:
Wooden handle. "3200 A.M. 9/0 DEP Germany" incised on back
of head. Height: 12½″ (left); 13½″ (right).

Maker, Origin, and Period
Left: Rabery & Delphieu. France. c. 1876. Right: Armand
Marseille. Germany. c. 1912.

Comment
The French words *marotte* and *folie* originally referred to a court
jester who wore a pointed cap decorated with bells. In the 19th
century, folie came to mean a gaily costumed carnival doll on a
stick, sometimes with a squeaker box concealed in its torso, and
marotte referred to more complicated musical dolls like those
shown here, whose torsos contain music boxes that are activated
by twirling the dolls on their handles. Today, the word marotte
is often translated as "a whim."

Hints for Collectors
The rarest marottes are complete dolls that stand atop music
boxes. These boxes are set atop handles of wood, ivory, or metal.

Autoperipatetikos

Description
Female mechanical doll. Papier-mâché head covered with sized
fabric. Molded and painted features and black hair styled with
center part. Black eyes, closed mouth, rosy cheeks. Wears white
satin dress decorated with pink tulle; white cotton underskirt.
Painted gold shoes. Doll walks when clockwork mechanism
(hidden in cardboard dome underneath dress) is wound with key.

Materials, Marks, and Dimensions
Cloth and papier-mâché head and body; kid arms and hands; tin
feet. "Patented July 15th, 1862; also, in England" printed on
round board beneath skirt. Height: 9¾".

Maker, Origin, and Period
Designed by Enoch Rice Morrison for Martin & Runyon. New
York City. c. 1862–65.

Comment
Walking dolls were quite popular in America in the mid-19th
century. *Autoperipatetikos*, the Greek word for "self-walking,"
was the term used by Enoch Rice Morrison for his well-made
walking doll, patented in 1862 in both England and America. The
doll was available with a cloth, china, bisque, or papier-mâché
head. The original box instructed the user to "clasp the board at
the bottom with the thumb and finger of the left hand. . . . With
the right wind [it] up, turning the key from you, and then set it
LIGHTLY ON ITS FEET."

Hints for Collectors
An autoperipatetikos doll in its original carton is a valuable find,
since the box is often printed with illustrations of the doll in its
original costume, as well as with information pertaining to its
distributor, date of issue, and other data that might otherwise
have been lost.

Lady at her toilette

Description
Musical mechanical doll with bisque swivel head. Wig of brown human hair styled with pink satin band. Molded and painted features, blue glass paperweight eyes with red dots at corners, painted lashes, shadowing on lids, open mouth showing teeth. Original costume of pink satin dressing gown over white gauze and pink satin underskirt. White cotton bloomers trimmed with lace, white silk lace stockings, pink satin slippers. Doll holds powder puff and hairbrush. Vanity mirror, celluloid brush, glass perfume bottle, several cloth and cardboard boxes, and a tin box arranged on dressing table covered with satin and lace. Key activates music box and clockwork mechanism concealed in brown velvet stand, causing doll to powder face as music plays.

Materials, Marks, and Dimensions
Bisque head and limbs, composition body. "Simon & Halbig/ S & H/6" imprinted on back of head. Height: 21″.

Maker, Origin, and Period
Head: Simon & Halbig. Germany. c. 1900–10.

Comment
A lady at her toilette was an especially popular subject for automata and was an image made all the more fascinating by the wonderfully complex array of toiletries that accompanies dolls like the one shown here. In contrast to her sophisticated accoutrements, this lady's mechanical movement of powdering her nose while the music plays is relatively simple.

Hints for Collectors
Collectors interested in the finest 19th-century automata should seek those made by Roullet & Decamps, Jean Rousselot, Jules Steiner, Fleischmann & Blödel, Phalibois, and Léopold Lambert.

Lady selling flowers

Description

Musical mechanical doll with bisque shoulder-head and swivel neck. Wig of light brown human hair. Molded and painted features, blue blown-glass eyes, pierced ears. Wears costume of brocade bodice with gold fringe over blue silk skirt. White satin shoes. Double-strand pearl necklace. Right hand holds silk flowers, left hand holds basket of flowers. When clockwork mechanism in torso is wound by key, music plays and doll's head moves from side to side while right hand offers flowers and basket lid lifts to reveal a miniature bisque doll throwing kisses.

Materials, Marks, and Dimensions

Bisque head and hands, composition and cardboard body. "Déposé Tête Jumeau SGDG 7" imprinted on back of head. Height: 24″.

Maker, Origin, and Period

Head: Jumeau. Clockwork mechanism possibly made by Roullet & Decamps. France. c. 1895.

Comment

The wistful-looking Jumeau doll pictured here goes through an elaborate mechanical routine that was calculated to delight audiences and to demonstrate the maker's technical skill. Jumeau manufactured fine bisque heads for Roullet & Decamps and other firms specializing in automata, and also purchased mechanisms from them in order to construct their own mechanical dolls.

Hints for Collectors

Automata with bisque heads were usually manufactured in the last third of the 19th century, while those with papier-mâché heads were produced earlier. These dolls are sought by doll fanciers and by collectors of antique music boxes and toys.

Bébé eating chocolate

Description
Musical mechanical doll with bisque head and wig of blond human hair. Molded and painted features, blue glass paperweight eyes, painted lashes and brows, open-closed mouth showing teeth. Original costume of pink satin and lace dress, lace collar, metallic braid trim at bodice and hem. White cotton gauze underskirt and pantaloons tied with pink ribbons. Black cotton stockings, satin shoes. Bébé sits on wicker basket with silk flowers at her side. Musical device and clockwork mechanism concealed within basket activate arms, upper body, and head so that girl appears to eat chocolate and read book entitled *Le Petit Fabuliste De La Jeunesse (The Little Storyteller)* while music plays.

Materials, Marks, and Dimensions
Bisque head and hands; composition torso and lower legs; hemp-over-wire thighs. Height: 16¼″.

Maker, Origin, and Period
Maker unknown. France. c. 1880.

Comment
The rare mechanical doll shown here is seated on a basket that may have originally contained chocolate along with the clockwork mechanism and music box, suggesting that the entire ensemble was intended as a gift. Such a charming toy was costly in its day, and would bring a very high sum in today's market.

Hints for Collectors
After purchasing a fine doll that, like this example, is in good condition, have it checked by a specialist in antique mechanical dolls to learn how to maintain its mechanism in working order. It may be necessary to activate and lubricate its metal parts periodically to prevent them from becoming brittle or immobile.

352 Bébé pulling dog cart

Description
Mechanical bébé with bisque socket head and brown mohair wig. Molded and painted features. Blue glass eyes, open-closed mouth showing 3 upper teeth, pierced ears. Original costume of pink silk dress with floral lace overlay; blue ribbon braid at waist, cuffs, and hem. Matching cape and hat, beige cotton stockings, black leather shoes with blue ribbon bows. When wound by large key, doll walks and pulls dog cart.

Materials, Marks, and Dimensions
Bisque head; papier-mâché body; composition limbs. "Limoges France" marked on back of head; shaft of key marked "6." Height: 12″.

Maker, Origin, and Period
Maker unknown. France. c. 1900.

Comment
Limoges, France, is one of the great porcelain-making centers of Europe. The "Limoges" mark imprinted on the neck of the doll illustrated is found on most porcelain items manufactured in the city during the past 100 years. This doll is operated by a winding key and spring. A similar device patented by Roullet & Decamps in 1892 may have been the model for this mechanism.

Hints for Collectors
It is not unusual to find a charming mechanical doll with its original costume in tatters. A collector will sometimes reclothe such a doll by carefully removing its original outfit, which may have been glued onto the body, and making a pattern from what remains of the garment. A suitable pattern may also possibly be found in one of the many recently published books on dolls' fashions, and appropriate 19th-century fabrics may sometimes be salvaged from antique clothing found at flea markets.

Grandmother knitting

Description
Mechanical doll with papier-mâché head; gray mohair wig and eyebrows. Molded and painted features, blue glass sleep-eyes, closed mouth, facial wrinkles. Wire glasses. Original costume of paisley shawl over long-sleeved brown linen blouse; pink coral and gold brooch at neck. Striped blue and white cotton apron over heavy blue and black woolen skirt, white lace-trimmed underskirt. White eyelet-trimmed cap. Blue and white striped stockings, black wooden shoes with brass button fasteners. Skein of blue wool in lap. Doll sits in wooden chair. Eyelids open and close and hands move in knitting motion when clockwork mechanism is activated by large metal key.

Materials, Marks, and Dimensions
Papier-mâché head, wooden body and limbs. Height: 19″.

Maker, Origin, and Period
Maker unknown. France. c. 1890–1900.

Comment
Although the elderly woman doll shown here wears a disproportionately large cap, she has a beautifully realized face, reflecting complete absorption in her work. Her coarse linen blouse, paisley shawl, rough wooden shoes, and thick stockings emphasize her peasant origin. "Grandmother knitting" was the subject of numerous dolls of all types and materials, including apple-head and wooden dolls, and even modern dollhouse figures.

Hints for Collectors
Keys for automata were often lost, but most keys fit many dolls. Sometimes metal or brass keys bear a firm's initials, but since they were frequently interchanged, it is not advisable to identify a doll by its key.

Description
Bébé with bisque head; molded and painted features. Blue glass paperweight eyes, painted eyebrows, open mouth with upper row of teeth. Long wig of red human hair. Jointed composition body. Pierced ears with pink glass earrings. Phonograph in torso plays record of "Polichinelle" when iron key in back is wound to activate clockwork mechanism.

Materials, Marks, and Dimensions
Bisque head, composition body. Back of head marked "Déposé Tête Jumeau II." Blue ink stamp on back of torso reads "Bébé Jumeau Bte SGDG Déposé." Record in torso marked "Bébé Jumeau Phonographe Bte SGDG, Polichinelle." Height: 24″.

Maker, Origin, and Period
Jumeau. France. c. 1895–99.

Comment
Thomas Alva Edison produced a phonograph doll in 1889, inspiring Jumeau to manufacture the example illustrated here, whose wax cylinder records were activated by a key-wound clockwork mechanism. The Jumeau doll's recording contained the following phrases, here translated from the French: "Hello, my dear little Mommy. . . . We will go to see Guignol to hear him sing. Knock, knock. Who's there? . . . It's Punch, that's who."

Hints for Collectors
Jumeau phonograph dolls are quite rare and bring high sums when found in working order with their original records. The phonograph in the bébé pictured here does not work, and its torso has been refinished and partially replaced. Although an unrestored doll in good condition is always more valuable than a comparable repaired example, tasteful restoration nonetheless enhances the value of a damaged doll.

Bru bébés

Description
Bébés with bisque heads and wigs of reddish-blond human hair.
Molded and painted features, blown-glass eyes, closed mouths.
Jointed bodies. Pierced ears. Original silk shoes with cardboard
soles. Left: Bébé Petit Pas has blue eyes, red glass earrings.
Clockwork mechanism in torso (activated by key on side) causes
legs to swing from hips. When metal ring at side is pulled, doll
says "Mama, Papa." Right: Doll has brown eyes, molded bosom.

Materials, Marks, and Dimensions
Left: Bisque head; composition body and limbs; kid at hip joints.
"Bru Jne R 11" incised on back of head. Paper label affixed to kid
strip on torso reads "BÉBÉ BRU Bte SGDG/Tout Contrafacteur
sera saisi et poursuivi/conformément à la Loi." "Bru Jne Paris"
printed on soles of shoes. Right: Bisque head, lower arms, and
hands; kid body; upper arms of kid over wood; wooden lower
legs. Back of head marked "Bru Jne 11"; on left shoulder, "Bru";
on right shoulder, "N. 11." Paper label on chest identical to that
of doll on left. Height: 24¾" (left); 23½" (right).

Maker, Origin, and Period
Bru Jne & Cie. France. Left: c. 1891. Right: After 1883.

Comment
Paul Girard, the head of Bru from 1891 to 1899, registered a
French patent for his key-wound, walking and talking Bébé Petit
Pas, pictured at left. The doll shown on the right is a somewhat
earlier, non-mechanical example.

Hints for Collectors
Many Bru dolls can be identified by their molded bosoms, a
feature seen on the doll at right. Because the quality of Bru work
declined during the firm's later years, dolls made after 1900
command lower prices than earlier examples.

Description
Mechanical girl dolls with composition heads, molded and painted features. Grinning closed mouths, red cheeks. Metal springs encased in cardboard bodies. Left: Black fur wig, painted brown eyes. Original costume of red and white checked cotton dress over navy blue sweater; dark blue stockings. Beige suede laced shoes. Right: Brown glass eyes, light brown mohair wig. Original dress of blue and red checks on white ground with white eyelet collar, cuffs, and band. Black cotton stockings, black leather high-laced shoes. Holds orange in right hand, flower in left. Springs wound by keys in backs cause dolls to move from side to side, while raising right arms to mouths.

Materials, Marks, and Dimensions
Composition heads; cardboard bodies; padded wire upper arms; bisque lower arms; wooden legs and feet. Left: Composition hands. Right: Bisque hands. Height: 14½".

Maker, Origin, and Period
Probably manufactured by SFBJ. France. Distributed by Abercrombie & Fitch. New York City. c. 1939.

Comment
These dolls were believed to have been made in the late 19th century until an Abercrombie & Fitch catalogue from 1939 was recently discovered to contain an advertisement for them, clearly dating them to that year.

Hints for Collectors
Do not assume that the store or doll firm that advertised a doll also manufactured it. Distributors sometimes affixed their own label or ribbon to the clothes or body of a doll produced by another firm.

Walking toddler

Description
Little girl mechanical doll with celluloid head, molded and painted hair and features. Blue eyes, closed mouth. Original costume of matching red and green plaid cotton jumper and bonnet, white cotton blouse, white cotton underskirt, white satin pants. Clockwork mechanism causes doll to walk.

Materials, Marks, and Dimensions
Celluloid head and limbs, metal body and feet. "Made in Japan" incised on feet. Tag pinned to jumper reads "MECHANICAL/ WALKING DOLL/WIND THE SPRING AT THE/SIDE AND PLACE THE DOLL/ON THE FLOOR./LOOK HOW SHE WALKS!/LIFT HER UP AND THE ME-/CHANISM STOPS. PLACE HER AGAIN AND/SHE RESUMES WALKING." Height: 13¾".

Maker, Origin, and Period
Maker unknown. Japan. c. 1950.

Comment
Japan produced its first dolls with Caucasian features about 1915, many of them unabashed copies of German dolls that were unobtainable in America because of the ongoing war. Production gradually declined after the end of the First World War, and not until the mid- to late 1950s did Japan resume large-scale manufacture of dolls for export. The doll illustrated is unusual because it was made around 1950—a time when few such figures were being produced in Japan for the American market.

Hints for Collectors
An unusual-looking doll with an unknown provenance occasionally surfaces at an auction or antiques show. It may turn out to be a good investment if it is reasonably priced and its origin can be later determined. Mechanical dolls usually increase in value over the years.

Doll Advertisements

While doll advertisements may seem quaint and amusing to modern readers, they are of historical interest because they document the popularity of certain kinds of dolls. Such advertisements, along with illustrated manufacturers' catalogues, also provide invaluable information about doll clothes, since they depict dolls in their original outfits. Furthermore, the name of a doll's maker or distributor, its patent date, mold number, and a description of its materials are sometimes printed next to its picture.

Catalogues and Magazines

Some of the earliest catalogues, produced in Germany in the late 18th and early 19th centuries, were salesmen's sample books consisting of hand-colored illustrations of dolls dressed in various costumes. Later catalogues often depicted unclothed dolls with limbs flexed to show the workings of their joints. By the mid-19th century, many periodicals, including fashion magazines, illustrated dolls in great detail. Journals such as the French *La Poupée* (*The Doll*) and *Gazette de la Poupée* (*The Doll's Magazine*) and the American *Doll's Dressmaker* were devoted entirely to dolls and the art of outfitting them. *Harper's Bazaar*, founded in 1867, featured illustrations of dolls and their clothes as early as 1869, followed in the 1880s by *Vogue* and *Ladies' Home Journal*. Since the mid-19th century, catalogues have been issued by prominent dollmakers and distributors, including Bru Jne & Cie, Kämmer & Reinhardt, Silber & Fleming, F. A. O. Schwarz, Montgomery Ward, and Sears, Roebuck & Company. Facsimiles of some early ones have recently been printed, but because these are published in limited editions, they are often difficult to find.

Advertisements and catalogues that include a descriptive text along with illustrations provide insights into changing styles and consumer demand over the decades. 19th-century ads show that an elegant dress, fine materials, and delicate proportions were a doll's most desirable features, but by the early 20th century, dolls were extolled mainly for their sturdiness and naturalism. For example, an ad for Martha Chase stockinet dolls, printed on p. 435, amusingly boasts of the dolls' realism by showing a photograph of a woman holding two Chase dolls and asking, "Which is the live baby?"

Illustrations

The advertisement for Arnold Print Works dolls on the facing page was published in the December 13, 1894, issue of *The Youth's Companion*. On the following pages, the ad on the left for the Schoenhut dolls appeared in *The Delineator* in December 1914; the ad for Martha Chase dolls on the upper right was featured in the December 1909 *Ladies' Home Journal;* and the Chase ad on the lower right appeared in *The Delineator* in November 1917.

A Merry Christmas to the Children.

Every child should have these popular toys manufactured by the **Arnold Print Works**, North Adams, Mass. They are **Inexpensive, Harmless, Lifelike and Amusing.**

Mail Orders

promptly filled in season for Christmas, Postage free. Order at once.

Patented July 5 and Oct. 4, 1892.
TABBY CAT, 10c.

Pat. July 5 and Oct. 4, 1892.
Little Tabby,
(4) 10c. (8) 20c.

Pat. July 5 and Oct. 4, 1892.
Little Tatters,
(4) 10c. (8) 20c.

Patented July 5 and Oct. 4, 1892.
Reg'd, England, Jan. 23, '95.
TATTERS, 10c.

Patented July 5 & Oct. 4, '92.
LITTLE RED RIDING HOOD, 10c.

Patented July 5 & Oct. 4, '92.
Reg'd, Eng., Aug. 23, '95.
PICKANINNY, 10c.

Pat. Jan. 31, '96.
SAILOR BOY, 10c.

Patented July 5 & Oct. 4, '92.
PITTI-SING, (4) 10c.

Patented September 26, 1893.
JOINTED CLOTH DOLL, 10c.

Patented July 5 and Oct. 4, 1892.
BOW-WOW, 10c.

Patented July 5 and Oct. 4, 1892.
JOCKO, 10c.

Palmer Cox Celebrated
BROWNIES

Twelve different figures of the popular little fellows, seven inches long. Printed in colors on one yard of cloth, marked where to cut out and sew together—**20 cts.**

Pat. July 5 & Oct. 4, '92.
Little Bow-wow, (4) 10c.

Patented July 5 and Oct. 4, 1892.
FLOSS, 10c.

Other figures not shown are HEN and 4 CHICKS, 10 cts.; ROOSTER, 10 cts.; OUR SOLDIER BOYS 6, 10 cts.; TOPSY 4, 10 cts.; LITTLE JOCKO 4, 10 cts.

Directions.

These figures are printed one each (except where (4) are marked) on half yard cotton cloth in natural colors and marked accurately where to CUT OUT AND SEW TOGETHER. Stuff with Cotton or Bran and put pasteboard in the bottom to make them stand up.
ANY CHILD CAN DO IT.

Pat. Jan. 15, '92.
UNCLE SAM.

Pat. July 5 and Oct. 4, 1892.
BUNNY, 10c.

Pat. July 5 and Oct. 4, 1892.
OWL, 10c.

Order them at once if you want them for CHRISTMAS—Postage Free.

SHEPARD, NORWELL & CO., Boston, Mass.

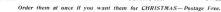

These are <u>not</u> real children, but
Schoenhut _{Wood} All- Dolls

They are the triumph of forty-two years of successful toy making. They are made all from wood, fully jointed—practically indestructible. The head is modeled of solid wood in real character style, natural and lifelike. It is not a "doll-face" head, but a production of art, modeled by a famous sculptor. Figures are jointed at neck, shoulders, elbows, wrists, hips, knees and ankles with steel spring hinges and swivel connections. The parts are held tightly, though flexible enough to be placed in any character position, and the dolls will hold any pose. *No rubber cord* is used in the joints. They never require restringing.

These wonderful dolls never break and cause heartaches. They can be played with every day without fear of destruction. The dolls are painted with natural oil colors and can be washed. They are dressed either in knitted union suits or in natural clothing. They come with hair carved on head or with fine quality mohair wig.

Schoenhut dolls being a new invention are not stocked by all dealers. If yours cannot supply you, we will send direct from the factory. Send for illustrated booklet.

Schoenhut's Humpty-Dumpty Circus Toys

Toys that gladden the hearts of our dear little ones—Appeal to boys and girls alike of any age

The funniest things you ever saw. The elephant can do tricks you never heard of. The donkey is better than any animal Barnum ever had. The clowns can make grown-up people, as well as children, laugh for hours.

The figures are made of solid wood, fully jointed with *elastic cord*, painted in oil colors. The clowns are dressed in fancy costumes. Will stand the toughest kind of treatment. There's no end to the fun—new tricks, each more grotesque than the last, are constantly discovered. You can search Toyland through and you'll find nothing to approach Humpty-Dumpty's Circus. Ask to see it at any Toy or Department Store.

Schoenhut's "Modlwood" Toys

All-wood construction toys for the small youngster whose unskilled hands cannot master the more complicated toys. They are made from clean, white wood (not painted). Can be constructed and dismantled at will, satisfying the boyish craving to know "what's inside." Locomotives, Automobiles, Touring Cars, Racing Cars, etc., can be made.

Get your dealer to show you these toys, also the Humpty-Dumpty Circus Toys. If he cannot supply you, send us his name, and we will mail you illustrated literature free.

THE A. SCHOENHUT COMPANY

Patentees and Manufacturers.　　2449 Sepviva St., Philadelphia

An American Toy Factory— largest in the world— modern, sanitary, well lighted.

Makers of the World-Famous "Schoenhut" Toy Piano and Humpty-Dumpty Circus Toys.

Schoenhut's "Modlwood" Toys

Glossary

Armature   Framework serving as a supporting core in a doll's body; usually metal, wire, or wood.

Articulated   Term applied to a jointed doll with movable limbs.

Automaton   Mechanical figure that appears to imitate the movements of humans; often operated by a clockwork device.

Bald-head   Doll with a smooth, dome-shaped head and no holes cut in the crown.

Ball joint   Articulated joint usually formed by a wooden or composition ball between two sockets that are connected by elastic or a metal spring to allow movement in several directions.

Bathing doll   Small unjointed china or bisque doll, usually white or black, with blond or black hair. Also called a *Badekind* or a *Frozen Charlotte*.

Bébé   Doll representing a young child; most commonly made by late 19th-century French and German manufacturers.

Bent-limb body   Baby or child doll with bent limbs allowing for a seated position; introduced in the early 20th century.

Bisque   Unglazed porcelain with mat finish, made from kaolin clay and usually tinted; often used for doll heads and sometimes for limbs.

Blown glass   Glassware shaped by blowing air into molten glass using a blowpipe; used for doll eyes.

Bonnet doll   *See* Hatted doll.

Breveté   French word for patented; often part of a doll's mark.

Brush marks   Small strokes painted around a doll's forehead and temples to suggest hair.

Buckram   Stiff, coarse cotton or linen fabric often used for the heads or faces of cloth dolls.

Celebrity doll   Figure portraying a movie or stage celebrity, such as Shirley Temple or Charlie Chaplin. Sometimes called a personality doll.

Celluloid   Highly flammable compound of cellulose nitrate and camphor introduced in 1870 and employed in dollmaking.

Character doll   Child doll with lifelike, realistically modeled features. First created in Germany in the early 20th century.

China   Glazed porcelain composed of kaolin clay, feldspar, and silica.

Clockwork mechanism   Machinery similar to the works of a clock and operated by a spring usually wound by a key. Found in many 19th-century automata.

Comb marks   Small molded ridges on a china doll's head suggesting hair that has been combed.

Composition   Mixture of wood or paper pulp, similar to papier-mâché but containing additional ingredients such as sawdust or plaster. Term is generally reserved for dolls made after the mid-19th century. *See* Papier-mâché.

Concha belt   American Indian belt with shell-shaped or disklike ornaments; often made partly of silver and turquoise. Miniature versions found on many Indian dolls.

Cottage industry   Any industry, such as that producing wooden dolls in Appalachia, with a labor force consisting of family members or other groups working at home with their own equipment.

Craft doll   Doll produced by a local cottage industry or crafts guild; usually designed for display rather than as a plaything.

Crazing   Network of hairline cracks that develops over the years on a painted or glazed surface as a result of changes in temperature.

Crown   Topmost part of a head; often cut away and left open on French dolls.

Cry box   Source of sound in a talking doll, generally employing bellows, reeds, or another apparatus and operated by pulling a string, pressing some part of the body, or moving the doll or one of its limbs. Also called a voice box.

Déposé   French word for registered, used with regard to a trademark or design; often part of a doll's mark and abbreviated *Dep.*, which is also the abbreviation for *deponiert*, the German word for registered.

Doll artist   One who makes dolls by hand, often as one-of-a-kind portraits of individuals or historical figures. May also refer to someone who designs dolls for a commercial manufacturer.

Doll-face   Term describing a girl doll with a standardized, sweet, smiling expression. Often applied to early 20th-century French or German bisque dolls.

Edwardian style   Ornate clothing style popular during the reign of Edward VII of England (1901–10), characterized by hourglass-shaped dresses for women and long, fitted suits for men.

Embossed   Raised in relief from a surface, as in design or lettering that often occurs in dolls' marks.

Fashion doll   French lady doll with bisque head and adult body dressed in fashionable or regional costume. May be a manikin figure made specifically to display new clothing styles. Sometimes called a Parisienne.

Fashion plate   Illustration, often a published engraving from the late 19th or early 20th century, depicting a stylish outfit or someone modeling such clothing.

Fired   Term applied to a ceramic product, including bisque or china doll heads, heated in a kiln for the purpose of hardening, binding pigment, or glazing its surface.

Flange neck   Doll neck usually with rim or lip at bottom edge for securing head to body; may have holes for sewing it to cloth body. Other types fit flush against top of shoulder piece and may be attached to body with a rod through the head.

Flirting eyes   Doll eyes that move from side to side by means of a weighted control mechanism inside the head.

Flocked hair   Hair simulated by gluing thin fuzzy or velvety fibers of wool or felt to a boy or baby doll's head.

Floss   Soft, loosely twisted silk or cotton thread for embroidery; also a fluffy, fibrous material sometimes used for doll wigs.

Folk art   Artworks or utilitarian objects generally created by self-taught, anonymous craftsmen and characterized by simplicity and boldness. Includes Appalachian poppets, Amish dolls, and homemade dolls made of such diverse materials as scrap-bag fabrics, clothespins, cornhusks, nuts, fruit, and shells.

Fork hands   Hands with sticklike fingers; found on early wooden dolls.

Glaze   Glasslike finish applied to porcelain and pottery, generally derived from feldspar and fired on in a kiln. Refers to glossy surface of china-head dolls.

Glue spot   Round painted area on a doll's pate thought to indicate where wig was to be affixed to the head; found most often on 19th-century china dolls.

Gofun   Fine oyster-shell paste, applied in layers and polished; found on the faces of some Japanese dolls.

Googly eyes   Large, bulging cartoonlike eyes, generally glancing sideways; may be glass or painted.

Gusset   An insert, usually triangular or diamond-shaped, placed in a seam to strengthen a garment and to allow for movement. After the mid-19th century, used often for joints on leather or kid doll bodies.

Gutta-percha   Milky substance made from the latex of certain Malaysian trees; resembles rubber but is lighter in color, heavier, and more brittle. When used for 19th-century dolls, it was combined with resins and other materials; some synthetic compounds were also given this name.

Half doll   China or bisque doll with molded one-piece head and upper torso; lower torso and upper portions of limbs made of cloth. Not to be confused with half figures, which are strictly decorative.

Half figure   Decorative figurine made of a one-piece head and upper torso attached to a household item such as a pincushion or tea cozy; often called a pincushion figure.

Hatted doll   Figure, usually bisque, with molded-on bonnet or hat.

Incised   Term applied to doll marks and letters, numbers, or designs carved or engraved on a surface.

Intaglio eyes   Painted eyes with incised, concave pupils and irises.

Kachina   Hopi or other Pueblo Indian figure representing a religious spirit; these spirits and the elaborately masked Indians who dress up to impersonate them are also known as Kachinas. Figures usually carved of cottonwood root or pine.

Kapok   Silky fiber from the seed pod of the ceiba tree, used as padding in cloth dolls as well as in mattresses and life preservers; also called silk cotton.

Kid body   Doll body entirely or partly made from the skin of a young goat.

Lathe-turning   Technique for shaping wood by applying a chisel to it while it rotates on a lathe. Used for Queen Anne and other wooden dolls.

Low-brow hairstyle   Coiffure characterized by wavy curls falling low on the forehead, popular during the late 19th and early 20th centuries on china lady dolls with molded hair.

Luster   Delicate pink or metallic shading on glazed porcelain.

Manikin   Model of the human form used for the study of anatomy or to display clothing; also refers to a miniature male figure.

Mask face   Rigid, molded or printed front of a doll's head, generally made of composition or wax and attached to a stuffed cloth backing.

Médaille d'or   French for gold medal. This award for dolls was won by Emile Jumeau at the 1878 Paris Exposition and is often indicated in his mark. Similar award won in 1889 by Jules Nicholas Steiner also included in his mark.

Mint condition   Term describing doll, clothing, or accessories in original, unused condition. Mint-in-box refers to a doll preserved in mint condition and in the container in which it was originally issued.

Mold   Hollow form, usually metal or plaster, into which porcelain slip, melted wax, or another liquid is poured; also used for malleable materials, such as porcelain clay or composition, which are pressed to shape doll heads or other body parts.

Mold number   Numerals indicating a type of doll or a series made from a particular mold; often included in maker's mark inscribed on doll.

Molded features   Hair, ears, teeth, clothes, or other doll features formed when material is pressed or poured into a mold and takes its contours.

Multi-face doll   Doll with a single revolving head having 2 or more faces that can be changed by turning a knob. Also, doll with a stationary head to which separate masks can be attached.

Multi-head doll   Doll with 2 or more interchangeable heads, often socket-type, that can be screwed onto neck or shoulder piece.

Open-closed mouth   Molded doll's mouth with lips parted, sometimes showing teeth or tongue, but no actual opening cut into head.

Paperweight eyes   Flat-backed eyes of blown glass similar to that used for paperweights; often found in bisque-head dolls.

Papier-mâché   Mixture of paper pulp, glue, and sometimes chalk, sand, or other substances that, once molded, dries to a hard mass. A type of composition, it was frequently used for dollmaking during the 19th century. *See* Composition.

Parian   White, untinted bisque thought to resemble and thus named for the white marble native to the Greek island of Paros. Parian-type refers to doll heads of this material; most often made in Germany in the 1870s and '80s.

Pate   Crown of the head. In dolls, often a solid bald area, or a cork or plaster covering placed over the cutaway portion at the top of the head; usually concealed beneath a wig.

Patent   Government grant to an inventor of the exclusive right to make, sell, or use his invention for a specified period.

Patent date   Date on which a patent is issued to an inventor for a new or improved product or process. Often included on dolls as part of maker's mark.

Patina   Mellow and worn finish a surface acquires with age; a desirable quality on wooden dolls.

Peddler doll   Doll dressed as a vendor and outfitted with trays or baskets filled with various small items. Popular in England during the 19th century.

Peg-wooden doll   All-wooden doll, partly carved and partly turned and having ball-and-socket or peg joints. Made in the Grödner Tal valley in the southern Alps from the late 18th to the 20th century.

Penwiper doll   Doll with a piece of clothing made of felt or another absorbent material used for wiping excess ink from a quill pen.

Personality doll   *See* Celebrity doll.

Porcelain   Any hard, nonporous ceramic ware, usually translucent, consisting of kaolin clay, feldspar, and quartz and fired at a high temperature. *See* Bisque, China, and Parian.

Portrait doll   Doll modeled after a recognizable individual, such as Henry VIII or Franklin D. Roosevelt.

Poured-wax doll   Doll with head and sometimes limbs made from wax that is poured into a mold in successive layers; most often produced in England.

Pouty   Character doll depicting a child with a pensive or pouting expression.

Premium   Item, such as a paper or printed-cloth doll, offered free of charge or for a nominal sum in exchange for the proof of purchase of a product or service. Often used as advertisement.

Provenance   The history of an artwork or object, including its origin, a record of ownership, and where it has been exhibited.

Pull strings   Strings or cords on the outside of a doll's body that operate a cry box or other apparatus concealed within the torso.

Quill-wrapping   American Indian decorative technique employing porcupine quills that are flattened by biting, then dyed and wrapped around strips of rawhide to create patterns.

Rooted hair   Natural or synthetic hair inserted in single strands or clusters into a doll's wax or plastic head.

Rosebud mouth   Small red mouth with pursed lips resembling the bud of a rose.

Saran   Thermoplastic resin derived from vinyl compounds and used for a variety of purposes, including doll hair.

Sew holes   Holes in a doll's rigid shoulder plate through which string or thread is sewn to attach it to a cloth or kid body.

S.G.D.G.   Initials for *sans garantie du gouvernement*—French for "without government guarantee"—meaning that no patent search has been conducted to guarantee government protection of a manufacturer's patent. Often part of a French doll's mark.

Shoulder-head   Head and shoulder plate made in one piece and
attached to a body made of another material.

Shoulder plate   Shoulder portion of a doll; may be the lower part of a shoulder-head, or a separate piece into which a socket head is inserted.

Side-glancing eyes   Stationary or movable eyes that look to one side; may be painted or made of glass or another material.

Sleep-eyes   Eyes that open and close usually by means of a weighted mechanism inside the doll's head; may also refer to stationary eyeballs with movable lids.

Slip   In ceramics manufacture, a liquid clay and water mixture cast in a mold or used for applied decoration or for cementing separate elements together.

Slit-head   Doll with head made usually of poured wax or wax-over-composition having a slit cut in the center of the crown for the purpose of inserting hair.

Socket head   Doll head with neck that fits into shoulder plate or body in a way that enables head to swivel.

Spoon hand   Rudimentary hand, usually wooden, carved in cupped shape and lacking separated fingers but often having an articulated thumb.

Spring-jointed   Having joints operated by internal metal springs. Characteristic of doll bodies made by such firms as Kämmer & Reinhardt, Parsons-Jackson, and A. Schoenhut.

Stockinet   Elastic knit fabric, usually cotton, employed in dollmaking, particularly for faces; sometimes stretched over a core of a harder material.

Stringing   Method of joining elements of a doll's body using cords or elastic.

Swivel head   Head that turns in a socket; also called swivel neck.

Toddler body   Short, plump, jointed doll body characterized by chubby thighs and legs.

Tongue-and-groove joint   Joint formed by a protruding tongue on one surface that fits into a groove on another surface.

Topsy-turvy   Doll with two heads, one at top and one at bottom, and a reversible skirt that conceals whichever head is not in use. Sometimes called a double-ender.

Trademark   Officially registered symbol, word, or name designed for exclusive use by a manufacturer to identify its products.

Tuck comb   Stand-up wooden comb carved as a decorative part of the coiffure of a peg-wooden or other doll.

Utility doll   Doll, usually homemade, with a body fashioned from a common household object, such as a bottle, broom, or feather duster.

Vendor doll   *See* Peddler doll.

Victorian style   Ornate decorative style prevalent during the reign of Queen Victoria (1837–1901).

Wax-over-composition   Doll head or limbs made of composition and coated with wax. Also referred to as waxed.

Public Collections

Dolls are exhibited in many American museums, particularly in those devoted specifically to playthings, folk art, or Indian artifacts. In addition, historic houses often have fine examples on display. Although dolls are part of the permanent collections of the sources listed below, they may not always be on display.

New England
Connecticut
Fairfield: Fairfield Historical Society. *Mystic:* Memory Lane Doll and Toy Museum, Old Mystic Village. *New Britain:* New Britain Youth Museum. *New London:* Lyman Allyn Museum.

Massachusetts
Boston: Children's Museum. *Kingston:* Major John Bradford House. *Plymouth:* Plymouth Antiquarian Society. *Salem:* Salem Children's Museum, Essex Institute. *Sandwich:* Yesteryear's Museum. *Wenham:* Wenham Historical Museum.

Vermont
Shelburne: Shelburne Museum. *Springfield:* Springfield Art Center.

Mid-Atlantic Region
New Jersey
Flemington: Raggedy Ann and Andy Doll Museum. *Morristown:* Morris Museum of Arts and Sciences. *Newark:* Newark Museum.

New York
Cooperstown: New York State Historical Association. *New York City:* American Museum of Natural History; Aunt Len's Doll and Toy Museum; Brooklyn Children's Museum; Museum of American Folk Art; Museum of the American Indian; Museum of the City of New York; New-York Historical Society. *Rochester:* Margaret Woodbury Strong Museum. *Yorktown Heights:* Town of Yorktown Museum.

Pennsylvania
Douglassville: Mary Merritt Doll and Toy Museum. *Lancaster:* Pennsylvania Farm Museum of Landis Valley. *Philadelphia:* Atwater Kent Museum; Perelman Antique Toy Museum. *West Chester:* Chester County Historical Society.

Washington, D.C.
Smithsonian Institution; Washington Dolls' House and Toy Museum.

South
Arkansas
Eureka Springs: Guether Doll Museum. *Little Rock:* Arkansas Arts Center.

Florida
St. Augustine: Lightner Museum.

Georgia
Atlanta: Atlanta Toy Museum.

Kentucky
Bowling Green: Kentucky Museum. *Lexington:* Headley Whitney Museum.

Louisiana
New Orleans: Children's Museum, New Orleans Recreation Department. *Shreveport:* R. W. Norton Art Gallery.

Missouri
Point Lookout: Ralph Foster Museum. *St. Louis:* Eugene Field House and Toy Museum.

Tennessee
Chattanooga: Houston Antique Museum.

Virginia
Richmond: Valentine Museum. *Williamsburg:* Abby Aldrich Rockefeller Folk Art Center.

Midwest
Illinois
Chicago: Museum of Science and Industry. *Normal:* Illinois State University Historical Museum.

Indiana
Indianapolis: Children's Museum of Indianapolis.

Michigan
Detroit: Children's Museum, Detroit Public Schools. *Grand Rapids:* Grand Rapids Public Museum.

Ohio
Cleveland: Cleveland Museum of Art. *Toledo:* Toledo Museum of Art.

Wisconsin
Madison: Wisconsin State Historical Society.

Rockies, Southwest, and West Coast
Arizona
Flagstaff: Museum of Northern Arizona. *Phoenix:* Heard Museum. *Tucson:* Arizona State Museum.

California
Santa Ana: Charles W. Bowers Memorial Museum. *Santa Barbara:* Santa Barbara Museum of Art.

Colorado
Denver: Denver Art Museum.

Montana
Browning: Museum of the Plains Indians & Crafts Center.

New Mexico
Santa Fe: Museum of International Folk Art.

Oklahoma
Anadarko: Southern Plains Indian Museum & Crafts Center.

South Dakota
Murdo: Prairie Doll Museum. *Rapid City:* Sioux Indian Museum.

Texas
Jefferson: Jefferson Historical Society & Museum. *San Antonio:* Witte Memorial Museum.

Utah
Provo: McCurdy Historical Doll Museum.

Bibliography

Anderton, Johanna G.
Twentieth Century Dolls
Des Moines: Wallace-Homestead Book Co., 1971.
More Twentieth Century Dolls. 2 vols.
Des Moines: Wallace-Homestead Book Co., 1979.

Angione, Genevieve
All-Bisque and Half-Bisque Dolls
Exton, Pennsylvania: Schiffer Publishing, 1981.

Angione, Genevieve, and Whorton, Judith
All Dolls are Collectible
New York: Crown Publishers, 1977.

Axe, John
Encyclopedia of Celebrity Dolls
Cumberland, Maryland: Hobby House Press, 1983.

Boehn, Max von
Dolls
New York: Dover Publications, 1972.

Bullard, Helen
The American Doll Artist
Vol. I. Newton Centre, Massachusetts: Charles T. Branford Co., 1965.
Vol. II. Des Moines: Wallace-Homestead Book Co., 1975.

Coleman, Dorothy S., Elizabeth A., and Evelyn J.
The Collector's Book of Dolls' Clothes: Costumes in Miniature, 1700–1929
New York: Crown Publishers, 1975.
The Collector's Encyclopedia of Dolls
New York: Crown Publishers, 1968.

Colton, Harold S.
Hopi Kachina Dolls, With a Key to Their Identification
Albuquerque: University of New Mexico Press, 1971.

Foulke, Jan
Focusing on Effanbee Composition Dolls
Cumberland, Maryland: Hobby House Press, 1978.
Focusing on Gebrüder Heubach Dolls
Cumberland, Maryland: Hobby House Press, 1980.
Kestner: King of Dollmakers
Cumberland, Maryland: Hobby House Press, 1982.

Fox, Carl
The Doll
New York: Harry N. Abrams, 1973.

Hillier, Mary
Dolls and Dollmakers
New York: G. P. Putnam's Sons, 1968.

Holz, Loretta
Developing Your Doll Collection for Enjoyment and Investment
New York: Crown Publishers, 1982.

Howard, Marian B.
Those Fascinating Paper Dolls: An Illustrated Handbook for Collectors
New York: Dover Publications, 1981.

Jones, Iris Sanderson
Early North American Dollmaking
San Francisco: 101 Productions, 1976.

King, Constance E.
The Collector's History of Dolls
New York: St. Martin's Press, 1977.
The Encyclopedia of Toys
New York: Crown Publishers, 1978.

Lavitt, Wendy
American Folk Dolls
New York: Alfred A. Knopf, 1982.

Manos, Susan
Schoenhut Dolls and Toys, A Loving Legacy
Paducah, Kentucky: Collector Books, 1976.

Noble, John
A Treasury of Beautiful Dolls
New York: Hawthorn Books, 1971.

Revi, Albert Christian, ed.
Spinning Wheel's Complete Book of Dolls
New York: Galahad Books, 1975.

Robinson, Joleen, and Seller, Kay
Advertising Dolls
Paducah, Kentucky: Collector Books, 1980.

Rustam, Phillis A.
Cloth Dolls: A Collector's Guide
Cranbury, New Jersey: A. S. Barnes & Co., 1980.

Smith, Patricia
Armand Marseille Dolls
Paducah, Kentucky: Collector Books, 1981.
China and Parian Dolls
Paducah, Kentucky: Collector Books, 1980.
Madame Alexander Collector's Dolls
Paducah, Kentucky: Collector Books, 1978.
Oriental Dolls
Paducah, Kentucky: Collector Books, 1978.

Walker, Frances, and Whitton, Margaret
Playthings by the Yard: The Story of Cloth Dolls
South Hadley, Massachusetts: Hadley Printing Co., 1973.

Westfall, Marty
The Handbook of Doll Repair and Restoration
New York: Crown Publishers, 1979.

White, Gwen
Dolls, Automata, Marks and Labels
London: B. T. Batsford Ltd., 1975.
European and American Dolls
New York: Crescent Books, 1982.

Whitton, Margaret
The Jumeau Doll
New York: Dover Publications, 1980.

Yamada, Tokubee
Japanese Dolls
Tokyo: Japan Travel Bureau, 1959.

Young, Mary
A Collector's Guide to Paper Dolls: Saalfield, Lowe, Merrill
Paducah, Kentucky: Collector Books, 1980.

List of Plates by Material

Dolls have been organized by head type and major body material.

Bisque head
Bisque body: 122, 170–172, 223, 224. Cardboard body: 347. Cloth body: 75, 78, 80, 87, 88, 93, 95, 127, 161, 166, 173–175, 180, 184, 190, 216, 217, 221, 222, 291, 296–298, 307, 308. Composition body: 63, 66, 67, 84, 167, 177, 185–187, 192, 193, 195–202, 204, 206–210, 212–215, 218–220, 300, 346, 349–351, 354, 355. Kid body: 48, 68, 176, 194, 200, 203, 205, 211, 220, 221, 301–303, 305, 309, 310, 355. Papier-mâché body: 342, 352. Wooden body: 191, 304, 306, 344, 345.

Celluloid head
Celluloid body: 258. Cloth body: 265. Composition body: 271. Metal body: 357.

China head
China body: 86, 169, 225. Cloth body: 287, 289, 290, 292, 294, 295, 299, 300. Kid body: 284, 285, 288, 293. Wooden body: 286.

Cloth dolls
9–11, 28–42, 50, 53, 54, 56, 73, 77, 91, 92, 103–113, 147–159, 236–253, 340.

Composition head
Cardboard body: 356. Cloth body: 47, 72, 83, 89, 94, 116–118, 120, 121, 126, 160, 163, 178, 181, 256, 259, 261, 264, 267, 325, 327, 332. Composition body: 64, 65, 96, 100, 123–125, 128, 129, 182, 259, 260, 262, 266, 269, 272–274, 276–278, 282, 337. Kid body: 263. Metal body: 338. Straw body: 60–62. Wooden body: 19, 119, 130, 131, 257, 331.

Leather head
Cloth body: 55, 330. Leather body: 69. Seal fur and hide body: 57.

Paper dolls
133–145.

Papier-mâché head
Cardboard body: 343. Cloth body: 71, 348. Kid body: 322, 323, 326. Metal body: 164. Wooden body: 353.

Plastic head
Cloth body: 281. Plastic body: 268, 275, 279, 280. Vinyl body: 98.

Rubber head
Cloth body: 115, 328, 329. Rubber body: 13, 168, 254, 255.

Vinyl head
Cloth body: 114, 162, 179. Plastic body: 99. Vinyl body: 283.

Wax head
Cloth body: 70, 79, 81, 165, 226–228, 324, 333–336, 339. Wax body: 90, 183. Wishbone body: 7.

Wooden head
Cloth body: 23, 24, 76, 82, 231, 235, 317, 319. Paper body: 146. Wooden body: 6, 21, 22, 25–27, 43–46, 85, 132, 189, 230, 232–235, 311–316, 318, 320, 321.

Miscellaneous head materials
Biskoline: 188. Buckskin: 8, 49. Cardboard: 270. Clay pipe: 12. Cork: 5. Cornhusk: 1–3, 52. Dried apple: 16, 17. Imitation fur: 127. Ivory: 58. Latex: 97. Lobster claw: 18. Metal: 229. Nut: 4, 14, 15. Palmetto fiber: 51. Scallop shells: 20. Sculpted porcelain clay: 74. Stockinet and foam rubber: 341. Wool yarn: 101, 102.

Building a Doll Collection

The first step in starting a doll collection is to realistically determine the amount of money, time, and display and storage space you can devote to it. You must decide if you want to put together a general collection that includes antique and modern dolls or if you wish to specialize in one area, such as bisque, folk, character, or even Bye-Lo Baby dolls. Budgetary limitations will, of course, play a part in your decision; for example, collecting antique bisque dolls will involve considerably greater expense than collecting printed-cloth dolls.

Experts generally advise beginners to buy what appeals to them and to buy the finest examples they can afford. In order to locate the best sources for your dolls, become knowledgeable about whatever field you have chosen. Many collectors begin with old dolls of their own or with those of relatives or friends. To further develop a collection, visit any of the thousands of doll merchants around the country.

Shops, Shows, and Auctions

The more valuable, older dolls are generally sold in specialized shops and at shows and auctions. Collectors often turn professional in order to support their interest in dolls and set up shop in their homes. Dealers who sell at home usually do so by appointment only, or by mail-order, advertising in such trade journals as *Antique Trader*, *Doll Reader*, and *Dolls*.

Doll shows take place in auditoriums, hotels, and meeting halls in communities of all sizes. These exhibitions give collectors a chance to meet many dealers at one time, see a wide variety of fine dolls, and locate rare examples as well as unusual doll clothing, doll parts, and related items. It is wise to arrive early, make a quick tour, and then inspect each booth at a more leisurely pace. Most shows last only a day or two, and because several collectors may be interested in the same doll, decisions must be made rather quickly. Since you can inspect hundreds of dolls in one visit, shows are good places to learn about the field. These events are usually advertised in local newspapers and regional publications. While you should be prepared to bargain, also expect that some dealers will have firm prices from which they will not budge.

The doll field has become so popular that auctions devoted entirely to dolls are now held from coast to coast. Some of the better-known auction houses that specialize in dolls are Auctions by Theriault in Waverly, Pennsylvania, and Richard W. Withington, Inc., in Hillsboro, New Hampshire. General auction houses, such as Sotheby's and Christie's in New York City, sell dolls along with other types of collectibles and antiques.

The unpredictability that makes an auction so exciting is also its major drawback, however. Buyers have only moments to decide upon a bid, and prices are set by the people who happen to be on hand. Buying at auction requires patience and self-restraint, since a particular sale may not offer the specific doll you are seeking, and it may be wise to wait until you find exactly what you want at a future auction. See the section called Buying At Auction (pp. 449–50) for information and hints about bidding.

Secondary Sources

Collectors who are interested in inexpensive dolls and who have time to seek out occasional bargains often frequent flea markets, garage sales, general antiques stores, and thrift shops, where dolls may sometimes be found along with inexpensive collectibles. Since the dolls are usually unidentified, at times they may be purchased for a fraction of their true worth. The more experienced collector has an advantage here, because he or she can recognize true bargains, dolls sold for their market value, and those that are overpriced.

Mail-order advertisements are another popular source for dolls. The classified ads found in doll magazines describe and often picture highly desirable examples; through these ads sellers offer to send complete lists of dolls to prospective buyers. The drawback in shopping through the mail is that photographs do not always reveal the flaws in a doll.

Shopping Hints

No matter where you buy, be cautious. Although dishonest practices are rare, any seller may occasionally be guilty of poor judgment or excessive optimism; deliberate deceptions are far less common than honest mistakes. It is wise to get a bill of sale describing the doll you have bought, its age, attribution, and any repairs done to it. Also ask for a guarantee stating that the doll can be returned should any of this information prove untrue.

Doll Clubs

Beginning and advanced collectors often find that joining a doll club can help them build their collections and further develop their expertise. At meetings arranged by the clubs, doll collectors become acquainted, exchange information about their dolls, and take part in museum trips and lectures offered by their organizations. In addition to holding regular meetings, some clubs arrange doll shows or "swap and buy" sessions. Many clubs are affiliated with the United Federation of Doll Clubs, or UFDC (8 East Street, Parkville, MO 64152), which publishes the magazine *Doll News*. UFDC also sponsors a national convention that is held in a different city each summer and attracts more than 1000 members.

Professional Organizations

In time, many collectors try their hand at dollmaking and restoring. For those who become professional dollmakers, a number of doll-artist organizations exist. Knowledge about these associations and their standards is important for anyone interested in contemporary dolls.

NIADA

In 1963 the National Institute of American Doll Artists, or NIADA (303 Riley Street, Falls Church, VA 22046), was established by eleven well-known artists specializing in original handmade dolls. To join NIADA a candidate must be recommended by three active members and submit dolls for an approval process; standards are high and membership about sixty.

ODACA

The Original Doll Artists Council of America, or ODACA (21 Hitherbrook Road, St. James, NY 11780), founded in 1976, is patterned after NIADA in that candidates for membership must submit original dolls to be juried. NIADA and ODACA dolls come with certificates and tags stating they were made by members. They are often sold at doll shows or through mail-order advertisements; doll artists may also be reached through any of the organizations to which they belong.

IDMA

Unlike NIADA and ODACA, the International Doll Makers Association, or IDMA (3364 Pine Creek Drive, San Jose, CA 95132), has unrestricted membership of about 500 and accepts artists who make original dolls or reproductions.

Buying at Auction

Many of the finest and most interesting dolls are sold at auction. Some auctions are composed entirely of dolls, while others contain a variety of merchandise. Rarities, often sold at record prices, are auctioned with much fanfare and press coverage. Museums occasionally dispose of their surplus dolls at such events. Many doll enthusiasts who at first attend auctions to learn more about dolls eventually try their luck at bidding and become regular participants. For those who know the rules of the game and are knowledgeable about dolls, buying at auction can be a very rewarding experience.

How an Auction Works
An auction is a sale of items to the highest bidder. The seller, or consignor, offers objects to prospective buyers through his agent, the auctioneer. The bidder offering the most money buys a "lot" (one piece or a group of pieces sold together). The auctioneer tries to stimulate bidding and obtain the highest price, since he or his firm generally receives a percentage of the sale as payment or commission.

The Viewing
The first step toward informed bidding is to attend the viewing, an advertised period of a few hours or a few days when the objects to be auctioned may be examined by the public. Never bid on a doll unless you have checked it thoroughly beforehand. Compare a doll to its description in the catalogue, if one is available. Always carry a pencil and notebook to jot down lot numbers, prices, and descriptions. Be certain to check a doll completely for marks and condition. Dolls are often locked in display cases that must be opened by an attendant. Many collectors subscribe to the doll catalogues of the major auction houses as a means of keeping abreast of current prices. The conditions of sale are usually listed in the catalogue, but if you have any questions about bidding procedures or forms of payment, speak to an auction house representative. Staff members are generally available to answer questions about the merits of the various dolls.

The Sale
Come to the auction prepared: Some auction houses accept only cash; others will take cashiers' checks, certified checks, personal checks with proper identification, or even credit cards. Since many auctions are crowded, arrive in time to obtain a seat and, if necessary, register for a numbered paddle with which to bid. Some auctiongoers prefer sitting up front, while others like to sit in the back where they can better observe the overall action. At most larger auctions, the auctioneer will provide estimated price ranges for the dolls in the sale. These are usually printed in the auction catalogue or on a separate list. Though dolls quite often sell for more or less than the estimates, these should give you some idea of what the auctioneer expects a doll to fetch. For future reference, mark down the prices of all dolls sold.

Listen closely because the bidding can be very rapid, with most auctioneers selling between 60 and 100 lots an hour. Be ready to bid when your item comes up. More than one person has lost out on a desired doll because it was sold before he expected it to be or before he could get in on the bidding. When the doll you want is up for bid, do not succumb to "auction fever" and pay more than you had intended. In the final analysis you have to make a judgment based on your knowledge and the amount you are willing to spend. Be aware that many large auction houses allow a seller to set a "reserve" on a lot—the price below which it will not be sold, frequently close to the low estimate. If bidding does not reach this minimum, the lot will be withdrawn and returned to the consignor for a small handling fee.

Successful bidding requires concentration, steady nerves, and discipline. As you gain experience, you will learn not to jump into the bidding too soon, not to overbid, and to bid on "sleepers," that is, lots that are underpriced. When bidding on a doll that you had not intended to buy, but cannot resist because of its low price, be sure it is one you examined carefully in the viewing. There may be a reason why there is little bidding for it. If you cannot attend the auction, you may leave an absentee bid with the auction house or pay a dealer to bid for you. Some auction houses allow mail or telephone bids; such bidding, however, is not recommended unless the bidder delegates someone to examine the doll prior to the sale.

Collecting Your Purchases

The fall of the gavel and the cry of "sold" mark a successful bid. Now the buyer must pay for the purchase and remove it from the auction premises within a stated time limit, which may vary from a few hours to more than a week. Some auction houses provide shipping and wrapping services, while others do not even keep bags or cartons on hand, so the buyer should come prepared.

Price Guide

In the past 20 years dolls have become one of the major fields of collecting, and as a result, the demand for them has caused their prices to rise dramatically. Traditionally, collectors focused their attention almost exclusively on fine 18th- and 19th-century European examples. Because these early dolls are now difficult to find and prohibitively costly—commanding as much as $20,000 —many other types of dolls have recently become popular. Nowadays, collectors' tastes and interests vary greatly and include such categories as infant, folk, cartoon-character, and printed-cloth dolls. National costume dolls, long regarded as a minor specialty, are gaining in popularity as well.

The tremendous growth of the doll field has made it difficult to keep abreast of current prices, yet such information is essential to collectors. To the novice, prices may seem unpredictable; they depend not only on supply and demand, but also on the preferences of the collecting public at any given moment. For example, 20th-century Madame Alexander dolls now bring higher prices than some antique china or papier-mâché dolls. Lenci dolls have also skyrocketed in value, well beyond the average increase in doll prices over the past 5 years; for example, in 1977 a Lenci sports doll might have fetched $200, whereas in 1983 one sold at auction for $800. A large Lenci flapper doll may bring as much as $2000 today. Because they are rarely mentioned in price guides, auction catalogues, or doll literature, folk dolls are some of the most difficult to evaluate. Such lack of coverage makes it possible, on occasion, to pick up an unusual example for a small sum.

Sleepers
One of the pleasures of collecting dolls is to find them at the best possible prices. While everyone enjoys discovering a bargain not recognized by the seller—known as a "sleeper"—keep in mind that dolls are generally bought at current market value. Sleepers are likely to be sold at flea markets, garage sales, and thrift shops, where most vendors know little about dolls. Do not expect to discover rare antiques at such sources; instead you will probably find modern dolls in well-loved condition.

Price Determinants
Damaged, repaired, or altered pieces cost less, of course, than those in good condition and may not be worth purchasing. A doll in mint condition is always worth much more than others of its type. For example, a 1964 Barbie doll in good condition can be had for under $100, whereas a vintage 1958 "mint-in-box" Barbie may sell for $1000. Although collectors of older dolls look for examples in mint or near-mint condition with all their original parts, they are more exacting about the heads of dolls than about the bodies. Many fine dolls have had their arms or legs replaced, but collectors still purchase them in spite of their altered state. However, dolls with replaced parts or other repairs are less valuable, so before you buy a restored doll, be sure to adjust the price given here accordingly. Other important determinants of price are attribution, marks, and rarity. A maker's mark or firm attribution will significantly add to a doll's value. Rare dolls are usually but not always the most valuable. A well-known doll sometimes attracts more interest than a rare but less familiar type. On the other hand, dolls made by firms with limited production, such as Bru or Thuillier, command the highest prices. Collectors interested in folk dolls will be willing to pay more for a unique homemade figure than for a craft doll that was produced in quantity.

Price Ranges

The prices given in this guide are nationwide averages for dolls in good condition. They are based on auction records, dealer and shop prices, and published mail-order lists. Keep in mind, however, that every buying situation is different, and that no 2 objects are identical. Therefore, a price guide can only provide an estimate of a doll's value.

Folk Dolls

Because subjective considerations play a large role in assessing folk dolls, their prices tend to be more uneven than those of more formal types of dolls. For the most part, folk dolls have increased dramatically in desirability and in value in the last few years. Dolls that could once be picked up in yard sales for a small sum now cost hundreds of dollars in fashionable antiques shops. However, it is still possible to find sleepers more easily in this area than in any other. Among the bargains are cornhusk dolls at $35 to $200, and dolls made of such unusual materials as fishnet, nuts, or shells, which may bring as little as $25. At the high end of the price range are carved wooden dolls, Amish dolls, and groups arranged in vignettes; these may cost $250 to $500.

1. Iroquois cornhusk doll $75–100
2. Cornhusk doll $35–65
3. Cornhusk lady $100–200
4. Walnut and leaf doll $75–150
5. Fishnet doll $25–50
6. Wooden moss man $35–75
7. Wishbone dolls $75–150 (pair)
8. Clothespin doll $35–65
9. Old-woman-in-a-shoe dolls $200–300 (set)
10. Dollhouse family $150–200 (set)
11. Linen-wrapped doll $35–65
12. Clay-pipe doll $100–150
13. Nipple dolls $25–75 (each)
14. Chestnut and pecan dolls $75–125 (left); $50–75 (right)
15. Walnut couple $150–200 (pair)
16. Apple-head couple $35–75 (left); $65–125 (right)
17. Apple-head jazz band $300–400 (complete 6-piece set)
18. Lobster-claw couple $200–250 (pair)
19. Shell dolls $200–300 (pair)
20. Shell wedding dolls $10–30 (each)
21. Wooden couple $250–350 (pair)
22. Carved wooden doll $100–150
23. Bedpost doll $500–750
24. Carved wooden doll $200–300
25. Wooden dolls $75–150 (left); $125–175 (right)
26. Wooden girl doll $50–100
27. Dancing stick man $200–300
28. Broom dolls $75–125 (left); $50–100 (right)
29. Sewing dolls $200–300 (pair)
30. Bottle dolls $100–150 (left); $200–300 (right)
31. Topsy-turvy doll $150–225
32. Black grandmother $250–400
33. Homemade Raggedy Ann dolls $100–150 (each)
34. Cloth sisters $350–450 (pair)
35. Amish cloth couple $450–600 (pair)
36. Cloth girl doll $175–250
37. Cloth boy doll $200–250

38 George Washington $125–175
39 Cloth boy doll $225–300
40 Betty and Martha Ann $450–550 (pair)
41 Pointed-head doll $100–200
42 Chinese doll $50–100

Indian Dolls

Once favored mainly in the West, Indian dolls now command high prices throughout the country. They are often sold at auctions of Indian artifacts, where museum curators, dealers, and collectors compete for rare examples that bring thousands of dollars. Antique kachina dolls are of considerable interest and seldom fetch less than $1000. Even modern examples start in the low hundreds and, if exceptional, can approach $1000. 19th-century Plains Indian dolls decorated with quillwork and elaborate beading are prized by collectors, who will pay anywhere from a few hundred dollars to more than $1000 for unusual examples. Eskimo dolls vary greatly in price, with early ivory figures bringing the highest amounts. For collectors with limited budgets, late 19th- and early 20th-century tourist dolls, often costing less than $100, are the best buys.

43 Zuni dolls $350–500 (each)
44 Hopi kachina $600–800
45 Hopi kachina $400–600
46 Hopi kachinas $350–450 (left); $400–500 (right)
47 Skookum dolls $50–75 (left); $65–95 (right)
48 Heubach Indian doll $700–950
49 Cheyenne doll $300–400
50 Indian play doll $75–100
51 Seminole dolls $200–300 (pair)
52 Seneca dolls $300–400 (pair)
53 Navajo dolls $200–250 (pair)
54 Sioux doll $200–300
55 Navajo doll $300–400
56 Cradleboard doll $200–300
57 Eskimo doll $200–250
58 Eskimo dolls $500–650 (pair)

National Costume Dolls

Antique costume dolls representing people of various countries or regions range in price from thousands of dollars to under $100. Doll collectors in America and Europe favor those by such famous European manufacturers as Simon & Halbig, Armand Marseille, and Kestner, which often sell for $1000 to $3000. On the other hand, most contemporary examples, especially craft dolls, are relatively inexpensive. Works by well-known modern doll artists, however, sometimes sell for more than $1000. Oriental dolls are of considerable collector interest; large examples cost several hundred dollars. The least expensive costume dolls are the small figures made primarily for tourists. These can often be purchased in their countries of origin or from import stores for under $25.

59 Door of Hope dolls $350–400 (each)
60 Chinese grandparents $200–300 (pair)
61 Warrior doll $150–175
62 Emperor and Empress dolls $175–200 (pair)

63 Kestner Oriental baby doll $1000–2000
64 Yamato Ningyo $175–300
65 Yamato Ningyo $175–225
66 Simon & Halbig Oriental doll $350–450
67 Steiner bébés $1000–2000 (each)
68 Jumeau Middle Eastern doll $1000–1200
69 Doña Juanita and Don Pancho $100–150 (pair)
70 Poured-wax doll $200–300
71 French peasant doll $250–350
72 Swedish dolls $150–175 (pair)
73 French peasant dolls $300–400 (pair)
74 Sir Harry Lauder $500–700

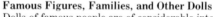

Famous Figures, Families, and Other Dolls
Dolls of famous people are of considerable interest, particularly
to collectors of works by contemporary doll artists. Such figures
range in price from the low hundreds to more than $1000 for
elaborately detailed examples. Antique peddler dolls, admired
for their array of minute wares, may also cost upwards of $1000.
19th-century dolls portraying Uncle Sam likewise may sell for as
much as $1000, while some contemporary dolls, such as a set of
Dionne Quintuplets, approach $2000, depending on their rarity
and popularity. 20th-century dolls in uniform, such as Red Cross
nurses, WACs, and G.I. Joes, are generally relatively
inexpensive at $25 to $100. Dolls that capture the mood of their
era range widely in price; for instance, the most common of
Mattel's vintage Barbie dolls sell for $25 to $100, while original
mint-in-box examples may fetch $1000.

75 French court ladies $400–450 (each)
76 Eleanor of Aquitaine $1000–1200
77 Elizabeth I $700–1000
78 Henry VIII $1000–1200
79 French court dolls $700–900 (pair)
80 Wedding-cake dolls $200–225 (pair)
81 Abraham and Mary Todd Lincoln $450–500 (pair)
82 Lee, Lincoln, and Grant $300–400 (each)
83 Franklin Roosevelt and Winston Churchill $250–350 (each)
84 Uncle Sam dolls $750–1000 (each)
85 Ringmaster $200–250
86 Chimney sweep $55–65
87 Peddler doll $300–500
88 Peddler doll $300–500
89 Vendor dolls $150–175 (pair)
90 Mammy doll $200–250
91 Gendarme $200–250
92 Quebec couple $75–125 (pair)
93 Dollhouse bridal group $75–100 (each)
94 Butler, cook, and housemaid $20–30 (each)
95 Red Cross nurse $250–300
96 Dionne Quintuplets and Dr. Dafoe $1200–1800 (set)
97 Angela Appleseed dolls $700–1000 (each)
98 Barbie doll $75–100
99 G.I. Joe $25–30
100 WAC and WAVE dolls $50–100 (each)

Storybook, Celebrity, and Cartoon-Character Dolls

The prices of the dolls in this section largely depend on the popularity of the characters they portray. Early characters such as Betty Boop, Little Orphan Annie, and Charlie Chaplin are favorites of collectors, who usually pay $75 to $300 for them. Later figures, such as Fred Flintstone, are still inexpensive at $25 to $35. Prices for dolls representing the same character may vary considerably according to the quality and rarity of individual examples. For example, early Raggedy Ann dolls cost up to $200, while later versions are priced under $50. Prices may fluctuate, however, since collectors are often willing to pay a premium to obtain all versions of their favorite character. Also, certain rather ordinary figures, such as the Gold Dust Twins or a Campbell Kid, may bring $100 to $200 because they appeal not only to doll collectors but also to the growing number of people interested in advertising materials.

101 Knitted doll $75–100
102 Knitted cowboy $35–60
103 Clowns $15–25 (each)
104 Clown $50–75
105 Harlequin $500–700
106 Little Pixie People $35–50 (each)
107 Golliwog $200–300
108 Gold Dust Twins $125–150 (each)
109 Raggedy Ann and Andy $75–125 (each)
110 Shrinking Violet $15–20
111 Nancy and Sluggo $100–150 (each)
112 Katzenjammer Kids $400–500 (set)
113 Popeye $150–175
114 Fred Flintstone $25–35
115 Steiff sailor and cowboy $150–175 (each)
116 Charlie Chaplin $175–250
117 Charlie McCarthy $75–150
118 W. C. Fields $75–150
119 Mortimer Snerd and Baby Snooks $175–225 (each)
120 Googly dolls $50–75 (each)
121 Billiken $125–150
122 Kewpie dolls $50–150 (left); $150–200 (right)
123 Campbell Kid $150–175
124 Buddy Lee and Black Magic $50–100 (left); $75–150 (right)
125 Little Orphan Annie and Sandy $175–200 (set)
126 Ella Cinders $100–150
127 Little Red Riding Hood and the Wolf $150–200
128 Snow White, Sneezy, and Grumpy $175–200 (Snow White); $125–150 (each dwarf)
129 Pinocchio and Jiminy Cricket $125–150 (each)
130 Betty Boop $200–275
131 Superman $100–200
132 Howdy Doody $75–100

Paper Dolls

These dolls comprise a separate collecting specialty. In the last decade interest in them has grown, and as a result, prices have risen dramatically, with the most impressive gains made by celebrity dolls. Whereas ten years ago a Shirley Temple booklet could be bought for under $10, it now costs $35 to $45. Occasional bargains can be found at flea markets and at shows specializing in ephemera. Although rare examples of early paper dolls, such as McLoughlin's Topsey, are relatively expensive, most paper dolls are affordable. Many popular characters, such as Kewpie, Dolly Dingle, and Charlie McCarthy can still be purchased for as little as $15 to $35.

133 The Heavenly Twins $65–85 (set)
134 Homemade paper doll $50–75
135 Dolly Dingle of Dingle Dell $20–25
136 The Kewpie Kutouts $18–20
137 Shirley Temple $35–45
138 Charlie McCarthy $25–35
139 Advertising paper doll $18–20
140 The Lettie Lane Paper Family $15–18
141 Sweet Sybel $50–65
142 Little Alice Busy-Bee $25–30
143 Topsey $100–125
144 Amelia $100–125
145 Fate Lady $35–60
146 Fortune-teller $250–350

Printed-Cloth Dolls

Printed-cloth dolls, usually priced at less than $200, offer collectors a fine opportunity for starting a specialized collection at affordable prices. Unusual advertising dolls and storybook figures made by well-known early fabric firms such as Art Fabric Mills and Arnold Print Works are the most expensive and hardest to find. For example, collectors will pay a premium for the first version of Aunt Jemima, but only a fraction of that price for a later example. Condition is all-important in assessing printed-cloth dolls; faded, limp dolls bring considerably less than mint examples. Many people will pay more for an uncut sheet version of a doll than for an assembled doll, with rare and desirable examples such as the Brownies ranging up to $400 a sheet.

147 Punch and Judy $185–200 (each)
148 Santa Claus $125–150
149 The Brownies $300–400
150 Quaker Crackels doll $100–125
151 Kellogg's Goldilocks $75–100
152 Miss Malto-Rice $125–150
153 Little Red Riding Hood $75–100
154 Aunt Jemima and Uncle Mose $75–100 (each)
155 Rastus $75–100
156 Kellogg's Snap $75–100
157 Liberty Belle $50–75
158 Topsy-turvy doll $75–100
159 Babyland Rag doll $175–200

Baby Dolls

Although most baby dolls were manufactured in the 20th century, some are difficult to find and therefore costly. Their rarity generally determines their price: Examples made in large quantities may bring less than $50, while scarce dolls will cost $200 to $1000. Another price determinant is the popularity of a doll at the time of issue; for instance, the Bye-Lo Baby, known in the 1920s as the "Million Dollar Baby" because of its huge and immediate commercial success, is especially favored by today's collectors. Made in many sizes, Bye-Los in large and hard-to-find versions bring the most money. Prices range from $200 to more than $1000. Other expensive baby dolls include the 19th-century Pierotti wax dolls, some of the first baby dolls on the market, and the ever-popular German character babies. These types usually cost more than $500. Lower-priced babies include many vinyl or plastic dolls made since the 1940s.

160 Lamkin $185–225
161 Tee-Wee $185–275
162 Gerber Baby $35–50
163 Bye-Lo Baby $250–400
164 Papier-mâché mechanical baby $175–250
165 Pierotti wax baby $500–800
166 Black Bye-Lo Baby $450–600
167 Black Dream Baby $200–400
168 Rubber baby $175–200
169 Bathing dolls $200–300 (each)
170 Scootles $200–400
171 Queue San and Chin-Chin Babies $75–125 (left); $125–175 (right)
172 All-bisque Bye-Lo Babies $185–250 (each)
173 Tynie Baby $200–250
174 My Dream Baby $200–300
175 Century doll $350–400
176 Tantrum baby $300–400
177 Kaiser Baby $350–500
178 Bubbles $100–150
179 Lil' Darlin $35–60
180 Bonnie Babe $550–650
181 Baby Grumpy $125–150
182 Patsy Baby in hamper $250–350
183 All-wax baby in basket $175–200
184 Multi-face doll $750–900
185 Japanese baby doll $125–150
186 Little Bright Eyes and Peero $300–400 (left); $200–300 (right)
187 German character baby $285–325
188 Biskoline baby $135–175
189 Wooden infants $300–400 (each)

Boy and Girl Dolls: China and Bisque

The dolls in this section represent the aristocracy of the doll world, commanding prices that are often astronomical. Collectors who can afford to spend anywhere from $250 to well over $20,000 will most often find these dolls at doll auctions or doll shows. The French bébés continue to set records at auctions, followed by German bébés, which bring steadily increasing prices. Bargains are hard to find in this area, since there are many more would-be buyers than available dolls. However, some very affordable dolls are also featured here, including the popular Snow Babies, at about $50, as well as small china bathing dolls and all-bisque figures in the $65 to $100 range.

190 Gesland bébés $2500–3000 (each)
191 Huret bébé $3500–4000
192 Schmitt bébés $3000–3500 (left); $2500–3000 (right)
193 Jumeau bébé $2500–3000
194 Bru bébé $7000–8000
195 Jumeau bébé $18,000–20,000

196 Jumeau bébé $2500–3000
197 Belton-type bébé $700–900
198 Long-face Jumeau bébé $7000–10,000
199 Belton-type bébé $700–900
200 French bébés $15,000–16,000 (large); $10,000–12,000 (small)
201 Lanternier bébé $700–900
202 Le Parisieh $2000–3000
203 Fulper doll $300–400
204 Girl doll $300–400
205 Florodora $250–350
206 Dolly Dimple $300–400
207 Kestner girl doll $400–500
208 Bleuette $250–300
209 Armand Marseille girl doll $250–300
210 Gretchen $1400–1600
211 Kämmer & Reinhardt boy doll $1400–1600
212 Simon & Halbig girl doll $800–1000
213 Just Me dolls $250–300 (each)
214 Poulbots $800–1200 each
215 SFBJ bébé $800–1000
216 Century doll $600–800
217 Whistling boy doll $350–400
218 SFBJ boy doll $500–600
219 SFBJ boy dolls $500–600 (each)
220 Heubach boy dolls $350–400 (each)
221 Parian-type male dolls $250–300 (each)
222 Betsy Sheffield and Little Brother $500–700 (each)
223 All-bisque dolls $65–85 (each)
224 Snow Babies $50–60 (each)
225 Dressed bathing dolls $85–100 (each)

Boy and Girl Dolls: Wax and Wood
The prices for wax or wooden boy and girl dolls vary as much as the dolls themselves. Many collectors avoid fragile wax-over-composition dolls, which are generally considered less appealing than their more charismatic bisque counterparts. These waxed dolls are usually moderately priced at $250 to $350. On the other hand, wooden boy and girl character dolls are quite popular and have risen sharply in value in recent years. Schoenhut figures that display the realism so desirable in character dolls are especially sought after. Prices for Schoenhut dolls start in the low hundreds and soar to more than $1000 for rare examples.

226 Multi-face doll $4000–5000
227 Motschmann-type doll $275–350
228 Wax-over-composition doll $250–300
229 Minerva doll $85–125
230 Wooden girl dolls $800–900 (left); $500–600 (right)
231 Wooden girl doll $75–125
232 Schnickel-Fritz $800–900
233 Tootsie-Wootsie $500–600
234 Doll-face doll $350–400
235 Wooden infants $350–400 (each)

Boy and Girl Dolls: Cloth

The growing fascination with folk art has stimulated interest in 19th- and early 20th-century homemade American cloth dolls, inspiring many collectors to invest in this once underpriced field. Examples by Izannah Walker, for instance, now fetch up to $5000. The dolls of lesser-known makers such as Martha Chase, Emma Adams, Julia Beecher, and Louise Kampes sell for prices in the low- to mid-hundreds. Many cloth dolls were products of cottage industries, which created them in limited numbers. The rarity and great appeal of these dolls suggest that they will continue to increase in price. Condition is very important, however, because fading or damage will sharply devalue even the rarest example. Other cloth dolls by early 20th-century European makers are appreciated for their realism, careful workmanship, and exquisite costumes. Dolls by Käthe Kruse now sell for as much as $500 to $800; Lencis range from $350 to $2000.

236 The Columbian doll $450–600
237 Missionary Ragbaby $450–600
238 Martha Chase hospital doll $250–350
239 Käthe Kruse toddler $500–800
240 Alabama Indestructible Doll $600–800
241 Philadelphia Baby $600–800
242 Izannah Walker doll $3000–4500
243 Izannah Walker doll $3500–5000
244 Martha Chase dolls $250–350 (each)
245 Rollinson doll $350–400
246 Priscilla $150–200
247 Tyrolean couple $350–500 (each)
248 Golfer $450–800
249 South Sea Islander $75–125
250 Little Shaver $250–300
251 Kamkins $350–400
252 Cloth girl doll $175–225
253 Princess Elizabeth and Princess Margaret Rose $250–300 (each)

Boy and Girl Dolls: Miscellaneous Materials

The dolls in this section, made of such varied materials as rubber, plastic, composition, and celluloid represent a wide range of collecting interests and cost anywhere from under $25 to about $500. All date from the 20th century, and an increasing number of collectors are willing to pay hundreds of dollars for these antiques of the future. While highly desirable types, such as Shirley Temple dolls, cost up to $500, lesser-known dolls of the 1940s and '50s are priced at under $50 and offer good opportunities for beginning collectors.

254 Amosandra $25–50
255 Rubber doll $20–25
256 Trudy $200–250
257 Margie $75–175
258 Celluloid dolls $35–50 (each)
259 Campbell Kids $125–175 (each)
260 Famlee doll set $350–500
261 Uneeda Biscuit Boy $200–300
262 Patsy Lou $250–300
263 My Darling's Baby Naughty $150–175
264 Little Sister $175–225

265 Gretel and Yerri $175–225 (each)
266 David Copperfield and Tiny Betty $175–225 (each)
267 Fern Deutsch dolls $300–400 (each)
268 Little Women $200–250 (each)
269 Scarlett O'Hara $200–250
270 Late Jumeau bébé $600–700
271 My Rosy Darling $225–250
272 Munich Art doll $200–250
273 Sonja Henie $175–225
274 Jeannie Walker $175–225
275 Toni $150–175
276 Shirley Temple $400–500
277 Shirley Temple cowgirl $400–500
278 Terri Lee cowgirl $125–150
279 Ginny $75–100
280 Nanette $75–100
281 Helene and Karlchen $125–150 (each)
282 Monica $150–175
283 Gregor and Sasha $150–175 (each)

Lady and Gentleman Dolls: China and Bisque

Most china lady dolls are moderately priced, although some unusual 19th-century examples with fine detailing may bring more than $500. Bisque lady dolls, particularly those made by well-known firms such as Bru, Jumeau, and Rohmer, are quite costly—a signed Rohmer doll may have a price tag in the low thousands, while those dolls accompanied by extensive trousseaus and trunks can fetch up to $5000. Parian-type dolls, which are made of untinted bisque, are often priced around $250 to $350.

284 Bald-head china doll $800–1000
285 China-head doll $800–1000
286 China-and-wood dolls $700–800 (each)
287 China-head doll $450–500
288 China-head doll $250–275
289 China-head doll $350–400
290 China-head doll $400–450
291 Parian-type doll $325–350
292 China-head doll $375–400
293 China-head doll $2000–3000
294 China-head dolls $325–350 (each)
295 China-head doll $250–300
296 Parian-type doll $400–425
297 Parian-type doll $150–200
298 Parian-type dolls $300–350 (left); $125–150 (right)
299 Dolls with printed-cloth bodies $100–150 (each)
300 Bisque-head doll with trunk $3500–4000 (set)
301 Bisque-head doll $5000–6000
302 Bisque-head doll $1800–2000
303 Black bisque-head doll $1800–2000
304 Bisque-head doll $2000–2500
305 Bisque-head doll $1800–2000
306 Bisque-head doll $2000–2500
307 Half-dolls $150–200 (each)
308 Hatted dolls $150–200 (each)
309 Bisque-head doll $800–1000
310 Bisque-head Gibson Girl doll $1000–1500

Lady and Gentleman Dolls: Wood

Wooden dolls dating from the 18th century that are in good condition and wearing original clothes rarely come onto the marketplace. These are beyond the means of most collectors, since their prices can approach $4000. Less costly are the various peg-wooden dolls that range from $100 for small, ordinary examples to more than $500 for very detailed early versions. While 19th-century inventors such as Joel Ellis were developing new methods of mass production, other carvers, usually anonymous, continued to make sculptural statements in wood that are now regarded as desirable folk dolls. The best of these examples can cost anywhere from a few hundred dollars to more than $1000. A few contemporary doll artists, such as Marta Finch-Kozlosky and Helen Bullard, still painstakingly carve wooden dolls; their $700 to $950 price range reflects the months of research and labor that went into them.

311 18th-century dolls $3000–4000 (left); $200–300 (right)
312 School for Scandal doll $350–500
313 Joel Ellis doll $250–400
314 Peg-wooden doll $350–400
315 Peg-wooden doll $750–900
316 Peg-wooden doll $175–225
317 Ship's prow doll $1000–1800
318 Scottish folk doll $350–500
319 Footman $600–800
320 Theodosia Burr $700–900
321 Gertrude Stein $800–950

Lady and Gentleman Dolls: Miscellaneous Materials

Prices of dolls in this group range from $75 for a 20th-century metal figure to $2000 for a Lenci cloth doll. 19th-century papier-mâché dolls cost anywhere from $200 to $1200. Composition dolls are generally inexpensive, but early versions, such as ones by Greiner, will bring $500 or more. Early rubber and rawhide dolls, the result of experimentation with dollmaking materials in the mid- to late 19th century, can reach $500, even though they were never very popular in their day. The prices of wax lady dolls vary tremendously according to the merits of the individual figure: Poured-wax dolls can cost upwards of $1000, while most bonnet dolls sell for under $200.

322 Papier-mâché doll $1000–1200
323 Pre-Greiner doll $350–500
324 Wax-over-composition doll $250–350
325 Greiner doll $500–650
326 Papier-mâché doll $250–350
327 Greiner dolls $500–650 (each)
328 Rubber lady doll $450–500
329 Goodyear rubber doll $450–500
330 Darrow rawhide doll $450–500
331 Springfield doll $250–400
332 Composition doll $250–285
333 Bonnet doll $185–225
334 Slit-head doll $350–500
335 Pierotti wax doll $750–1000
336 Poured-wax doll $850–1200
337 Gibson Girl $500–750

338 Metal doll $75–100
339 Wax lady doll $225–275
340 Lenci flapper doll $1500–2000
341 Aunt Connie $300–400

Mechanical Dolls

Mechanical figures have always been among the most expensive dolls. Toy and doll aficionados vie for the rarer ones, which seldom cost less than $1000. On the other hand, some 20th-century examples and very simple *marottes* occasionally can be obtained for less than $500; moreover, mid-20th-century American and Japanese walking dolls can be had for as little as $75 to $125. The magical appeal of mechanical dolls ensures a continuing rise in prices.

342 Black banjo player $1500–2000
343 Clown mandolin player $1500–1800
344 Boy and girl in boat $500–750
345 Bébé with puppet show $1800–2200
346 Boy blowing bubbles $3500–5000
347 Marottes $300–400 (left); $185–225 (right)
348 Autoperipatetikos $450–600
349 Lady at her toilette $3500–5000
350 Lady selling flowers $6000–8000
351 Bébé eating chocolate $5000–7500
352 Bébé pulling dog cart $890–1000
353 Grandmother knitting $500–750
354 Jumeau phonograph doll $5000–7500
355 Bru bébés $6000–8000 (each)
356 Tata dolls $900–1200 (each)
357 Walking toddler $75–125

The Price Guide was written by William C. Ketchum, Jr.

Picture Credits

Photographer
All photographs were taken by Schecter Me Sun Lee.

Collections
The following individuals and institutions kindly allowed us to reproduce objects from their collections:

Aunt Len's Doll and Toy Museum, New York City: 90, 107, 109, 132, 162, 178.
Author's Collection: 2–4, 7, 8, 11–14 (left), 15–17, 27–34, 37, 38, 40–42, 50, 101, 102, 134, 148.
The Brooklyn Children's Museum, Brooklyn, New York: 1, 5, 6, 20–23, 39, 43–47, 49, 51–55, 57, 58, 69, 73, 79, 82, 83, 88, 89, 92, 94, 95, 110, 114, 115, 117, 122 (right), 168, 177, 179, 180, 196, 204, 207, 255, 258, 264, 265, 268, 283, 297, 316, 317, 319, 322–324, 326, 333, 334, 338, 341, 352.
Ladies' Home Journal, © 1909. Reprinted with permission: 140.
Made In America, New York City: 26, 35, 36, 91, 103, 104.
Private Collections: 14 (right), 76, 99, 320, 321.
The Margaret Woodbury Strong Museum, Rochester, New York: 9, 10, 18, 19, 24, 25, 48, 56, 59–68, 70–72, 74, 75, 77, 78, 80, 81, 84–87, 93, 96–98, 100, 105, 106, 108, 111–113, 116, 118–122 (left), 123–131, 133, 135–147, 149–161, 163–167, 169–176, 181–195, 197–203, 205, 206, 208–254, 256, 257, 259–263, 266, 267, 269–282, 284–296, 298–315, 318, 325, 327–332, 335–337, 339, 340, 342–351, 353–357.

Drawings
Dolores R. Santoliquido: pp. 464–471.
Paul Singer: pp. 32, 34, 36, 38.
Mary Jane Spring: pp. 16–25.

Makers and Marks

This table is a selection of the dollmakers and designers featured in this book, accompanied by a representative sampling of their trademarks. The name of the firm or individual is followed by the location and approximate dates of operation; the words "and after" following a date indicate that it is not known precisely when a particular maker ceased being active.

Maker or Designer

Emma E. Adams
Marietta Adams Ruttan

Alexander Doll Company (Madame Alexander)

Louis Amberg & Son

Arnold Print Works

Arranbee Doll Company (R&B)

Art Fabric Mills

Averill Manufacturing Company

Julia Beecher

Carl Bergner

Berwick Doll Company

George Borgfeldt & Company

Bru Jne & Cie
affiliated with SFBJ

A. Bucherer

Buschow & Beck

Cameo Doll Products Company

Cellba Works

Century Doll Company

Chad Valley Company

Martha Jenks Chase

Co-operative Manufacturing Company

Grace Corry (Grace Corry Rockwell)

Darrow Manufacturing Company

Dean's Rag Book Company

	Location	Dates of Operation
	Oswego, NY	1891–1900 1900–c. 1910
	New York, NY	1923–present
	New York, NY	1911 and after
	North Adams, MA	1876–1919
	New York, NY	1922–58
	New York, NY	1899–1910
	New York, NY	1915–65
	Elmira, NY	1893–1910
	Sonneberg, Germany	1890–1909 and after
	New York, NY	1918–25
	New York, NY and Europe	1881 and after
BRU·J^{NE} R 11	Paris and Montreuil-sous-Bois, France	1866–99 1899 and after
	Amriswil, Switzerland	c. 1920 and after
	Reichenbach and Nossen, Germany	1888 and after
	New York, NY Port Allegany, PA	1922–30 1930–70
	Germany	c. 1920–52
	New York, NY	1909–25
	Birmingham, England	1923–present
	Pawtucket, RI	1891–1951
	Springfield, VT	1873–74
	New York, NY	1920 and after
	Bristol, CT	1866–77
	London, England	1903–present

Maker or Designer

Door of Hope Mission

Grace Gebbie Drayton

Cuno & Otto Dressel

EFFanBEE (Fleischaker & Baum)

19©24
EFFANBEE
DOLLS
K·TALK·SLEE
MADE IN USA

Joel Ellis

Freundlich Novelty Corporation

Fulper Pottery Company

Georgene Novelties, Inc.

Gesland

Goodyear Rubber Company

Ludwig Greiner
Greiner Brothers

GREINER'S
PATENT DOLL HEADS
No.7
Pat. mar. 30 '58 ext '72

John B. Gruelle

Hasbro Industries, Inc. (Hassenfeld Brothers)

Hertwig & Company

Gebrüder Heubach

E. I. Horsman
E. I. Horsman Company
Horsman Dolls, Inc.

Maison Huret

Ideal Novelty & Toy Company (Ideal Toy Corporation)

Jumeau
affiliated with SFBJ

Kämmer & Reinhardt

Joseph L. Kallus

Louise R. Kampes

Marion Bertha Kaulitz

	Location	Dates of Operation
	Shanghai, China	c. 1917–25
	Philadelphia, PA	1909–36
[logo: POLE-MAIER / D]	Sonneberg, Germany	c. 1873 and after
[logo: EFFANBEE DOLLS / WALK-TALK-SLEEP]	New York, NY	1910–present
	Springfield, VT	c. 1858–74
	New York, NY	c. 1940–50
[logo: AMBERG DOLLS THE WORLD STANDARD / FULPER / MADE IN U.S.A.]	Flemington, NJ	1918–21 (doll heads)
	New York, NY	c. 1930–64
	Paris, France	1860–c.1924
[logo: GOODYEAR]	New Haven, CT	c. 1851 and after (dolls)
[logo: GREINER'S IMPROVED PATENTHEADS Pat. March 30th '58]	Philadelphia, PA	1840–74 1874–83
	New York, NY and Norwalk, CT	1915 and after
	Pawtucket, RI	1926–present
	Katzhütte, Germany and London, England	1864 and after
[logo: 8132 Germany Gebrüder Heubach / G H]	Lichte and Sonneberg, Germany	1820–1925 and after
	New York, NY	1865–1901 1901 and after present
[logo: HURET 68 RUE DE LA BOETIE]	Paris, France	1850–1920
	New York, NY	1902–present
[logo: JUMEAU MEDAILLE D'OR PARIS]	Paris and Montreuil-sous-Bois, France	1842–99 1899 and after
[logo: K. R]	Waltershausen, Germany	1886 and after
	New York, NY and Port Allegany, PA	1912 and after
	Atlantic City, NJ	1919 and after
	Munich, Germany	c. 1908–20

Maker or Designer	
Kenner Products Company	
J. D. Kestner, Jr. Kestner & Company (porcelain factory)	JDK
Käthe Kruse	Käthe Kruse. 9771
Josef Kubelka	
Léopold Lambert	
A. Lanternier & Cie	
Lenci (Enrico and Elena Scavini)	
Bernard Lipfert	
Armand Marseille	Armand Marseille
Martin & Runyon	
Mattel, Inc.	
Mary McAboy	
Enoch Rice Morrison	
Charles Motschmann	
J. F. Müller & Strassburger	
Nelke Corporation	
New York Rubber Company	
Rose O'Neill	KEWPIE GERMANY COPYRIGHT ROSE O'NEILL
Parsons-Jackson Company Parsons & Parsons Company	
Edward S. Peck	
Jacob Petit	
Pierotti	
Grace Storey Putnam	

	Location	Dates of Operation
	Cincinnati, OH	1947–present
	Waltershausen, Germany Ohrdruf, Germany	1804–1932 1860–1932
	Bad Kösen, Germany Donauworth, Germany	1910–39 1939–present
	Vienna, Austria	1884–1909
	Paris, France	1888–1923
	Limoges, France	1885 and after
	Turin, Italy	1920–present
	Germany New York, NY	Before 1912 1912–74
	Köppelsdorf, Germany	1890–c. 1939
	London, England	1862–65
	Hawthorne, CA	1945–present
	Missoula, MT	c. 1913–55
	New York, NY	1862 and after
	Sonneberg, Germany	c. 1855–70
	Sonneberg, Germany	1863–93
	Philadelphia, PA	1917–c. 1930
	New York, NY	1851–1917
	Wilkes-Barre, PA and Day, MO	1909–40
	Cleveland, OH New York, NY	1910–18 1918–19
	Brooklyn, NY	1884–86
	Fontainebleau, Seine-et-Marne, and Belleville, France	1830–62
	London, England	1780–c. 1925
	Oakland, CA	1922 and after

Maker or Designer

Rabery & Delphieu affiliated with SFBJ
Rheinische Gummi und Celluloid Fabrik Company
Rohmer
Gertrude Rollinson
Saalfield Publishing Company
Sasha Dolls (Sasha Morgenthaler)
Schmitt Schmitt & Fils
A. Schoenhut & Company
Simon & Halbig
F. Simonne
Celia & Charity Smith
D. M. Smith & Company
Ella Smith
Société Française de Fabrication de Bébés & Jouets (SFBJ)
Margarete Steiff
Jules Nicholas Steiner
Sun Rubber Company
A. Thuillier
Raphael Tuck & Sons
Vermont Novelty Works
Victoria Toy Works (Norah Wellings)
Izannah Walker

	Location	Dates of Operation
	Paris, France	1856–98 1899 and after
	Mannheim-Neckarau, Germany	1873 and after
	Paris, France	1857–80
	Holyoke, MA	1916–17
	Akron, OH	1900–76
	Switzerland and Serie, England	c. 1939–present
	Paris, France	1863–77 1877–91
	Philadelphia, PA	1872–c. 1930
	Gräfenhain, Germany	1869–1925 and after
	Paris, France	1847–78
	Ithaca, NY	1889–1911 and after
	Springfield, VT	1879–86
	Roanoke, AL	1904–24
S.F. B. J. 237 PARIS	Paris and Montreuil-sous-Bois, France	1899–1958
Steiff	Giengen, Germany	1877–present
	Paris, France	1855–1908
	Barberton, OH	c. 1937–57
A 10 T	Paris, France	1875–90
	London, England	c. 1881–present
	Springfield, VT	1869 and after
	Wellington, England	1926–60
	Central Falls, RI	c. 1855–86

Index

Numbers refer to entries.

Staff

Prepared and produced by Chanticleer Press, Inc.
Publisher: Paul Steiner
Editor-in-Chief: Gudrun Buettner
Managing Editor: Susan Costello
Project Editor: Lenore Malen
Assistant Editor: Marian Appellof
Art Director: Carol Nehring
Art Assistants: Ayn Svoboda, Karen Wollman
Production: Helga Lose, Amy Roche, Alex von Hoffmann
Picture Library: Edward Douglas
Drawings: Mary Jane Spring, Dolores R. Santoliquido
Visual Key Symbols: Paul Singer
Design: Massimo Vignelli

The Knopf Collectors' Guides to American Antiques

Also available in this unique full-color format:

Folk Art
Paintings, Sculpture & Country Objects
by Robert Bishop and Judith Reiter Weissman

Furniture 1
Chairs, Tables, Sofas & Beds
by Marvin D. Schwartz

Furniture 2
Chests, Cupboards, Desks & Other Pieces
by William C. Ketchum, Jr.

Glass 1
Tableware, Bowls & Vases
by Jane Shadel Spillman

Glass 2
Bottles, Lamps & Other Objects
by Jane Shadel Spillman

Pottery & Porcelain
by William C. Ketchum, Jr.

Quilts
With Coverlets, Rugs & Samplers
by Robert Bishop